LOSING
MARIPOSA

Published by ECW PRESS
2120 Queen Street East, Suite 200, Toronto, Ontario, Canada M4E 1E2

NATIONAL LIBRARY OF CANADA CATALOGUING IN PUBLICATION DATA

Little, Doug
Losing Mariposa: the memoir of a compulsive gambler / Doug Little.
ISBN 1-55022-533-2
1. Little, Doug. 2. Compulsive gamblers — Canada — Biography.
1. Title.
HV6710.3.L58A3 2002   616.85'841'0092   C2002-902166-9

Cover and text design: Tania Craan
Production: Mary Bowness
Typesetting: Wiesia Kolasinska
Printing: Transcontinental
Front cover photo: © Pierre St. Jacques / Imagination Photo Services

This book is set in Sabon and Franklin Gothic

The publication of *Losing Mariposa* has been generously supported by the Canada Council, the Ontario Arts Council, and the Government of Canada through the Book Publishing Industry Development Program. **Canadä**

DISTRIBUTION

CANADA: Jaguar Book Group, 100 Armstrong Avenue, Georgetown, ON L7G 5S4

UNITED STATES: Independent Publishers Group, 814 North Franklin Street, Chicago, Illinois 60610

EUROPE: Turnaround Publisher Services, Unit 3, Olympia Trading Estate, Coburg Road, Wood Green, London N2Z 6T2

AUSTRALIA AND NEW ZEALAND: Wakefield Press, 1 The Parade Way West (Box 2266), Kent Town, South Australia 5071

ECW PRESS
ecwpress.com

LOSING

The Memoir of a Compulsive Gambler

DOUG LITTLE

MARIPOSA

ECW PRESS

This book is dedicated to all the *Little* women,
past present and future in my life;
And to the compulsive gambler who still suffers.

ACKNOWLEDGMENTS

This is a much different, and much better book than I started to write thanks to the help of all these people. That it is not perfect is a tribute to my humanity. *Thank God.*

I was given a great deal of encouragement and support in writing my story by other compulsive gamblers and friends, many of whom read the manuscript in its various draft forms and made positive contributions.

Paul Palango and *Saturday Night Magazine,* Charlie Angus at *HighGrader Magazine,* and Gladys Pollack of *Reader's Digest* furthered the telling of this tale by publishing parts of it. Also, Phil Lange of the *Electronic Journal of Gambling Issues: eGambling* published excerpts and provided reassurance.

My mentor in the Humber School for Writers program, "Coach Q" — Paul Quarrington — helped me unlock my narrative voice and discover the structure of this story. Thanks to school director Joe Kertes for still believing in me and for developing such a great program.

In Ottawa, my good friend David O'Malley offered suggestions, page by page, as did the wonderful Patricia Kemph. The faith and inspiration of my boss and best friend, Michel Gauthier, and the reinforcement of my colleagues at the Canadian Tulip Festival were critical to the completion of this journal.

The literary expertise of my daughter Melanie Little as a writer and editor made this a much better book. Her encouragement and enthusiasm throughout my writing helped me rediscover the creativity I feared I had lost. She will always be my Muse.

My thanks to ECW Press editor Paul Vermeersch for his work on the book and for making the fearful process rewarding. Thanks to publisher Jack David for his belief in this story and that phone call on such a mournful November day. Thanks to my agents, Margaret Hart and Lynn Kinny, for all their work on my behalf, now and in the future.

Finally, but foremost: my undying love and gratitude to my Lovely Louise, who is truly my gift in recovery.

INTRODUCTION

This is my story. It is my interpretation of what happened during my gambling addiction, and what led me to this place. It is the result of looking back on a lifetime of 48 years for the first time, without the fear of what I might see. I have stopped running.

Is the story true? To the best of my ability I have recounted what happened but sometimes the memories are recalled through the eyes of a six-, eight- or 12-year-old, some 40 years later. They are memories of a frightened young boy, running to survive, or of a confused teenager experiencing his first infatuation with love — and first love with alcohol and escape into what he could be when drinking. They are stories seen first through parting the veil of drugs and alcohol. Then I am looking back through a workaholic haze, where I lived as a caricature of myself, an image I projected to the world, because I was afraid it might find out who I really was. Finally, they are the stories of the two-year gambling binge that completely destroyed my life and brought me to the place where I had nothing more to lose by looking at myself, learning about myself and finally, loving myself.

These stories are not about the other people in my life, and whatever I say about them is not true, for it is only my story, my interpretation of what happened, and not necessarily what happened. They are all heroes and heroines in their own right and nothing I will say herein is meant to portray them in any other manner. I blame no one for my life. I take all the blame, all the responsibility.

I, too, I am my here, every day that I have the courage to live in the real world of who I really am. This is my story.

I don't know whether you know Mariposa. If not, it is of no consequence, for if you know Canada at all, you are probably well acquainted with a dozen towns just like it.

Busy — well, I should think so! Ask any of its inhabitants if Mariposa isn't a busy, hustling, thriving town.

Stephen Leacock
Sunshine Sketches of a Little Town

CHAPTER ONE

For me the war is over. Three times I charged into the fray, three times I

retreated. Out to the van in the parking lot, past the smiling, nodding security guard — "Good night, Sir" — to get more ammo. More loot! More fuel! "If only I had enough legs," I told myself. *Ha! Ten thousand dollars worth the legs — the shinbone-thighbone-assbone legs — twice for Christ's sake — and it still wasn't enough.* I want to scream. I want to run up and down the banks of slot machines and yell: "Fuck! Fuck! Fuck!" Let me grab one of those dealers' chip trays and fling it across the blackjack pit. Then we'll see some action. Let me tear off tonight's ruinous roulette wheel, and spin it through the air. *Legs.* Let me put my failed feet through the screens of those video-gambling sluts.

But, I won't, will I? *A skunk doesn't piss in his nest.*

Staggering! This is what it — what I — have come to. Staggering like a Sunday-morning wino, zigzagging around the casino floor. Not because I'm drunk — I haven't had a drink in 18 years — but, because I am whipped. Beat. Broke. Empty. Ten thousand more dollars lost in a final desperate chase. But, even more than that, I am pierced, wounded, defeated — a casualty of another senseless night of combat. Where are the gaming medics? I hear there's a nurse's station around here somewhere, in case of heart attacks. What about heartache? What about heartbreak? *Shit!*

I

At least if I *was* drunk people would understand. Somebody would look after me. Here, on this battlefield, I'm not even allowed to show my wounds. Hell, there's not even a place to sit in a casino once you've lost. All I can do is wander, around and around, hoping to be struck by some kind of merciful lightning bolt from out of the neon skies. Or, failing that, to meet some familiar fellow warrior who'd arm me with another couple of hundred bucks so I can go back to war.

Outside the casino, my tantrum over, I marvel at the difference between my comings and goings to this place. When I came here tonight, my pockets full of money, everything was possible. "Tonight's the night," I told myself, half cheer and half incantation. All I had to do was believe: "Luck be a Lady tonight!" Now, crossing the almost-empty parking lot at 3:30 in the morning, I'm a loser. My final $1500 stash is gone. I'm stripped naked and feel like I've been dragged — *staggered* — around the Casino Rama floor as a living spectacle of defeat. Not that the casino would do that to me. They only display winners. They just want me out. No, it's me. Me, in my wallowing ruin. Punishing myself.

Another $10,000 of other people's money gone. How much is that now? $70,000? $80,000? I don't know. I've stopped counting. Now it's not about how much I owe or how much I have lost. This is the painful truth that comes in the darkness of early morning, when the dream world of winning my way out of trouble smacks up against the reality that, once again, I have lost my way further into it. The chips are down. I can't take back my bets. I am gambling my life away.

What makes this anguish all the worse is the prospect of not being able to return to lose my mind among the bells and whistles and the sound of impending victory.

Despair washes over me as I think of crossing the Atherley Narrows Bridge. This is the place where the warm waters of Lake Couchiching are sucked into the frigid northern basin of Lake Simcoe, creating a narrow, shallow channel a hundred feet below the bridge. The Narrows are considered sacred lands by the Chippewas of Rama, the owners of Casino Rama. Chippewas of Mnjikaning — fish-fence-minders — is what they call themselves of late, reclaiming their traditional native tribal name. They are now the custodians of the ancient, 4,500 year-old fishing weirs — wooden stakes that lay underwater in the shallow passage. In 1615 Samuel de Champlain watched the original inhabitants, the Huron Indians, spear thousands of fish here — fish corralled in the channel through this elaborate system of underwater fences. The Hurons were known as fierce gamblers, often willing to gamble away weapons, homes, even families, in a game of chance. *Even families.* That was before they were erased from this region we still call Huronia by the Iroquois shortly after Champlain's visit. Centuries later the Chippewa, part of the Anishnabe Nation, moved down from the north to occupy the then-empty territory. Of course, this was also before the white settlers in the 1800s forced the Chippewa onto the reserve in Rama where the casino now stands.

I drive down tonight's Rama Road away from the Casino, my hands gripping feverishly at the steering wheel, as if the van is keeping me on the road rather than the reverse. I turn onto Highway 12 and the ominous concrete railings of the bridge appear.

The wooden weir poles that were here during Champlain's time are still here today. I can picture them, sharp and pointed in the shallow canal below, their historic importance receding. Even in this desperate hour, I can't help but see the grim humour in my being skewered on these ancient and sacred pylons. A fitting end to my fall from grace in the native casino. That I am a founding member of the Fish Fence Circle and one of the leaders of the Community Casino Task Force only adds to the irony of my predicament as I contemplate acceleration, not over, but through, the approaching sacred Atherley Narrows Bridge.

When I was a kid, my father told me a story of how, during the war, he had to retrieve the bodies of some soldiers whose jeep had gone over the bridge on the Mispec Road. That was near my birthplace, Saint John, New Brunswick, on the way to our favourite beach, Mispec Beach on the Bay of Fundy. It was a tale of my father's wartime service in the military police that we heard over and over again. His graphic details are too deeply imbedded in my subconscious to ever allow me to actually drive off the bridge but, as I drive over, the wonted thought of this ultimate escape is always there and has been there almost every night for the last three months. Maybe it's the image of Staff Sergeant Douglas A. Little, or someone like him, pulling my lifeless body from under the bridge that stops me.

"How could Melanie live with *that*?" I ask myself, talking out loud, as I do so often these nights. I couldn't leave her to live with my suicide. Melanie is my 27-year-old daughter, now a graduate student at the University of British Columbia, doing an MFA in creative writing. What is this now, her tenth year of university? An Honours BA from McGill, a Masters from U of T and five years towards a Ph.D. in Toronto before she said screw it to the old-boys club and English Literature and left without finishing her thesis. Her mother and I still argue about whether she can go back and finish it later, with me on Melanie's side. But, like many things I argue about, I don't really know.

Now that I'm across the bridge, the reality of not killing myself sinks in. It means I have to live and face another hopeless hour before I can anaesthetize my brain enough to get to sleep. Life beyond that mustn't exist. Sleep is a big enough challenge. The van turns onto the bypass towards my home, a ten-minute trip from Casino Rama. There was a time when I thought this would be my salvation, living so close to a casino. Over the past two years, before Casino Rama opened, I had taken five excursions to the major casinos in Windsor and Sault Ste. Marie, Michigan. Each time I lost everything and came home broke. Yet I couldn't wait until Casino Rama opened. I told myself I lost those other times because I was away. *You don't quit when you're losing because you can't return the next day, or next week, like you'll be able to once the casino comes to Orillia.*

"I'll be able to quit when I'm losing at Rama," I'd say. I tried to convince my wife Roberta that my hometown gambling would be different than the frenzy she had witnessed when she came with me to Sault Ste. Marie earlier in June. "Here I can go back later, when my luck has changed. And I'll be able to quit when I'm winning, because I can always return another day."

In the seventy-seven days since Casino Rama opened, I have never quit — winning or losing — unless I was too broke or too exhausted to keep going. The only time I've ever left with more money than I came in with was the night I had to leave early because the next day I had to pick up Melanie in Montreal. Even the memory of that $5,000 win doesn't help me on this hopeless night. Slapping me in the face is the reality that I owe $50,000 more now, just two months later, than I did that night.

Reaching home does nothing to dispel my sense of impending doom. My first prayer is that Roberta is asleep. Battle-weary, the last thing I need tonight is a confrontation. Still, it is amazing how little I have cared lately when she has confronted me, and come to think of it, it's equally surprising how seldom she has tried.

Remember the knock-em-out battles we had about my drinking twenty-five years ago? The smashed telephones, the screaming, and the beating fists when I would come home drunk after staying out with the boys. But that was then, and even Roberta has mellowed, or maybe she has just given up. Still, I pray she is sleeping.

To which god am I praying tonight? The God of my youth is the one I pray to in these desperate hours, between losing and sleeping. Part of my anaesthesia is saying the Our Father and the Serenity Prayer, over and over in my head, as I lie in my bed, blocking out all the spinning and menacing thoughts.

"God grant me the serenity to accept the things I cannot change, the courage to change the things I can and the wisdom to know the difference." This is the legacy of five years of meetings and fellowship after I quit alcohol eighteen years ago in the hard-drinking and hard-gambling gold-mining town of Timmins in northern Ontario. The Lord's Prayer is the residue of a three-year sojourn during my high school years at a minor seminary studying, of all things, to be a priest. My first great escape.

Tonight my prayers will need reinforcement. The daily lottery tickets and a couple of instant scratch tickets that I bought earlier today will help get me through the night.

Luck, you see, is my other deity.

As I pull into Maple Leaf Crescent, I curse these newfangled vehicles whose headlights are automatically lit whenever the motor is running. I want to turn out the lights and slink up the driveway. Not only do I want to avoid attracting the attention of my sleeping wife at four o'clock in the morning, but also my next-door neighbour George, my banker. He already made a remark a couple of weeks ago when I was in the bank.

"Is there something wrong with your headlights?" he asked.

"I don't think so," I said, relieved he hadn't asked me about my $5,000 overdraft.

"Because the other night when you were leaving, backing out of the driveway, your headlights weren't on."

"I'll check on it," I said. Of course the reason the headlights weren't on was that I was backing out of the driveway without turning on the van's engine, coasting so that Roberta and the neighbours wouldn't hear me sneaking off to the casino in the middle of the night. *Was he razzing me?*

Now I fall out of the van, my body limp with exhaustion and misery as I cross the driveway to my doorstep. I cast a backward glance over my left shoulder to see if George is peeking out from behind the curtains. I put my key in the door and start to push with practised care against the heavy resistance. *No, it's not Roberta.*

"Meow . . ." I hear through the crack of the door.

"Grrrrrr . . . shut up Tuffy," I growl, fearing that if I don't wake her, he will.

He's not always there. Sometimes he's sleeping in her room, but the memory of the night he shrieked as I opened the door too quickly keeps me cautious. Tuffy is the only thing that I did right during these two years of gambling. A purebred Himalayan, a fur-ball with the famous pushed-in face, he was Roberta's birthday gift last year. Since that time he has become her second child.

Sleeping in my wife's room is a privilege I lost years ago due to a combination of my snoring, the fallout from my alcoholism and its successor, workaholism, and mutual stubbornness. Now Tuffy not only gets to sleep in my matrimonial bed, but he also has in-and-out privileges and is often propped up against the door guarding against my return home. I am, however, an expert at clandestine comings and goings. In the aftermath of the most catastrophic event of my life — to date — the question I got most often was, "How could you not wake Roberta?"

Five years ago, on August 2, 1991, I awoke in the middle of another lonely night with hell burning in the middle of my chest. "Ahhhagggaaahh," I cried in pain, a searing fireball rousing me from my bed. I was soaked, the pillow was drenched, even the sheets. An aching throb was smouldering at the top of my stomach, not unlike the ulcer attacks I had years ago. *Tagamet*, I thought; surely somewhere I had some ulcer pills. I got up and sat on the side of the bed for a moment, peeling off my saturated undershirt. *This is a pretty severe ulcer attack.* That didn't surprise me considering the stress I had been under. I was between day nine and day ten in my thirteen-day Leacock Heritage Festival, and it was the eve of the busiest day of the year, the Leacock Sunshine Sidewalk Sale. It had not been an easy year, with controversy over my shopping out of town for Festival t-shirts and lower-priced sound equipment, and I could tell that the admission money was not coming in the way it should.

I was startled to see by the clock beside the bed that it was only 1:30 in the morning. I had just gone to sleep. After each day's events during the Festival, my committee and some of the entertainment — often the writers and readers — went to a hospitality suite at the Sundial Motel for refreshments and snacks. Often it was the first opportunity I'd have all day to eat. That night it had been hot wings — something new, Kentucky Fried Chicken Hot Wings — and, of course, beer. In my case, root beer. I had gone home about 12:30 a.m., tired of being nudged awake as I sat on the motel room couch, the wings gone, nursing my third root beer, and nodding off like a Lady Laurier barroom sot. Once home, I passed out quickly.

Now I slowly got up from the side of my bed, shuffled over to the dresser and got a new t-shirt. The breeze made my clammy skin feel cold. I customarily slept with the windows wide open so the cold morning air would wake me for the next day of festival organizing. I couldn't help myself and wondered for a moment what the weather was going to be like for tomorrow's sidewalk sale.

I eased my way out of the room on the third floor of our split-level town house, holding on to the walls and then the banister as I coaxed myself down the stairs to the bathroom just off Roberta's bedroom. At this point in the story, people often wonder aloud how I managed to get up, get dressed and drive myself to the hospital without waking Roberta. I've often thought it was a good thing. My cool-headed, solitary functioning, fuelled by a denial of what was really happening, staved off the panic that might have killed me. Certainly Roberta would have panicked.

The bathroom mirror told me I looked like crap, but that was no surprise. Still, the pasty white ghost-look was new for me, and my reaction was a precursor to the nurse's first question, "Do you always look so pale?"

The ulcer pills were not in the bathroom and were more likely in a kitchen cupboard drawer, although it had been a while since I'd seen any. The ulcer was ancient history, an ailment that materialized after I quit drinking and started worrying. The drugs usually got it under control, until I stopped taking them. Then it would flare up again, and once more I would start taking the medicine. A couple of Tagamet pills and a glass of milk would usually settle things down enough to get me back to sleep.

Sitting in the kitchen, waiting for the magic pills to work, I asked myself, *Was this different?* I couldn't deny that the pain was more intense but then, so was the pressure, so was the strain. The Leacock Heritage Festival was in its third year. I was its founder, chairman, and de facto manager. The Festival was also tied into my job as manager of Downtown Orillia, as the Downtown Management Board was its major sponsor and its financier. A celebration of Canadian humorist Stephen Leacock, and of the historic town of Orillia (which he called "Mariposa" in his classic, *Sunshine Sketches of a Little Town*), it was an award-winning event, both at a national and provincial level. Making it pay for itself, as with most festivals, was an ongoing challenge. For my employers, the Main Street merchants, the success of the Festival all came down to the next two days — the sidewalk sale. If it was a success, I was a hero. If it flopped . . . well, it never had, at least not in my time, but it was all about weather. If the sun shone, people came in droves. If it rained, the sale would be a wash and so would the Festival. The sale used to be called "Leacock Daze." I in my hubris changed the name to the "Leacock Sunshine Sidewalk Sale." The Downtown had another one-day event in May, the "Great Garage Sale." I expanded it to two days and renamed it the "Greatest Garage Sale Under the Sun." I somehow didn't recognize how insane it was to take credit for the sunshine and blame for the rain.

♥ ♦ ♣ ♠

My mother told me they had an old newspaper photograph on display at the Rockwood Court reunion showing me playing marbles when I was eight years old. I remember this picture, because it solidified my reputation as the "Marble King" of Rockwood Court.

"It's Official Now. . . . Small Fry Welcome Spring," the *Saint John Evening Times Globe* headline announced above the picture. "Sure sign that spring is here to stay is to see a group of youngsters playing marbles," the picture cut-line read. "Here the camera lens has caught Karen Hutchison, Babe MacDonald, Doug Little (shooting), Janet Stephenson, and Ronald Meahan all grouped on their knees engrossed in shooting marbles."

"All the children live in Rockwood Court which houses 500 families in the Northeast sector of the city, but these scenes are typical of the entire Saint John area nowadays."[1]

Rockwood Court was where I had spent the first happy eight years of my life. I remember us living at Number 10, but I understand we also lived at numbers 6, 4, and 2. We were among the first families to move into the new row-housing complex during the war and as our family grew — there were eight of us by 1952 — my mother kept moving us to bigger and bigger units.

"Keep this up," my Baptist grandmother told my mom one day, "and you'll soon have lived in the whole damn building."

I'm not sure if I actually earned the title of Marble King or whether, like so many other hand-me-downs, I really inherited it from my older brother David along with his barrels of alleys, glassies, and crockies. Whether or not I passed them on to my sisters when I moved on to trading and playing for baseball cards, I don't recall. When I was eight years old, before the next spring, we moved from Rockwood Court to a house in Milford. The contrast between the joy I recall from Rockwood Court and the fear I experienced in Milford and East Saint John makes me wonder if I hadn't figuratively, as well as literally, lost all my marbles in the move.

Had the thought of my heart and a heart attack even entered into my head? Oh yes. But it was testimony to my inherent capacity for denial that I had not reckoned with the words. I recognized the symptoms described in minute detail by my father when he had his first heart attack when I was 19 years old. The fireball in the middle of the ribs. The crushing weight, like a lead safe, sitting on your chest and making it impossible to breathe. He was driving in his car and, father like son, he too drove himself to the hospital.

I was going back to bed, an act of faith in the miracle cure. I crawled back up the stairs as I realized, for the first time, how weak I felt. I sat on the side of the bed for a few moments, willing the pain to subside. I laid down.

"Ahhhagggaaahh . . . damned . . . ahhhagggaaahh," I wailed against the dark, wrenching fist that was squeezing my heart, a radiating pain that shot throughout my chest. "Jesus," I swore, invoking the rejected religion I was quickly reconsidering. "Christ, that hurts."

I sat back up slowly, deliberately, and the sharp paralyzing spasm subsided to a chronic but severe ache. Finally, *This is no ulcer attack* broke through my denial and *HEART ATTACK* flashed in my brain like the neon sign of my father's bygone "Little Inn" restaurant. Then I detected an increase in the beat of my heart and as soon as I acknowledged its presence, it accelerated even more, sounding now like battling bass drums in my chest. Adrenaline! Panic! I knew nothing about medicine but I instinctively knew that panic and rapid heartbeat were not the ideal responses at the moment. I sat purposefully still on the edge of the bed, breathed deeply, and tried to calm myself down.

"No way it's a heart attack," I lied to myself, fooling terror into remission. My drums calmed, I started to think about getting dressed, just in case the hellfire returned. The pain hadn't gone: it was just simmering in my chest, an aching, burning sensation I thought would never go away.

"I'll just get dressed so I'll be ready if it gets worse," I told myself, as I took socks and clean underwear from the drawer. Somewhere through the pain I felt a smile as I thought *Mom would be proud* — clean underwear if I'm found dead somewhere. Leg by leg, arm by arm I got dressed in slow motion, just in case. The simmering soreness continued but the bolt-of-pain-from-hell had not returned. I decided to go downstairs again. *Maybe I'll take another Tagamet pill.*

Sitting in the kitchen I contemplated going for a ride until the burning passed. There was no way I was going to try laying down again until it did. *Maybe I'll drive by the hospital, just in case.* The drive to the hospital was a blur. I saw a policeman on the way and wondered if he would stop me for erratic driving. If he did, I would have to tell him I was having a heart attack.

The next thing I knew I was sitting in the parking lot of the emergency ward of Soldiers Memorial Hospital, debating with myself as to whether I should go inside. *It's the busiest day of the year. If you go in it will be all over the news.* Orillia being a small town, me being who I am and this happening during the Festival, my ex-reporter instincts told me true.

If you didn't think you needed to be here, you wouldn't have driven to the hospital and you wouldn't be sitting here now. The truth of this statement penetrated my smokescreen of denial. I got out of the car and walked through the emergency doors.

The "Do you always look this pale?" nurse wheeled me into an emergency room. Five hours later, I called and woke Roberta from her sleep, telling her I had just survived a heart attack.

I push Tuffy out of the doorway and enter the darkness of the house. I wonder at this memory of my heart attack. How black my despair is now compared to the tranquillity I had experienced in the hospital ICU. If I died, I had thought then, I would have accomplished some things. Melanie, I was so proud of Melanie. The Festival. Downtown Orillia. I marvel at this peacefulness now and suspect the euphoria of the morphine.

I quietly empty my moneyless pockets of keys on the dresser in my separate bedroom. To think that tonight, just five years later, here I am leaning precariously on the brink of self-destruction — *losing Mariposa.* The Festival that meant so much to me is about to be destroyed. The downtown will be irreparably damaged, not by some newfangled mall or Big Box killer, but by me — its guardian, its "Czar."

What about Melanie?

"I'm gambling them all away," I hear myself whisper as I head to the kitchen, open the refrigerator and reach for my French Vanilla ice cream and my chocolate syrup. From my back pocket I pull out my bundle of lottery tickets.

I have to check my numbers.

CHAPTER TWO

All of it — the after-gambling desperation, the thoughts of sui-

October 22, 1996 — 7 a.m.

cide, the self-loathing, the all and sundry moaning and groaning — completely disappears the next morning as my mind focuses on the task at hand: *Where can I get more money to go back to the casino and win back what I've lost?* I am already back in action. Everything is possible. I just need some money — some fuel — and some luck. A new day — a new chance.

Don't be negative. Don't be a loser. Gambling is my religion. Luck is my god and the first commandment is to believe. Lady Luck is out there, stashed somewhere in Casino Rama. All I have to do is find the money so I can keep looking for her. All things are possible. All I need is another stake.

Looking in the mirror as I quickly shave — gotta get out of here before Roberta wakes — there is no hint of contrition, no regret, no acknowledgement that I lost another $10,000 of "other people's money" over the weekend. It was money I "borrowed" from the Leacock Heritage Festival charity casino funds that I was supposed to bank on Saturday morning. I banked it all right: directly into the Bank of Rama. That was more than easy. Getting it back out — that'll be the challenge.

I'll pay it back. I'll pay it all back. I cannot afford doubt. It's too late. "Today's the day. I can feel it," I chant. I give myself a wink and a kiss in the mirror, part of the ritual. *Stay positive!*

I hurry to complete my shower and dress in my basement bathroom, far away from Roberta's bedroom. Sneaking around has been harder since she lost her job. Now she sleeps reasonable hours — in bed by 11 p.m. and up by 8 a.m. Quite a contrast with the 4 a.m. to 7 a.m. slumber routine I'm keeping these days, and that's on the nights I actually come home to rest.

When my gambling started — in, of all places, a bingo hall — she was working the afternoon shift as the membership coordinator at the Midland YMCA, an hour's drive from Orillia. She was gone from 11 a.m. to 10 p.m. almost every day, leaving me free to fill my nights. So what? For the past 18 years all I filled them with was work anyway. Community meetings, municipal committees, council meetings, election campaigns, board meetings, executive meetings, tourism committees, provincial meetings, national associations, festival organizing, speech writing, desktop publishing, and downtown managing. On February 3, 1978, I took my last drink and conquered my addiction to alcohol. Immediately, work became my new drug of choice. My work defined who I was.

Like the planets aligning for some celestial convergence, several unrelated occurrences happened in December 1994 to set in motion my two-year gambling binge. First, I was burned out at work. Six years as the manager of the Downtown Orillia Management Board, six years as the chairman of the Leacock Heritage Festival, six years with a myriad of committees, events, and associations and I was toast. I also felt trapped. After my heart attack in 1991, I went "on staff" (rather than on contract) with the Downtown, which actually made me a City of Orillia employee, with all the medical, pension and disability benefits that such a job provides. I could no longer just up and quit when I wanted. I had security and a heart condition that made me need it.

Second, I had also been diagnosed with sleep apnea, a sleeping disorder. The snoring that was a factor in my bedroom banishment was but a symptom of the apnea. I stop breathing when I am asleep, and my mind, intent on staying alive, wakes me up to get my breathing going again. This happens about twice every minute, all night long, making me at best sleep-deprived, and at worst dead. Sleep apnea was likely a contributing factor in my heart attack. Now, after living with apnea and being sleep-deprived for God knows how many years, I was sleeping with an air pump called a C-PAP (see-pap) machine that kept my air passages open when I slept. I was no longer sleep-deprived. Translation: I needed less sleep.

Next, the Ontario government announced that the Chippewas of Rama, the Native community that lives adjacent to Orillia on the other side of Lake Couchiching, had been awarded the right to construct a world-class gambling casino on their reserve to serve as a source of economic development and revenue for all of Ontario's First Nations. This was the culmination of a year-long bidding process. My letter of support from the Downtown Management Board was, if not the first, then among the first, praising the project. As a promoter of economic development and tourism for the Orillia area I believed a casino would be great for the local economy.

"Jackpot," read the headline in the December 6, 1994, edition of the *Orillia Packet & Times.* As the manager of Downtown Orillia

I was quoted as saying "I think it's fantastic. It's going to be a boon for the native community . . . but it'll also have a great spin-off for the rest of the community. Our objective must be to get them [casino patrons] to come in and enjoy the rest of the community."

No doubt some of the "spin" going around in my head was that of the roulette wheel. I had fallen in love with roulette while on vacation in the Dominican Republic a few years back and the idea that I would soon be able to play any time in my own backyard had me excited.

Last among my cosmic catalysts, but not the least: Bingo! — and the new Magic Dabber Bingo Hall in Downtown Orillia. The only experience I'd ever had with bingo was when I was a kid playing it at home or watching my mother at the fall Exhibition in Saint John. Downtown Orillia already had one bingo hall, a converted movie theatre called the Geneva. Our Downtown offices were in a building adjacent to the hall. More than once I had to go in and get some bingo player or another to move his or her car out of my parking spot. It was a dingy, smoked-filled hovel, full of little old women and overweight housewives gambling away their pension and welfare cheques. You wouldn't have caught me dead in the place. Guys I knew in the Rotary and Lions clubs, which sponsored bingos at the Geneva, joked about having to remove their smoke-polluted clothing outdoors before they were allowed in the house after volunteering for a night at the bingo hall.

Magic Dabber was different. For one thing, it had a non-smoking room, and while it was in a former grocery store building, it had been completely renovated. It was a state-of-the-art bingo palace, owner Fred Snook would tell you: electronic boards, electronic monitors, padded seats, and carpeted floors with room for 800 customers. There was also a snack bar and a Nevada ticket booth, dispensing the paper break-open gambling tickets that proliferate throughout Ontario in every corner store, tobacco shop and, it seems, bingo hall. The 200-seat non-smoking area was a big selling point to City Council during the debate over the bingo hall's licence, which was opposed by the Geneva, and originally, by me, on behalf of the DMB. (We were afraid bingo players would take up all the downtown parking.) The management board won some concessions — no daytime bingo Monday to Friday, and shoppers could use the hall's parking lot during the week. These were conditions the hall owners agreed to under duress, in order to get their licence, and I, as the mouthpiece of the downtown merchants, was not very popular with the bingo crowd in either hall.

So I was surprised to get a phone call a few days before the hall was to open in early December from Gord Pye, a sergeant with the Orillia City Police. He was also president of the Magic Dabber Bingo Hall Sponsors Association.

"Is the Leacock Heritage Festival interested in running a bingo at 10 p.m. every Sunday night at the new bingo hall?" he asked. One of the planned sponsors couldn't get a charity license and at the last minute the hall needed another organization to sponsor the last spot. The group also had to get a license quickly, in less than a week. As Gord knew, as the downtown manager and the mayor's campaign manager, I had the connections to speed the process along.

Sponsoring a bingo could mean $25,000 to $50,000 a year to a charity sponsor. I jumped at the chance. Technically the Leacock Heritage Festival was not a charity but simply a non-profit organization, but because it presented programming for the good of the community it qualified to sponsor charity gambling licenses. I had no trouble getting the approvals from the province and the city, and on December 10, 1994, I began supervising a Sunday night bingo in order to raise money for the Festival. This meant I led the volunteers working the bingo every Sunday night from 9 p.m. to 1 a.m.

After two or three weeks of Sundays operating the bingo — and seeing other people win $1,000 and $2,500 jackpots — I decided to give bingo a try myself. I had to play, though, at another late-evening session, as you are not allowed to play during your own organization's bingo session. When I sat down in the non-smoking section on that first night I knew I had arrived. Here was a place where I could relax. A place where all the thoughts about work, home, and troubles disappeared. All that mattered was listening to the caller and marking those bingo numbers. Here was my escape.

So began the six-month "bingo-phase" of my gamble-mania. At the end it would not only devastate my life as I knew it, but would also destroy my masterpiece, the Leacock Heritage Festival, which, ironically, had unlocked the Pandora's box.

"You're a real gambler, aren't you?" the older woman who was standing behind me said. We were waiting in line to buy our bingo cards for the 10 o'clock, Wednesday-evening session at the Magic Dabber Bingo Hall. The fact that I was ripping back the pull-tabs on a handful of Nevada tickets as I waited in the bingo line may have been her first clue. She had seen me in the bingo hall before, as both of us organized our own charity's bingo on other nights and met at the Magic Dabber Bingo Hall Charities Association meetings. She ran late-night Thursdays, one of my favourites. I often got in a double dose of bingo on those nights since I didn't have any business meetings and Roberta worked until 10:00 p.m., allowing me to attend the 7:00 p.m. session, too.

The woman was a crusty, matter-of-fact, no-nonsense taskmaster, at least according to the runners that helped at her session. But this night, her less-than-subtle hint bounced off my consciousness, or lack of consciousness, like the rain flowing off the windows on the outside of the bingo hall.

I know what I am doing. I convinced only myself, but didn't care what she or anyone else said about my new obsession with bingo. I knew it was a town joke that I played bingo almost every night. "You don't know," I said to anyone who dared hint that it was a bit unusual for a person of my position to be playing bingo every night. "It's really electronic gambling. It's not the same old church bingo anymore."

Certainly for me it was more than the church bingo of the old days. Nightly jackpots were $1,000 and $3,500 per session. I sat in the pristine non-smoking section, my $56 worth of bingo cards spread out over half a table that normally could seat eight people, a $20 pile of Nevada tickets on my left, and a couple of $5 scratch lottery tickets — for between bingo games — on my right. It was my mini-casino. I was getting ready.

As the bingo numbers were called I bounced the liquid dabber from number to number on the eighteen cards with the precision of a robot punching holes. When I was finished I looked up, squinting, at the lighted caller board, looking for the next number as my left hand reached for a Nevada ticket. When I was in high school I thought it was very cool to teach myself to light a match with one hand. Now, with that same hand, I cracked the cardboard Nevada ticket open with a snap, and with a twist of my thumb peeled back the five pull-tabs, ready for my split-second glance before I let it fall into the waiting waste-basket at the end of the table. Immediately, I brought my focus back in time to mark my bingo cards for the next number.

"The natural reflex is to the garbage can with these things," I said to the other players as we stood around the large wastepaper basket during a break or after bingo, pulling the tabs of what can only be described as 50-cent paper slot machines. More than once I would end up going through the garbage at the end of the night looking for a missing gold bar winner. Behind each slot — each chance — there were three symbols, usually random fruit shapes: the losers. The winners — three cherries in a row — were worth a buck; three lemons, $5; three prunes, $10; three bells, $25; and the ultimate — three gold bars — $100. This was Nevada's holy grail, the bars.

Back at the bingo table I had a winner in my stack of Nevada tickets. The rush of adrenaline was matched by the lightning speed of my right hand crossing the table to my left, ripping the tabs from the ticket and squirreling the "gold bars" away in my shirt pocket. Cherries, lemons, and prunes were reinvested for more tickets. Bells and bars were strategically cashed in during the breaks or at the end of the night. Often I would keep a bar or two in my pocket until the end so everyone else would think they were still in the box and keep chasing, increasing my odds of winning the next set of bars. In the break-open ticket game the advantage was to know how many bars were still in the box in relation to the number of tickets left. In a new box there were four winning sets of bars among 2050 fifty-cent tickets. Like so much of gambling, you had to have your "system."

"Have you got one stashed in your pocket, Doug?" Fred asked

as he whisked by, making change for his snack bar during the break. It seemed I always had one "stashed" in my pocket. Actually, my wins were a reflection of the hundreds of dollars I spent each night playing Nevada. That particular night there seemed to be no end to the bars. I'd won six times, for $600. The fact that it had cost me over $400 to win that much was only incidental and hardly worth considering. Not worth considering at all was how much it cost on the nights when I only won one, or worse, none. I put down the twenty dollars for two more fists full of tickets. Funny how I seemed to remember only the excitement of those big wins in both Nevada and bingo.

Did I win at bingo? It was a question I got all the time and one I would go to great pains to answer in the affirmative, whether it was Roberta asking, or anyone else. Well, I never lost. According to the bingo regulars, I won all the time. That's a common illusion in gambling. Winning is very public, broadcasted and shouted from the rooftops, not only by the gambler, but also by the gaming operator. (*Gaming.* That's the new corporate and government-sanctified, sanitized name for gambling now that they've taken over from the mob.) Losing, on the other hand, or the extent to which you've lost, is easy to keep secret. Nobody wants to know. Everybody loves a winner, and conversely, nobody likes a loser.

Winning was how I justified what I was doing, to Roberta, to my friends and to anyone who was watching. Winning and relaxing were my rationalizations. Now, not only did I need to win enough to keep paying for my gambling, I also needed to win enough to maintain the façade of winning. This included an occasional fifty dollars or hundred that I left with a note on the kitchen table for Roberta, ". . . from last night's game." It also included paying for the rare dinner and movie for my friends Bob and Mary-Anne, the "Bank of Bob" as I came to call him before this journey was complete.

Bob and Mary-Anne Willsey — they both were my bosses over the years as chairmen of the Downtown Management Board — owned four main-street businesses in Downtown Orillia, known as the Mariposa Market stores. Bob was certainly Orillia's best merchant, and perhaps one of Canada's best, having expanded his businesses and opened three new stores during the recessionary early 1990s. First he fine-tuned his main store, the Mariposa Market, a combined general store, bakery and café. Then he beat The Body Shop to Downtown Orillia by opening a unique bed and bath operation called The Scent Shoppe. This success was followed by the Mariposa Kids Clothing Store just in time for Bob and Mary-Anne's own kids, Elizabeth and Stephanie. Next came Seasons, a store that could be transformed with the changing weather — a Christmas store in fall and a gardening store in spring.

Bob was not only the hardest working guy I have ever met, he was also among the smartest, a fact that he shrouded well behind a mask of bemused innocence, and the fact that he had better things on his mind. A running gag Bob and I had was about the how-to retailing book he and I were going to write for the less successful merchants on the street. The gag was how few pages it would have. One page: "Clean your windows." Another: "Sell good stuff." And another: "Be nice to customers." One day after listening to a merchant complain about how slow business was while across the street customers were trying to get into her locked store, we added: "Open your doors."

Bob was chairman of the DMB when I was hired in 1989 and he stayed on the Board continuously until a few years ago when he put Mary-Anne in place to protect his interests, and mine. Mary-Anne, hiding nothing behind her biting harpy tongue, occasionally accompanied me to bingo for a night of insanity. I should have known there was something wrong with me when I started avoiding inviting her because she didn't take the game seriously enough.

"Are you going to bingo again tonight, Doug?" she asked during my daily free lunch with Bob. "I don't know," I lied. "You know," she'd say, "you just don't like company. It interferes with your being able to keep track of your numbers. 'Don't talk! Don't talk! Mr. Little's trying to hear the bingo caller.' God help us if we have a good time."

Bob and Mary-Anne were actually very tolerant of my bingo, and were quick to my defense if anyone made a snide remark or questioned the propriety of my newfound obsession.

"He does it to relax. Who else do you know who only goes to the 10 o'clock bingo session after his regular 12-hour day of work and evening community committee meetings?"

"Besides, he wins."

This morning the office looks foreign to me, too confused to be comfortable, too foreboding. Ever since the Festival ended in August, I have been so consumed with gambling and my need to win that I have had little time for cleaning up and reorganizing my life. In the past few weeks I have avoided coming to the office as much as I could. It has become a constant reminder of the growing chaos in my life.

On my desk there is a sea of pink. Messages from Leacock Heritage Festival creditors who haven't been paid. A message from Mr. Casino: "Where's the cheque?" Messages from bank managers about overdrafts. A message from Bob. There is also a note from Doug Bell, who is my manager of the Leacock Heritage Festival. "The city called about the bingo reports — again!"

Doug began as manager near the end of my bingo phase in June of 1995. Also a former chair of the DMB, he went out of business as a jeweller and took computer retraining. I was able to hire him for the Festival on a job placement program that paid most of his wages for a year. When I quit playing bingo, I also quit the Sunday night volunteering and bingo became this other Doug's weekly task.

The reports he is talking about are the weekly summaries that need to be filed with the City of Orillia lottery licensing department, itemizing how much was made at the bingo session, what was deposited, and what was spent and where. We are probably three months behind in reporting, which is better than the five months we were behind in August, but back then I had how busy we were with the Festival to blame. Now with the City, like everywhere else, my excuses are wearing thin.

In the beginning we religiously filed the reports within three or four weeks and made all the deposits on time or almost on time. The need to make that regular weekly deposit was keeping things under control. At first I always made deposits the night of the bingo, so the reports would show the deposit slip dated the same day. After, as I got into "borrowing" some of the money for my own bingo expenses, I'd make the deposits in a day or so, once I found a source of new cash to replace the money I had borrowed.

A day grew to a week, and eventually weeks became months. As necessity made me bolder, I started filing backdated deposit slips. This went on for a good year and the reports were finally made when the deposits were caught up and the money was in the bank. Only recently, as the pressure, and the losses, grew, did I start filing the reports without having the money deposited. Still, my hope was to make the deposits, replace every cent, and no one would be harmed, or the wiser.

Harmed. I am mindful enough to know I have to protect Doug Bell from my money manipulations. In the after-losing hours of creeping reality and increasing desperation, I know I can go to jail for what I am doing but I have no right to drag along innocent bystanders. I make Doug complete the preliminary reports and turn them over to me, along with the weekly deposits. I am responsible for the reporting and the banking. Sure Doug knows something is wrong; but he also knows I have a good track record for solving problems and have pulled things out of the fire before. What he doesn't know, and what even I don't know yet, is that the slippery slope of compulsive gambling is not like any previous inferno I have ever confronted.

Compulsive gambling is the inability to stop gambling, and the inability to win at gambling because you can't stop. It is an addiction like drug abuse or alcoholism, where money is the substance you abuse. My abuse of money has been lifelong. Then again, so have my addictions, stretching back to childhood.

"Just lay there and clear your mind," the priest said, walking slowly around the room. I was at a retreat. Earlier he confessed to us that he was an addict too, addicted to sex. That, I have learned around recovery rooms, can mean everything from masturbating too much (which, for a priest, may not be that often) to abusing children.

Still, as I lay there it was not the old priest who used to kiss me at Cub Scouts for bus tickets that came to mind, or my vague memories of another young priest trying to fondle me in bed. It was my father, in our garage on Milford Road, and boxing gloves, that I saw.

Within my program of recovery this retreat was recommended to me as an aid to getting in touch with your Higher Power. Considering where my gambling addiction had taken me, I was completely open to all treatment. My belief in this program that had worked for others like me was my faith in a Higher Power.

"Just let yourself float," the priest said. "Don't try to control your mind, just let things come and let them go."

What a contrast, I thought. For years I would never allow myself to look at who I really was. I was too busy getting things done.

"Relax. Sleep if you need to, if you are tired."

Early in group meetings I would speak about being two images of myself. One, the respected community leader — the manager of the downtown, the president of Festivals Ontario, the chairman of the Leacock Heritage Festival, blah, blah, blah — who worked 80 hours a week making things happen.

"There are no rules, just calm yourself, breathe easy and let your mind float."

The other, the gambler, who snuck out in the middle of the night, playing feverishly all night long, laying it all on the line. Both were caricatures.

"Just let those thoughts go. Allow yourself to float deeper. Back and back . . ."

Milford Road. What am I, nine or ten? It must be Grade Three. Dad has just bought me boxing gloves, and he is going to teach us how to box. I can see the makeshift ring he's built in the middle of our garage. Who's there? Another guy named Perry? I'm not sure of his name. He's kind of the neighbourhood wimp. He could use some boxing lessons. And Joey. The toughest kid in Milford. With some boxing lessons from my dad, I could beat even him.

As a former military police sergeant during the war, Dad knew all kinds of holds and blows that could paralyze a man twice his size. Ju-jitsu, he called it.

There were lots of times on our living room floor when Corporal David and Private Douglas were brought to heel, and often to tears, by a rough-housing Staff Sergeant Little, with just a twist of his hand. He had strength and power, and we never knew him to fear anything.

Corporal David, my older brother by four years, seemed to get it. He, too, was tough and fearless. Before we moved to Milford we lived in the "Old Buildings" of Rockwood Court and fought daily with the kids from the "New Buildings." We were the Little Gang, and my brother was the leader. In Grades One and Two, I would get out of school before the older kids and I'd have the job of setting things up for the rock fight over the fences between the Old and the New. I'd rush home and sneak into the New Building's courtyard and steal all the lids from the garbage cans, taking them back to the Old courtyard to act as shields in the daily battle. Often by the time the older kids got home I was already into it, blasting rocks across the fence at anything that moved. I was so proud.

In the garage I can't wait for my dad to show me some moves, some ju-jitsu secrets. Just having the gloves on makes me feel indomitable, like Superman in his cloak, indestructible. I'm bobbing and weaving around the ring as I wait for my dad to finish tying up Joey's gloves.

Joey climbs into the ring.

"Okay," Dad says, "No kicking or biting. No low blows. Break, and go to your corners. When I ring the bell come out fighting."

Whoa! What about the moves? The secrets? Ju-jitsu?

Clang! Dad rings the bell. I bounce out into the middle of the ring, swinging and jabbing just like I've seen on TV. Joey calmly walks into the middle. I watch him put his arm up in the air and he gives me one roundhouse — right in the stomach.

I'm doubled over. I can't breathe. Tears well in my eyes but not a sound comes from my mouth as I stagger around the ring trying to catch my breath. Joey walks calmly back to his corner and puts his arms on the ropes to wait.

Finally I catch my breath, and from my doubled over position in the middle of the ring I cry: "Ring the bell, Daddy, ring the bell."

Ring the bell, Daddy, ring the bell, came out of my mouth, and my childhood, as I knew it, ended.

There were tears in my eyes as I lay on the retreat room floor. This was the demarcation line in my life. From this point on it was my father's mocking "Ring the bell, Daddy, ring the bell" that defined our relationship.

I don't know whether it was before the boxing ring or after that my father's boss died and alcohol became a dominant factor in our home. My father worked as a restaurant manager for a man named Louis Green who owned "Green's at the Head of King Street." It was an institution, not only in our life, but to all of Saint John. It was a tobacco and magazine store with a soda fountain restaurant at the key corner at the top of King Street, on King's Square in the heart of the city. In my memory my dad had worked there at least seven or eight years in the 1950s.

When we lived in Rockwood Court, and went to school at Holy Trinity, I would sometimes walk or take the bus to Green's after school and wait for my father so we could go home together. Green's had the greatest comic book section.

"Hey there, young fella," an old man with yellow glasses and a balding head said to me one afternoon, "you can't just sit around here reading comic books all day. You have to buy something."

"I can so," I shot back in a matter of fact tone, "My father is Doug Little."

"And who are you," he said, amused at my brashness.

"I'm Doug Little Junior."

Our family mythology paints Louis Green as a benevolent grandfather to us all and surrogate father to my dad whose own father died when he was three. Dad and his seven brothers and sisters were raised by his widowed mother and a cantankerous and abusive stepfather we just called Brownie. If Nanny Brown seemed like a saint, Brownie was the devil and caused my dad to leave home, and live with relatives at the age of fifteen.

My father seemed to change with Mr. Green's death. Again family myth said Mr. Green left my father a share of the business along with his two sons. But it wasn't true. The sons inherited the business and eventually my father was fired, or quit, because they couldn't get along.

Physical punishment was no doubt a part of our family's disciplinary regime before Mr. Green's death, although I have no recollection of beatings before that time or in Rockwood Court where we lived until I was eight. After that, physical hitting, whether it was the back of the hand to the head or the leather belt to somewhere behind, seemed to be the response to every situation. My father, who had always been somewhat of a benevolent tyrant, became a mean bully and someone to fear. My mother and he fought regularly about his drinking. He often came home in the middle of the night drunk. He was in a bad mood almost constantly.

I retreated more into myself, became more secretive. I was confused — and guilty — about what was going on at cub-scouts. The priest. The kissing. Maybe touching. For bus tickets. I couldn't tell anyone. I took the bus tickets. Who would believe me anyway?

"Ring the bell, Daddy, ring the bell" became a teasing taunt that told me I didn't belong. Beatings reinforced the message. I started to run, and to do whatever I could to get out of the house and out of his way. At nine years old I began a lifetime of escape — and a lifetime of doing whatever it took to effect that escape.

CHAPTER THREE

The intercom in my office buzzes. It's Jennifer. Even before she speaks

October 22, 1996 — 9 a.m.

I know something is wrong. How distant and sombre she has become lately. So has my other assistant Susan. It's like they're watching something very bad happen and they can't figure out what to do about it. What I don't realize, or won't realize, is that it's happening to them, too.

"It's Bob."

"Thanks," I answer. I put the phone receiver back down, look at the pink message from yesterday, and stare at the blinking outside line. *The Bank of Bob.* The thought hits me like a heart attack.

When I talk about my gambling binge over the next few years I'll often describe myself as juggling eight bank accounts all at the same time, only one of which was my own. Well, the balls are about to fall.

I pick up the phone. "Bob?"

"My bank returned eighteen hundred dollars of your cheques."

"Fuck."

"Some of them are from two weeks ago, and they say there's more," Bob snaps angrily.

"My overdraft. The bank must have kicked back my fucking overdraft," I say. "They didn't even call me."

Well, they didn't call me yesterday, or on Friday, that much is true. But my neighbour, the bank manager, has pleaded with me throughout the last couple of weeks to get the overdraft covered, saying that $5,000 was over his authorized limit. "Don't worry, George," I told him, "I'm just waiting for the festival to get the cheque from the casino's sponsorship — they owe me money — and I'll get the overdraft covered." Did he believe me? Probably not, but who I am and what I've done earns me the benefit of the doubt. This is the personal currency I exchange for cash on a daily basis up and down the main street of Orillia in order to continue my gambling.

"Jeez, I'm sorry, Bob." I am genuinely sorry. Sorry I haven't won enough to cover this and the other overdrafts. "Let me call and see what I can do. Don't worry about it, I'll get them covered one way or another." *Don't worry about it.* One of the books I would read about families and compulsive gamblers would say if the gambler were to wear a t-shirt, it would say "Don't worry about it." Mary-Anne would tell me later that Bob was up all night the night before, sick to his stomach.

"I'll call you," I say, but it sounds hollow so I add, "no, I'll come down."

"My bank is upset about this, you know," he says, more sorrowfully than I have ever heard him say anything.

"I know, Bob. I'm sorry. I'll get it looked after." I don't dare tell him my luck has been lousy lately. We aren't going to acknowledge that I have been gambling with his money.

"He was so upset because he let it happen, that he let you do it," Mary-Anne would say.

I hang up the phone and feel my own bout of nausea coming

on. "Shit! Shit! Shit! Shit!" How could the bank do that? How could they kick back cheques they'd already accepted?

Of course I didn't call George to find out. In fact, George called me. No, he called the "other Doug," as I call Doug Bell. One of the cheques he kicked back was on the Leacock Heritage Festival account and the Royal Bank bounced it right back. Now, because Doug Bell's signature was also on the cheque (I have him sign them blank) he is being threatened with being held liable for the $1500 cheque. While that is just nonsense — as it is a corporate account — he is sick to his stomach, too.

I'm sitting at my desk, my head in my hands, literally paralyzed with fear. I am trying to keep the impending sense of doom at bay. I wonder if I am shaking on the outside, whether the trembling that is emanating from my chest and stomach can be seen by those who are close to me. No, I lie to myself, they can't: I put on a brave front. But I know my mask is beginning to slip. I can see it in the faces of the people around me, hear it in their voices, and feel it in my own isolation. It creates a kind of anger in me. A determination: I can't fail at this. *I'll show them.* My answer has always been to try harder, work harder, get the money, and make it happen. What I don't realize is that gambling is not like other things. The harder you work at gambling, the worse things get.

"I know, I'm working on it," I bark at Doug Bell as he puts his head through my office door and tells me he has to file some bingo reports with the City of Orillia. They called again. In our unspoken code he is really asking if I have money to make the deposits as the bank slips have to be included along with the reports. In the end, to get the City of Orillia off his back and mine, I resort to dummying the deposit slips. Another crime.

"I am trying to borrow some money to get caught up," I tell him, but I can't look him in the eye. He knows the only borrowing I am doing is from the bingo float each night, and from last week's deposits, as I desperately try to win back my losses. What he doesn't know is that my "loans" also include thousands of dollars in cheques I cashed on the accounts and two ten-thousand-dollar deposits from the charity casinos that I told him I had put in the bank.

Whatever borrowing I can do, I have already done. They are called bailouts, and I have had a few. The last one was eight thousand dollars, from a loan shark in Toronto before Casino Rama even opened.

"There was a call for you yesterday," Roberta said as we both moved around the kitchen on the June Saturday morning, a week after we came back from our trip to the casino in Sault Ste. Marie. "A guy named Johnny. He said to tell you 'Johnny called.'"

"Okay," I answered, trying to act casual while inside all my vital organs seized up in horror. *Johnny called.* You'd think the guy could be a little more subtle.

"Who's Johnny?" I knew she'd ask and I try to free my brain from its panic in order to concoct a plausible reply.

"Some guy I used to gamble with at the charity casino in Barrie." I slid close to the edge with my response, hoping to give it credibility. "He probably wants to borrow money."

The last thing I wanted to do was to tell her that Johnny was a loan shark and that his purposeful call to her was no less than a veiled threat.

"Why would he want to borrow money from you?"

"He thinks I win all the time and therefore I have money. He's just a loser."

"How did he get my number?" she asked, knowing the phone is in her name; I'm not listed in the phone book.

"I gave him my Little & Associates card once. I thought he might have some marketing work. He works for Honda in Alliston." God, I wanted to shut up. The more I talked, the more convoluted the story got. It was time for offense. "He didn't leave a number, did he?"

"No, he said he would catch you later," Roberta replied.

"See, he's just some loser calling around trying to borrow money." Believable? Who knows. But it did the trick of shifting the spotlight from the inexplicable "Johnny" to the tired old chestnut, "my gambling."

"I hope your gambling isn't getting us into trouble again," Roberta started.

"Look," I attacked, "I gamble to relax, and I win more than I lose. Blackjack is not bingo. I can handle it." Ouch, I shouldn't have mentioned the bingo. It conjures up last year's crisis and the loan from her father. "Besides, it's summer, Canada Day, Farmers' Market, Leacock Heritage Festival, and on top of it all the final Task Force stuff for the Casino Rama opening. I haven't got time to gamble."

She knows that has been true in the past. Last year I quit bingo in June and didn't really gamble at all — except for lottery tickets and playing on my computer — all summer long. Gambling at the charity casinos didn't start in earnest until the fall of 1995, and compared to bingo, it was relatively easy to hide.

"I have to go check out the Farmers' Market," I said heading for the door, dodging any more questions about "Johnny."

I met Johnny through a friend of mine who shall remain for-ever nameless in his innocence. He was someone who bailed me out personally the first time things had come to this kind of a head, although at the time he thought he was lending me some money to help my daughter Melanie get into Columbia University in New York City. She did have a combined scholarship and loan offer from Columbia for about $25,000 but with the tuition at $30,000 and living expenses in New York City, we couldn't swing it, so she turned them down.

This time I knew I needed to take the direct approach, and who knows, maybe I was sincere. I knew then I had a gambling problem. I owed about $20,000 to various organizations and it just seemed to get worse every time I gambled. I thought maybe I should quit, but first I needed to get the $20,000 under control or my life was going to explode.

I met with my friend in a Tim Horton's in Barrie and I spilled my guts about having a gambling problem. I told him I borrowed $10,000 from the charity casino that the Festival ran and lost it all in the casinos in Windsor and Sault Ste. Marie.

"If I don't get that money deposited in the bank real soon, I won't be able to file the reports or pay the casino operators. I'm going to be splashed all over the newspapers," I moaned. "And I'll go to jail," I added for emphasis.

"Last year," he asked, "was it gambling?"

"Yes," I confessed. "It was bingo and I quit bingo, cold turkey. But I got in trouble again when we visited these other casinos in Windsor and Sault Ste. Marie, trying to assess the impact so we could get ready here in Orillia." Partially true. I always saw my visits to these big casinos as the answer to my problems, at least when I was on the way there. Leaving, I was always broke. My friend's first bailout — the university deposit — was partly spent on my first visit to what I called a "real casino."

When I approached him for the first loan, I was about six or seven thousand dollars in the hole, owing some to the Leacock bingo float and deposits, some to Winter Carnival and some to my overdrawn bank account. This was April 1995, relatively early in my overall gambling spree, but I was heavily into the bingo and Nevada by this time. I was covering my losses with borrowing from the bingo floats, my petty cash and travel advances, and a revolving cheque-writing scheme between the several bank accounts I would soon describe as my "gambling cycle."

He actually gave me $4,500 as an advance on some marketing work I could do for him in the future. To protect his anonymity I won't say more.

With this first bailout I paid off the overdraft on my own account, deposited money into the Winter Carnival account to cover the cheque kiting, made some bingo deposits, and restored the float. I also kept five hundred dollars for gambling at the native casino we were going to be visiting in Sault Ste. Marie during the Festivals Ontario Conference held there. The conference was in Canada. The casino, Vegas Kewadin, was in the United States. It was owned by the Sault Ste. Marie Tribe of Chippewas, tribal relatives of the Chippewas of Rama who would be opening our own casino near Orillia the next year. Of course I had to check it out to see its economic impact. The economic spin-off. Sure, that's what I said, but we know which particular spin I had in mind.

In my gambling there were more surprises than just calls out of the blue from "Johnny." There were things that make all gamblers believers in all the nonsensical superstitions we cling to, like wearing the right shirt, or sitting at a certain table, driving down certain roads, or having a lucky charm — we had little trains in the bingo hall that you would push when you won and they'd whistle "whoo whoo." Things like lucky numbers (7, 17, Melanie's birthday), and certain people you'll play with and others you won't. How about looking around the casino for just the right machine — the one that talks to you?

With gambling, unlike the other alcohol and drug addictions I have known, you win, and you win at the strangest of times. In my irreverent faith in luck, I assigned magical meaning to the wins.

The night before I was to leave for Sault Ste. Marie, and my first visit to a "real casino," I had my biggest night of winning at bingo. I had often joined the first bingo session of the night, which normally starts at 6:45 p.m., halfway through, buying my cards during the break. That gave me until about eight o'clock on any given night to get my board and community meetings over. The bingo rules said you had to be there before the second half starts and you still had to buy a full book of cards, wasting four games. This gave me a shot at the $3,500 Super Jackpot, the $1,000 jackpot, the bonanza game and three regular games and one special.

That night, right off the bat, I won a regular game, along with seven other people, splitting the $50 prize seven ways — $8. In bingo payouts, we always rounded up. Then came the Super Jackpot.

The Super Jackpot could be had in 49 numbers and my dabber was perched, waiting over the I-21 number on my card. It was the only number I needed. My heart was pounding like a jackhammer.

This was the closest I had ever come on the $3500 Super Jackpot, right down to the last number. *God, how I want twenty-one.*

"Twenty-one, twenty-one, twenty-one, twenty-one," I kept saying over and over under my breath, my eyes, with my new glasses, focused completely on the monitor where the next ball would appear, seconds before the caller hollered it out. I was trying to will twenty-one into the slot.

The previous ball disappeared as he called it and up came the new number. I stopped breathing as it came into focus.

N-32.

"Phewwww," I let my breath out and sighed. "Shit, I only had one left," I said to the other bingo players sitting in the non-smoking section.

"Too bad," some of my twenty or so fellow non-smoking players lied. In bingo, you always hate it when someone else wins, because it means you've lost, or at least, you have to share the prize if there's a tie. At these early sessions they get more non-smokers. At the 10 p.m. session I could be alone in the whole room or, at most, there would be six or seven other players. Unless, that is, the Super Jackpot could be won at 55 or 56 numbers. That would keep those from the first session there and attract players from the other bingo hall after its seven o'clock session. Not this night, though, as the second session would have 50 as the magic number, a long shot at best.

Three numbers later, I-21 popped its ping-pong head onto the TV screen and I yelled, "Bingo!"

"Bingo," I yelled again so the runner would hurry to the non-smoking microphone and announce bingo for the caller and the rest of the players to hear out in the smoke-infested main part of the hall. Immediately the crusty old woman who had become my constant companion in the non-smoking section snarled at me, "It's the next number." She added under her breath, "Idiot." In my excitement I had forgotten — you didn't call bingo until the number was actually called.

"False alarm," the bingo caller laughed, "please check your numbers."

"I-21" he finally called and I hollered, rather anti-climatically, "Bingo."

So I won the Super Jackpot game in the first session, but not the Super Jackpot itself. I won the consolation prize of $400. I waited to see if there were others who would share in the four hundred bucks, but no, it was all mine.

"I see you won again, Little. You're so lucky," one of the wiped-out women said to me as she was going out the door after the first session. "Did you get the bars, too?" she snapped, walking past the spot where I was perched placidly in front of the garbage pail cracking back a handful of Nevada tickets. In fact, I *had* got the bars, but they were hidden deep in my shirt pocket, a $100 bonus to my bingo wins.

During the ensuing late-night session I bagged a $25 early-bird game, a $100 Special all alone, and split another $50 regular game with two other winners. I also won a $125 Bonanza game, where they sell cards all night long on 45 numbers that were already called, with the caller completing the rest of the numbers — anywhere up to sixty — before the last game of the night.

The last game was the Regular Jackpot, a $1,000 prize that someone wins every night for a full card. They call numbers until someone wins. Paying out this one-thousand-dollar prize, Sunday night after Sunday night at the Leacock Heritage Festival bingo session, was pivotal to the breaking down of my initial prejudice against playing bingo; that, plus the non-smoking room, and of course, Nevada tickets. I started playing Nevada as a joke — 50¢ a try. Who cares about a buck or two? Until I snagged a hundred dollars for 50¢ and I was no longer laughing.

Again, I was hot. It was the first time I had ever won the jackpot but so did two other people and we split the thousand-dollar prize, $334 each. This night alone raised my reputation as a winning gambler to the level of legend throughout both bingo halls and, via the rumour mill, throughout Orillia. I couldn't have cared less. I was flying.

Seven wins in one night, plus a set of bars in Nevada — $1,109 in total — all on the night before I went for my first visit to a *real* casino, plus I still had $500 left from the bailout.

Hey, I thought — coming down to earth — what an opportunity to bank some pro-bingo points at home. That night I left Roberta a note, with $409: "See! I do win at Bingo!"

Surely, twelve hundred dollars was enough to make a killing in Sault Ste. Marie, especially on a winning streak.

My secret friend had money, but due to personal and business happenings in his life he didn't have that much cash to help me at the time. I told him I had to have $10,000 to buy some time until Leacock's sponsorship money came in and they paid me what they owed me. It was easy to convince anyone that the Leacock Heritage Festival owed me money because everyone knew that I created it, that I raised the money, managed it, and made it happen. It was my festival. But, and it was a big but, it was also a non-profit organization and I was its voluntary chairman. Other than my receipted expenses, it never paid me a cent in eight years; that is, not counting what I stole. In defending me, after I crashed, Bob's wife, Mary-Anne would argue, "It was his money anyway." It wasn't an argument we used in court.

My friend gave me $2,000 cash — another gift. No talk of future work this time. He said he would arrange to have a friend of a friend — Johnny — lend me $8,000 but he warned me, "Don't miss paying this guy back."

I met Johnny in another donut shop in the northern part of Toronto. He gave me eight grand cash and I gave him seventeen post-dated monthly cheques for $500 each with no name written on the payee line. My three per cent interest rate was not at loan-shark levels due to my friend but Johnny emphasized that if I missed one payment all the rules changed and the full amount came due.

"Do you understand what I am saying?" Johnny said quietly. He leaned across the donut booth and looked into to my frightened eyes.

"I understand," I said. I felt the same flush of blood pressure, of excitement and anxiety that I'd come to crave in gambling. On the way home, it was just like winning. I was euphoric.

Hey, I have eight thousand dollars, I thought. *Maybe I can double it at a charity casino.*

Doug Bell knows I am in trouble, but even he has no idea how deep that trouble is, or how despairing I am becoming. Still, we are growing apart and he spends more and more of his days in front of his computer doing God knows what. I have distanced myself from all of my employees during these last months. Everything is spiralling out of control and my answer is to isolate, deny, distort, minimize, and full-out lie. There isn't a lot of work being done by me or anybody else in our operations, at least not that I notice. My concentration is shot. Not even an impending deadline, no board meeting, or special event, can bring me into focus on my work. I am on automatic pilot.

Now my day job is to find money — money from anywhere — to get back to the casino. I quake at, and quickly dismiss, any thought of not winning. That I have to rely on payroll advances, petty-cash funds, moving cheques from one bank to another, and downright stealing are all secondary to the imperative: "I need money." Maintaining my job and my façade as a community leader have became unimportant in comparison to my quest for gambling fuel; even friendship and family have succumbed.

Over the past month, failing all else, at the end of the day I've been calling Bob's mother-in-law, Donna. I ask her to keep $500 cash out of the daily deposits from his Mariposa businesses and I bring her a cheque. On the weekends she holds the cheques and if I win, I replace the cash. If I lose — the norm — the cheque contributes to that growing, unsecured overdraft in my own bank account.

Think, Mr. Big Shot, think. I've got to get money to Bob. I've got to buy time. Bingo! The Bingo deposits and the float from this Sunday night — I haven't touched them yet. Each week we have a cash float for the Bingo of about $800, which we keep in the office (when I haven't already borrowed it). There should also be the deposit from Sunday night's session. Doug doesn't make deposits any more but brings me the money so I can catch up on a previous deposit and we can file the report. It is an endless game of rob from Bingo to pay back Bingo, or Nevada, or Bob, as the case may be.

"There is no deposit," Doug tells me as he hands over the cash box. "We lost money." My mouth drops. "I had to go into the float to pay out the prize money," he adds.

Ever since the casino opened three months ago there has been a steady drop in bingo players. At our Sunday night session we have been affected more than others because it was already one of the quietest nights.

No wonder that a year later, at a meeting of the Ontario Coalition Against Gambling Expansion, I would learn that the Ontario Bingo industry was offering to finance OCAGE's legal challenge of the Province of Ontario's charity casino expansion plans. I was a guest at the meeting as a compulsive gambler. I urged them to be at least the one group — along with Gamblers Anonymous — not to be in the pockets of some facet of the gambling industry. Sadly all treatment, research, community assessment, and awareness of problem and compulsive gambling was, and is, being financed (and, therefore, controlled) by the gambling industry and its government partners, the very beneficiaries of gambling expansion. I was shocked to learn even the Canadian Foundation for Compulsive Gambling was beholden to the casinos and the government for its funding. No wonder there is so little criticism of the expansion of gambling in Canada. Everybody is at the trough.

"How much is there?" I ask, abandoning any pretense as to what I was going to do with the cash.

"About $550," he says. "Don't forget I am going to need $800 on Friday to get change."

"Yeah, I know," I say, taking the cash box back into my office.

It's not anywhere enough to satisfy Bob — and what am I going to use to get back to the casino tonight?

The idea of running away has entered my head more than once. One desperate fantasy has me going up and down Orillia's Mississaga Street, visiting each of the two hundred merchants that are my Downtown Management Board members, cashing one or two hundred dollar cheques at each, and then running — after one last night of playing at the casino of course. What would that be, ten to twenty thousand dollars? But that would be out-and-out theft, not something I could rationalize. No borrowing, no *I'll pay it back*. No tomorrow. I'd have to admit I was a crook.

Other times, like after the last visits to Windsor and Sault Ste. Marie, broke, I thought of just driving across the bridge at the border and not turning back. Somehow, though, grand theft auto — the van belongs to the Downtown — and robbing convenience stores for food and gas money couldn't pass even my warped reality check. Driving through the bridge to end it all seemed a more viable solution.

There is about $300 in bills in the cash box: fives and tens, as well as about $250 in coin: loonies, toonies, and quarters. I can't give Bob loonies and toonies and I can't go to the bank. At least not to my bank, or Leacock's bank or the Winter Carnival's bank. Or, come to think of it, Bob's bank. I'm running out of banks. The Orillia Winter Carnival has one of the eight bank accounts I control, also overdrawn, and no longer cashing cheques. "Don't worry," I told the bank manager, "Leacock Heritage Festival owes the carnival some money and we are just waiting for a cheque from the casino."

A year and a half later, my story splashed across the cover of

Saturday Night Magazine, one of the Orillia Royal Bank officials will get a big laugh in the local paper by saying: "When he said he was waiting for money any day from the casino, we thought he meant a donation, not the roulette wheel."

By the time most of us compulsive gamblers are done, we are also compulsive liars. I was. It was how I stayed in action, how I got money, how I took the time from home or work. It became second nature. It became easy. What was hard was keeping all the lies straight.

But how did all this "borrowing" start? As manager of the DMB I had two advances from which I paid my expenses. One was a petty cash advance of $100 and the other was a travel expense advance that could have been anywhere from $200 to $500 depending on what my travel needs were at any given time. It was for meals, gas, miscellaneous stuff when I was going out of town on downtown business, or for meals if I was working overtime which used to be a great deal of the time. The office also had a $100 petty cash which was used for things we needed to buy on a day-to-day basis. I tried to stay away from this one because the staff got upset if there was no cash when they needed supplies. Often it took me weeks, sometimes months, to get around to filing my petty cash receipts and having my money accounted for, replenished or reimbursed.

The Orillia Farmer's Market had a petty cash and I was also its manager, under a contract with the City of Orillia. Then there was the Leacock Heritage Festival petty cash and the expense advance I had for its needs. In the months leading up to, and during, the 11-day celebration at the end of July, I had hundreds of dollars in cash expenses. At the beginning of July there were the Canada Day celebrations of which I was the coordinator. Although there was an outside treasurer and a little more day-to-day control, I still had expenses and petty cash.

Winter Carnival had both petty cash and expense cash advances. Carnival got ridiculous, as we had to pay snowplow operators and snowmobile race competitors in cash. I was not only the coordinator of the carnival but also its treasurer.

The Leacock Heritage Festival had a separate treasurer throughout most of the years, but he resigned early in 1996 because he had no control over what I was doing.

Both the Downtown and the Farmers' Market used the City of Orillia's accounting department and, ultimately, its treasurer as well. Their accounting procedures were pretty straightforward and their books were verified by annual audit. Throughout the years the treasurer and the City auditors raised questions about my payroll advances and about the DMB's loans to the Leacock Heritage Festival, but the loans were on the up-and-up and dealt with by the Downtown Board long before my gambling became a factor.

In total, I had six petty-cash advances and five expense advances under my control for eight years, give or take an event or so. And, while the DMB and the Farmers' Market had the sophisticated accounting department, the Festival, the Carnival, and Canada Day were all made up of volunteers, me included, and accounting certainly was not my priority. My priority was always to get the job done, make the event happen, to use whatever resources were available, and let the accountants pick up the pieces and do the counting later.

The Leacock Heritage Festival's bingo, Nevada, and Charity

Casino proceeds were shared with Canada Day and the Winter Carnival. To me it was all community development. If Leacock had it, and Winter Carnival needed it, then sure, give it to them.

So it didn't matter to me if it was the DMB's travel advance, Leacock's petty cash or the Winter Carnival's expense advance I had in my pocket: when I needed to pay for something, I used it. Somebody kept track of all this stuff, but it wasn't me. I always kept receipts for everything I did, everything I paid, and who owed whom, but it was the bean counters who kept it straight and me out of trouble. That was, before my gambling started.

At least once a year we'd account for all the petty cash accounts, all the expense advances and all the cash expenditures and expenses. Most years some of the organizations would owe me money; sometimes I owed them a little. It all came out in the wash, and, to get things done, it seemed an okay way to operate — before gambling.

Doing whatever it takes to make things happen: that is my winning formula. It has been since I was a young child.

"Don't you touch me!" My mother's yelling woke me from my sleep. We were in our house on Russell Street, in East Saint John, on the second floor where the bedrooms were, and it sounded like my father was drunk, again. It had been happening with such regularity lately he'd taken to staying away from home, living in one of the boarders' rooms upstairs over the restaurant, where we used to live when we first moved to East Saint John.

The Little Inn, at Kane's Corner, was actually just up the street, on the corner of Loch Lomond Road, where Russell Street ends and Bayside Drive begins. We moved there from Milford when my father opened his own restaurant with, we all thought, the money he got for his share of Green's. But no, he borrowed heavily to renovate and open the restaurant. It became his hell, maybe hell for all of us, as it sucked the life out of not only him, but my mother and my older brothers, and sister. That was not the way it was supposed to be.

The first job I ever had was as a busboy in my father's new restaurant when I was ten years old. The hand-rubbing anticipation of all the tips I was going to make was the same heart-pounding excitement I'd feel years later, the first time I stood in the underground gold mine where I worked in Timmins, and again now, every time I sit in front of a roulette wheel.

In the gold mine, my head spun and my palms sweat as I saw bright yellow nuggets of gold everywhere I looked. I couldn't help it. I just wanted some of that gold in my pockets. There was so much of it stuck in the rock walls; no one would ever miss my little bit.

I told the restaurant patrons they were my first customers and their tips were going to be my first tips. I don't know where I got the idea the busboy, when he cleaned the tables, got the tips. What disappointment I felt when my mother told me the tips belonged to the waitresses and not to me. I could hardly believe her. I suspected she was just telling me that because she was a waitress. The busboy job lost a great deal of its appeal that day.

As a newspaper reporter in the mining community of Timmins for several years, I had heard stories of high grading and the fanciful tales of successful businessmen who had made their initial fortunes that way. High-grading was taking the large "high-grade" gold ore from the mines where you worked, smuggling it out in lunch pails or in clothing and even in various body crevices. The fables of successful high-graders in Timmins are like the legends of successful bootleggers in other communities.

By the time I reached the 1400-foot level of Pamour Porcupine Gold Mines in the early 1970s, there was a great deal of security against high-grading. Not that it was needed at Pamour, regardless of my sweaty palms. Pamour was proud of its status as the lowest-grade gold mine in the world. High-grade, if it existed at all, was scarce.

Gold mine security: First, they checked your lunch pail. You also walked through a metal detector, like those used in airports. Underground clothing was left to hang in the "dry" and you walked naked to the locker room to get changed into street clothes.

All of this was racing through my brain as I stood awestruck in the rock cave — the stope — my eyes darting through the dark from wall to wall, the yellow metal glittering in the bouncing beam of my underground head lamp.

How do I get it out? The question continued to haunt me as I moved about the stope, assisting my partner with the engineering survey of the mine workings. I couldn't find the answer, but neither could I ignore the shining nuggets lying scattered at my feet. It was too much to resist.

Alone in one corner of the mine stope I bent down, my head lamp bobbing, and picked up a nugget about an inch square. I slipped it into my jacket pocket. Another, a little smaller. And another.

My partner was talking to someone on the other side of the stope, laughing. I turned to see what they were so amused about and I heard him yell across the muck, his words echoing off the hard rock walls: "It's pyrite! Fool's gold!"

I wondered if this was the first place they took all the rookies in the underground mine. Gold mining lost a great deal of its appeal for me that day.

"Wow, your parents own their own restaurant, you must be rich," was a common refrain among the kids at school. I didn't understand why we weren't, or why, if we were, I didn't have the toys that other kids had. The one thing I did have, however, was food — hamburgers, hot dogs, and milkshakes. One day I invited the richest (I thought so anyway) and most popular guy in my school, Perry Nice, along with his friends — his gang — to come to the restaurant for free hot dogs and hamburgers.

"This will make me part of the gang," I told myself, standing in front of my mirror. I could never figure out how my mother could say no to something I wanted even before I asked. Years later she would tell me she had always overheard me rehearsing everything in front of the mirror.

Perry Nice and the gang enjoyed the free eats and afterwards we went off together to do whatever gangs do, but Perry turned and said: "Stop. It doesn't make you our friend, or part of our gang," he said, pushing me away.

"But," I stammered, "the hot dogs, the food. I thought . . ."

"My father always says, if someone wants to bribe you to do something, take the bribe but don't do it anyway."

God, I hated the feeling I had that day.

By the time we had the restaurant a few years no one in our family had any illusions left about it making us any money, not to mention any friends. Mom worked there every day, from morning to night. She was gone before we got up in the morning because she had to serve the breakfast crowd. At lunch, there was the lunch crowd. And at dinner time, she served dinner to the dinner crowd. I suppose she got a few hours off in the afternoon, but I was at school. When we did see her at night she was usually hollering at us for one thing or another, or just crying in her bed. My sister Veronica spent most of her time looking after my four younger brothers and sister, as well as bossing the rest of us around. It was like she was the mother now.

"Don't touch me or so help me I'll . . ." I heard my mother scream. I opened the door from my bedroom to see my father, from behind, staggering in front of my mother, who was standing poised like Mickey Mantle with a baseball bat — except she had a bunk-bed board that looked like a two-by-four.

"Don't you touch her!" I shrieked, running and jumping onto my father's back, grabbing him around the throat, desperately trying to recall one of the jujitsu moves.

"Dougie, don't, go back to bed!" Now my mother was yelling at me.

My father was completely stunned by what I did, and spun around in circles trying to catch me as I hung on to his neck.

"Doug, be careful. Don't you hurt him," Mom cried at him.

On the third turn, with his hands reaching menacingly over his head, I saw my chance to jump. I scrambled down the staircase and out the front door. Terrified, I stayed hidden in the backyard until I was sure it was over and he had gone to sleep.

Maybe he didn't threaten me. He didn't have to. I was afraid enough for both of us. That night, 12 years old and shivering in my backyard, I made up my mind I would do whatever it took to get away.

Shortly thereafter I got religious.

"Do you want to be a Priest?" I saw the ad for the Redemptorist Fathers and Saint Mary's College in an issue of *The New Freeman*, a Roman Catholic newspaper that was kicking around the house. In our family we always went to Mass each Sunday. It was invariably a major production and a source of turmoil each week as my mother tried to round up anywhere from six to eight kids and herd them off to church. Mom had the zeal of a convert — she was a Baptist when my father met her — but the rest of us seemed to be going through the motions.

"Forgive me Father, for I have sinned. It's been one week since my last confession."

"Go ahead." The gruff tone of the response from our parish priest, Father Kinsella, told me I was in deep trouble.

Shit — he's pissed and I haven't even said anything yet. What's he going to say when I tell him about stealing from my mother's purse, and taking quarters from dad's dresser? I've already got the strap at home, but what the hell's he going to say?

"Sorry Father, . . . umm, . . . umm. I hit my sisters, I yelled at my brother, I said bad words, and I took the Lord's name in vain." No way I was going to give him the big stuff.

"Taking the Lord's name in vain is breaking the Third Commandment and is a Mortal Sin damning your soul to the everlasting fires of Hell. How dare you take the Lord's name in vain!" he snarled.

Whoa. Holy Mackerel. I'm in for it now.

"What else."

"Nothing Father, nothing. That's it. I didn't do any . . ."

"Oh, shut up, Little," he hissed through the darkness of the confessional screen window, darkness that was supposed to make you feel at ease, as if you were talking to God, not a priest or a man. Only God is supposed to know it's you.

"For your penance say ten 'Our Fathers' and ten 'Hail Marys' and make the Stations of the Cross every day after school for a week." Beads rattled and I felt the wind of his absolution blessing on my face.

Jesus, I thought.

"Go," he said when, still in shock from the "Stations of the Cross" penance, I didn't move. I scrambled out of the confessional and went to the pew near the front of the altar to say my "Our Fathers" and "Hail Marys."

Christ, I thought as I moved my lips to make like I was praying, how the hell was I going to come all the way over here every day after school to do the Stations of the Cross without Mom and Dad finding out and thinking I'd done something really bad to deserve it. Our church, Stella Maris, was at least a half an hour's walk from my grade five school.

"They'll never believe I was just swearing," I mumbled out loud.

"What's swearing?" my little brother Joey asked my sister Veronica as we all walked home from confession.

What attracted me most about the "Do you want to be a Priest?" ad was that the contact address was St. Peter's, the same church where I had gone to Cub Scouts when we lived in Milford. At least I wouldn't have to deal with Father Kinsella. It was, however, the church with the "kissing priest."

Saint Mary's College was a minor seminary in Brockville, Ontario where young boys from "Grade Nine to First Arts Preparatory College" came from all across Eastern Canada to study for the priesthood and initiation into the religious order known as the Redemptorists.

"If you are interested see your Parish Priest or contact the Redemptorist Fathers at St. Peter's." Hiding out behind the garage in terror of my father may not have been a spiritual experience, but I certainly had a religious conversion the day I found that priesthood ad. From that point on in my 13-year-old, grade-eight life, it all was about getting accepted into Saint Mary's College.

Suddenly I was religious, rushing to church, not only on Sunday but also during the week once I became an altar boy and began assisting with the Mass. Father Kinsella thought I was just trying to get on his good side, put up to it by my parents. Little did I know that he held the mortgage on my parents' Russell Street home, a mortgage he would threaten to foreclose a few years later when my father's health, and the restaurant, failed.

I suddenly cared about school and improving my behaviour. I'm sure the Simonds Junior High principal couldn't understand my absence at what had become our regular meetings at the end of his strap.

I was making it happen.

CHAPTER FOUR

I look through the flood of messages scattered across my desk. One is a call

from Dan Landry. He's working with me to have an electronic kiosk for tourism promotion put into the casino. With it we hope to attract, into the rest of Orillia, some of the hundreds of thousands of people — perhaps millions — that will go to the casino. The economic spin-off.

Lynn from the Orillia Community Futures office has called reminding me there is a meeting of the Community Casino Task Force in my office tomorrow, Wednesday morning. This is the umbrella group we put together to have all the community organizations work with the Chippewas of Rama and the casino operators to make sure the entire area benefits. I represent the Downtown on the committee, and I am a vocal supporter of the economic impact it will have on our community. It's an irony that will soon make national headlines.

Just last week the *Toronto Star* quoted me, as the Downtown Manager, saying, "The casino is an economic engine." The article continued: "He predicts spin-off from the casino and the newly opened Ontario Provincial Police headquarters will 'change the face of the community — no doubt about that.'"

We formed the Community Casino Task Force a year ago to host an Opportunities conference searching for ways for the region to benefit from the casino. Our keynote speaker told us we had to learn to "Dance with a Gorilla." Today I feel like it's the morning after a little more than dancing.

Carnival Hotels and Casinos from Florida were announced a few days before the conference as the operators of the casino and its officials showed up at the event with a pledge to work with the community to make sure everyone benefits.

It is easy to support the casino in Orillia. Everyone does. Not only does it mean all those tourists, 14,800 a day on average in the first month of operations, but there are also some 3,000 jobs for the region, not to mention the multi-million dollar payroll that will be spent in the community. There is little, or no, opposition. A separate group concerned about the social impact of gambling on our local residents split off earlier this year from the Community Casino Task Force, but tomorrow morning they are scheduled to meet with the task force to discuss ways of lessening any damaging impact. No, they will tell us, there is no treatment locally for gambling problems. Is there a demand? They'll say they don't know and need $25,000 to do a study to see if there is a need. The casino will put up part of the money. Another group will be co-opted with gambling money.

For the past year the task force has met weekly in my offices. In the last three months there have been times when I've left the casino just in time to go home, shave and shower, and show up sleepless for the meeting, often with casino officials, including the vice-president of marketing Ed Leichner, in attendance.

In his reference letter Ed will write: "I have known and interacted with Doug Little since January 1996 when I arrived in Canada to work on the Casino Rama Project. Doug approached me and asked that I become involved with the community

Casino Task Force which was formed to help spin off economic development from the Casino's anticipated success to the surrounding communities.

"In all my contact with Doug over a nine- or ten-month period (at least weekly) I have found him to be an extremely dedicated and hard working member of the community. He was sincerely concerned that the surrounding communities, as well as Orillia, benefited financially from the about-to-open Casino and the anticipated numbers of visitors it was projected to generate.

"Doug was a major driving force in ensuring Casino Rama and its executives were involved in the community and aware of their corporate responsibilities as a member of it. He was instrumental in organizing the community Casino Task Force and its benefits for the area businesses."

He concludes: "I always found Doug to be terrific to work with, bright and tireless, and a full-time promoter for Orillia and the surrounding areas."

My love affair with roulette began on a vacation I didn't want to take. In 1992, I recovered from my heart attack and was able to resume my job responsibilities and community activities full bore. About the only thing that got waylaid was a plan to start a Winter Carnival in Orillia. It was postponed for a year or two. I also quit as president of Festivals Ontario, but stayed on as past-president. I resigned as vice-president of the Canadian Association of Festivals and Events and Ontario's representative on its board. In 1991 I had a co-chair of the Leacock Heritage Festival — a woman named Pamela Sunstrum who had moved to Orillia in 1990 from Toronto where she had worked with the government as communications manager. After my heart attack in the middle of the 1991 Festival, Pamela carried the Festival to its end.

In 1992 I hired her as the paid executive director of Festivals Ontario, on a part-time basis, but with enough time that I could have someone else step in and become the voluntary president. Pamela also took over my seat on the national CAFE board.

While I unloaded some things for health reasons, I also took a few new projects into my workaholic life, including serving as campaign manager of Clayt French's successful mayoral election bid in November of 1991. Then, in 1992, wearing my patriotism on my sleeve, I naively became the chairman of the Simcoe North Yes Committee in the Charlottetown Accord Referendum.[2] I thought it would be a rah-rah, national unity, love your country and mom's apple pie campaign. It turned out to be anything but. We lost, as our region, like most of the country, said no.

While all this was going on Roberta was plotting a family vacation at Christmas time in the Dominican Republic. She put the non-refundable deposit on her Sears' card. We had no choice but to pay the balance and go. Not, however, before I did some plotting of my own.

Although work was still my drug of choice at this time, gambling and casinos were not complete strangers to me. During the past three or four years I had travelled across Canada for festivals meetings as board member of CAFE. In Winnipeg and Vancouver I discovered charity casinos during my once-a-year visits and I had tasted the fatal excitement of blackjack.

"Let's check out the new casino," someone suggested and we all headed over the overpass that connected our hotel to the conference centre in Downtown Winnipeg. Don Blair, manager of Folklorama, one of Canada's largest multi-cultural festivals, told us his organization was making thousands of dollars a year as one of the beneficiaries of the casino's winnings.

If I was expecting Las Vegas, I was sadly disappointed. It was a conference ballroom filled with portable blackjack tables, a few poker tables and a couple of crown-and-anchor wheel games, the kind my father would gravitate to during the Saint John Exhibition while we ran around from ride to ride.

Did I mention that Dad was a gambler? Today at 77, living in New Brunswick, he has been saved from destruction at the hands of the corner store video lottery terminals (VLTs — the "crack-cocaine" of compulsive gambling) by Alzheimer's disease. He can't find his way to the store any more.

At thirteen I was still looking for ways to impress my father. My friend Brian Stewart worked around the stables at the Exhibition Raceway on weekends. He and I were inseparable in Grades Seven and Eight, often banished to the hall together for horsing around in class and often watching each other wince at the hurting end of the school's corporal punishment policy.

"I got a tip at the racetrack," he said to me one Monday morning. "I overheard these jockeys saying Bertie's Lightning is going to win in the seventh race on Wednesday."

"How?" I asked.

"By racing, you dickhead. How do I know how, I just know what I heard."

I knew my father liked to go the races. That's where he often ended up when he took us to the Ex, as long as my mom wasn't around.

"Brian got a tip at the racetrack," I told him when we were alone in the kitchen of the restaurant. "He works there on the weekends and says he heard some jockeys talking about Bertie's Lightning winning in the seventh race, but I don't know, Brian can be such a BS'er too."

"What night?" he asked.

"Wednesday."

"Don't say anything to your mother. We'll check it out together."

I couldn't believe how excited I was for the next two days.

"I'm going to the track with my dad, Stewart, that tip better be good or I'll knock your block off."

"Yeah, you and what army?" he said, taking position and shadow boxing with my head. Brian liked to think he was a tough guy, but when push came to shove the few times I saw him in a jam, he was just like me: it was his mouth that did the swinging.

"My old man, how about his army? — It had better be right."

"Hey, man, ya bets yer money and ya takes yer chances. You want guarantees, go to Simpson-Sears, not me."

Well, it was right and my father won $237 dollars that night on a $10 bet. It was the happiest day I had with him since the times we'd go fishing together when I was six years old and he'd end up carrying me on his shoulders wading through waist-high rivers, deep in the God-knows-where of New Brunswick.

Hot dogs and pop galore. It was as if everything was okay now.

I was his son again, the good and worthy one. And Brian, he was a hero, and always welcome in my father's eyes. My tenure was somewhat shorter.

In Winnipeg we all tried a hand at blackjack, not really knowing what to do. What the hell, it was only a buck or two. We also tried the crown and anchor but no one played poker; it looked far too serious for tourists and besides, everyone was more interested in hitting the bars — or, for some, the sheets.

"I'm going to bed," I said as we headed back across the bridge to the hotel. Since everyone knew I didn't drink, I didn't get pressured to go to the bars. Occasionally, when I did go, I was treated as somewhat of a celebrity.

But that night, bed was the last thing on my mind. I headed back to my room, called Roberta to check in, and as soon as I thought the coast was clear, I headed back to the casino. Playing blackjack, for a couple of bucks a hand, I stayed until closing at four o'clock in the morning. I may have lost a hundred, or even two hundred dollars, but I had a helluva lot more fun than sitting around a bar watching people start to talk stupid.

"What did you do last night, Doug? — you look tired," my friend Michel asked me the next morning at breakfast.

"I went to bed, but I watched a movie till three," I lied.

"Hey, we were out to three at the bar and I don't look as tired as you. Must be getting old!" Funny how he could tell me nonchalantly he was out drinking until three and yet I was reluctant to say I was out gambling.

♥ ♦ ♣ ♠

I knew if I was going on vacation to a casino resort then I had to have money with which to gamble, money that no one else knew anything about. So, when we arrived in Puerto Plata I had an extra $500 US in travellers' cheques that Roberta didn't know about. I had gambling fuel.

The resort was nice enough. The food was better than the Mexican resort where we'd gone a few years earlier, though the beach was neither as isolated nor as beautiful. On the plus side, a section of the Dominican beach was for topless bathing. I couldn't get too excited about the flattened pancakes of women lying on their backs, but since the casino didn't open until eight o'clock each evening, the topless beach provided some diversion during the day.

It was also great having Melanie along. It was a break for her as she had just completed her twelve-month Masters in English Literature at the University of Toronto, and was continuing on with her Ph.D. studies. Also, she was company for Roberta while I gambled.

I couldn't wait for the casino to open on the first day so I snuck away from the beach, where Rob and Melanie were sun worshipping, and went to scout out the premises. I found it was a small casino with about a dozen blackjack tables, a craps table, and two roulette wheels. I was disappointed there were no slot machines as I had been looking forward to trying them. Up until then I had only seen slots in movies and toy stores.

I used my opportunity to exchange one of the hundred-dollar travellers' cheques at the resort currency exchange for pesos with which to gamble. I could have gambled in U.S. dollars, and been paid my winnings in U.S. dollars, but because I needed pesos for everything else at the resort, Roberta would have wondered where I got the American cash.

"I am just going to bet 200 pesos on any night, win or lose," I lied at dinner. "You can keep all the other money." That's a little less than $20 U.S., maybe $25 Canadian given 1992's more favourable exchange. "You and Melanie can come with me, and bet a bit if you want."

"We're going to the show," Roberta said. "Come with us, it's the first night."

"It's also the first night at the casino," I answered, promising to go to the show the next night. Every evening at this all-inclusive resort they had a variety stage show to entertain the guests. The performers were mainly day employees doing double duty and the shows were hokey. I wouldn't have put them on any of the stages of my events, even in Orillia, but here — with the beach, the sun all day and the free drinks — they were quite popular.

When eight o'clock finally came I first had to deposit the women at the show and then I actually skipped and ran to the casino, careful not to be seen. I had my 200-peso daily ration in one pocket and the other 1000-peso stash in my socks. Before I got inside I nonchalantly reached down and pulled out a one hundred peso note to add to my stake.

"I'll get all the chips early," I said to myself. "That way if Roberta comes and I am down I won't have to quit." As a matter of fact I pulled out another hundred pesos and decided to keep some chips stashed in my pockets just in case.

The casino only had a few people when I arrived shortly after eight, and they were all around one of the roulette wheels. No one was playing blackjack yet so I joined the group and watched the spinning wheel. I was anxious to get my 400 pesos converted into chips so I climbed up on a stool along the table next to the wheel and announced I wanted to learn the game, putting my four bills on the table.

"Chips," I asked. The Spanish pit boss or roulette boss (later I learned they were called croupiers) questioned whether I wanted it all in roulette chips or casino chips. "Both," I answered, quickly seeing the difference. The casino chips, like the chips in the charity casinos in Canada, were in five, ten, twenty-five peso denominations right up to 1000 pesos — about a hundred bucks. The roulette chips came as a thinner round wafer, and could actually carry whatever value you wished to buy.

I was a beginner and I signed that I wanted one hundred one-peso roulette chips and three hundred pesos in casino chips in twenty-five peso denominations — green. For my roulette chips I chose "lucky red."

The head croupier spoke English and explained I could place the quantity of chips I wanted to bet on the number, or numbers, I wished to choose. The table had thirty-six numbers, corresponding to the thirty-six numbers on the roulette wheel, plus the zero and double zero. If the ball on the wheel stopped on any of the numbers on which I had a chip, I would be paid thirty-five to one.

"Señor may also bet on the lines or corners of numbers, or for red or black," he said, pointing to the coloured squares on the outside of the table, or for "even or odd numbers." Enough talk, I thought, and let him know by placing a few chips on the board, watching what the other players were doing.

I looked over the green felt roulette board and placed my red chips on several numbers at one end of the board. One, four, six, seven, eight, nine, and seventeen all got one chip "straight up" and I played the splits between six and nine, seven and eight, and a trio bet on the seven, eight and nine row. On the outside I wagered two chips on four boxes: the "First twelve"; "One to eighteen"; odd; and red. In all, I bet eighteen pesos — about two bucks.

As everyone placed their bets and the Dominican croupier spun the wheel and twirled the white ball in the opposite direction, I placed another two chips on the splits between zero and double zero, and another two on "Lucky 17" — Melanie's birthday. Silently I watched my first roulette gamble with all the calmness of James Bond in Casino Royale. I don't see what's so exciting about this, I thought, as I waited for the wheel to finish its interminable spinning. I wondered when blackjack and the real action was going to start. Finally the wheel started to slow and the croupier waved his hand over the board calling, "No más apuestas" — no more bets.

Suddenly the white ball dropped *clink* against the inside of the wheel and began *clink* jumping *clink* around the numbers *clink* in number zero, and out *clink* across twenty eight *clink* and *clunk* — it finally stopped in the number nine.

"Nine!" I yelled, jumping out of my chair. "I win!"

"Nueve, rojo, nine, red."

"I win!" I shouted again. Maybe this game was not so boring after all. The croupier cleared all the losing bets off the table, gathering the failed chips into a big mound in the corner of the table beside him where another casino worker sorted and stacked them into their proper colours. The losers out of the way — out of sight, out of mind — he began adding up my winning payout.

Everything done in a casino is choreographed, designed to

maximize the win for the casino owners. Get the losing chips out of the way first so prospective new customers walking by will only see winners on the table and money being paid out; the reality that there are seven or eight times the chips lost by the other players is swooped quickly into the corner. At Casino Rama, as I have learned, everything, right down to the colour of the paint on the walls, is the result of a carefully weighed executive decision, as is its design with no windows (you can't tell whether it is day or night), no clocks, and blasts of cool, oxidized air pumped in at four o'clock each morning to help keep the all-night players awake.

My red winning chips left on the table told me that I had won more than I'd realized and my excitement grew as I watched the croupier pile up my profits. All together the croupier was pushing seventy-three new chips my way. This was great.

"Imagine," I said to the rest of the players at the table — who were watching somewhat less enthusiastically — "if I had been playing American dollars."

Having paid all the winners, the croupier announced, "Place your bets," and we began again. I placed an additional chip on all my bets and doubled up on number seven (July) and placed four more chips on number seventeen. I added a chip to numbers twenty-two (Melanie's age), nineteen (the century), and another to number seventeen.

The croupier again twirled the white ball around the roulette wheel as we contemplated our bets, all of us searching the table for some hint as to the number we'd missed that was just bound to win. As he was about to say "No más" I dropped another chip on the last winner, number nine.

"Si señor, numbers often repeat in roulette," the pit boss said across the table, eyeing my bets — especially my mini-stack on seventeen.

"My lucky number, my daughter's birthday," I responded to his unasked question.

"It is the most popular bet in roulette, señor."

"Lucky 17," I said as I placed the first bet, on the first spin of a roulette wheel in Casino Rama. I told Roberta, sitting next to me at the gala opening, "You gotta believe."

Opening night at Casino Rama, July 29, 1996. It was a special night, by invitation only. I had the inside track on invitations through my relationship with the casino on the Community Task Force and with the marketing department, not only through Ed, the vice-president, but perhaps more importantly, through his secretary, Margaret Ayers, who once was my Festival Coordinator. I got all the invitations I needed for just about everyone who asked. I got them for my merchants, for my board members and for my gambling buddies, who were mostly from Barrie, including some of the charity casino dealers. I was a big shot. The only people I didn't get them for were my Leacock Heritage Festival committee members because the opening was right in the middle of the Festival and someone had to mind the show.

Everyone was dressed to the nines. Roberta and I had shopped for a new suit for me, a classy black one with a stylishly loud black and white tie. She was ambivalent about coming with me, having experienced my casino fever first hand in Sault Ste. Marie just a month earlier.

"I hated you in Sault Ste. Marie," she would one day tell me, recalling my running from slot machine to slot machine, my feverish search for one that would give me back all the money I had lost over the two-day visit. But that was when I was away, when I couldn't quit because I couldn't go back the next day or the next week.

Banish the negative thinking: Casino Rama has arrived.

"Come on 17, lucky 17," I cheered loudly and excitedly, to Roberta's embarrassment, as the Rama croupier spun the ball on the very first roulette game in Casino Rama and passed his hand over the table and shouted, in English, that familiar "No more bets."

Whirl, Whirl, Whirl. The ball sped around the wheel, held in its track by centrifugal force, the way the motorcycles used to hang sideways on the sheer round walls of the Exhibition stunt show. The wheel began to slow and the ball dropped from its track, *clink* it bounced among the numbers, *clink* in one hole *clank* and out again, *clink* across the incline of the wheel to the other side, *clink* my breathing had stopped. I had stopped. Everything had stopped, in suspended animation, awaiting the final drop of that ball — *clink* — number 17! "Yes!"

The first winning number of the first roulette spin in Casino Rama was 17 — Melanie's birthday. *It was a sign.*

"Lucky 17!" I yelled. "My lucky number. The first spin." Even Roberta was excited: after all, it was Melanie's birthday, and my five-dollar chip was paying $175. Everyone else at the roulette table just smiled politely like all those other parents did on the original "Lucky 17" day at the Peterborough Civic Hospital, when we were all looking through the nursery window and I was boasting: "Isn't she the most beautiful baby you ever saw?"

"I'll keep these," Roberta said as she scooped up the 35 red casino chips and put them in her purse. Nothing's changed from Puerto Plata, I thought. Oh well, at least I'd have some freedom to gamble since she has the winnings safe in her purse.

I didn't win every spin in the Paradise Casino that first night in the Dominican Republic, but between what I had on the table and what I had stashed in my pocket, I felt like a winner and to everyone else I was one, too. Roberta and Melanie came to see me after a few hours when their show was over.

"I'll take some of these for you," Roberta said, grabbing about half my chips.

"No," I said, "You can't take those red ones away from the roulette table. Take the green ones. They are worth 25 pesos each. The red roulette ones are just one peso."

So, as I anticipated, Roberta took five of my "winning chips" and slipped them into her purse. I was careful not to move my legs for fear that any clatter from my pockets would have been costly. I didn't mind the 125 pesos but that was enough. Those "winnings" were my licence to keep gambling, the price paid to buy my "freedom to wager."

In November of 1999, Bernard Landry, then Quebec deputy premier, would say that fifteen suicides attributed to problem gambling so far in the year in that province were the price we have to pay for the "freedom to wager." By the end of the year the Quebec provincial coroner's office reported the price had increased to 27 known gambling-related suicides.

After watching me win and lose a few spins Melanie and Roberta became bored and decided to go to bed. "Don't stay up all night, Dad," Melanie said as they left. "You'll be too tired and cranky tomorrow."

"I won't, I'll be okay," I said, waving goodnight. Besides, the casino closed at 3 a.m., less than four hours away, I was surprised to realize. Wow, did those three hours ever go by fast.

The next four hours and the next nine days all went by fast. Maybe I won that first night. It must have appeared that way in the casino because on the way to my room a young Dominican girl accosted me.

"Would señor like a blow job? Just one hundred pesos."

Without hesitation I said no. Even though sex between Roberta and I was not to be a vacation highlight, any more than it was now a home highlight, I had no interest in sex. I was gambling.

As my gambling took over more and more of my life and my time — every night if I could — Roberta asked me if I was having an affair. "Hell no, I'm gambling. It's more exciting than sex." A little insensitive, perhaps, but, it was true: when I was gambling, nothing else, not even sex, mattered.

In Puerto Plata I spent every night in the Casino from opening until closing, except for the few hours I spent appeasing Roberta and Melanie by going to the occasional show or lingering at dinner. I left them sitting by the pool area and walked away calmly until I was around the corner. Then I broke into my run to the casino.

The last night I was incredibly lucky. I can't recall how many times number seventeen hit, and seven. By then I had graduated to playing stacks of chips on each spin, hundreds of pesos. That was after the women had gone to bed. It was not unusual to have twenty, even thirty pesos on number seventeen, and half that amount on seven. I also had five chips on an ever-expanding list of numbers for an ever-expanding variety of reasons — whatever the pursuit of luck fancied.

By the last night on each spin of the wheel I was betting between 250 and 300 pesos on twenty-two of the thirty-eight numbers plus the lines, corners, and the occasional column bet. If a straight-up five-peso bet hit, I'd win 175 pesos back, just over half of what I was betting. But if seventeen, or even seven, hit, I was huge.

Seventeen seemed to come in every second spin with seven coming up almost as often. It was an incredibly lucky night and I was the talk of the casino, among both the dealers and the patrons. I was even more popular than the high rollers at the craps table as I stacked chips like skyscrapers on seventeen and seven.

"Seven-seventeen, come on seven-seventeen," I chanted as the ball spun around the wheel and started to fall. To the dealers and to many of the guests I was "Seventeen."

"Come on, come on, seventeen," I'd hail as the ball danced from hole to hole.

"Yes! Yes! Seventeen," I celebrated, pumping my arm in the air as if I'd just won the Olympic gold medal. The payout with a twenty-five-peso tower on seventeen and the piles of five on the surrounding lines and corners was 1,437 pesos — about $150. Boy, did I ever wish I was playing dollars. The payout for the number seven winners was about 600 pesos or $60. By the end of the night I had won back about half of all the money I had lost over the past ten days. I went home with almost three hundred dollars U.S.

That I left with two hundred dollars less than when I arrived did nothing to dampen my enthusiasm and my feeling of being a winner. That I spent some seventy hours over ten days glued to a roulette table every night, not only didn't seem like a waste, it seemed like an accomplishment. Just being there had been winning.

In the sober, second-thought days, before my gambling binge, I told myself: *You had the luckiest day possible and still only won back half of what you lost in the ten days before.* It was an observation I thought would help me moderate my gambling in the future. I couldn't have been more wrong. Instead I remember the dangling carrot aspect of my "luck," which always gave me hope when I should have been losing it.

CHAPTER FIVE

"David Shaw is on the phone for you," Jennifer bleats through the

October 22, 1996 — 11 a.m.

intercom as I bang my head on the desk trying to figure out where, or from whom, I can get money. Money to pay Bob; money to buy time; money to get back to the casino so I can win my way out of this trouble.

Lately I had been playing the sucker games in my desperation to win a big jackpot. Caribbean Stud and Let It Ride were both poker games with jackpot payouts, not unlike the slot machines, only bigger. Not that there weren't big jackpots in the slot machines but they required a big ante, twenty or a hundred dollars a turn, and double or triple that to play maximum. I'd watched people play the hundred-dollar slots, just as everyone did. (That was all I needed all over town: "Did you see Doug Little playing the hundred-dollar slots? What a big shot! Wonder where he gets all the money?") They went though hundred-dollar tokens as fast as I could go through dollars. It was all relative. If I was on a roll elsewhere in the casino, then occasionally I threw a twenty into those machines, and once I even wasted a hundred dollars. But more than likely, it was the five-dollar slots I'd hit on the bathroom run between shuffles, or the dollar slots when I needed to replenish my ante for the table games.

However, I thought nothing was wrong with chasing the $50,000 jackpot in Let It Ride with a five hundred or thousand-dollar stake. I also played for the Caribbean Stud progressive jackpot which grew as high as $100,000 a couple of times in the three months that Casino Rama had been open.

"Those games have the worst odds in the house," my blackjack buddies told me.

"I know," I said, " I'm just taking a shot at the jackpot because I can't seem to win at blackjack lately." That was true. The changes in the game rules from the charity casinos to Rama had spooked me and I rarely won. I had no confidence left in my ability to control the game so I only played on a hit-and-miss basis, going from table to table like a cherry picker going from grocery store to grocery store, buying only the specials, trying my luck, and moving on quickly whether I was winning or losing. If I was winning I was afraid some jerk was going to come along in one of the other seats at the table and do something stupid to screw it all up. If I was losing I had no confidence that I could wait until the end of dealer's shoe — the stack of cards in the current shuffle — for a change of luck, and opted for a change of table, or even a change of games, looking for that elusive yet essential instant win.

I knew too much about blackjack the way it was at the charity casinos. There I could play all seven spots on the table, control the game, and not have to put up with rookies and tourists coming to the table and screwing up the whole game by splitting tens or hitting on seventeen. In Rama I was only allowed to play two squares maximum, which meant there was the potential of five other people helping the casino by screwing up the game. Sometimes, I would run into some of my old charity casino friends, especially my blackjack partner, Arnold, and we'd take up all the seats at the table. But even then it seemed everyone was screwing up or just that Lady Luck had deserted me at the blackjack tables.

The other thing I hated about Casino Rama blackjack was that the dealer took both cards before the play, one down and one up. In the charity casinos the dealer always took his second card after the play, meaning that whoever was playing anchor — the end player — could influence the dealer's cards by deciding to "take one for the table." Lots of times when I was playing "VIP" — all seven spots — I would take an extra card on the last square to stop the dealer from getting a face card to match another face card or ace that was showing. In Rama, that face card seemed to be always already "in the hole." You didn't even get to play if the dealer had blackjack, because they checked the hidden card with a table mirror first.

"Dealer has Blackjack," the dealer, trained to show the least amount of emotion possible, said calmly, as he reached out to collect the bets of everyone on the table.

Fuck. My mind growled, but I was trained too, and I said nothing, smiling as he took my fifty-dollar bet on each spot.

Gambling is about systems: developing a manner of playing that gives you an edge — or so you believe. Because it's also about faith — faith in your system. I had no faith left in blackjack in Casino Rama, which lead me, incredibly, to have faith in the long-shot poker games.

This was incredible — I'd always been a terrible poker player, and I knew it. There were times in the charity casinos, when my blackjack luck wasn't working, or when it was and I "sensed" a turn in my luck, that I picked up my chips and went to the poker pit, it being the only other gambling choice.

"Is this seat free?" I asked as I sat down.

"It's yours now, but it's not free," the smart-mouthed house dealer said. In "Texas Hold'em Poker," played in the charity casinos, the house supplied the dealer and took a rake off every pot. The players were playing each other, not the casino operator.

"Welcome to the game, Dougie," the other players said almost in unison, salivating like a pack of wolves into whose den a plump sheep has just wandered.

"What's the ante?"

"Five and Ten." The small game, I was relieved to hear — the big game being Ten-Twenty: a $10 minimum bet and a $20 maximum. All of these limits can be quite deceiving as I was about to learn.

"How much are you bringing to the table?" the dealer asked. "There is a one-hundred-dollar minimum."

"Three hundred," I said, to everyone's delight. I caught the grinning looks and the knowing eyes. In Hold'em Poker, everyone — there could be anywhere from seven to eleven players at the table — antes up $5 to start, and the dealer gives everyone two cards down. Three cards are then dealt up in the middle, the so-called flop. These three common cards, along with two more turned over after more betting, are used in combination with each player's two hidden cards. Each player bets his best five-card poker hand made out of the total seven cards.

I picked up my two pocket cards and saw they were the Ten of diamonds and the Four of spades. The guy next to me told me to keep my cards down and hidden so that "no one else could see them from the sides." I put the cards down near my lap and studied the Ten and Four like there was some message hidden in the numbers.

"Keep your cards above the table," the dealer impatiently barked.

"Whoa, he's new, take it easy," the player to my right admonished the dealer as everyone bobbed their heads in agreement. "Don't upset the new sucker" was barely shrouded behind their poker faces.

Betting in Hold'em begins from the left, with a dummy chip being passed clockwise from player to player at the start of each hand to designate who bets first (not unlike a speakers' baton of the Roman Senate or the speakers' stick in group therapy). The first player must bet five dollars, check or fold, forfeiting his ante in the pot. We went around the table, everyone betting another five dollars.

The players finished betting on the first two cards and the dealer whacked the three cards face-up into the centre of the table. "Three of hearts, Four of diamonds and Queen of spades. Possible Pair of Queens. Possible Straight to the Five. Betting is open."

The first player bet. "Five dollars."

"See five and raise five," the next player said, meaning the rest of us had to put in $10 in order to stay in the game and see any more cards.

"Check ten," the next player said, throwing two red chips into the pile.

"Fold."

By the time it gets to me two players have folded and everyone else is in for the ten bucks. I have two Fours the way I read it, with two cards to come. In blackjack I would have bet $70 by now. "See ten and raise five."

"Beginner's luck," one of the players said as he threw his cards into the middle, signifying he was folding. Everyone else had to put up another five bucks to stay in the game. By my quick calculation there was $230 in the pot. Boring old poker was getting exciting.

The dealer picked up his pack of cards and flipped another card — the turn — onto the line of the first three. "Seven of hearts," he announced; "possible Straight to the Seven."

"Check." The first player passed, as did everyone else around the board until it came to me.

In blackjack there was no passing: I had to bet on every spot. "I bet five," I said to the puzzled looks of some players and to the knowing looks of others.

"You have to bet double on the turn," the dealer said contemptuously.

"Dougie's hot," the guy who keeps calling me Dougie said. I was thinking his name was Dave but I was waiting for someone to verify it.

"Oh yeah, sure, I bet ten then," I said, causing two of the other players to throw their cards into the middle, folding. Later I would learn that you aren't supposed bet unless you have at least a Pair of Tens or better, but still, what I was *supposed* to do never stopped me.

Everyone else threw in their Ten and the dealer flipped over the last card — the river: "Four of clubs." I could hardly contain my glee. Three Fours. Poker face, poker face, I kept saying to myself as I looked around the room trying to read everyone else's expression. I didn't see anything.

"Pair of Fours on board," the dealer called. "Bets?"

The guy who started betting from the beginning wagered $10, causing another two guys to fold before it got to me.

"See ten and raise ten," I said.

"Full House, he's got a Full House," a guy across the table said as he threw in his cards.

Full House. Three of a Kind and *Two of a Kind.*

The other two remaining players anted up the final ten and the dealer called: "Show, gentlemen."

I put my cards down. "Three Fours," I said, and saw a few eyes rolling.

"Straight to the Nine," the guy across from me said, bettering my Three of a Kind.

"Pocket Queens," the guy who started the bidding in the first place announced. "Full House." Three Queens and my two Fours. Shit. He reached for the pot of about three hundred and sixty dollars, fifty-five dollars of which was my money.

And so it went for a few more hands, with me chasing cards with five and ten dollar bills and the guys in the poker pit cheerfully rubbing their hands as the three hundred dollars in chips in front of me moved inescapably around the table to the piles in front of them. I did luck out and get some half-decent hands, but I was useless at hiding it so the pots I won were small: everyone bailed out. Finally I took winning as a sign from the Gods and quit. I went back to blackjack to replenish the stock.

"Doug Little here," I answer the phone.

"Douglas," the voice relied, "Ralph is after your nuts."

David Shaw is one of the members on my Downtown Orillia Board, one of the more reasonable members. At first I thought he would be trouble given his links to the Orillia Chamber of Commerce and the Visitors and Convention Association. The

Downtown was always at loggerheads with these groups. The Ralph he is talking about is Ralph Cipolla, who also sits on my board and who is somewhat of a nemesis for me.

I've known Ralph since I first came to Orillia in 1983 and was the manager of the regional tourism association. Over the ensuing thirteen years we have had this strange relationship where I would allow him to use me in order to keep him, not so much as an ally, but as a benign antagonist. Even so, Ralph was dangerously unpredictable and certainly not someone I could trust. Now, since I have abandoned all pretense of being his ally, he is my out-and-out enemy, hell-bent on my destruction.

Bob and Mary-Anne cheered my apparently gutsy move of quitting Ralph's provincial election campaign last year after I had successfully engineered his nomination for the Liberal Party — a task they knew I had only taken on in the interest of my own political manoeuvring. They would joke about it in terms of my ability to "get a dog elected."

Once, in Timmins, I got an undertaker elected to city council. I was sitting in my office one day when this guy came in and introduced himself as Bob Laporte.

"I want to be an alderman. How much is it going to cost me?" he asked flippantly, successfully impressing me with his bravado. "I have the money. I just sold my funeral home."

What's the cost of a funeral, I wondered, trying to find a figure that would sound right. "$5,000 for the campaign," I said, "and $5,000 for me."

He put $5,000 cash on my desk and an hour later he returned with another $5,000. "Let me know when that runs out," he said.

As the municipal election campaign progressed I gradually realized that he was a nut bar, and that I was unleashing him onto Timmins. I would joke about it privately with the other members of council that I knew. "You have no idea what I am doing to you."

For one thing, while Laporte could not speak well publicly, he also had trouble thinking publicly. Every word he uttered during the campaign, I wrote. However, in a small-town election in the late seventies, $5,000 bought a lot of advertising and name recognition, which is all it took to get elected into one of the five aldermanic seats in the old Town of Timmins ward.

He won, and fortunately was an ineffective but harmless member of council. The last time I saw him he was playing the stock market heavily in Timmins. The last I heard of him, however, was several years later when I read in the newspaper about a former City of Timmins alderman being convicted and sent to jail for trafficking in drugs.

While Bob and Mary-Anne saw my quitting Ralph's campaign as gutsy, I knew two other factors — my gambling, and Ralph's veiled threats — were the catalysts in my decision. By the time the 1995 provincial election campaign was gearing up, I was fully into the nightly playing of bingo and was looking for fewer evening meetings, not more.

After I missed a few committee meetings and seemed reluctant to join Ralph's campaign team — now being lead by Ralph (you know the expression: "If you run your own campaign, then you have a fool for a candidate") — we had a meeting.

"I just want to warn you that there is a lot of talk about you playing bingo all the time," Ralph told me, "and there are rumours about your finances and money with the city."

I couldn't believe my ears. *This guy wants me to help him get elected?*

"I want to be able to protect you on the board against those who are spreading these rumours but I need your co-operation," he said.

Sure, I thought, and I know who is spreading the rumours.

Feeling like I was being blackmailed, whether it was real or perceived, had always made me act irrationally, made me drop my defense and coping mechanisms, and shed my masks, and give up my Machiavellian manipulations. I played directly into the black-mail threat.

When I was a kid my older brother David would often black-mail me with threats of telling my parents about things I did — like stealing money — if I told them about him smoking in our room or hitting me. He exercised his tyranny well and added more fuel to my determination to escape from my family's chaotic Russell Street home. He also instilled in me a lifelong abhorrence of blackmail and a resolve to never allow myself to be its slave again.

"I enjoy bingo — I play to relax," I said angrily. "I am not worried about my financial reputation nor about money with the city. Everything I've done is documented and approved by the Downtown Board."

"Hey, I'm just trying to warn you, I am on your side," Ralph said.

"I am just too busy to continue on the election committee, too busy to debate every direction with the people you now have involved and I've done all I can do."

He was about to respond but I didn't give him a chance.

"I'm out." With that I got up and left, going directly to Mariposa Market to bask in the adulation of Bob and Mary-Anne and inhale a peanut butter chocolate layer cake to soothe my anxieties.

"Ralph knows about some money from the Farmer's Market that you used for gambling," David tells me as I listen numbly on the other end of the phone. "He's trying to get the Board to fire you over it, and to call in the police."

Chicken Little. The sky is falling! The sky is falling!

Jennifer, I think to myself. Jennifer told Ralph. Whether this is true or not I don't know. Jennifer also worked on Ralph's election campaign so she may have gone to him. Or, she and Susan, my assistant who coordinates the Farmers' Market, may have simply gone to Board Chairman, Mike Knight, for fear of their own jobs. I certainly can't blame them.

David told me about a secret Board meeting where Ralph advocated firing me and calling the police. However, David and the other members had agreed to treat it as a "family matter" and to confront me and get me help for my gambling problem.

"I'm telling you this so you can diffuse whatever Ralph's up to and so that you watch your back. Mike Knight and Lance Edwards are supposed to meet you and report back to the board."

"Thanks, Dave," I say, "Ralph's still pissed off that I quit his election campaign and he lost."

"Yes, well you've certainly given him the opportunity to get his revenge, haven't you?" he says. "You'd better deal with this gambling stuff."

"I will, I am. Thanks."

"Yeah," he says and hangs up.

Another juggling ball falling from the sky. I probably owe the Downtown about a thousand or so dollars in missing Farmers' Market deposits, petty cash, and sidewalk sale cash deposits that I "borrowed" and still haven't repaid. While David's call almost makes my heart seize in fear, especially knowing Ralph is out there stirring the pot, it is also hopeful that the board is sympathetic and willing to help. *Maybe they would be willing to lend me the money to pay off Leacock?*

The next question in my head is this: how much does Ralph really know? While I don't blame Jennifer or Susan for telling — it has to be them — I am worried how much they have said. They know that something is amiss at Leacock. The daily calls from the banks and the threatening messages from creditors are telling. However, I decide I can only act on what I do know for sure, but act I must.

I call Mike Knight and tell him I need to talk to him as soon as possible.

"I can't meet right now," he says, "I'm busy in the store."

"I hear Ralph is after my ass," I say.

"Don't worry about him, but we do need to talk and to get things straightened out. The board is behind you."

"I'm glad to hear that," I say. "I'm trying to deal with my problems." My voice trembles, my fear resonating in the mouthpiece.

"I know. Look, I can't talk now. Lance and I are supposed to get together with you in the next few days to discuss this whole thing and set up some new procedures. I'll call you when I get a chance to set a time to come and see you with Lance. Okay?"

"Okay. I'll see what I can do in the meantime," I say.

"Never mind," Mike says. "Just relax. We'll get through this. We'll work something out. Bye."

I take comfort in what Mike says, but I get the sense from the conversation that the Board only knows the Downtown part of my problem — which is good — but it still leaves me to deal with the other $79,000 I owe, not to mention a hostile loose cannon mouthing off all around town.

This is not the first time I've had a Board go to bat for me due to my unorthodox "borrowing" habits, and it's not the first time I've left myself vulnerable to my enemies.

"Bigger than the rules." I once attended an Alcoholics Anonymous (AA) conference where a speaker shouted, "Bigger than the rules" to describe his innate ability to justify his actions, regardless of what he did.

Bigger than the rules was the doorway to my becoming a thief. Yes, I'd always had trouble handling my personal finances, and there are countless examples of my breaking the rules in that regard too. But "borrowing," the euphemism I used for my stealing money for gambling, began long before my two-year binge — perhaps more innocently — because I was bigger than the rules. For me the end justified the means. I needed to get this done; therefore I could do whatever was necessary to see that it was accomplished.

I made my own rules. Proper accounting and procedures were for bureaucrats and people who worked nine-to-five. I was getting things done and, if needed, that meant cutting corners.

In 1982 we left Timmins for Orillia to pursue the figure skating dream for my daughter Melanie at the best skating school in the country — the Mariposa School of Skating. It was then the school of world champion and Olympic silver medallist Brian Orser (more recently, it's produced champion Elvis Stojko). The figure skating story is Melanie's to tell. All I will add is a question my psychiatrist asked me one day about the thousands and thousands of dollars we spent on skating. "Do you ever wonder if you were gambling with Melanie's figure skating?"

I never worked in Orillia when we first moved there, but I worked out of Barrie, thirty kilometres to the south. From what I saw Orillians tended to fight amongst themselves about everything and seemed to eat their own. First, I worked as the Manager of the Huronia Tourist Association, and second, I ran my own marketing business with the largest regional mall as a client along with the hot air balloon festival in Barrie. I resigned as manager of the Huronia Tourist Association after three years of record-breaking success largely due to my "bigger than the rules" attitude and my priority of paying for figure skating. A year earlier, in 1995, I had been called on the carpet for obtaining payroll advances and for borrowing — I'd leave a note — from a cash account I controlled, for my own use. Oh, yeah, I also bounced a cheque at one of my board member's businesses, which I had replaced. I offered to resign but the Board refused my resignation, asking for my promise that it wouldn't happen again. The next year, an element within the executive — notably a disgruntled supplier — used the incident to force my resignation. This story was among the rumours Ralph was spreading.

♥ ♦ ♣ ♠

Throughout September and October, I would go to Casino Rama to play Let It Ride or Caribbean Stud with five hundred dollars in my pocket but by the time I got a seat among the overcrowded tables I'd be down to a couple of hundred bucks. After losing at roulette and the slots, I would have no staying power — "no legs." It was a just a matter of ten or fifteen hands and I would be broke again. Not this past weekend though.

On Wednesday, Thursday, and Friday the Leacock Heritage Festival was sponsoring a charity casino at the Highwayman Inn, operated by a couple of local businessmen under the name "Mr. Casino." As I have said, the charity casinos were a big part of my gambling prior to the opening of Casino Rama, what I describe as the 'charity casino phase' of my betting bender. While I deluded myself into thinking I was a pretty good blackjack player, by the time the phase ended and Casino Rama opened, I was already $25,000 in the hole.

Sponsoring a charity casino meant obtaining a special Monte Carlo Event licence from the Ontario Gaming Commission, selling the chips to the gamblers, handling all the cash, and depositing the money in the charity's bank account. The operator, in this case Mr. Casino, supplied all the equipment and dealers, and operated the blackjack tables and poker pit.

On Wednesday the set-up was typical, with about eight black-jack tables that could seat seven players each and two poker tables for between seven and eleven players. With the exception of casual gamblers, who came in for the novelty or because they happened to be in the hotel, the gamblers at the charity casino were pretty well regulars. Sure, the opening of Casino Rama hurt the attendance at these fundraising events as it did attendance at bingo, but it also added a new, and potentially lucrative market — the casino dealers themselves. Ontario law prohibited employees of a casino from gambling at their own casino. Rama dealers and staff attended the charity events, replacing some of the gamblers lured away by the opening of the *real* casino.

There were also the poker regulars who came for the Texas Hold'em Poker, a game not yet allowed in Ontario's major casinos. Like bingo and Casino Rama, the charity casinos seemed to attract the same core of players night after night regardless of whether they were held in Orillia or Barrie.

All charity casino events seemed to make approximately the same amount, about $3,000 to $3,500 a day, out of which the expenses had to be deducted, which in practice meant the whole amount. The organization sponsoring the charity casino ended up with about five per cent, or $500, for the three-day event. The low return to the charities, the high cost of operation, plus some doubts about the integrity of some operators would soon cause the Ontario government to abolish the private operators of the charity casinos across the province, and ultimately to take them over itself through the Ontario Lottery Corporation. Of course, the government was also influenced by the millions and millions of dollars of profit it was already making from the permanent casinos in Windsor and Rama.

The most important thing the charity sponsor did, however, was to bank each evening's proceeds and then pay the operator's invoice a week or so later, once the accounting was done. I still had an outstanding invoice to pay from September's Monte Carlo event, begging the operator's patience while I worked out Leacock's cash flow as we waited for that infamous "cheque from Casino Rama."

"We're overdrawn in the main Leacock Heritage Festival account," I explained. "The bank is using the balance in the charity casino and bingo accounts as collateral for the main account overdraft until we get the Casino's sponsorship cheque, which I expect any day."

It was a line that would soon wear thin, but so far it was still working. After all, it was not the first time that we were delayed in paying Mr. Casino and we'd always came through in the past. Little did they know that some of the accumulated $30,000 overdraft in the Leacock bank account at the Royal Bank came from paying them $6,000 for the June event because I had gambled away those proceeds.

The first night of the charity casino, Doug Bell took the early shift, allowing me to gamble at Casino Rama until midnight. Then I worked until closing at 4 a.m. and took the $3,000 home with me. The next night I worked the early shift, giving me time after midnight to do some gambling at Rama. Doug closed the charity casino and put the deposit in my drawer at the office. I now had $6500, give or take a few hundred I spent gambling along the way, and a little I used, here and there, to repay some other cash I borrowed.

On the final Friday night, Doug worked the early shift and I took over at midnight. When I left at 5:00 a.m. I had just over $10,000 in bank deposits that I could "borrow" in order to win back all the other money I had "borrowed."

Once again, I had "legs," enough money at one time to be able to gamble at the level I needed to win my way out of trouble. That it hadn't worked the last time wasn't a thought that was allowed into my psyche. *I have to stay positive.*

At five o'clock in the morning, already tired from staying up all night running the charity casino, I drove directly from the

Highwayman Inn to Casino Rama and parked my Downtown Orillia mini-van around the back, slipping in the side door. When I first started coming to Casino Rama I used valet parking — it was a free service us regular high rollers got as part of the "comps" or complimentaries given by the Casino. After coming and going three times in one night as I replenished my gambling fuel from various desk drawers in my office, I became a little sensitive to the "Back again?" observations of the valet captain. Parking in the back at least gave me the illusion of anonymity. With 530 overhead cameras throughout the casino I'm sure my every visit was duly noted.

The Downtown leased the van in 1995, at the beginning of my bingo gambling. I was supposed to sell advertising and get it painted with bright "Shop Downtown Orillia" signs all around. Somehow I was always too busy to have it done. Having it conspicuously parked outside the bingo hall, the charity casino locations and finally Casino Rama every night made the addition of garish Downtown Orillia signs a low priority on my agenda.

"Hey, Doug Little, how come every time I come here, I see you?" I cringed when I heard these words from a woman I didn't even know, but who knew me from television or the newspaper as a result of my work for the Festival or the Downtown.

"How come every time I'm here I see *you?*" I laughed, and quickly followed up with standard betting banter, "Are you winning?"

I hit the casino floor with $2,000 leaving the rest locked in the van in the parking lot. The theory was to get ahead and never have to go back out to the truck to get more money. "I'm playing with the casino's money," was my practised response to anyone asking me, "Are you winning?"

Roulette. I always hit the roulette tables first to see if my luck was running. With a ten-grand bankroll I wanted to make a killing right off the bat. My habit was to buy one hundred singles and see what happened. Now it was one hundred five-dollar chips.

"I'll play colour, nickels," I announced as I spread five one-hundred dollar bills on the table. The action reminded me of the high roller I watched at my table the night Casino Rama opened. He'd whacked ten one-hundred-dollar bills on the roulette table calling for "colour, black." Black chips were one-hundred-dollar denominations. He put all ten chips on the red square on the outside, in a classic double-or-nothing bet. If the ball landed on a red number he would win another thousand, doubling his money. If black came in, he would lose it all.

"Twenty-nine, black," the croupier had called out as if we couldn't see. We all lost. "Sorry sir," the croupier said to the man as he cleared the ten black chips off the table along with all of our one-dollar chips.

"Again," the high roller said as he counted out another thousand. *Whack, whack, whack, whack, whack, whack, whack, whack, whack, whack.* Ten chips on red.

"Red is due," I said, optimistically looking at the electronic board that showed the numbers that had won in the last fifteen spins. Black had won in the last six straight. I believed the odds should be that red would come up for the next six, or at least the next one, or so we wished. This was delusional thinking. What my flush friend and I were not recognizing was that each spin of the wheel was a separate event, totally unconnected to the last spin, or any other spin. There was a fifty-fifty chance it would be red, and the same odds it would be black. No more, and no — in fact it *was* less than fifty-fifty because of the zero and double zero slots which had no colour, where he would lose whether he bet red or black.

Clink. "Zero. Red loses."

Whack, whack, whack, whack, whack, whack, whack, whack, whack, whack. "Again." Another one thousand.

Me, I'd have been running to another table or to another game, or to the washroom to throw up. I was glad I didn't have to make the red versus black decision on the next spin. I was attracted to black but I thought red was due.

Clink. "Four, black."

My high-rolling friend finally took his luck, or lack thereof, somewhere else. Even my ten-thousand-dollar "legs" were not large enough to imitate this all-or-nothing memory.

In roulette, I still played all my numbers — seven, seventeen, and a myriad of others chosen for whatever fanciful reason. But, since dollars — and five-dollar chips — were not pesos, I had cut back on all the splits, corners and rows I'd played in the Dominican. Still, that meant covering 20 or 21 of the possible 38 numbers, and in some cases I placed multiple chips on each number.

This morning I had to be bold. I needed to win big. I put five chips on seventeen and three on seven. I placed two chips on some numbers and one chip on the rest. A total bet of thirty $5 chips or $150 every time the wheel spun. It may not have been a thousand dollars, but, for me, it was plenty of action. At 5:30 in the morning I had my pick of the four roulette wheels in Casino Rama that were open. Before I'd decided I had wandered from table to table assessing what numbers had already won with an eye to discovering whether my numbers were hot or, conversely, due. Especially seventeen. I was looking for luck.

I was also looking for croupiers that weren't going to give me grief. Playing twenty or so numbers took a little time to set up and on a surprising number of tables of late I had not been able to get all my bets down before the ball was put in play and the croupier was waving no more bets. Of course I went absolutely nuts (on the inside — remember gaming decorum) when a number I would have bet came up and I didn't have a chip on it.

I was not as animated this morning as I usually was while I watched the white ball spin around the wheel. I dropped a couple more nickels on number seventeen and tried to will the ball into the seventeen slot. "Seventeen, come on, come on seventeen. Do it!"

Clink, it bounced on twenty-four, *clink*, it hit seven — my heart jumped and so did the ball — and *clunk* — it stopped in double zero. *Shit*. But, hey, I won. Thirty-five to one: $175 on a $160 bet. But I still had the $5 bet too, I told myself, putting the disappointment of the near-number-seven win — $525 — behind me.

One of the books I read on gambling as I was trying to learn how to beat the casinos warned about playing with "scared money" — money you couldn't afford to lose. The last thing I wanted to admit this morning was that this was *terrified money*, the last big gamble to win my way out of what was looking more and more like total destruction. *Horrified money. Petrified.* It was hard to feel enthusiastic under such pressure.

The new rule in my ever-changing system for roulette was to play until my numbers didn't hit at a table and then to move on. This happened on the next spin, as number thirty-four came in. Three spots from seventeen on the wheel; there was a time when I would have played thirty-four. I gathered up my nickels and moved tables in disgust.

At the new table I covered all my twenty squares on the board, along with number thirty-four and the last number that won at this table, number ten, for good measure. I had $170 wagered by the time the wheel began to twirl and I threw another nickel at seven, seventeen and twenty-seven. I needed all the Melanie luck I could get.

"No more bets!"

Clink. The ball bounced in and out of seventeen. *Clink,* it hit thirty and then shot across the wheel and landed, *clunk* in 29. I lost. $185. I moved tables again. Two losses in a row: it was time to take this show on the road. There would be more time for roulette later.

My private line rings in the office, shocking me out of my stupor. "Doug Little here, " I answer.

"Doug?" It's Roberta's voice. I can sense the alarm.

"Yeah, what's up?" I reply, unable to muster the energy to shroud my own anxiety.

"That guy, Johnny, called," Roberta said.

I can't even answer.

"He said you bounced a cheque on him."

CHAPTER SIX

I can hear the fear in Roberta's voice and want, some-how, to make sure

October 22, 1996 — 12 noon

she can't hear the terror in mine. *Idiot! You bounced a cheque on a loan shark!* My mind is panicking but I need a plausible sentence to come out of my mouth to smooth over the crisis.

"Oh, it's just a couple of hundred dollars I borrowed from him at a charity casino one night," I bluff. "I gave him a postdated cheque. I forgot about it."

"He said it was $500, and he wants it straightened out today," Roberta replies with her familiar angry edge: she's not buying my bullshit. "Where are you going to get $500?"

"I don't know. But I'll deal with it. Don't worry about it."

"Doug, are we in trouble again?" she asks with a mix of anger and sadness. I have to get off the phone. As much as I would like to allay Roberta's fears with an instant solution I don't have one. Telling her the truth certainly won't do that.

It's lamentable that Rob and I had a 27-year marriage that began and ended with lies — my lies. I hitchhiked to Timmins after a disastrous year at the University of New Brunswick. When everyone asked why the hell I was going to a mining town in the

99

middle of the Northern Ontario wilderness I told them I had a job at a newspaper there.

Oddly, it was a prophetic lie. I was going to see a woman I had met and almost married in Toronto the year before when the haze of alcohol and loneliness made me fall in love with the first woman I slept with, who then told me she was pregnant by another guy.

I knew the jerk. We had both worked in the management training program at Kresge's in Toronto — a job I got right out high school because I couldn't afford to go to university. He introduced us at a party — their breaking-up party, I suppose. We hit it off but she went back to Teachers' College in North Bay the following week. A few days later I got a phone call.

"I need to see you, to talk to you," she said. "Can I come to Toronto?"

"I don't have anywhere for you to stay," I told her, as I cursed myself for not moving out of the room on Weston Road where I was living. I was now working at the Chrysler parts plant in Islington — maybe the best job of my life — and could afford an apartment.

"I can stay at my cousin's or maybe we can just get a hotel room. I have money." I have no qualms admitting that desire, or lust, or whatever you want to call an 18-year-old's hormonal thrust, influenced my actions and decisions with Josephine, but so did compassion and love, regardless of how immature it may have been. I have learned that most of my emotions are immature, and that I'm scared half to death of the rest.

She came. We stayed in the King Edward Hotel and I lost my technical virginity. I had done everything else in my wild and crazy grade-12 year at Simonds Regional High School in East Saint John after fleeing the priesthood at the end of Grade 11.

I worried out loud about getting her pregnant just before the conclusion of my short-but- sweet introduction to going all the way.

"We don't have to worry about that," she replied, permitting me to abandon all restraint and revel in the euphoria of my first unencumbered orgasm with, definitely, a woman. I was in love.

The physical attraction complete, the emotional bonding began as we talked about how lonely we both were. She finally screwed up enough courage to divulge what she had come to tell me — she was pregnant. No wonder we didn't have to worry.

The words were no sooner out of her mouth then these were out of mine: "We'll get married, then."

We didn't, of course. But it did create a great deal of drama in her life and mine, and it likely made telling her domineering mother and adulating father a little easier. At least we did it together and she wasn't alone.

When I called my mother to tell her I was getting married to this girl I had got pregnant, she said no way, that I hadn't been in Toronto long enough to get someone pregnant, and she sicced my older brothers on me. They came storming into Toronto, armed with a priest.

Josephine went back to Timmins to have her baby boy, David-Todd (named, can you believe it, after my older brother, who stopped us from getting married). I stayed in touch with her, even spent Christmas in Timmins, or more accurately, South Porcupine, where Jo and her family lived.

I moved in with Josephine's cousin, sharing an apartment with her and another girl, but Jo and I drifted apart without con-clusion, her with immediate maternal concerns and me with my sea of alcohol, sexual promiscuity, and self-absorption. After having an affair with the roommate, I lost my job — my great union job — due to absenteeism at Chrysler. There was a bar across the street from the plant where we went for lunch. I had a long liquid lunch one day and ended up in Fort Lauderdale, Florida for spring break. Then, in April of 1967, living in a flophouse in Downtown Toronto, I got a call to go home. My father had just had a heart attack. It was time to beat it back to Saint John.

In describing the consequences of the gambling that took me literally to the doors of prison, insanity, and death, I would often say I lost my family, my home, my job, my reputation, and my community. But as I looked back on my whole life I was surprised to realize that, due to alcohol, I had lost all of these things several times by the time I was twenty-one.

In Saint John that summer my father recovered, although his restaurant business was toast. I also survived — thrived, in fact, falling head over heels in love with a stunningly beautiful young woman — Robin — for whom I, hippie that I was, played Sonny to her Cher, or so we thought. She, certainly, looked like Cher — not today's plastic model, but 1967's *genuine* Cher.

I discovered drugs, not in Toronto, but in my down-east hometown where I saw my high school friends — now in university, and now also hippies — trying them and not turning into madmen. In Toronto, I'd never been sure, so I'd stuck to beer and the occasional bout of glue sniffing. Heaven help me as I age.

I joined my friends attending university and I became the editor of the University of New Brunswick in Saint John student newspaper, a job I got as a result of my desire to be a journalist and my claim that I'd worked part-time for a Toronto newspaper during my year up there. I'd even had the audacity to name the *Toronto Star.* To my consternation someone whose father knew someone at the *Star* checked: there was no record of me. The paper was really the *Weston Times*, and I wrote one article for them although they had invited me to write more.

If I wasn't all I should have been to be editor of the UNBSJ *Equinox*, it wasn't all it should have been as a university newspaper, either. In its second year of operation, UNBSJ was a branch plant of the main university in Fredericton. It only offered two years, freshman and sophomore, and thus it was easy for a sophisticated big-city bullshitter to talk his way into the editor's position.

I still have some of those university newspaper issues and I am amazed at how similar these bombastic, self-righteous, muck-raking articles were to the style I used as a small-town columnist ten years later writing the weekly scandal and rumour-mongering columns that everyone in Timmins just couldn't wait to read.

My editorship was short-lived anyway as the combination of booze, marijuana, and campus politics overtook my desire for the position. I had all I needed anyway. Later I would be able to tell a real newspaper I'd been the editor of the University of New Brunswick newspaper, which is in fact what I did in Timmins. It got me the job.

Which of my addictions cost me my relationship with Robin? To be honest, I'm not sure. A combination of alcohol, grass, and a life of lies is not a recipe for a protracted relationship — or for a sustainable memory.

I was heartbroken when she broke up with me and I descended even deeper into the morass of drinking, drugs and self-pity. The only two Saint John girlfriends I remember after that were both, for lack of a better word, weird, linked forever in my memory because I threw both of them out of my apartment. One was a Jean Shrimpton look-alike with big hair and an underdeveloped body. I learned later she was ill. I learned it from a student nurse who debunked the rumour this ex-girlfriend was spreading that she had miscarried my child. The second "girlfriend," another soft, dark-haired beauty, scared the hell out of me sexually.

My one year in university was pretty well a wash. I didn't even stick around for my marks. It was time to flee back to Ontario.

I called Josephine in Timmins and told her I was coming to see her. I wired her $35 so I would have money when I got there and I started hitchhiking. In May of 1968, it was "Love-in on the Mountain" in Montreal, and I stayed three weeks, finally leaving but taking a dose of the grabs along as souvenirs of my sojourn.

The night I arrived in South Porcupine, Josephine was out on a date and that summed up the condition of our relationship. We agreed to be friends and she helped me get settled in Timmins. I started looking for a job.

The first place I went was the Timmins *Daily Press*, the famous Lord Thomson of Fleet's first newspaper. *Ha!* Around Timmins he was known more for the number of cheques he bounced than as a press baron. This oft-spoken fact likely cost Timmins a Thomson Empire memorial to its initial newspaper. Instead, the company scoffed at heritage efforts to save and restore its 1930s Daily Press building and tore it down.

I remember during the newspaper job interview how proud the managing editor John Wilson was of having "Just run the NDP out of town." On June 9, 1968, Trudeaumania swept Canada, and on its coattails, Liberal Jean Roy swept NDP Member of Parliament Murdo Martin out of office. I learned later (first-hand from his wife when I lived in his house) that Murdo's philandering in Ottawa likely helped.

"My sister got to kiss Trudeau," I piped in. "My father drove him around Saint John during his visit. I come from a long line of

Liberals." In New Brunswick you were either a Liberal or a Conservative. I didn't even know what an NDP was at that time. I would learn soon enough.

There were no jobs open at the *Daily Press* but I impressed John with my university newspaper editorship, my political moxie and, no doubt, my desperation, which would make me a good candidate to work long hours for little money. A tendency to be a workaholic was a prerequisite at the first, and likely all, Thomson Newspapers, at least in those days.

A few days later, when I was about to take just any job, I got a call from "Mr. Wilson," as I came to call him. "Jack McLean, our Town Hall reporter, just took a job as the economic development officer with the Town of Timmins, and that creates an opening here if you are still interested."

"Yes, Yes, when can I start?"

"Well, we can't have him reporting on Town Hall when he's going to work for them so he's gone and the job's open now. When can you start?"

"Today!" I was too young and too poor to worry about being over-eager.

"Tomorrow, then," he said. "We start at 8 a.m. but we are on deadline until 9:30 so you'll just have to hang around and not get in the way."

"Great, I'll be there," I said, jumping up and down in the rooming house where I lived, just two blocks away from the newspaper office.

The next day I learned about obits, Bygone Days, and Bits and Bites. I found out how difficult it was to type with two fingers on an antique Underwood typewriter (at least UNBSJ had an electric typewriter) and that I was going to be making $35 a week. I also learned that the guy who got Jo pregnant also worked there, in fact he came from a family of newspapermen, most of whom had also started at the Timmins *Daily Press*. While I may have had to work with him — and, as it turned out, drink with him — I never did like him. People that I did like were also there. Dick Cameron was my city editor, a genuinely nice guy. Dick was often excited, but rarely upset. He also had a quirky way of asking obvious questions like they were a wonderment: "Is that beer really only your first?" The only fault that I can recall about Dick — aside from the fact he didn't drink — was that he tried to teach me how to drive.

One of the tools reporters used to chase stories (and at the *Daily Press*, located beside the Timmins fire hall, we literally chased stories) was the *Daily Press* car. This shared mode of transportation was something everyone fought over — signing in with their needs early each day. Everyone but me. I didn't know how to drive. Maybe it was the fact that I was away from home at Saint Mary's College during those formative car-obsessed years of fifteen and sixteen. Perhaps it was seeing my older brother's nose broken by my father one day because he had taken off in the Little Inn delivery van with his girlfriend and missed an important delivery. Possibly, it was providential.

Dick, like a few other men in my journalism career, took teaching seriously. Unfortunately for him, that extended to driving. On a return trip from a reporting assignment, over the winding, twisting semi-asphalted Frederick House Bridge Road near Connaught, Dick decided it was time I had a driving lesson.

"Okay, let's do it," I said — somewhat too enthusiastically, Dick should have realized — as I took over the wheel.

"Good, good, you're doing okay," Dick said as we moved down the road. "Keep your eyes about thirty feet in front of the car and steer towards that point, ever so lightly. Don't look at the road, just in front of the car."

"This isn't so hard," I said — as always, getting a little cocky.

As time went on we ended up behind a transport truck travelling at a reduced speed, which was warranted given the curves, the soft shoulders and broken pavement.

"Okay," Dick said, "Look for a chance to pass him. Remember you have to be able to see well ahead and judge that you have the room to pass. At best it's a guess, but it's important that it be a good guess."

Now Dick was teaching me, and it was good advice he was giving me for highway driving. For straight highway driving. For the road to Connaught he should have said it needed to be a *great* guess.

Cautiously, I pulled out into the oncoming lane and began to accelerate, easing the Daily Press car beside the slow-moving transport. I looked over at Dick, grinning, expecting his nod of approval. Instead I saw his eyes popping out of his head and I turned my eyes back to the road to see an oncoming oil truck suddenly on the road ahead.

I don't know if I got it from the hot-rod talk of my Grade 12 classmates, but my instincts reacted to the fear by slamming the car into gear — up into gear — as I imagined all those race car drivers did and putting the pedal to the metal.

I'm not sure whether it was Dick's scream or the screech of the grinding gears that made me realize in that split second that I should have slammed the gear shift *down* and not up — I'd thrown it into automatic reverse. I pulled the gear back down, saving the transmission from falling completely out of the car. But, it was too late to pass the transport. I slipped the car in behind the transport just in time to avoid the oil truck that passed us with its driver mouthing obvious obscenities. The car, following its own instincts, coasted to a stop at the side of the road.

"Get out," Dick shouted, "I'll drive the rest of the way. You can take taxis."

Greg Reynolds was the wire editor when I first started at the *Daily Press*, but in later years, after Dick retired, he became my City Editor. He was also a drinking and, I now realize, a gambling companion. Every day we finished putting the newspaper to bed at noon and headed across the street to the Lady Laurier or Victory House to celebrate. Well maybe not to celebrate, but to "have a few" with lunch or, more likely, *as* lunch. This was my kind of job and these were my kind of people. And Timmins was my kind of town, reputed to have more taverns per capita than any other place in Canada. When I first told my mother I was planning to go to Timmins she was worried about all the gambling that was supposed to go on in gold-mining towns. I remember laughing at her exaggerated concerns then, and even later in Timmins, as I sat around the barrooms playing something called Bullshit Poker with dollar bills.

"Somebody go to the bar and get some fresh bills," Dan Kelly said, talking to the circle of news and politico types that were gathered around the two tables pulled together in the Victory House Tavern. This was our daily bar, and often our nightly haunt too. Dan was a radio announcer at CKGB, the radio station across the hall in the Thomson Building, as it was formally called. Lord Roy actually started his media empire with a radio station in North

Bay, and this Timmins station was his too. Kelly was also a town councillor and — it is now safe to reveal — my constant inside source for what was going on behind closed doors at Town Hall. Not that he was alone in that role, but he certainly was the most consistent over my twelve years in the Timmins news business. He was my Deep Throat.

Another councillor, Eddy Couture, was also there. He too provided a great source of daily information for my stories and columns through the years. He was the proprietor of the Esquire Grill, the downtown Timmins headquarters for rumours and scuttlebutt — my stock-in-trade. As much as the Victory House was my beer and gambling Bethel, the Esquire Grill was my coffee and news cathedral. Twice a day, morning and afternoon, I'd join the local wags and prattlers to learn the latest hearsay and scandal, the starting point for many of my better journalistic endeavours. Ed himself was also a trusted raconteur. Ditto for dental therapist Councillor Don Collins and prospector Don McKinnon (a soon-to-be very, very rich prospector who would find the Hemlo goldfields near Lake Superior), a councillor who I would later help in his unsuccessful run for the Mayor's chair.

Greg and a number of other news types — mostly radio and television reporters — filled out the chairs and traded in their old bills for new ones when I returned from the bar. Bullshit Poker is so called because the object is to use the serial numbers on each person's dollar bill to call the highest poker hand, without getting caught bluffing, or in this case, bullshitting.

Dan Kelly, having won the last round, started. "Three tens," he announced, looking out from behind his carefully folded-up bill. I didn't know what he had but I didn't have any zeros on my bill, so I would call "bullshit" if the bet stayed in the tens. If a bettor was caught bullshitting he had to pay everyone the ante, anywhere from a dollar or two up to ten and twenty dollars depending on variables such as who was playing, the time of the night and the number of drinks we'd all consumed. If the bettor could make the called hand using his own bill plus all of the other bills in play at the table, then all the players had to pay him the ante. Our bet was up to five dollars, given that it was after the council meeting and the men's side of the tavern would close at midnight.

The next bettor either had to call something higher than three tens, pass, or call bullshit. If everyone called bullshit then the person with the final bet had to make his hand.

Ed bet four Tens and then Greg bet four Tens, Ace high. The next player, someone from the radio station who remains in the fog, passed. Don Collins said bullshit, indicating that he too had no Tens. The television reporter bet four Aces, Ten high. That put a new twist on things for me as I had two ones and I had to assume he had at least two, if not three. But, the name of the game was Bullshit Poker, so I bet: "Five Tens."

Kelly looked at me out of the corner of his eye and he knew I was bullshitting. But, considering his bet, as well as Eddie's and Greg's, there was a good chance there were five Tens among the seven hands counted together. "Six Tens," he said.

Ed said bullshit. Greg: "Bullshit." Radio guy: "Bullshit." Don Collins said, "I know you're bullshitting, Kelly." CFCL-TV news studied his Ace-rich hand and then, seemingly reluctant, announced bullshit, leaving it to me. My bet, my risk, at this point was five dollars. *If Kelly's bullshitting, I win five dollars; if he's not, I lose another five, on top of the twenty I've already lost and owe Greg.*

If I have two ones, I thought, and the TV guy has two, or three, chances are good that at least two of the other five guys have one each. Seconds later my mouth said, out of the blue, "Six Aces."

"Bullshit" and shaking heads all around. "Show," Kelly grinned.

"No, no," I said, "everyone else has to show first." They did. Kelly none. Ed, bless his soul, one. Greg also had one and I was rubbing my hands with glee. Radio guy, none. Collins: "None." It all came down to the TV reporter's hand. Did he have two or three?

He threw the bill on the table and announced, to resounding laughter, "None."

"Little," Greg said, knowing I would be coming for another loan as I put my bill on the table, "you should give up gambling."

The person whose job I took at the newspaper was also responsible for my meeting my future wife. In September of 1968, after four months on the job, I was covering an Ontario Housing Workshop at the Empire Hotel. It was one of those think-tank things where various elements of the community are brought together to discuss possible solutions to town problems, in this case, housing.

Jack McLean, as the town's economic development officer, was participating, along with other members of council and city officials. A class from Northern College, the local community college, was also attending as observers. At one point they divided the workshop participants into several round-table groups, each of which was to discuss some aspect of the housing problem and report back later to the full assembly. I sat in on one of the round tables to follow the story.

"We need a secretary," Jack announced as we were all taking our seats. "Doug, go get us a secretary."

Across the room, several of the college students were sitting together at one table. I went over and tapped the best-looking one on the shoulder. "We need someone to take notes at our table," I said as she turned. "Could you . . . ?"

I couldn't finish my sentence. I was tongue-tied like the school boy I should have been by this little girl who was looking wistfully back at me with her dreamy green eyes and saying, "Yes."

Her name was Roberta Major, she was taking a year of college before going away to university and she was beautiful. Me, I told her, I was *a writer*. "I hitch-hiked up here after university to work in the newspaper where I'm the town hall reporter."

"What a drag," I know I said to her — she told me — probably about the workshop.

That night wasn't the first time I wrote a story intoxicated — some of my best stuff was written that way — but it was the first time the intoxication wasn't due to booze or drugs.

What a fucking day! I don't dare ask what else can go wrong for fear of the answer.

Roberta gives me the number Johnny left and I tell her I'll call her later to let her know what happens.

All this pressure makes me want to run. No, not run away, but run into the casino where I want nothing more than to hide in a corner and gamble the rest of my life away. Failing that, I'm not sure I want to live. The board's talk about getting me some help and the karmic messages like Johnny's call that have been slamming me in the face all day all point to my quitting gambling, and yet what do I feel? An even stronger urge to get back to the casino. No, not to win back what I have lost, nor to, as I like to say, win my way out of trouble. No, now despondent, I just want to bury myself there. How different I feel now from just a few short days ago when, with thousands of dollars in my pockets, everything seemed possible.

Giving up on roulette, I decided to get right down to the business at hand: winning the $101,254 progressive jackpot at Caribbean Stud. This was the biggest jackpot that Casino Rama had ever had and with all the play it was getting it was growing at a rate of about $10,000 a day. To win the progressive you had to put a buck in the special jackpot slot at the Caribbean Stud table, and then get a Royal Flush. I didn't know the probability of getting a Royal Flush, or, in the terms I understood then, "the odds against it," but I figured they were pretty high. To me the odds didn't matter. Somebody had to win and as long as I had money to play, that somebody could be me. That was all the information on odds I needed.

My Casino Rama vice-president friend, Ed Leichner, said to me one day just after the casino opened, "You know you can't win here — in the long run everyone loses."

"I know that," I answered with my mouth while my brain disowned the words. I was different. I had to be different, and that need made me different. I just needed enough money, enough time, and enough luck to make it happen. Sitting around the Caribbean Stud table at 7:00 a.m., October 19, 1996, I knew I was running out of all three. The only way I could drown out the frightening truth of these thoughts was to gamble more, to gamble higher, and to gamble wilder.

The play of Caribbean Stud is two-tiered. First there is the ante, which can be, depending on the table minimum at a given time, anywhere from $15 to $50 or higher. If you ante $25 then you can bet an additional two times that amount once you see your cards and the one card showing in the dealer's hand. If you fold, you lose the ante. If you stay, you have the potential of winning based on both the $25 ante and the $50 bet. In this game there are a couple of hills to climb. First, your hand has to beat the dealer's hand, and then, to win the second bet, the dealer has to qualify by getting an Ace-King or higher in his hand. If he doesn't qualify you get paid even money for the ante and you get to keep your bet. If he does qualify and you beat him, your payout is based on the poker hand you have, with, of course, the Royal Flush paying the ultimate progressive jackpot providing you have paid the one dollar in the progressive slot.

I sat at a $25-minimum table. In the morning there are $15-minimum tables but when the jackpot is over a hundred grand the table minimum eases up throughout the day; by tonight none of the twelve Caribbean Stud tables will be at less than a $50 minimum. And you can bet they'll all be crowded, with people lined up waiting behind your chair.

That's the joke about casino operators claiming they simply offer an entertainment alternative comparable in cost to dinner and the theatre. With tables at $50 minimum — quite usual for Friday and Saturday nights — the $200 entertainment alternative lasts about two minutes in poker, blackjack, or roulette.

I anted up my $25 and my one-dollar progressive bet. Just as in other poker games, traditional wisdom tells you not to bet — "keep your option" — on anything less than a Pair of Tens, because you need to be bigger than the dealer's hand to win.

Unfortunately, the desperate pursuit of luck upon which I had embarked precluded wisdom of any kind, let alone that of the traditional variety.

Five cards were dealt down to each player, with the dealer receiving four down and one up. I picked up my cards and carefully looked at them. You aren't allowed to show each other your hands or talk about what you have in this game.

A Pair of Queens. All right, I thought. Pocket Queens. *I'm in.*

The dealer, however, showed a King, which could have been part of a Pair of Kings or could have been matched with an Ace to make sure the dealer qualified. Each player now had the option to fold or play.

The guy on the left of the dealer folded, forfeiting his $25 ante. The next guy stayed and bet another $50. Fold, stay, fold, until it came to me and of course I played my two ladies — *love those ladies.* I pushed $50 into the circle and the dealer revealed his hand. Two Threes. I won, even money on both my ante and my winning pair.

One of the other players got a Flush, and was paid five-to-one — $150 — *not bad.*

I once watched one of my table mates win ten percent of the progressive jackpot on a Straight Flush only to get pissed off when the dealer didn't qualify on his $100 bet, costing him the added $5,000 at fifty-to-one.

I recognized one of the players at my table as part of a couple I had played with during a previous all-night session of Caribbean Stud, the night I learned the game about six weeks ago when I was still working through the remnants of the last "borrowed" ten-grand.

"Hey, man, it's good to see you. How's it going?" I asked,

looking around expectantly for the inevitable return of his wife looking for more money for the slot machines.

"Not bad," he said. "I've been here all night and I'm thinking about getting them to give me a room where I can get some sleep."

"Where's Christine? The last time we were here she was really hot."

"Gone," he said. "She just took off in the night about two weeks ago. Ripped me off for a couple of thousand dollars."

"No kidding," I said shaking my head. *She loved to gamble.* That previous night, I had thought, jealously, how great it must be to have a wife who loved to gamble too. I often marvelled at the Asian customers at Casino Rama who always made gambling a social or family affair. Not the local date-night casino gawkers who walked hand in hand around the playing floor drinking in the noise, the lights and the madness but remained untouched save for twenty or so dollars in a slot machine. "Win or lose" types. No, these Asians were high-stakes gamblers, thousands on the line each hand at baccarat, mini-baccarat or Pai-Gow, or on the spin of a wheel in roulette. They'd be there, guys with girlfriends, families, gambling in groups, as a social outing. Me, and everyone else I knew that was a serious gambler, gambled alone or with strangers who became our casino "friends." What we were really doing in the casino remained hidden from our families and our friends. Often, like my middle-of-the-night excursions, the fact that we were in the casino at all was kept hidden.

I couldn't hide the fact I had stayed out all day and night that Saturday. It was just so obvious that gambling was the cause. I went directly from the charity casino to Casino Rama, meaning I'd already been up almost 24 hours when I started gambling at 5:00 a.m. When I left the casino, 28 hours later, I had gone 50 hours without sleeping and probably could have kept going had I not made the mistake of stopping for breakfast. I was falling asleep as I ate.

Desperation had overtaken any caution or concern that I normally would have had about going home after being out all night without so much as a phone call to say where I was. It was unnecessary information, anyway, because Roberta knew where I was and what I was doing — although not with whose money.

When I left Sunday morning, October 20, I wasn't broke. I was badly bent, but not broke. Of the charity casino's ten grand I was down six, but that left me $4,000 for a comeback once I got some sleep. Arriving home shortly before 10 a.m. in the morning I was confronted by my worn-out, tear-stained wife. I fed her my standard "I was down, and couldn't leave" line, then, "but I came back and I won a couple of hundred dollars — here!" Now I was down to $3,800.

"I'm exhausted. I can't talk now. I have to get some sleep." I couldn't deal with a long, dragged-out discussion.

"You're going to kill yourself. You'll have another heart attack," she said to me, her eyes welling up with tears. When we were young, and I came home after a 28-hour drinking binge, I would have been afraid she would kill me. Now, she's afraid I'm going to kill myself.

She was right to worry, too, because certainly the thought of a heart attack had crossed my mind during many of those late-night hours of despair. Even as late as that weekend, during my gambling marathon, I caught myself thinking that perhaps a heart attack would be a good way to go.

It would be less damaging on the living than suicide — better for Melanie, I'd think in between shuffles, spins or whirls, when denial failed, and reality didn't just bite, it snapped. Then I realized they'd find all the money missing and figure I killed myself anyway. That was when I cranked up another, or two, slot machines, side by side, playing all three like a goddamn piano-playing monkey, just to keep thought at bay.

CHAPTER SEVEN

I don't have to call Johnny. My friend — I'll call him *F.* for friend — came

October 22, 1996 — 1 p.m.

knocking on my downtown door. "Jeez, Doug, I told you, you can't not pay this guy and, shit, you can't bounce a cheque on him either," *F.* says to me as soon as I open my office door.

"I know. It's my fucking bank. They cancelled my overdraft and kicked back cheques from the last two weeks. I'm scrambling to deal with it now."

"Well, you'd better deal with it. This guy is pissed and he's not the kind of guy you want upset."

"I'm a bit upset with him for Christ sakes. Why does he have to call my house and get Roberta on my case? He knows she isn't part of this. She doesn't know I owe him any money."

"Doug. Use your fucking brains. He doesn't care about your problems. He just wants you to repay him the money you borrowed, without these hassles. Now he's worried about the rest of the cheques."

"I'm trying to raise some money to cover his cheque and the others that bounced."

"Are you still gambling?" he asks, looking me directly in the face. I know this is one time I shouldn't lie.

"Yeah, I'm trying to get even, to pay off the rest of the money I owe."

"You know you're never going to get even, or pay off anything as long as you are still gambling. I thought you were going to get some help?"

I was. Three months ago to the day, July 22, I met with my family doctor and told her I was destroying my life with gambling. She was surprised by what I was telling her: gambling out of control, using money that I shouldn't be using, not caring about the consequences — my position in the community, my reputation — not caring what happened between Roberta and I. A year earlier, in July of 1995 when I quit bingo, I had told her I was tired of wrestling with my addictions.

"I thought you were talking about nose spray," she said, recalling the conversation, "not gambling." It didn't surprise me. My recollection of that earlier visit was of my whining about Roberta. It was just a few weeks after I'd told her about my bingo debts and her having to borrow from her father to bail me out. She was making my life hell.

"I wish I had killed myself rather than tell you," I spat at her one night as she reminded me of the trouble I, once again, had got us into. "I will never, never tell you anything again," I swore.

I didn't spit out my gambling problem to Dr. Strickland during that first visit, however. I had talked about vague "addictions" that I was tired of wrestling with, but what I really focused on was that I had a "wife problem." What an amazing coincidence. Eighteen years earlier, I didn't have a drinking problem: I had a wife problem.

Now I was spilling my guts to my doctor about my out-of-control gambling but I had no intentions of stopping. Maybe I did when I made the appointment a week or so earlier, the day after a major loss at blackjack. I was frightened of how I was growing more and more distraught in the middle of the night as I drove home broke again. The dark thoughts of suicide were beginning, and the fanciful thoughts of being able to talk my way out my troubles were on the wane. Truth sneaks in during those desperate early-morning hours.

However, *now* it was a week before the opening of Casino Rama, and nothing was going to stop me from being there. We parted with Dr. Strickland agreeing to look into any possible treatment, saying she would call me. The next time she saw me, it would be to monitor my heart condition and mental health as I grappled with those same consequences I didn't care about that afternoon just a few months earlier.

"I'm trying to quit, *F.*, but it's not that easy. I need help. I'm trying to find it," I say, telling him that I have admitted to the Downtown Board chairman that I have a gambling problem and that the board has said that they are behind me in getting help. "Maybe they'll even pay for treatment," I venture, seeing I've hit a responsive chord. "I just have to get through the next few days, get some of this financial crap under control so I can breathe and deal with the gambling."

F. is encouraged by the fact that the Downtown knows about my problem. "Do they know money is missing?"

"Yes," I hedge, "but they say it's a 'family matter' and we're going to work it out together." Like the Downtown Board, there's no way in hell I am going to tell *F.* about all the other money I've taken from Leacock and the Winter Carnival. I saw hope in his eyes, and I wanted to keep it there, because in his hope I was able to find a little for myself. A little, but not enough.

"I have a client who owes me some money," I lied (he's another guy I can get an advance from for future work). "I'm hoping I can get it this afternoon. I'll pay Johnny the $500 to cover the cheque."

"You better make it six hundred," *F.* said. "I'll call him and get back to you later this afternoon." With that he left me with the problem of not only finding $600 for Johnny but also a similar amount, at least, for Bob, in order to get my juggling act back on the road.

One of the events I created at the Leacock Heritage Festival was called the Leacock Street Performers Fair. We brought eight or nine big-city buskers to small-town Orillia to busk on the main street and across the city's waterfront. Most of the buskers were jugglers, juggling everything from balls — even bowling balls — to knives, chainsaws, and fire in their efforts to charm money from the pockets of their audiences. Along with jugglers, we also had magicians who climaxed their acts by escaping from straitjackets.

To promote the second year of the festival, two of the buskers — magician Tom Baxter and stuntman Rob Evans — devised a publicity stunt to be done high above the main street of Orillia. They would hang upside-down suspended from a crane and race to see who could get out of the straitjacket first. It was supposed to be a dragged-out, slow motion, lots-of-talk stunt, narrated by one of the best buskers in the business, Johnny Toronto. He was the artistic director of the Street Performers Fair and helped me get the rest of the buskers to Orillia. The real art in busking was the spiel: the running commentary gathered the crowd with the jokes, the suspense, and the buildup to the stunts. The pièce de résistance, the climax of the show (Johnny Toronto's was juggling three fire torches while wheeling around on a ten-foot unicycle) was completed with the pitch — asking for the money in the hat.

"Ladies and gentlemen, boys and girls, 100 feet high in the air, above the hard pavement on the streets of Downtown Orillia, I give you magician extraordinaire Tom Baxter and his adversary, master stuntman Rob Evans, in a death-defying grudge match to see who can escape first from these securely padlocked straitjackets, genuinely certified and locked tight by none other than your very own Chief of Police," Johnny Toronto pitched through the PA to the hundreds of townsfolk who had come to see the spectacle.

"Never before has such a competition taken place in such a dangerous venue, high above the street without a safety net. Harry Houdini did it alone, over water, but never over pavement." (Houdini did it underwater, with not only a straitjacket, but also chains. To his credit, this is the way Tom Baxter had conceived of the stunt when he first approached me, but Rob was not too keen on the chains or the water. Also, I was the manager of the Downtown streets, not the waterfront).

"Now as the cranes lift our brave, daredevil challengers to the 100-foot level, I ask the audience for complete silence so each of our protagonists can hear the starter's signal which will begin the race to escape from these tightly bound straitjackets, normally reserved for the insane." Then Johnny Toronto added, "Of course, once the pistol has been fired, you may cheer riotously for your favourite prestidigitator."

It all looked very impressive, and was going very smoothly. The two cranes, supplied by a community-minded welding company, sat side by side, spanning Mississaga Street, next to the picturesque and historic Orillia Opera House. By now a crowd of several hundred people had gathered, straining their necks as "those crazy boys" were lifted aloft, dangling upside-down by their feet, suspended from ropes attached to each crane's metal hook.

It was my job to determine when the two were ready for the contest to start. I estimated they were high enough — nobody was going to check — and red enough, as all their blood drained into their heads. I took Tom's calm nod and Rob's frantic shake as signals they were both ready. I gave the word to the starter who fired the blank pistol. "Bang!"

Johnny Toronto started off his play-by-play commentary calmly enough on what was supposed to be a minute or two's struggle. "Ladies and Gentleman we have Tom Baxter twisting and turning as . . ." then the panic set in.

Rob was in trouble. Far from the choreographed, slow-paced competition we had planned, Rob was racing out of his straitjacket like his life depended on it. Tom, hearing or sensing something was wrong, joined in the acceleration.

"But wait, here comes Rob Evans like a bat out of hell, he's got one arm out! Now Baxter's got his arm out. They are moving at the speed of light getting out of those jackets. This is going to be a world record!" Johnny screamed.

I can't remember who won. That wasn't supposed to be the point. It was a publicity stunt. It turned into a race, not just against each other, but also against fear. Rob, who was doing the stunt for the first time, had felt the rope around his ankles slip. He wanted out of there and down as fast as he could.

Like Rob Evans, I could feel my rope slipping, and, I wanted to escape.

Ken Burgess, my other client, and friend, owned a small chain of video arcades and pool halls across central and northern Ontario. He was the one client I was able to transfer from Timmins to Orillia when I first moved down in 1983, as he had businesses in both places. That year, for the first few months anyway, he saved my family and I from starvation by giving me contract work and cheques in advance.

In July of 1982 we enrolled Melanie in summer school at the Mariposa School of Skating in Orillia, where Canadian and World Figure Skating Champion Brian Orser trained under coach and school director Doug Leigh. Although Doug taught her on occasion, Melanie's principle coach was Neil Carpenter, who also coached champion skaters and had skated in the Olympics himself. It was at his urging that we came to Orillia for a summer school in the first place, as he had come to Timmins the year before to teach a skating seminar. Competitive skating is a bit of a progressive addiction and a slippery slope in and of itself. First it started as a recreation — learning to skate. I was pretty big on this idea as I had been an early skater. I was a speed skater when I was five and a half years old, and — I have the newspaper clipping to prove it — a champion. In this picture, my nine-year-old brother David and I hold medals we had won at the Maritime Speed Skating Championships. David won his medal beating the competition in his ten-and-under age group. I won mine for getting up off the ice when I fell. I was the only competitor in the under-six class and raced, as they told me, "against my shadow." Fortunately, my shadow was slower at getting up.

Melanie's skating soon became a diversion from, of all things, school. Thanks to a father who dreamed of being a writer — making books and authors special in our home — and a mother who made learning and reading fun, Melanie was reading at three. She had been going to the story time at the library since she was a year-and-a-half old. When she was about three and a half, story time at the library was filmed as a Christmas special at the Timmins television station. During the filming Melanie, in between stories, stood up in her red-and-white, crinoline-fluffed dress, and with her arms spread high in the air, announced: "I love books. I have a million books." A slight exaggeration, but if we spent a fortune on figure skating, we spent the first one on books and toys.

When she entered school, Melanie was light years ahead of her classmates to the point that in Grade One they put her half days into the grade two reading and spelling classes where she still led the class. Halfway through the year we noticed she was having difficulty finding a peer group of friends, as she was neither completely a grade-one student nor a grade-two. With her teachers and the school, we made the decision to accelerate her learning again and complete all of the grade two material by the end of the year. Melanie did the two years in one and went on to Grade Three with her advancing Grade Two peers. The problem I saw with this was my fear that it would continue to happen and that Melanie would end up some academic freak, say 12 years old in university. Her mother wanted her in a special Montessori school, but I was opposed to this, fearing it would also isolate her from the real world and not allow her to grow up like a normal child. Today the only explanation I can imagine for my opposition, along with my complete ignorance of Montessori Schools (I never let my ignorance of something interfere with my ability to express a strong opinion about it — after all, I was once a newspaper columnist), was my recollection of the snobby Netherwood girls who attended private school, in Rothesay, near my New Brunswick hometown.

The solution was less school and more figure skating. Melanie was already in skating — she started when she was five — but now we started to add Fall Schools, Spring Schools, and Summer Schools to the mix along with private lessons. Now she needed not one, but two pairs of the handmade world-class Knebli figure skates (one for dance and another for figures) that cost upwards of $350 each and could only be purchased through a private fitting with Mr. Knebli himself at his shop in Toronto. How much money did we spend on skating? The truth is I don't know. The receipts I kept for 1981, the year before Orillia, added up to over $16,000. After that I stopped counting. My philosophy was simple: nothing, not even poverty, was going to deprive my little girl of every opportunity in the world. I was "bigger than the rules" for her, too.

The diversion worked. With these special skating schools, travel, competitions and practice, Melanie missed school half the time (in Grade 11, the last year she skated, she missed 44 days of school in the first semester) and she still maintained marks that always were the highest, not only in her class, but in the entire school.

By the time we got to Orillia, Melanie had a number of medals and trophies, and had just achieved, at 12 years old, a Canadian Figure Skating Association gold medal in dance. By this time figure skating was a dream — her dream and our dream. The thought of the Olympics motivated her, but, I'm not sure what else. Perhaps it was fame, definitely it was fun and travel. For me, it was pride and love. Certainly Roberta shared my love and pride, and perhaps too, Melanie's desire for fame, living her life, as she did, through Melanie. She also saw a practical side to it all, a way to make money, if all else failed, by teaching skating. After all, we had spent a small fortune paying young women up to $24 an hour for private lessons, and that was before Orillia when the world-class ante jumped to $32 an hour.

I never believed in skating as a way to earn a living. I had seen too many of her previous teachers in Timmins working part-time as grocery store cashiers because there weren't enough skating students. For this college dropout, after 15 years of doubting my own abilities, more education was, and still is, my maxim. I may have had a profound impact on Melanie's life in this regard — encouraging her to pursue her education and believe in herself. Having an impact on her life was certainly what I intended when I decided to stay in my disastrous marriage — ruined by my alcoholism and stupid naiveté — after I sobered up in 1978.

We decided to move to Orillia in the middle of that figure skating summer school of 1982. Regardless of whether skating ended up being her career or not, we agreed it would be a colossal step backwards for Melanie to return to skating in Timmins after experiencing the excellence of the Mariposa School. In Timmins she would have been the proverbial big fish in the little pond and that would have hurt her drive for excellence in whatever she decided to do. Roberta and Melanie moved in the fall of 1982, in time for Melanie to start high school in Grade Nine. I was to follow in 1983 when I found someone to take over my small marketing

business with my two key clients, the 101 mall, where I was promotion coordinator, and Downtown Timmins, where I was the
downtown manager.

The first time we went to Orillia for summer school, Roberta
and Melanie stayed in something called Paradise Cove. It wasn't.
In fact it was a run-down collection of ageing cabins on the north
shore of Lake Simcoe that brought Roberta to tears as she tried to
clear away the spiders from every corner and crevice. To be fair to
the cabins, ten years later we would rent a relatively luxurious
house, also on the north side of Lake Simcoe, and the battle with
the spiders there was just as monumental and continuous (as were
Roberta's tears — though the tears were no longer about spiders).

In the fall they rented another cabin down the road from the
first, which was in a little better condition and had smaller spiders.
I remained living in Timmins, in the attic of Roberta's parents'
house. We sold our house after taking out a fourth mortgage to
pay for skating and being informed by our insurance broker that
no company would insure a house with four mortgages. I warned
the guy who held the third mortgage that the second mortgage
holder was going to foreclose. To protect his investment he bought
the house and paid off all the mortgages. We walked away having
used all the equity to finance our collective figure-skating dream.

While I remained in Timmins to work and sleep, I travelled
to Orillia every second weekend to be with my family and to help
them find more permanent housing. We settled on a townhouse
complex, on Lankin Boulevard, not far from the Twin Lakes
Arena (years later I was part of a city committee that had the
arena renamed as the Brian Orser Arena in recognition of his
achievements), and, you guessed it, on the spider-infested north
shore of Lake Simcoe.

In Orillia, Roberta got a job. Now that Melanie was in high school and we were ensconced in the best skating school in the country, the need for her to be at home, or available to travel with Melanie to this skating school or that, diminished in comparison to our need for money. Through a friend in the car business in Timmins, I bought Roberta a new, no-money-down 1982 Toyota Tercel, a car that served her well until 1991 when it died, causing her (while I was flat on my back in intensive care with my heart attack) to go and buy a sporty Chevy Cavalier Z-24.

"That cold-hearted bitch," she once overheard a faceless voice in a crowd say, "he's in the hospital with a heart attack and she goes out and celebrates by buying a new car." Of course such behaviour is not that uncommon among people under catastrophic stress — some even begin to gamble compulsively. The old car was finished partly due to the mileage I put on it going back and forth to Barrie in 1983 to 1986 as tourism manager for the region after I had to sell my own car early in 1983 to keep the bank from repossessing it. But, then again the bitch-calling lady never knew the whole story.

That I missed my family, holed up in the attic above my in-laws in Timmins, there was no doubt. I was also tiring of the fourteen-hour drive back and forth every other weekend to Orillia. It seems I spent my life on such journeys. First, to and from North Bay, where Melanie and her Mom spent two summers and falls in figure skating schools. Then it was Scarborough, for a month — a disaster off the ice as they billeted with a family whose daughter was jealous of Melanie's skating ability. Lots of tears. Then came the pursuit of the gold medal in dance when Melanie was 10 years old. Scarborough was part of that as was a month in Fredericton, New Brunswick where Melanie and her mom stayed with my parents and skated with a coach she had met in North Bay. In order to get your gold medal in dance you had to pass five separate dance tests, each set to different music and performed in a different style. In addition to dancing each perfectly yourself, you also had to dance with a partner. At these higher-level dances — bronze, silver and up — that was almost always with a professional. So, in order to pass these tests you not only had to chase training schools, you also had to chase partners and test days which were held about twice a year somewhere throughout your region — in our case, the vastness of Northern Ontario. Training in North Bay, test days in New Liskeard, and dance practice every weekend in Espanola with her professional partner, George O'Reilly. Melanie had her silver medal in dance when she was nine. The tiny, incredibly beautiful nine-year-old dancing the sultry *Blues* was the talk of the figure skating world in Northern Ontario. Melanie proceeded to pass the first three gold dances in the next year, and it looked like she was headed towards being the first ten year old in anybody's memory to achieve a gold medal in dance. Then the famous skating "politics" which you hear so much about at the international level kicked in at the regional level. No matter what anyone tells you to the contrary, they're there at every level.

Melanie had no partner. Not that we didn't look in North Bay, Scarborough, and Fredericton, and not that Melanie's reputation didn't speak for itself. The awful truth we had to face was that there were very few male figure skaters period, and even fewer dancers. This scarcity left the males who did exist completely in the driver's seat as to where they skated and with whom — and as well able to dictate who paid. Whether I liked it or not, after six years of scraping to pay for skating, there was no way we had enough money or the ability to find enough money to play in the partners' game of competitive ice dancing. Melanie seemed to sense the end of our Olympic dance dream and began to concentrate on the individual free skating and figures portions of her training. "No way I am going to share the limelight with some guy," she rationalized and began the climb as a free skater, which brought us to Orillia and the best free-skating school in the country.

In the fall of 1982, my two Timmins clients decided to go to war with each other. The Downtown was opposed to the 101 mall's proposal to expand under the provincial Downtown Revitalization Program and bring a Sears store into Downtown Timmins. I had to pick sides and as I was only the promotions manager at the mall, and the overall manager of the Downtown, I carried out my management duties opposing the mall's expansion in a presentation before City Council. I lost the mall as a client; it lost its bid to expand. Sears located outside the downtown in the suburban Timmins Square. Whether the downtown made the right choice is still debated in Timmins today.

It also became clear that my remaining client, the downtown, was not willing to sign a new contract unless I would guarantee that I would be there for the next year to carry out the role myself. Of course it was apparent that I would not, since I had sold my house, moved my family, and was becoming increasingly absent in my thinking, if not my presence, as I looked yearningly south to Orillia.

Timmins and Northern Ontario, being resource-based, often did well compared to the rest of the country in recessionary times. Timmins had gold, which was used as a hedge against inflation, keeping the economy relatively strong throughout the recession of the early eighties. Not so Orillia, a declining manufacturing town and tourism area. Orillia was in the grip of the recession when I arrived there full-time in January, 1983, looking for clients. I found only small contracts: a mini-mall in Midland, selling ads in the new weekly newspaper — the Orillia *Sun's* economic development issue — and a logo design and some marketing campaigns for the small main-street shoe store where Roberta had found work as a salesperson. I became loosely associated with a small advertising company, Huronia Promotions, which operated out of the Elmvale offices of Andrew Markle, from where we also sold ads for his summer weekly newspaper, *Huronia Happenings.* During this same time, Markle's house of cards was coming crashing down as he and others were charged with real estate fraud, bank fraud and insider dealing. Still, he seemed a nice enough guy to me.

It was a tough time, culminating in a few clandestine visits to a pawnshop in Barrie with my 35-mm camera and the limited family jewels. Yep, I hocked the wedding ring, except it wasn't the wedding ring diamond anymore, because when we were separated in 1975 — for the second time in six years (I always say I was married for 27 years, give or take a few years) — Roberta had the engagement ring made into a heart necklace. When we were separated for a year in 1972 I threw my wedding band away. When I came back in 1973, my friend, Rheal, with whom I had been living for the first six months of my separation, had retrieved it and saved it for me. I still have it, even today, stored safely in a box with an old set of false teeth: novelties that, while I never intend to use them again, remind me of life's lessons every time I open the box. The teeth are hideous, almost worn right down to the plastic gums (it looked like I had no teeth when I opened my mouth). They were my gambling teeth: I had more important things to do with my money and everybody else's than to get a new set of false teeth. So unreal was my world in the last six months of my gambling that I spent the entire time with a bottom-row tooth — one of my own — broken at the root and capable of being pushed forward ninety degrees by my tongue, to hang precariously by its attachment to the gums. Every night when I went to bed, not only did I have to worry about my gambling debts and my sleep apnea, I also had to worry about swallowing my lower middle tooth and waking up looking like a complete idiot.

Interestingly, thirteen years before, in 1983, I dared not open my mouth and bare my top teeth because of the cavities there. Back then, with figure skating, I also had better things to do with my money than to spend it on normal expenditures like dentists. I remember calling every person I knew in the world at that time looking for money, but I either already owed them or they couldn't quite come to grips with lending me a couple of hundred dollars for rent or food when I was spending about a thousand a month on figure skating. Go figure. I finally ended up at the welfare office, oddly enough, after I had found a job.

I was helping out selling ads in the *Huronia Happenings* newspaper when I came upon an ad by the Huronia Tourist Association, the regional tourism board for the County of Simcoe and the Cities of Orillia and Barrie, looking for a manager. I learned later they had fired their last manager for alleged incompetence and that she'd sued them for wrongful dismissal, a mess I was subsequently left to clean up by way of settlement. It would, however, prove to be good experience for negotiating my own departure three years later. After an interview, I was hired, or so I thought, by a committee, but was not to start until the end of July when I would meet the entire board. Meantime we were out of options for food, so I headed to Midhurst, to the County of Simcoe administration building, where they handled welfare for both the county and the City of Orillia. It was the same building where the tourism committee had interviewed me, and the place where I would have my offices for the next three years.

I was able to arrange a meeting with the acting director of the welfare office and I explained my situation — omitting the figure skating of course — and he authorized an emergency cheque of about $400, which he said I could repay when I got on my feet in my new job. It was all done with a great deal of compassion for which I was grateful. He went on to be the director and we crossed paths many times in the building and at department head meetings and events over the next three years. He never mentioned our first meeting or the fact I never paid the money back. Unfortunately, I never got on my feet.

I had called Ken Burgess earlier this morning and simply told him I was in trouble and needed $500 fast. He said he would call the arcade in Orillia and arrange for the manager to give me $500 from the safe. We agreed to meet later that week to talk about my trouble and to see what I could do to pay him back. While Ken had always been there for me I worried about his ever finding out about my stealing. He had countless problems with employees in his video arcades breaking into machines, disappearing with deposits and "borrowing" the store float for their own use. I had often seen his frustration in dealing with the police and courts trying to recover his money, but I had also seen his empathy and even willingness to give his thieves a second chance. As I did all of Ken's letter writing over the fourteen years we worked together, he didn't write a letter of support to the courts for me but he was there in court, and although he knew what I did was wrong, he never abandoned our friendship or his belief in me.

Bob was another person who didn't abandon me but as I sat in his office that afternoon, handing over the $500 I had just picked up at Top Hat, I knew it was the closest he ever came to violence in his whole life.

"I'll get you the rest as soon as I can, Bob," I say. "I'm going to try to borrow some money from my older brother to get this mess straightened out."

When I did make that call it was the shortest fifteen seconds of my life.

"Jimmy, I am in big legal trouble because I was gambling. I need to borrow $80,000 or else I could end up in jail."

"That's too bad, Bub," he told me, "but I'm retired now, and on a fixed income. I can't help you."

"Okay, I understand," I said. "Don't say anything about this to anyone. I'm trying to work it out."

"Okay, Bub," he said and he hung up.

That I made that call testifies to the level of my desperation. That I had an illusion he could help me, and that earlier this summer, shortly after Casino Rama opened, I had planned a trip to New Brunswick with Melanie for the express purpose of asking him to loan me $25,000, was evidence of the level of insanity that gambling had taken me.

I think that my desperation, and perhaps even my insanity, are apparent to Bob this afternoon: his anger starts to recede.

"What are you going to do about the gambling?"

I start to answer but it's a rhetorical question and he keeps up his head of steam. "You sure as fuck can't keep losing my money. You are cut off. No more cheques. Not in the store. Not from Donna." I go to speak but he keeps yelling. "I had no idea you were cashing a cheque with her almost every night. You should have heard the names I called her over it."

"It's not Donna's fault, Bob. I told her I was depositing my winnings each morning to cover yesterday's cheques."

"I know exactly whose goddamned fault it is." He was getting red again. "You just weren't around to hear the names I was calling you."

"I'll pay you back, one way or another, I promise."

"You're damn right you will. Look out when Mary-Anne gets her hands on you."

Curiously, Mary-Anne, when I did see her a few days later, was just sad, as if she were in mourning. Maybe it was the fact she now worked at the Casino and had a job enticing guys like me to gamble more and more. She was Manager of VIP Services, which meant she looked after people who had a lot more money than I had, or than I could steal. Later she told me that Bob never believed my compulsive gambling was anything more than an excuse.

I leave Bob's office feeling sheepish and depressed. I want nothing more than to gamble myself senseless. Across the street from his store, the Casino Rama Shuttle Bus that I helped bring to Downtown Orillia is idling, waiting for its next customers. I want to just board and tell the guy to drive, drive, drive — but what's the use? While he may have the fuel to get me there, I don't have any for when I arrive.

Money. Where can I get money? I stop on the corner of Mississaga and Peter streets, looking up and down my downtown street like I'm late at a Sunday brunch and can't find the food. Where's the beef? Looking one way, I see Bob's Mariposa Market, where I owe a couple of thousand dollars. Behind me, on West Street, is David Shaw's travel agency and his ominous warning about Ralph. Kitty-corner is the Royal Bank, Leacock's bank, from where the account manager is calling me daily about the $30,000 overdraft. Down the street is my bank, the National Bank, where I am sure I would now have trouble getting a soup bone. At the corner, on the other end of the street, is the Laurentian, the Winter Carnival's bank, where its overdraft means my cheque-cashing privileges are also cancelled. Around the corner and up West Street is City Hall, where I could once get payroll advances and petty-cash advances, but no more. Across from it is the bingo hall, where maybe I can borrow a couple of hundred dollars from Fred, or cash a cheque for more, but knowing what I know about my bank, do I dare?

Back on Mississaga Street all that's left is to look east to the section of the downtown where the businesses of my antagonist Ralph are located. I shiver in distaste and fear. Ralph Cipolla knows. Christ, what a field day he's going to have with this.

Looking up and down the street in my hopeless search for the money to at least pay off Johnny, my eye latches onto City Tickets. This is a hole-in-the-wall shop that sells nothing but lottery tickets of every variety, and a selection of break-open Nevada tickets — three different boxes, thanks to my marketing advice.

I generally spend anywhere from twenty to a couple of hundred dollars on everything from scratch tickets to Lotto 6-49 and Super 7 draws, as well as on the Nevada tickets. While I've calmed down a bit of late in my purchase of such tickets — with the casino I don't need them as much — today I want whatever lottery tickets I can buy just to give me the hope I will need to get to sleep later, and for now, to maybe win at least part of the money I need to pay off Johnny.

"How's it going," Silvia says to me as I walk into the store. I am sure my face reflects a story and she's curious.

"Oh, I've had better days," I answer, turning my back as I fill in the Pick 3 lottery form on the shelf against the wall. This is straightforward: pick three numbers, in my case 7-1-7 (what else), and if they come in during the evening draw, you win. I bet five dollars a day, three dollars on the exact order and two on any order. I won once with 7-1-7 and it paid $1,525. I drove to the Ontario Lottery Corporation office in Toronto to get the cheque. I remember looking around that prize payout office — talking to a $50,000 Bingo ticket winner and whispering about the $220,000 Lotto 6-49 winner who was then at the wicket — swearing to myself, *I'll be back.*

A week ago I took a day off from my gambling obsession to re-establish the possibility that there really was life outside of gambling. Thanksgiving was on October 14, the day before Roberta's birthday. Throughout the Huronia region, among the awesome fall foliage of the Medonte Highlands, a special Thanksgiving Artisan Tour was being held. I took Roberta around the circuit as a combined birthday present, Thanksgiving celebration, and peace offering.

Added to the turmoil of my gambling was Melanie's decision to quit her Ph.D. studies at the University of Toronto after five years, with only a thesis to write, and go to the University of British Columbia to take another master's degree, this one Fine

Arts in Creative Writing. *Oh great, another writer!* The bloom was certainly off that rose.

In addition, for some reason, for all my connections — or perhaps because of them — Roberta was not able to break into the job market at Casino Rama in any kind of position that suited her abilities, her desires, or her stamina. She did get a job at the casino when it first opened, not working for the casino corporation, but for the native community economic agency which ran the souvenir store. The terrible pay was outdone only by the terrible 12-hour shifts, often from 7 p.m. in the evening to 7 a.m. in the morning. Surely the insanity of my actions was confirmed when during the middle of the night Roberta was working in the casino gift store for $7.50 an hour and I was sneaking around, not a hundred yards away, losing thousands of dollars at the blackjack tables. I didn't blame her when she quit. It was another ignominious humiliation in a lifetime of living with an obsessive-compulsive.

The night the most precious person in my world was born I thought nothing of running out and buying a mickey of rum to celebrate. To be fair to me, I was on some other kind of errand at the time, although I can no longer remember for what. I imagine we weren't sure this was going to be the night and I was running out to get Robbie some ice cream, or whatever else the current craving demanded. Maybe I just bought the bottle so I'd have it "in case." What I do know is that I ended up in the maternity waiting room having a celebratory rum and coke the night Melanie was born in the Civic Hospital in Peterborough. To my credit it was only after the birth of my daughter was over, and I knew mother and child were both going to be okay. I was grateful for the drink as a relief because their being all right was in doubt as the night had progressed.

Roberta was a classic baby having a baby. The day I tapped her on the shoulder and picked her out of her class at the Empire Hotel, she was just seventeen. Very likely, on October 15, 1968 — nine months and two days before Melanie's July 17, 1969 birth — for her eighteenth birthday, I gave Roberta a child.

It was one of those intoxicated situations that would be quite funny but for the knowledge of the solemn biology that took place that night. I was living in a semi-private furnished attic room that had its own nearby bathroom. Its semi-private status meant I had to travel up the stairs through the landlady's home and I wasn't supposed to have guests at night. It was private enough, however, that I could. Not that we were fooling anyone. A few months later when Roberta and I announced we were getting married, my landlady merely said she thought we should.

This birthday celebration was like many of our nights since we'd met about a month earlier. I was likely half-snapped when I picked her up following my afternoon in the tavern after putting the newspaper to bed. We had dinner in a restaurant and had a few beers at a friend's apartment — my few to her one — and then we headed for Main Street, with a joint on the way and a few more drinks of rum or vodka silently in the room and into bed. I'm not going to comment on my sexual performance except to take solace that I didn't pass out in the act, because, whether it was the dope, the booze or just my natural desire for sleep after sex — or all three — I did fall asleep or pass out, at the very next-worst opportunity.

Of course, I had to pee. Now, this being an attic, the roof sloped on an angle over the toilet, just perfect for resting your head when you were standing taking a leak. After I finished, I went back into the bedroom to find Roberta gone. Gone? *What'd I say? What'd I do?* I looked at the alarm clock next to my bed and was amazed to see it was after 1:00 a.m. Perplexed, I got dressed and went after Roberta, who I supposed must have just left and was walking home. I hurried out the door and headed up Main Street to Mountjoy Avenue, which linked her Way Street home to my room over six or seven blocks. I couldn't understand why I couldn't catch up with her, and wondered if she had taken one of the side streets. When I finally got to her parents' house I was beside myself for fear that something had happened to her so I knocked on the door. After a few minutes, her father Roy came to the door.

"Roberta and I got separated tonight," I told him — the less said the better. "I just want to make sure she got home all right."

"Roberta's in bed."

"Thanks. Sorry to wake you. Bye," I said in rapid succession as I closed the storm door and turned heel without waiting to hear his response. I am sure his thoughts about me that night were justified time and time again over the next 30 years.

I learned the next day that when I didn't come back from the bathroom for 15 or 20 minutes, Roberta had come looking for me — but I'd locked the door. She'd knocked lightly and whispered frantically but she was afraid of waking my landlady. Looking through the keyhole she could see the back of me standing with my underwear half down my legs, leaning, she was sure, with my head propped against the ceiling. There I had fallen asleep.

CHAPTER EIGHT

Was I addicted to lottery tickets? Because I was spending some-

October 22, 1996 — 2 p.m.

where between $300 and $500 a week on the 17 different games, I have to wonder. This was the period in which I was getting ready for Casino Rama, when there were only infrequent visits to the Windsor Casino and a final visit to Sault Ste. Marie. I went to play blackjack at the charity casinos when they operated every other week. Lottery tickets, scratch tickets, and break-open Nevadas filled in when the other gambling was not quite as accessible.

I have met people who are addicted to lottery tickets, usually people on a limited income caught up in chasing the "Imagine the Freedom" fantasy promoted in the incessant and (it must be said) enticing television ads, or in the newspaper articles spinning the excitement around a $15 million jackpot draw and trumpeting the stories of the winners.

Rather than widespread addiction to lottery tickets per se, what I have seen is compulsive gamblers going back to gambling — the first bet like the first small drink — by succumbing to the media hype around those major jackpot prizes. It's a mind-set. Winning. Winning your way out of trouble. The dream world. The false hope. For most of us, one taste is all we need to send us back on a compulsive bender that will only end once we are out of money, have no balls in the air, and are facing total destruction. I have seen many gamblers use the lotteries as their door back to hell.

"Any big ones left, Silvia?" I ask, sizing up the three boxes of different Nevada tickets, each of which has $100 main prizes to chase. Fruit, Diamonds, and Super Nevada with its gold bars are the general themes of the three boxes.

(Over the next few years the government will quietly allow the expansion of this type of incipient gambling — paper slot machines I call them — by allowing for increased prizes, up to $300. Lots of people are addicted to these break-open tickets.)

Before I got into my gambling spree I'd go into the corner store to get Roberta a pack of cigarettes or to pick up milk on the way home and shake my head at how despondent the people looked standing around the garbage can ripping open the tabs on these cardboard tickets, looking for the winners. It looked so humiliating! I was convinced it was something only poor people did, desperate to turn fifty cents into ten, fifty, or a hundred dollars. I had no idea people stood around these stores for hours, or went store to store, spending ten dollars here and twenty dollars there, eventually paying hundreds of dollars to win — what? A hundred dollars? I had no idea until I, too, found myself standing there ripping open tickets.

We have a circuit, same people, same places, like we are bar-hopping, going from City Tickets to The Crows' Nest to Art's Clothing in the downtown, betting anywhere from ten to twenty dollars at each place, and more if we feel lucky, or if we do win. Winning, most of the time, just means putting it all back, chasing the next set of bars or diamonds, or whatever gives us the jackpot. Even the humiliation is bearable.

At first I was careful. I just bought the tickets, and because of who I was — Mr. Downtown Orillia — I could take them with me as I walked the streets, stood in line at the bank, or sat at lunch with my friends. With one hand in my pocket I would slowly rip the tabs off the tickets, and quickly sneak a peek at the tab-less ticket hidden in the palm of my hand to see if it was a winner. In this way I would check the twenty or so tickets, discarding the losers in the nearest garbage bin — my ultra-clean downtown had lots of them — and return to the store to trade in my winners for more tickets. If it was a big, one-hundred-dollar winner I would take the cash, or what cash was left after I bought a couple of lottery and scratch tickets.

"There's at least two big ones left in the bars, maybe three but I've got some tickets out, so I don't know for sure" Sylvia says. "The Diamonds are all gone but the Fruit still has a hundred and a fifty with the box almost empty."

Knowing the owners — it's not difficult since I am there everyday — and knowing what's left in the box is my Nevada system, the way I change the odds, at least in my mind, to my advantage. Sylvia and her husband, who is managing one of the nearby chain stores, bought City Tickets recently and quickly took my marketing advice, adding two more boxes of Nevada tickets. The previous owner, Jim, resisted having more than one box, complaining that it was too complicated to keep track of all the separate tickets and money.

Today I only want to spend ten bucks anyway so I tell her to give me five dollars from each of the Fruit and the Super Nevada boxes. For me this is pretty conservative but I don't have much money left, except for the already depleted bingo float that I still may have to use to repay Johnny.

Oh yeah, sure, I can hear myself: "Here, *F*, here's six hundred dollars for Johnny, sorry about all the loonies and toonies, the bank was out of bills."

In the casino, however, I often use rolls of toonies, loonies, and even quarters, simply taking them to the cashiers and exchanging them for tokens for the slot machines. It doesn't seem out of the ordinary there. Rolls of coin; bundles of five-dollar bills, fifty at a time; ten-dollar bills in bundles of $500; and twenties — bundled by the fifty. A thousand dollars. This is the bingo float, and the bingo proceeds that I borrow from on a weekly basis to feed my gambling fever. I can't begin to count how many bundles of five-dollar bills I've fed into the Casino Rama slot machines over the last 77 days. I can't remember a week when I didn't have to run around like a madman trying to buy five-dollar bills from somebody so there would be enough change in the bingo float for Sunday night. Most weeks I've had to replace the entire $800 float, usually by cashing a cheque at one bank drawn on an account in another. Before all the banks got testy about the overdrafts I'd cash a Leacock Festival cheque at the Winter Carnival's bank, or vice versa, or either of them at my bank, usually just before noon on Saturday, when I'd run out of other options, and luck. The bank tellers weren't too excited about the last-minute requests for the change, especially for the fives.

When I was five my big sister got polio. My parents were in Niagara Falls, on what was a kind of second honeymoon — a somewhat belated one, considering they'd had six kids by that time; and a somewhat odd one, too, in that they'd taken my father's mother, Nanny Brown along. My mother's mother — Grammy MacKinnon

— was staying with us. Also, at home they left Jimmy, the oldest, who would have been twelve by then. David was nine. The sick sister, Veronica, or Wonky as we called her, was seven. There were also two younger sisters, Mary, three, and Marjorie, the newcomer at one year old. While I know Grammy MacKinnon loved us, she had a hard time being patient with so many kids. Not being Catholic — my mother was a Baptist convert — my Grandmother must have wondered how the hell that many kids happened.

Grammy had to call Ontario and have relatives track my Mom and Dad down with the news that their darling daughter had the most dreaded disease of all, in the middle of what turned out to be the most devastating epidemic our country had ever experienced.

I remember going to the sanatorium where they had Wonky in isolation and standing by the road next to this frighteningly forlorn, grey-blue wooden manor, waving to her as she looked out through the window of her lonely room. All the polio victims were sent to this asylum, cloistered in behind the Saint John General Hospital. Many of them never came out again or if they did, they were, in the vernacular of the day, sadly *crippled*. Veronica was "lucky" — we would have said miraculous at the time — she came home after several months in the hospital with no visible legacy of the paralysis that once seized half of her body. I say visible, for she still had a slight numbing in her left cheek, and today, with post-polio syndrome, she experiences an infrequent and temporary seizing in her left hand and face. This, and the fact that a mechanical toy horse one Christmas morning wasn't for me, are the only troubling images I have from my early childhood.

A year later we had a major car accident in which everyone was thrown from the car (one brother jumped) except my mother, my baby sister, and me. Baby Marjorie was sitting in a car seat looped over the back in the middle of the front seat. Mom held on to her and I held on to my mom's neck, standing in the back. Dad came down Rothesay Avenue, near the Fernhill Cemetery, not far from Russell Street where we were to live five or six years later. It was a wet and slippery night. The car went into a violent spin, somehow causing the doors to open — maybe we hit something — throwing my father and brothers and sisters away from the car. My four-year-old sister Mary was sleeping in the back seat and was thrown through the rear window onto the pavement. She was the only one hospitalized — she was in a coma — but in a few weeks she recovered with no long-term damage.

I know I was a pretty good kid because everybody liked me and I liked everybody. I was the assistant bus driver, on the city bus, on the way to school in the mornings. The bus would even stop and wait for me at my front door on the days that I was late. I'd bound in full flight up the steps and slide under the bar at the front of the bus to take my designated place beside the cash box. There I dutifully pushed the lever that allowed the cash and tickets to fall into the box below. Somebody had to do it and *I* was that somebody.

My hometown newspaper had a columnist who wrote under an anonymous moniker: "The Man on the Street." My mother told me he once wrote a column about the city bus waiting for me in the morning:

> Our bus-riding habits always produce a little anecdote we think our readers would like.
> This morning, for instance, the bus had just

begun moving away from the stop when a sudden hissing of air brakes warned us there was still one more passenger to come.

The front door opened but nothing happened. We saw no sign of anyone rushing across the street, waving his arms to wait "just one more minute." Impatient passengers began to mumble disgruntedly, after a 30-second wait. Then all but the most tired of faces were wreathed with uncontrollable grins.

The other passenger had arrived. We should say, the newcomer was half there.

A tousle-headed blonde of seven was clambering aboard. In one hand he held his coat. In the other, a heavy winter jacket. Perched atop his half-combed blonde curls was a tipsy cub hat.

He was in a hurry, anyone could see that. As the bus moved away from the stop once more, the young fellow was eagerly tugging at his pocket for his five-cent fare.

As he began his hunt for a seat, the smile wreathing his scrubbed face was a bright "good-morning" to bleary-eyed, early morning office workers like "The Man on the Street."

The last we saw of the latecomer, he was being helped into his winter jacket by a motherly feminine passenger, while a fatherly hand straightened the Wolf Cub hat.[3]

In Grade One I was a rambunctious little guy. I just couldn't stop talking in school so I spent most of the year under Sister Noberta's desk, staring at her long black habit. Was I hyperactive?

Oh, yeah, but they didn't know that then. I was just, well — as an ageing Sister Noberta would say to my mother on a bus thirteen years later, when as a university student I got on with long hair, a knee-length grey fake-fur overcoat, a six-foot red and blue scarf, and cowboy boots — I was "just looking for attention."

In Grade Two I graduated from under the desk to the cloakroom. My Grade Two lay-women teachers didn't have those long black skirts. Our regular teacher was ill and we had a substitute teacher. Every day we were warned to be good or we'd upset our sick teacher when she got the daily report on our behaviour. I was in love with my Grade Two teacher and I was on my best behaviour for fear of hurting or upsetting her. My best behaviour . . . well, everything's relative.

I started driving the substitute teacher crazy, always having to go to the bathroom in the middle of classes each morning.

"Miss! Miss! Please! Miss!" I'd whine, up out of my chair, leaning over my desk, my arm extended over my head, hand waving. "Miss! Miss! I have to go! Miss!"

"Go!" she'd say, exasperated by my theatrics and her own suspicion that I was "just looking for attention." One's reputation precedes you in a school like Holy Trinity.

After a few days of these disruptions, and her instructions that I go to the bathroom at home or before class, my grunts and groans were met with genuine anger and threats of the cloakroom instead of the bathroom. Still my pleas continued, made all the more urgent by my fear of asking. Always I waited until the very last moment, hoping for a school bell to free me to zoom down the hall to the bathroom.

"Miss, ugh! Miss, ugh! Miss, I gotta go! Miss, ugh! Please! I can't hold it!"

"Douglas, I have had about all of this I am going to take."

"But Miss!" I was on the verge of tears, in pain and in fear of having an accident in front of the whole class.

"Okay, mister, you asked for it. Into the cloakroom! We are not going to put up with your racket any longer," she said as she grabbed me by the ear and ushered me past her desk, and through the cloakroom door.

"No, I really have to go and I can't hold it," I was screaming as she closed the door. I ran around the room for a minute or two, trying to get control of myself, but it wasn't working and I felt myself slipping. I started crying and screaming, and banging on the cloakroom door. I don't know what kind of light bulb went on but my teacher finally realized I wasn't faking.

Eventually they put me in the hospital and diagnosed me with an acute case of diarrhoea (I thought they said "a cute case"). I was in there for several days melting crayons on the heat registers with the real sick kids as the doctors puzzled why I was having these daily bouts with my bowels. In the end it was discovered.

Each school morning milk was delivered to our doorstep in Rockwood Court; with six kids, as many as four quart bottles a day. In the winter the cream, sitting on the top part of the bottles, would freeze and rise like little stacks of wafered chips or stovepipe hats out the top of the bottles. Every day I was the first one out of bed and I would get to those milk bottles first, and eat the "iced cream" off the top . . . and every day I would have "a cute case" of diarrhoea.

I have often wondered what I missed during that two weeks away from school. Likely phonics or some secret spelling trick, for I was an atrocious speller and grew to understand that I was also a terrible reader. But, looking back on those early years in school, the two weeks in the hospital probably didn't matter compared to all the times I just wasn't paying attention, my mind bouncing from one place to another. The possibility of attention deficit disorder has been raised in my adult life to explain some of my childhood actions as well as the fact that to this day, I am a slow reader, and must fight to control my attention. Perhaps this is why I work best on deadlines, under pressure, and in crisis situations.

City Tickets is just across the street from my office. I know my staff look out the window to see if I am over here: I often look up to see them dodging back from the sills of our large Edwardian windows. The office is located in one of the oldest buildings in Orillia, owned by a man named Sheldon Godfrey, who at one time was the chairman of Heritage Canada Foundation and is a proponent of the preservation of historic buildings. I moved the downtown business offices into his building almost as soon as I became the manager in 1989. To me it was important. If the organization was going to promote a heritage downtown and encourage the restoration of building façades, then it should set a good example by being located in a heritage building. It was the beginning of a great relationship with Sheldon, one where we helped fill his offices and where he allowed us to use extra office space if it was available or leased it to us at a reduced rate. The latter was the case with the Leacock Heritage Festival, which rented the offices across the hall.

Regrettably, a good number of the pink messages among the chaos on my desk are from Sheldon looking for his Leacock rent, which by this time is several months in arrears. Business colleagues, friends, and family are all getting caught up in my whirlwind, and for the first time, I am coming up against the reality of not being able to do anything to stop it. The faith that Doug Bell, and others, have in me to be able to solve this problem — to pull it out of the fire — is beginning to dwindle, as is my own confidence in my ability to get this thing done.

Father MacDonald, the Rector of Saint Mary's College, came to Saint John to interview my parents and I about my attending the minor seminary in the fall of 1962. This was the last step in what had been a year-long process. I had responded to the "Do you want to be a Priest?" ad and carried out a continued correspondence with the school registrar, Father Connell, forwarding marks, completing questionnaires, and building a case as to why they should choose me.

"No, my parents don't have the money to pay tuition or board, but they are committed to paying for my travel expenses, providing me with a wardrobe, and having all my teeth fixed before I go." My father once worked for the Board of Health, inspecting restaurants, so we had the contacts at the health office to get cheap dental work.

I took to visiting regularly with the Redemptorist priests at St. Peter's Parish. They became my advocates, promoting my candidacy — including the kissing priest, who looked upon me as his vocational discovery and protégé. The kissing was our secret, or at least it was mine because I was no longer sure of his sanity. Also, I reasoned, we'd been cheeky little eight- and nine-year-olds back then, and we did want those bus tickets. The question remained in my thirteen-year-old mind: who had been taking advantage of whom? We, somewhat less-than-ideal cubs conning a near-senile old man, or him, a dirty old man kissing little boys? At this point in my reasoning, my mind always reeled. *Yuck!* It was disgusting. Him sucking my lips and probing with his tongue!

Right from the beginning of the interview Father Rector seemed a strange man. He had very mechanical facial expressions and body movements, exaggerated, robot-like. These seemed affected because at other times, he was as normal and gentle as one of those saints he, and all of us, aspired to become. He was an enigma, and one of his most puzzling deeds, despite all of my machinations, was his acceptance of me as raw material to become a priest.

Saint Mary's College was a pastoral haven on the shores of the St. Lawrence River, between Brockville and Prescott, in a hamlet known as Maitland. The first view I had of my new home was from the window of the railway train we had taken from Montreal, after transferring from the New Brunswick Canadian Pacific train.

"There it is," one of the older students pointed out as the train passed by. "See the chimney stack?" The brick chimneystack was smaller than the one we had in Saint John from which, years before, a workman had been dramatically rescued in a basket dangling beneath a helicopter. The workman had been repairing the brick when the metal ladder attached to the chimney walls gave way beneath him, forcing him to climb to the top of the smoke stack. This one was not as high, but I nevertheless made a mental note not to climb up the chimneystack.

Behind the chimney rose a gigantic grey granite building, four stories high, and as wide as a football field. It had a green metal roof, huge windows with curved arches, and even from behind, it looked like a castle. And it had land. Property on both sides of the railway tracks belonged to the College. The north side was a wooded area with mammoth climbing trees where I would spend many joyous hours in the next few years; the south, cultivated fields where we harvested potatoes every fall.

We were met at the train station by Brother Malachy, a tall and stern-looking man who was so quiet I imagined he had found holiness within and decided to stay there. Brother John, "Little John," as we called him, was the opposite: short, laugh lines dancing around his eyes and mouth, and so sprightly that I imagined, wrongly of course, that he had a little of the devil in him. He was the cook — the chief cook, for when you are cooking three meals a day for 120 teenage boys, there are lots of cooks. As it was between meals, Brother John was helping out with the student pickups at the train station in Brockville. Brother Malachy, I would learn, was like the plant engineer, running the boilers, the farming, and the building maintenance. There were half a dozen Brothers at Saint Mary's, but by and large they worked under the leadership of Brothers John and Malachy. Brother Edward, the senior member of the Saint Mary's College Redemptorist family, was both holy and joyful, and even though he was officially retired, he participated in the daily chores, as we all did.

There were six of us on that train from New Brunswick, including another boy, Paul Kennedy from Dorchester, who was entering grade nine. Paulibus, as I came to call him, was my best friend for the next three years, and the person who, with total innocence, introduced me to my next great escape.

When everyone arrived, either by train or car, there were fifteen grade niners in my class. They came from as far away as Prince Edward Island — Alan Doucette — and as close as Prescott — Gordie Peters. Scott Follis came from Ottawa. Michael Flynn, who I had a fight with later, came from Belleville or Peterborough, or some other small southern Ontario town. Flynn belonged to a clique made up of Steve McInnis and Frank Kindellan, who are probably corporate presidents today, along with a couple of class clowns named Larry Cassidy and Mark Sharron. John Legault, who spoke with a stutter, was liked by everyone but joined Gord Moorey, Jim Quick, Robin Webb, and hapless Joe Saunders, as not really belonging to any group. While Peters could interact with everyone, Alan Doucette, Scott Follis, Paul Kennedy, and I made up the other, less prestigious group, the ones, it was felt, with the brains.

We all lived together in a large open dorm the first year I stayed at Saint Mary's. The older students lived at one end of the building with the younger ones at the other. Our beds were positioned in rows along the walls and up the middle of the room, like in hospital wards you see in war pictures or dormitories in orphanages. Our bathrooms were big cavernous places with rows of sinks, marble urinals, and common showers.

Clang! Clang! Clang-a-clang! Each morning we were woken at 6:30 a.m. by Father Scanlan, our Subsocius, ringing a bell that was designed for the outdoor schoolyard up and down the long dormitory. If you were having trouble getting out of bed, Father Scanlan might give your toes a friendly shake. If you made it a habit you likely ended up with the Socius[4], Father Thomas Callaghan, clanging that bell directly in your ears. Father Callaghan was tough as nails, looking, walking, and sometimes acting, like James Arness of *Gunsmoke*. He was the sheriff of Saint Mary's College and when he called me "Little," I jumped.

Each day we got up, washed and showered in silence. It was called the Code of Silence and it lasted until after breakfast. Like many things in a religious order it was meant to give you time to reflect, meditate and pray. We went to Mass each morning in the

College chapel, the place where we not only prayed three times a day, but where we also had the riot act read to us with regularity. Mom would tease my brothers during my college years about the seat of their pants wearing out while "with Dougie it's the knees from kneeling down."

For two and a half years Saint Mary's was like an Eden for me, a perfect sanctuary. Scholastically I did better than I ever had, or ever would again, coming near the top of my class, just behind my friend Paul Kennedy, who I always believed was a genius. Paul was a nerd almost before the word was invented. He would often stare out a window, seeming distant and deep in his own thoughts, only to fool a pouncing professor by having the precise answer at the ready, having heard every word in some compartment of his brain. In the three years I attended Saint Mary's, only at the end, in grade eleven, did I ever have to write a final exam — and then it was only one, French. St. Mary's had a tradition of "Recommends" which meant that if you maintained a high enough average throughout the year, you didn't have to write the final exams, and could go home a week before everyone else. Paul and I always took the train back to Saint John early together.

In Grade 10, Paul and I developed a science fair project on carpenter ants, carrying out various biological tests to assess their behaviours and their societal instincts. The project won the Brockville and Region Science Fair, and we were invited to participate in the Canada-Wide Science Fair in Montreal, where we would stay in residence at the University of Montreal. I say "we," but only one of us was officially allowed to participate in the Canada-Wide Science Fair, which didn't allow joint projects. The other went as an observer. The Brockville show officials told us we had to decide who should represent the project but that "it was obvious who had done most of the work." I was sure they meant the brainier Paul but the College stepped in and said we both must go. Father Callaghan flipped a coin to see who would be the official representative. Paul won.

Montreal was all the sweeter because we lived such a cloistered life at Saint Mary's, never leaving the school grounds unless for an organized outing or a visit to the hospital. Going to town, to restaurants, or even off college property was strictly forbidden.

Paul and I had a ball in Montreal. While he was the official spokesman for the judging, we shared duties explaining the project to the public and even did a television interview together with two young girls who were hosts for a Montreal English station's youth program. Shades of things to come (at least in my life), we invited the girls to the Science Fair banquet and they came. I think there is something about a man — or in this case a couple of boys — studying to be a priest that makes him a challenge for women. Or maybe they just felt safe.

Next year, in Grade 11, Paul and I went our separate project ways. Oddly, I finished mine, a series of experiments with earthworms — slicing and dicing, regeneration and all that, and Paul didn't. I entered the Brockville Fair, and while I did not win I was given an honourable mention. Then, the show officials decided to send two participants to the Canada-Wide Science Fair in Winnipeg, and I was on my way.

No winners at Downtown Tickets. I go around the corner to see if Fred is in the bingo hall. "I didn't like ya when I first met ya," Fred would joke for anyone within earshot, "and I don't like ya now."

Our relationship did start on a bad note with me as Downtown Manager opposing the new bingo hall in front of City Council. But that was two years ago, before an uncountable number of games of bingo for both the hall and for me. I still have a hard time admitting, even to myself, that all of this started in a bingo hall.

If Fred and I did get off on a wrong foot, we more than made up for it with the nonsense we got into together. As I walk over to the hall I am trying to remember whether I still owe him any money from the times we split the cost of scratch tickets. These days there are a gazillion scratch ticket games — Bingo, Keno, Battleship, Christmas Stocking, and of all things, the family game Monopoly and the kids' game, Snakes & Ladders. They've even got a 6-49 Happy Meal at McDonald's — "for adults." Yeah, right. One agency of the government is producing these tickets while across the hall, another department is pontificating on protecting children from gambling. It's all about the money.

Of course no one protected Fred and I from each other, and by the time we were done we owed his business three thousand dollars, the cost of our losing scratch tickets. Night after night I would take handfuls of tickets home after bingo and scratch them in the middle of the night (If you think I was bad, I know a guy named John whose fingers turned blue and green from his addiction to scratch tickets).

We hit the three grand level about the same time I crashed at bingo and quit. Fred would call me every once in a while about paying up my share — he always had his financial crisis too — but he was amazingly patient. All in all he was a pretty good guy for somebody who didn't like me the first time we met. The only way I got him paid off was at Casino Rama one night when I was on a hot streak playing Let It Ride! poker with him at my table. For every two hundred I won I paid him one hundred and by the end of the night I was down to only owing a couple of hundred bucks. The money flowed from the dealer to me, from me to Fred and from Fred back to the dealer, in a clear triangular path. Somehow, it still felt like winning to both of us.

I know Fred is okay to cash a cheque — provided it doesn't bounce which it certainly will now — but there is not a lot of hope in trying to borrow any money from him. His troubles have only compounded since the Casino opened. With bingo crowds being down, revenues in the hall are off sharply and he's had a falling out with his business partner/wife. Subsequently she has brought a controller into the business. Poor Fred can't even have a cup of coffee without keeping a paper trail. As much as Fred liked gambling — bingo, blackjack, poker, and whatever at the casino — he also liked to play other games. Not everyone takes that *no sex please I'm gambling* stuff seriously.

By the time I am standing on the street outside the bingo hall I accept the futility of asking Fred for a loan so I don't go in. This problem isn't going to be solved by borrowing a couple of hundred dollars, I tell myself as I walk, dejectedly, back to my office.

The search for money, and for the way out of my increasingly menacing predicament, grows more and more desperate. I visualize the Casino bailing me out — and saving me from jail — by giving me the money to pay off the money I owe. After all, look who I am — Mr. Downtown Orillia, the casino's biggest supporter. They can't let me implode. They're vulnerable, too. Can't you see the headlines: "Casino Booster Boosts Community Funds to Gamble" or "Casino Promoter Gambles his Life and Loses"?

With nowhere else to turn I call Ed Leichner, the marketing

vice-president who I work with at Casino Rama. I ask him if he would meet with me to discuss a personal situation, somewhere away from the Casino. We are to meet for coffee at the Euro Café, at the foot of Mississaga Street; it's one of the new businesses attracted by the revitalization I wrangled out of the government. The million-plus project, finally connecting Orillia's historic downtown with its beautiful waterfront, is the pinnacle of my tenure as manager of the downtown. I am trying to make sure it doesn't become my monument.

Ed is sitting at a table in the corner of the café when I arrive. He reaches out his hand and says, "How are ya doin' Doug? It's startin' to get cold again." Ed came to Orillia from New Jersey, via Florida where he worked with Carnival Cruise Lines' sister company, Carnival Hotels and Casinos, which has the contract to operate Casino Rama for the Native community and the Government of Ontario. Although he came in January, in the depth of Orillia's snowy winter, he's never gotten used to the cold.

"I've been better, Ed. I've got a big problem. In fact I've got quite a few big problems." I wait until the waiter has finished bringing us our coffees and then I open the floodgates of confession to this high priest of my luck god's temple, looking no longer for a win, but for mercy and a way out. Ed is the first to hear the story of the sordid mess. I am addicted to gambling. First bingo, then visiting the other casinos, the blackjack at the charity casinos and finally roulette and poker at Casino Rama. I tell him about the balls in the air, the eight bank accounts, my "borrowing" and my borrowing to pay back my borrowing, my losing. I tell him I owed eighty thousand dollars and it is going to be spread all over the newspapers if I don't get the money paid back very soon.

"Every night I go home I think about just killing myself, and then the next day all I want to do is get enough money to get back there, to win it all back." My voice is trembling as I speak — in fact my whole body seems to be shaking at the terror of what I am laying on the line, of what I am gambling here with Ed.

Ed is a good listener and kind enough not to say I told you so, because he did. "The only person who ever wins here," he once said, "is a person who comes in once for a night out, throws a few dollars in a machine and wins a jackpot. If she puts it in her pocket, walks out the door, and never comes back, then she has won. But, if she does come back, and they almost always do, we'll get back everything she won plus a big chunk of her money." I remember at the time shaking my head in feigned concurrence, all the while thinking somehow I was different. I was going to beat the odds. *Hey, somebody has to win, why not me?*

What I couldn't accept back then, and what I am having to come nose to nose with now, is the truth that I cannot win because I cannot quit, and because I can't quit, I can't win. When I was gambling frantically every night at the casino and coming home distraught but wired like a pinball bouncing off the walls, in between my prayers, I would read to get to sleep. One of the books I read in bed to get away from my troubles was Michael Crichton's "The Lost World," the dinosaur sequel to Jurassic Park. In one section Crichton talks about "Gamblers' Ruin," the idea that, winning or losing, gamblers always go back for more, leading to their inevitable demise. I remember praying that this prophetic warning wouldn't turn out to be true as I hurriedly moved on to the parts where the velociraptors tore the hired help to pieces.

"You are the second person this week," Ed says to me, "that is having a lot of trouble. I just got a call from a very good friend of mine in Atlantic City who's having his problems and is probably losing his family."

Having worked with me for the past year on the task force Ed is well aware of my abilities and my contacts throughout the region. We discuss the possibility of my working under contract for the marketing department carrying out some special assignments.

"Do you think the Casino could lend me the money to pay off what I owe, and maybe I could do some marketing work to pay it off?"

"Only Bobby could authorize any loan or money," Ed says, talking about Casino Rama President Bobby Yee, who I also know, and who knows me but not as well as Ed does. "But I think he might do it: I know he has a great deal of respect for you. You are going to have to meet with him and tell him everything you told me, and just ask him. I am sure something can be worked out."

"Can you arrange a meeting for me today?" I ask, my desperation grasping onto this life preserver of hope that Ed is throwing me and pulling for all its worth.

"He's away, but I'll talk to him as soon as he gets back and make sure he calls you. Meanwhile, try to relax."

I thank him for listening, for his understanding and his willingness to go to bat for me with Bobby.

"You know," he says before we part, "I have been in this business for 25 years, and I can count on one hand," raising his hand he spreads the five fingers between our faces, speaking in genuine sorrow, "on one hand, the people who are still gambling that started back then. Sooner or later, we get everyone."

"How, then, can you do it?" I ask. "Knowing that, how can you work in the casino?"

"Well, we just believe you'll either lose it with us or you'll lose it somewhere else, so it might as well be with us."

As I walk back to the office, I think, that must be the mantra of the gambling industry.

CHAPTER NINE

Ken McMullen is expecting me at his house. I had called him and I told him

I needed to talk to him. I am sure the urgency in my voice was palpable, so he said come right over.

As if it were preordained, I first met Ken and his wife Pat almost eight years ago at the Stephen Leacock Memorial Home on December 30, 1988 at the annual party held to celebrate Leacock's Birthday. I had just been hired to be the new manager of the Downtown Orillia Business Improvement Area and was talking about creating a festival that would celebrate Leacock throughout Orillia, with the idea of re-creating the turn-of-the-century Mariposa he wrote about in *Sunshine Sketches of a Little Town*. The Leacock Home was his charming summer cottage, now converted to a museum, on gorgeous lush grounds on the shore of Lake Couchiching. Orillia always had a love-hate relationship with Leacock. Some say it was because he made fun of old Orillians in *Sunshine Sketches* and others say it was because he was the town drunk. His fans, of which I am one, argue that he came to Orillia to relax — it was his cottage — so he drank. No one can write some 60-odd books and rise to be the most popular writer of his time in the English language world by being the town drunk. I had an answer, however, for even the most rabid Leacock detractors in promoting the idea of the Festival: "Use him. Seize the incredible marketing legacy he left us with Mariposa and exploit it as a tourist attraction."

The idea of a Leacock Festival was not new. In my three years as the manager of the regional Huronia Tourism Association, I knew there had been a Leacock Festival of Humour which had folded in the early 1980s. It still owed Huronia money when I arrived there in 1983, and I had the impossible task of trying to collect from the non-existent committee. Most of the thrust for the Leacock Festival of Humour came from Toronto, principally through the efforts of comedian Don Cullen. Part of its demise was that it had never been fully embraced by Orillians, who seemed eternally unable to take their town's potential seriously. After all, this was the community where the Mariposa Folk Festival began in 1961 but was run out of town after three wildly successful years because local officials feared the hippies it attracted.

In 1987 I ran the Hot Air Balloon Festival in Molson Park in Barrie, which was also then the home of the ever-mobile Mariposa Festival. I became friends with its executive director, Rob Sinclair. Rob and I, with others, founded Festivals Ontario as a network to help develop the province's festivals and events industry. In 1990, for the occasion of Mariposa's 30th Anniversary, I helped produce a Mariposa Homecoming Concert at the Orillia Opera House, featuring Sylvia Tyson, who had performed at the first Mariposa Festival in Couchiching Park in 1961. In November of 1989, I personally asked native Orillian Gordon Lightfoot, to take part in the Mariposa Homecoming when I met him after a benefit concert he gave for the Opera House and Soldiers Memorial Hospital.

"No, I can't do that," he said in an abrupt conversation backstage that shocked both Roberta and I. "Mariposa did me wrong."[5]

Ken and Pat had just moved to Orillia, buying a home there after he took early retirement from a career as an accountant with Union Carbide. They had come out to the birthday party to meet people and to see how they could get involved as volunteers in their new community.

Manna from heaven. Ken became a co-founder and treasurer for the Leacock Heritage Festival for all of its eight years, except for 1991 (the year I had my heart attack) when he took a contract to run an American cottage collective in Muskoka, and the last year, when he resigned because, as he wrote in his resignation letter: "I no longer have any influence or control over the direction or finances of the Leacock Heritage Festival."

Up to my ears in the charity casino phase of my gambling binge, and about as deeply in debt to all those Leacock accounts, I took Ken's letter, shrugged and planned to honour him and Pat at the 1996 Festival. Actually, by this time, none of the Leacock Festival Board had any influence or control over the Festival, the money or me. I was a bulldozer, even without the gambling, so anybody of a contrary mind was already gone from the organization, or was too busy with other things to know what I was really up to. Most people thought I had engineered the Festival successfully for seven years and they didn't need to come to board meetings just to hear me tell them how I was doing it. They simply showed up at the event and carried out the roles I needed fulfilled.

Not that Ken didn't have some idea what I was doing. In

April of 1995 he and Ron MacLean, the Chairman of the Orillia Winter Carnival, went with me to Sault Ste. Marie to the Festivals Ontario Conference and witnessed my first immersion into a *real* casino.

My wallet fat with winnings from bingo the night before and the residue of my first bailout from *F.*, I hit the Vegas Kewadin Casino in Sault, Michigan, with Ken and Ron in tow, the first night we arrived. All the way driving there in the van, all I talked about was roulette, giving them the self-censored, winning version of my Dominican holiday introduction to the game. I didn't have to mention the heart-pounding, adrenaline-pumping excitement I felt when I played roulette. Saying it would have been redundant.

Ken and Ron, like so many other people who knew me, were mildly amused by my enthusiasm — no, my fanaticism — for gambling. They knew, however, that I was obsessive about everything I did, whether it was Downtown Orillia, the Festival, or the multiplicity of things in which I was involved. I was always passionate, excited, and people seemed to enjoy the glow of my fervour.

Surprisingly, in the four days we were in The Sault — visiting the casino every night — I never played roulette once. I never got past the slot machines.

Previously, my first tortured introduction to slot machines had left me with an elephantine, unsatisfied craving. It was with Roberta and Melanie at another resort in Puerto Plata during that trip of 1992. We went to the Jack Tar Resort, on more of a walk than anything, just to look around. The Paradise, where we were staying, had only blackjack, craps and roulette, but the Jack Tar, with a much larger and brighter casino floor, had all the bells and whistles. Unfortunately I wasn't prepared for the excursion — you know, with a hidden cache of coins I could ferret out of my back pockets, socks, armpits, and other bodily orifices. Under the watchful eye of Roberta I was allowed to play only a couple of rolls of quarters, and failing to win instantly I had to stifle my hankering to interbreed with these machines. Only my contentment with roulette, reinforced by my fear of going outside the resort compound at night in the poverty-stricken Dominican Republic, stopped me from sneaking back to Jack Tar after Roberta and Melanie went to bed.

Earlier, I had a couple of other episodes with gambling machines. In 1972, during one of the liquid intervals from my marriage to Roberta, I went back to New Brunswick where my father was the chef in a private steakhouse-bar-dance club called the Cosmopolitan. Under some strange provincial licencing, as a private club, the Cosmo had a couple of gambling machines (membership really did have its privileges). Two were really just the garden-variety pinball machines where you played for money instead of free games, but the other was a precursor to today's Video Lottery Terminals, what the British call a Fruit Machine. If I can remember anything about that six months of beer, double rum and cokes at happy hour, and smoking anything that burned, it is the hours I spent in the dark corner of that club, night after night, gambling for nickels. I should say late night after late night, because my mom managed the dining room for lunch and dinner, and so those times were out of bounds. Before and after she was there, I would have had to draw lots with my father to get on a machine. He seemed glued to them until he went home at nine each night. The gamblers' secretive character pattern seems to have reached across generations as well as decades, at least for Doug Littles.

The other experience I had was of more recent memory during a vacation Roberta and I took to Prince Edward Island and Nova Scotia in August 1994. On the Ferry to P.E.I., I encountered, for the first time, the infamous VLTs that then populated every bar, laundromat and corner store in the province of my birth. My mom would tell me how she wrote the Liberal Premier of New Brunswick begging him not to allow the introduction of these electronic "widow-makers" into the province, knowing all too well they'd prey on the addicted and those that couldn't afford to play them. Her pleas having fallen on ears deafened by the sound of money, my mother gave up being a Liberal.

I certainly didn't have any problem with VLTs during that trip, other than that I was disappointed not to find them in every nook and cranny of P.E.I. and Nova Scotia. On the ferry I played the machine every second I could, either by eluding Roberta or feigning frequent trips to the bathroom. Of course I won. One thousand, one hundred and forty-eight dimes was the result when all the whizzing, whirling, whistling and wheeling was finished, neatly paid in a computer printout for $114.80, which I took to the restaurant cashier, but not before sharing the printout with Roberta as another instance of my seemingly never-ending good luck. I don't recall how many ten-dollar bills I fed into the machine but I do remember Roberta thinking we had an extra hundred-dollars for the vacation and we ended up considerably short of that.

By the time I hit the floor of Vegas Kewadin in the Sault, the floodgates of my pent-up demand for slot machines were bursting.

I literally ran from one machine to the other, up one row and down another, feeding first quarters and then dollar tokens into the slots, alternately pulling the one-armed levers and pushing the spin buttons searching for the secret recipe to make those babies cook.

Ken, the retired accountant, your quintessential bean-counter, and Ron, a God-fearing, Church-going member of Orillia City Council, wrestling with his own financial chaos, tried to act as brakes on my *loco*-locomotion.

"Okay, Doug, now that you've got that pail filled with dollars," Ken said after a particularly good spin down a bank of *Lucky Sevens*, "let's cash it in and go look for that roulette wheel while you're ahead."

"This machine is hot. I can feel it in my bones," I told him as I poured another handful of dollars down its slot. I was so adroitly able to feed the coins one after another the slot now seemed more like a spout or funnel.

Clink. Clink. Clink. Whap! I hit the maximum bet button ("play maximum" being the advice I was given from my slot playing advisors). *Whirl, whirl, whirl,* the three reels spun hypnotically as I watched, mesmerized by the action. *Kachunk!* The first reel on the left stopped at two bars. *Kachunk!* The right slot came up "Wild" and my heart started to pump as if synchronized to the speeding pulse of the passing icons on the last reel.

"Come on bars, come on double bars! Do it! Do it!" I cried out loud, rattling Ken and Ron, who looked from side to side, waiting for the guys in the white coats to come and get me.

Kachunk! "Two bars — Yes!" I yelled. "Double bars."

How far my gambling has come from that body-twisting, palm-sweating, blood-pumping night, dancing in front of those slot machines. Hell, back then a double bar win of just forty dollars had me screaming "Yahoo!" Now I look contemptuously at the amateurs who get riled up by winning a few coins while I bounce across three machines like a damned automaton, programmed, controlled, and enslaved. When I was young I was afraid to try heroin or other so-called "hard drugs" for fear of becoming addicted. I had to be in control, I told myself as I smoked my joints and drank my beer. Sure I tried acid occasionally for the trip, the experience, but I knew that it wasn't addictive. They said it fried your brain, but my gift for denial easily dealt with those harbingers of doom. I even tried cocaine (or what I was told was cocaine) once or twice, but mercifully it didn't seem to do anything, or enough for me, to keep me interested.

It came as quite a shock to me at thirty years old when, in order to quit drinking and thereby not permanently lose my daughter, my marriage and my home, I had to accept I was hopelessly addicted to alcohol and had no control once I started to drink. Now, eighteen and a half years later, I am being brought, kicking and screaming all the way, to the reality that here again I am hopelessly addicted, this time to gambling, and have no control once I make the first bet.

Ken answers the door, his latest pet project yapping wildly, closeted behind the basement door. Cats and dogs, never their own, but some stray or rescued adoptees, have been part of Ken and Pat's life on a revolving basis ever since I first met them. I suspect they are Pat's passion since Ken often exhibits more bemusement than affection for these interlopers. Pat and Ken, both widowed from their first marriages, have brought new enlightenment into each other's lives, often shared with a bit of gentle humour on both sides. Of late, grandchildren seem to be their new challenges.

"Come on in, Doug," Ken says as he swings the door wide open. "I put Skippy in the basement or else she'll drive you nuts jumping all over you, but there's a cat around here somewhere too."

"I'm sure it'll smell Tuffy's scent on me," I say as I take my shoes off at the door. Whether that will scare it or enrage it, I don't know. With our old cat, Goblin, no other animal, neither dog nor cat, dared come near the house except back when she was in heat. Tuffy, on the hand, with all the pampering Roberta gives him, is I suspect, a bit of a wuss.

Ken offers me something cold to drink — "Sorry we're out of root beer, my grandson Josh just left" — and suggests we go out into the backyard to talk. I ask for some water knowing how I dry up when baring my soul, and considering the dog's continuous yelping and scratching, I agree the backyard seems appropriate. The pool may even add a dash of pathos when I tell him about the thoughts of jumping off the bridge at the Atherley Narrows.

We sit down, angled opposite each other on two garden benches, each clutching our glasses of water, waiting for me to start. Ken's eyes show empathy and an awareness of what this must all be about. Having been my friend and ally for eight years, and having no small knowledge of what I have been up to for the last two years, he knows my world is finally crumbling. Looking at the sadness in Ken's eyes I recall the end of last year when I was three thousand dollars short on the bingo deposits. Ken and I decided to loan me $3,000 from the Leacock general account to make up the shortfall so he could file the reports with the City of Orillia and close the year-end accounting.

173

"I quit playing bingo in June," I professed at the time, "but I have never been able to get caught up with the money I owed." True, all true, but for the lies of omission: blackjack at the charity casinos had become my new *entrée du jour* in September; I paid my first visit to Casino Windsor in October; and I was now also juggling the Orillia Winter Carnival's accounts, where, Lord help me, I was the treasurer, and poor Ron MacLean was the chairman. When there were further delays in turning over the bingo receipts and deposit slips in the first few months of 1996, Ken sent me his letter of resignation.

Here in his backyard, I know the answer before I start, but I know I have to tell one good friend the whole tawdry tale — and listen to what he has to say. Of all the people I know, Ken is my choice. Of course he isn't going to lend me any money, although he is kind enough to explain that all his money is tied up in pensions, annuities and GICs. (Hey Bub! Retirement. Fixed income. Duh!) Not that my loan application is all that enticing: I am addicted to gambling; my employers want to meet with me to discuss my pilfering from the petty cash; a loan shark is expecting a $600 payment in an hour; I owe about eighty thousand dollars to eight bank accounts, only one of which is my own; and if I don't get everyone paid back soon, I'm going to have legal problems.

"I think you need to start thinking about how you are going to deal with all this, Doug," Ken says when all else is said and done. "You are going to have to face some tough questions and some tough consequences as a result of what you have done. You need help just to be able to face up to the truth."

"I know," I say, the truth of what he is saying grabbing my emotions. "I told my doctor some of it in July and she called around looking for some program or someone, but she called me back to say she couldn't find any treatment specifically for gambling, although Simcoe Outreach Addiction Services said they were looking into it."

"It's unbelievable that they could open a casino the size of Rama in a little town like Orillia," Ken says, doing a slow burn, "and on an Indian reserve, to boot, without putting some kind of social services safety net in place first, or at least, at the same time."

"We were told the gamblers would be coming from out of town, out of the region," I say. "Less than ten per cent were supposed to be local, and they were only going to lose less than five per cent of what Rama made in a year." I know these figures by heart, having used them so many times to promote the economic benefits of the casino in speeches, in newsletters and on the street.

"I hate to point this out, Doug, but you are part of that losing percentage."

Ken gave me the name of an Orillia psychologist he knew socially, who he said was a good listener. I took the name and had my doctor refer me to him. After an hour of telling him my troubles, the psychologist charged me a hundred dollars to tell me what I already knew: that there was no one qualified in Orillia to provide me treatment; that I had to see someone experienced in dealing with multiple addictions; and that my wife, afflicted by my actions, would need treatment too.

The news of Robbie's pregnancy arrived by osmosis, finally penetrating the thick layer of denial and ignorance that we shared and which led us to have sex without any birth control in the first place.

"You were supposed to pull out," I can hear Robbie whimpering through her tears, on the umpteenth night in November,

1968 as we tried to figure out what to do. "I thought I did," was my answer, but the fog of smoke and booze that permeated our two-month-old relationship meant anything could, and obviously did, happen.

"We'll get married," came out of my mouth as if I had rehearsed it. A friend of mine, Kurt Johnston, another reporter at the *Daily Press*, also got his girlfriend pregnant around the same time. (What the hell was it with reporters?) I remember some protracted arguments, all of them pretty much arriving at the same conclusion: "Why, hell yes, we have to do the right thing and marry those girls." Twenty-five years later I ran into the former Renee Parke, Kurt's ex-wife, at the announcement luncheon for the 1993 Leacock Medal for Humour, won by her new husband, *Hamilton Star* columnist, John Levesque. During the Medal for Humour Weekend, when he was awarded his silver medallion and given the $5,000 cheque at a gala dinner in Orillia, I hosted Renee and John, as I did all the Leacock Medal winners from 1989 to 1996. During that weekend Renee and I had a chance to talk about old times, and I met, for the first time, her daughter, Christine, who is about a month older than Melanie.

How Roberta convinced her parents that she was going to marry me, and that it had to be that spring, is still a mystery to me. She would not tell them she was pregnant, and did everything she could, including taking diet pills, to make sure she didn't show. I wouldn't have believed they didn't guess if it weren't for the fact that I was there five months later when, with tears all around, Roberta told them over the phone from Peterborough she was going to have a baby — soon.

In early December, Thomson Newspapers transferred me to the *Peterborough Examiner*, where I was to be the City Hall reporter, with a salary increase from $35 a week to $65. Considering that I was about to get married and have a new child in rapid succession, and that all the lies I told Roberta when I was courting her about having money in the bank were just that, this "promotion" appeared to be a godsend. They needed me right away, but I could come home for Christmas. Great, I thought, practically jumping up and hugging John Wilson when he told me the news.

"There's just one problem," John said — too bad, I'm thinking, get yourself another boy in Timmins, I'm going — "the *Peterborough Examiner* is on strike."

Oh.

"So what's that got to do with the reporters, we still have to be able to cover the news and write our stories, even if the pressmen are on strike. Christ, we're management."

"The reporters are on strike." John explained that it was something new; the Newspaper Guild had formed a union of the editorial staff just after Thomson bought the paper.

"Shit."

"They can't force you to take the transfer," John says, "but if you don't, it will pretty well dead-end your career, and you'll be here in Timmins earning $35 a week for the rest of your life."

"I can't believe there's a union for reporters," my left-leaning guilty conscience started to whine because, given the circumstances, there was not one iota of doubt I was going to Peterborough. *A strikebreaker. A scab.* Having been a United Auto Worker at Chrysler, and living for the past eight months in a Northern Ontario mining town, I knew what those words meant. Over the next five or six years my strikebreaking in Peterborough was to be one of my deepest and darkest secrets. I would work as a gold miner and a member of the United Steel Workers of America; a staff worker for that union; and a campaign organizer for the New Democratic Party in the 1971 Ontario election and the 1972 and 1974 national elections. For part of 1974 I even lived with the former NDP Member of Parliament, Murdo Martin. In 1975, during my second year-long separation from Roberta, and in this case, Melanie, I was a campaign manager for the New Democrats in London, Ontario. But my shame went beyond politics and I have carried it buried, as one of the saddest deeds of my life. At the time I rationalized it, like I can so many things, by saying I didn't believe in unions for writers, but in reality it was my depressing economic condition and my addiction that dictated my actions. In the end I fooled myself into believing that after eight months I quit the *Peterborough Examiner* in protest because they were not treating the strikers fairly (I even told my editor that when I quit). It was, as you will see, another lie.

If alcohol was part of my daily routine in the hard-drinking, hard-rock mining town of Timmins, it was worse in Peterborough, where a collection of misfits, alcoholics and desperados were under siege in the newsroom by day and holed up in a hotel by night. Thomson paid for our hotel rooms for a few months, almost to the time I got married, but that wasn't the only hotel the reporters called home. The great tradition of hitting the tavern after the paper was put to bed was reinforced by our siege mentality, our need to shore up our egos, and the deleterious example of some of the veteran hard-drinking newspapermen whose past with the bottle had landed them right where they were. My drinking was exacerbated by my not having Roberta around to keep me in check and by my paralyzing fear that this time, at 20 years old, I really was going to get married. No one was going to rescue me. The child Roberta was carrying really was mine. I was scared to death.

And if I was scared, imagine Roberta's nightmare. An 18-year-old child, all alone with her secret in Timmins, insanely dieting to maintain her already ridiculous 110-pound weight so she could fit into her "Jones of New York" wedding dress, wondering what the hell I was doing every night in Peterborough (jealousy was to be one of Roberta's life-long burdens). She now knew that not only did I not have money in the bank, but I was already a walking financial disaster area. Neither of us had any idea where we were going to live in Peterborough, what we would use for furniture or even how we would pay for the doctor and hospital bills — my medical plan at work had some nonsense about a nine-month gestation period. In addition, Roberta also brought her own baggage to the relationship. The Jones of New York wedding dress was, given the circumstances, but a symptom of the problem.

Roberta, like all 18-year-old girls, had dreams. She got me: worse than broke, an alcoholic with a pretense and a passion to be a writer, and a propensity to run like hell when things got too hot in the kitchen. I guess Peterborough was, in a sense, an escape, but amazingly, I came back, as I always would, because something was about to fundamentally change in my consciousness.

Along with the New York wedding dress came a big wedding on March 15, 1969 (I can't resist my life-long joke: *"Beware the Ides of March" — me and Caesar"*). I took out a loan for the diamond ring and Roberta's parents paid a gazillion dollars for the wedding: big church, sit-down reception, live-band dance, and Jones of New York walking suits with fox-fur collars for the honeymoon, two of them. My father came from New Brunswick to represent my side of the family. The night before the wedding, some friends had a small stag for me at the Empire Hotel at which my father and I celebrated my marriage and our mutual addictions with a night of gambling and alcohol, guaranteeing that I was appropriately hung-over on my wedding day, one of the many sins for which I have never been forgiven. I had already borrowed from a finance company for the honeymoon, and we did receive some cash at the wedding, but in the end I had to borrow $500 from Rob's parents so we'd be able to do things and eat during the two weeks. For if Roberta was taught to believe she deserved the best, I grew up with the conviction that I was entitled to what I wanted, when I wanted it, and I gave myself permission to do whatever it took to get it.

Did I love Roberta? Yes, unequivocally, yes. Did I know, at twenty, what love was? Assuredly no, but I would learn at 21. Roberta was the most beautiful girl-woman in the world to a boy-man who was wired to believe that who you were was in large part determined by the beautiful girl you had on your arm, the beautiful girl you brought home to Daddy. I had seen it with my oldest brother Jimmy's girlfriend Sheila and a whole string of girls that David brought home, all beautiful, all squeezed and teased by my flirtatious and charming father. I was a player with Donna in Grade 12, and with Robin in university, strutting them around school and parading them home. Many others didn't measure up, and consequently, I didn't bring them home regardless of how much they loved me. Roberta, on the other hand, was the prize and, both my father and I agreed, she was a keeper. I was always so proud when Roberta was on my arm: she made me somebody, at least until my work took over.

Beyond beauty, or as an extension of it, there was sex, which I was definitely in love with in theory but was pretty lame at in practice. For one thing, I thought alcohol and drugs were aphrodisiacs, and not just the panty-removers I used them for. Drunk or stoned, I performed poorly in bed, totally ignorant of a woman's physiology. They didn't teach that at the priesthood preparatory college or anywhere else back then. (When I was ten, I threw rocks at my next-door neighbour, Hazan Middleton, because he said my parents did "it." "Where do you think all those kids come from?" he yelled under my barrage of boulders.) I was a typical pre-ejaculator and totally frustrated by Roberta's inability to orgasm. The word selfish comes to mind, perhaps only because one day I would realize self-centredness was a central theme of my life, but ignorance is probably more true. I wanted to satisfy her, I just didn't know how to do it.

Unfortunately, by the time I found out, after a couple of separations, a lot of erotic reading, and even a couple of affairs at the end of our marriage, Roberta was so jealous about where I had learned it and so uncomfortable with what I learned, our sex life continued to be a disaster, for pretty well twenty-seven years. There were two other factors that bear mentioning, then I'm getting off this sex stuff because it is all subjective and all you are hearing is my interpretation, as you are, of course, in this whole journey. (I am not sure I would want to read Roberta's version.) First, alcohol continued to be a factor in our sexual relations even after I quit drinking for good in 1978. However, now it was significant by its absence. Secondly, Roberta withheld sex as a punishment, which I saw as "blackmail," and acting according to form — I withdrew my need rather than be held up to ransom. Our sex life, however, is only important in that it was a metaphor for our entire relationship and our twenty-seven years (not counting my few sojourns along the way) of marriage. The damage that I did in the early years could never be forgiven or repaired. Roberta and I lived in an accommodation, rather than a marriage, every now and then being supportive of each other, and every now and then not giving a damn, about each other or ourselves. But, my journey is getting ahead of itself.

The honeymoon went as these things do, although in retrospect, and given the chance to do it all over again, I would have remained in Montreal, where we spent the first half of the trip. We stayed at the Queen Elizabeth Hotel and were fêted as newlyweds at the Irish Hunter's Horn on St. Patrick's Day. The trip to New Brunswick to meet my family was a disaster, starting with us trying to "do it" in a railway train sleeping berth. In New Brunswick Roberta and my family observed each other as aliens from another planet. Except for my father (she met his requirement) and my Grandfather MacKinnon — my mom's dad — who told Roberta to keep her eye on me. Rob liked him.

Just to top things off, the proverbial frosting on the wedding cake, or in this case, the honeymoon, was iced on the last leg of our trip back home, at the Toronto airport. I finally told Roberta about the bathroom. You have to understand, she was in Timmins and I was in Peterborough and it fell to me, very inappropriately and for the last time I might add, to find the family home. In between working and drinking, I did look. I even rented an apartment and was ready to move in when Roberta made it very clear she was not prepared to live without furniture, and I let the rent deposit cheque bounce (in the subsequent small claims court case several months later a sympathetic judge agreed I had the right to discuss the conditions of the apartment with my fiancé. Fortunately he didn't know about the circumstances of the next apartment or else he could have called Roberta as a witness for the plaintiff).

The new furnished apartment was on Water Street, just a few blocks from the *Examiner* in what I believed was a nice area of the city, albeit one with heavy traffic, close to downtown. Maybe I should have questioned this belief when, walking to work one morning, I witnessed the aftermath of a murder just five or six houses down the street from ours, with the victim's body sprawled across the front lawn. My story got a byline and a front-page headline in that day's newspaper. It was great.

Since the house was within walking distance of everything — except the hospital — it was good for Roberta and I, as we didn't drive. (In that regard, the *Peterborough Examiner* was perfect for me — there were no company cars; everybody used taxis to get to assignments.) Our first home was an upstairs apartment, furnished, with a big living room, a bedroom, and a kitchen. There was also a storeroom that Roberta eventually talked the landlord into vacating and we fixed it up as a nursery.

The bathroom was pretty ordinary — sink, toilet, bathtub — the usual. What was so unusual, and what I kept from Roberta until the honeymoon was over, was that we had to share the bathroom with the family downstairs, another couple, slightly older (wasn't everyone) with a daughter. That not being bad enough, there really was no door per se to our apartment: the open staircase emptied unto a hallway to which all of our various rooms, including the bathroom, were linked.

"They're really nice people, Rob," I pleaded, trying to get her to stop crying in the airport lounge. "You'll make friends with her and you'll have someone to talk to while I'm out working." I hated it when she cried and usually I would do anything to get her to stop, ranging from begging forgiveness and promising her anything, to putting my fist through a bathroom door. If I had known of Roberta then even one-millionth of what I know today, I would have realized I had committed *the* cardinal sin, one that hasn't been forgiven or forgotten to this day. Ask Roberta about the highlights of our honeymoon and you'll get the Hunter's Horn, horse-drawn carriage rides in Old Montreal, and the news of the shared bathroom, which ruined it all.

In twenty-seven years I have learned the bathroom is Roberta's room: her sanctuary during her prolonged nightly bath; her refuge in times of weeping distress; a fortress to her intransigent anger; both a nursery and a war zone in the care of her daughter; a nunnery to her vestal modesty; and a spa, beauty salon, hairdresser and house of haute couture to her interminable morning ritual of getting ready to face the world. How could there possibly be any room for our own family, let alone another family, in such a bathroom?

My life after March 15 changed, except I didn't know it. I got on with being the intrepid reporter, the hard-drinking, chain-smoking, nose-to-the-grindstone newspaperman I had always imagined. I was living up to the image. Roberta spent most of her time alone, afraid of being away from home for the first time in her life, and scared to death of what was happening in her body. She'll tell you her obstetrician had to take a tranquillizer after she left his office. At home she was learning all those things they don't teach dreamers, even in Timmins. Boiling water, holding a broom and dust pan at the same time. Not to wash all your black, coloured, and white underwear together in the bath tub. We lived on wieners, baloney, fried potatoes and beans, maybe because that was all we could afford, but it was also all she could cook then. One night — one of the few I did arrive in time for supper — I found Roberta semi-conscious on the hallway floor with little strands of black soot floating all over the apartment. Once I got her out of the fumes and into fresh air she was okay, but what had happened? She had decided to cook a roast as a treat. Not being familiar with a gas stove, she somehow turned on the broiler in the drawer below the oven, the place where all our Teflon, plastic-coated pots and pans were stored. While that plastic may not melt if you heat the outside of the pot, we learned that day it will burn and turn to soot if exposed directly to the blue-flame of a gas broiler.

When we finally told Roberta's parents we were having a baby in a couple of months, after all the acrimony and tears subsided, her mother, Roberteen, agreed to come and live with us in Peterborough for a couple of weeks before and after the baby was born, to help out. Okay with me, I thought, less pressure on me to be around all the time. More time for work, and of course, more time for after work.

The *Peterborough Examiner* was Canadian literary icon Robertson Davies' award-winning newspaper, until he sold it in 1968 to Thomson Newspapers. While Davies was the publisher, the master behind the nationally recognized excellence on the ground was Editor-in-Chief G. Wilson Craw. Craw was still at the *Examiner* when I was there, although he was dying of cancer. Without, I hope, insulting his memory or his incredible talent as an editor, I like to think I was his last protégé; his last student in journalism; the last person he whined and growled at about how to write; and the last reporter at whom he threw inadequate copy across the newsroom floor attached to wooden clothes-pins, to be rewritten by the nine o'clock morning deadline. Then he'd come behind my desk to look over my shoulder and whine and growl some more. I have long realized that, while I am not Hemingway, I owe G. Wilson Craw thanks for encouraging my ability to write even when I didn't understand it myself.

Writing has helped me cover up and compensate for my poor reading ability all my life. Either through my own irresponsibility, my copious addictions, my out-and-out laziness, or perhaps through my unrecognized childhood disability — attention deficit disorder — I have had the life-long difficulty of being a slow reader and a person who cannot fix his attention on routine tasks. Writing, centred on deadlines, campaigns, projects, events, and festivals — loaded with stress and crisis — has not only been a way of life, it has been a way of coping.

CHAPTER TEN

On my way back to the office I decide to keep the "confession-a-thon" going.

October 22, 1996 — 4 p.m.

Oddly, I find talking about my problems both therapeutic and exciting, as if I am still wagering when I am rattling on about my troubles. Possibly it's because I'm still looking for money, like the door-to-door salesman logging enough *no's* until he gets that one *yes*, and that in itself is like being in action.

Also, in gambling, the higher the stakes, the more exciting the game. For sheer excitement — living on the edge — there is nothing bigger than coming clean to my employers, the Downtown Board, confessing to Leacock's former treasurer, and confiding in the vice-president of the very casino where I am self-destructing. For pure terror there is nothing like knowing my arch-enemy, Ralph Cipolla, is out there on the streets of Downtown Orillia, loading the dice. As far as therapy is concerned, everyone I have talked to has given me some hope, even Ken with his suggestion that I get ready to face the consequences if I don't solve the money problem. A "Plan B," a contingency in case of rain: for an event organizer like me this has its appeal. But God, I'm praying for sunshine.

Charity casino operator Mr. Casino is a company owned by Orillia construction businessman Darren Burns, and real estate agent and building owner Mike Timpano, whose family owns several businesses in Downtown Orillia. I have known both of them, as I know most business people in Orillia, for several years. Now I also know them as a frequent player at their charity casino events and a sponsor of those events through the Leacock Heritage Festival. I also know them as gamblers who have frequently seen me — and played with me — at Casino Rama. It will come as no surprise to them to hear I have a gambling problem.

In June of 1996 I was at the apex of my gambling frenzy. I was $20,000 in the hole to the eight bank accounts and the bingo and Nevada reports were piling up. Anxiety and panic attacks were sweeping over me with regularity and my concentration at work and everywhere else was shot. Sweating in bed at night I worried about getting caught, going to jail and having my life defined by the fact I was a gambler and a thief.

I'm not even going to make it to the opening of Casino Rama. On those 4:30 a.m. drives home from gambling in Barrie, I worried I would get caught first, or worse. After three nights of losing at the charity casino, I wanted to ram my van into one of the grey-concrete overpasses on Highway 400.

For the twenty-three kilometres of the trip back I would talk to myself, cursing my stupidity, my bad luck. Why hadn't I quit when I was up? If only I hadn't run out of time. If only they hadn't changed dealers. I was on a roll, then everything changed. "Oh, why didn't I quit, take my chips and go home?"

The charity casinos closed at 4:00 a.m. Whether I was winning or losing, they closed. The last-half hour was pure insanity, a kind of reverse, bleak "happy hour" where instead of drinking twice as much, you bet with even greater hysteria. If I was down, I needed to get even. If I was up, it was never high enough to cover off all I had previously lost. All that I owed. All that I had stolen.

Why didn't I go home at two o'clock? I thought to myself as Sherrie shuffled the cards to get ready for the next shoe. If I had gone home, I would have been up a thousand on the night and only $3,000 in the hole — this week. Now I was down $5,000. How the hell was I going to pay that back by Friday? Those bank deposits had to be made within a week or else there would be no plausible excuse.

How I hated the shuffle in a charity casino. That break in the action allowed the real world to come wheeling into my mind. *I'm here to gamble, not think.* In a bona fide casino there are lots of distractions during a shuffle: drop a couple of green quarters on number 17 in roulette, slip $50 into a five-dollar slot machine on the way to the washroom; watch the Asian guys bet $20,000 a hand in the VIP Baccarat Room playing a game that amounts to little more than high-stakes card cutting. Here, all I could do was wait.

Michael the pit boss knew I was down. *Can he see the desperation in my face or can he just do the math?* In charity casinos, the action is small enough that the house knows who is winning or losing at all times. Especially VIP players like me.

VIP Blackjack: I bet all seven spots on the table, me against the dealer. It was the only way I played now, ever since partnering with Arnold went sour a few months earlier. Nothing really happened, I just couldn't win with him any more. We'd either both lose or I'd lose alone. Earlier, he saw me at the table and came over.

"Want to play together?" he asked, gesturing at the seven spots on the table and searching for his three.

"No," I said, avoiding his eyes. "I'm down. I gotta stay on my own. I haven't been winning lately."

"It's okay, it's okay. I'll play over here. Go get 'em." He walked away. I knew he felt bad. Maybe it was recreation to him; maybe he could afford to be nice. I couldn't. *Shit. He taught me the game.* Arnold owned a golf course in Barrie and had been a regular at the charity casinos ever since I started playing at them last year. On many nights we'd been a team, dominating the table, playing like we could do no wrong, stacking up the chips, breaking the house. "You're on fire," one of the guys standing around said. "It's like you can read the cards." Recalling those heady days, it's hard to understand how I could be so down, how I could owe so much money.

"Are you almost ready, Sherrie?" I asked, annoyed with my own angst.

"Almost, darling, and I feel a good shoe coming on." Sherrie and most of the dealers liked me. For one thing they knew me because I sponsored the Leacock charity casino nights that their company operated. Also, I tipped. On the surface, I was a good loser. I never blamed anyone else, never got mad, swore, or threw things like some of the guys. I thought that kind of behaviour was an invitation to bad luck, negative vibes, bad karma, that sort of thing. Inside I was screaming. Did they genuinely feel sorrow when I lost? I wanted to think so, but then, my losses paid their salaries. Having been on the other side of the table, as a sponsor, I knew one hot gambler playing VIP like me could mean a losing night for the operators in a charity casino. Sure, that meant the sponsor didn't make any money either, but it really meant the operator lost because he had to pay the staff and overhead. In Toronto and even in Barrie, at the other casino company, they hated to lose and tried all kinds of tricks — some of them, I'd have bet, illegal — to stop a player on a roll. Once, at Huronia

Casino, a woman — a regular named Donna — and I were having a good night controlling a table, each of us up several hundred dollars. Then the owner of the company asked if we minded if he dealt for a while. I don't know whether she cared but I sure as hell did. I didn't want to play against the damn owner, but my gambler's ego wouldn't let me say it. I finally quit when I had about two hundred dollars left. I never went back to Huronia's events. It was these types of shenanigans that would give the government the excuse it needed to take over control of all gambling.

Finally Sherrie was ready for me. I had felt tired during the break but now I was animated, bobbing and weaving, standing in front of the green felt table, my chips lined up along the padded sides. Watching her bury the hole card, I was wide awake, ready for another round. Ready for redemption.

"Okay, let's do it," I said, and all the worry of the outside world — everything but Sherrie Darling, me, and the cards — disappeared.

I had two five-dollar chips in each of the seven circles — the maximum ten-dollar bet you were allowed to make in charity casinos. I was really making a $70 bet per hand but let's not quibble on the fine points. I had ten piles of five-dollar chips in front of me — $500 — and a pocket full of green quarters, $25 each, the remainders from earlier in the evening when I was up a grand. Twenty. I always knew how many. It was another thing I did during the shuffle to keep my mind occupied.

Snap, snap, snap, snap, snap, snap and *snap,* Sherrie whacked my first cards beside the circles. My eyes were on her card. *Snap.* A Seven. Good. I had a chance. I feared an Ace of course: Blackjack is an Ace and Ten, it didn't have to be a Jack. I also feared any face card or Ten. Now I could watch what she was giving me, and the battle was underway.

A King on a Queen. "Good," I said, as I waved her off.

"Don't want to split those Tens?" Sherrie joked as she gave me a Three on a Four on the next square. "Yuck."

"Hit me," I said, scratching on the green felt with the middle finger on my right hand, the one with the tell-tale band-aids covering the dried, cracked skin from too much of this very scratching.

Eight. Fifteen. "Hit me," I scratched.

Queen. Bust. "Oops, sorry," Sherrie feigned as she scooped up those cards with her right hand and slammed them in the crib, deftly sliding my $10 from that circle into her tray.

Next came an Eight on a face card. "Eighteen." I waved Sherrie off.

Snap. Another Three on an Eight. Eleven. "Double down," I said as I placed another $10 at the back of that circle. Another card. Ten. "Yes! That's better, Sherrie — keep it up."

A Six on a Six. *Shit, what do I do?* I searched my brain for the computer prompt or the book instruction or Arnold's voice. *Always split Sixes or is it never split Sixes?* I couldn't remember. Sixes against a Seven? I split them. *It's another all or nothing night.* I moved $10 more to the side of the circle. Another Six. "Split," I said and I moved another $10 out.

Nine. Fifteen. A scratch of the finger: "Hit me." Four. "Stay." A wave, and on to the next hand.

Ten. Sixteen. "Hit," scratch. Ten. "Too hard." Swoop cards, discard, slide money into Sherrie's tray.

Five. Eleven. "Double down." Another $10 from my tray.

Jack. Twenty-one. "That's one you're not going to get, Missy,"

I said as I exhaled some anxiety and twisted out a kink in my neck. I could feel the heat in my blood. My throat was dry.

"Don't get cocky," Sherrie said as she slapped a Five on my eleven. I paused, knowing what was next as soon as I thought it. Shit. *Sixteen, I have no choice.* "Hit me."

Seven. Bust. *Swoosh, slam, swoop,* and *clink* in her tray. I played with a cyst on the back of my neck, twisting my back against my other hand. I looked, I am sure, like one of my straitjacket contortionists.

The sixth spot. A Two. A Three. *Three small cards: it'll be a face.*

"Hit," I said and scratched the table. Close, a Nine. "Now a face," I said with resignation, regretting the prediction as soon as it passed my lips. *Positive, you idiot.* Ace.

"I could have used that next, Sherrie," I chided. "Hit me," I scratched.

Ten. Bust. "They're always together, eh?" Sherrie sympathized as she swooped up the cards, and my money, from the table.

My last spot. Another Ten. Three. "Ten and Three, thirteen," Sherrie said. I looked at her Seven, thinking about what she needed, what I wanted her to have. *A Ten — she has to stay on seventeen.* "Lucky Seventeen," I murmured out loud, prompting Sherrie to repeat, somewhat sarcastically, "Thirteen!"

The object here was for me not to take the card I wanted her to have. This was the players' advantage in the charity casinos: you could influence the dealers' second card by taking or not taking a card on the anchor spot. When you have several experienced people playing at a table, sometimes the person at the end, in the anchor seat, will "take one for the table." In the big casinos, the play is different: the dealer gets both his cards off the mark, taking away this players' edge.

I didn't want a Ten. "Hit me," I scratched.

Six. Another nineteen. Six would have been good for her, giving her thirteen, I thought, second-guessing myself. *No, I've seen too many thirteens topped with Eights.*

"What's it going to be, Dougie?" Sherrie taunted me.

I waved my hand to pass and returned the jab: "Ten, come on, Sherrie, you can do it."

She turned a Four. "Eleven," my mouth said, but my mind cringed as I took the first shot of the inevitable one-two combination. I looked back at the cards already on the table, grimacing, trying to see but not wanting to think the worst — to forecast the worst. To make it happen. What would have happened if I had given her the Six? Seven, Six and Four. Seventeen. *Damn.* Now we've had Four, Six, and Three. Damn, my mind moaned. *Don't say it; don't even think it.* But, it was too late: *Tens are due.*

Ten. "Dealer has 21," Sherrie said very succinctly, knowing I was on the ropes.

We pushed, or tied, on three hands of twenty-one, meaning I got to keep three ten-dollar bets. I lost seventy more dollars.

So it went for the remainder of the shoe and I was down another $500. My brain couldn't take the torture of watching and waiting for another shuffle so I went over to next table where there were a couple of empty spots and plopped my ten-dollar chips on each. I was now literally running from my thoughts. I won. I lost. I won. And on and on.

Finally Sherrie was ready for me and as we took our positions, aggressor and defender — or the illusion thereof — Michael stepped over and announced: "Last shoe." Closing time.

I couldn't win. I'd had near-perfect shoes before. You can only win about eight hundred dollars. I was already down $1500 for the night and $5,500 for the three days. Despair washed over me. My concentration was gone. Not even the action could keep my wretched feelings at bay. I played a couple of hands on auto-pilot, hardly knowing what I was saying.

"That's it for me, Sherrie. I'm beat," I said as I picked up the last of my red chips to head for the cashier booth before the four o'clock poker crowds. The last thing I needed was a whole bunch of "How much did you win, Little?" questions from those guys.

I had $240 left. Enough to leave Roberta a hundred dollars on the kitchen table when I went to work, pretending I won, and some money for lottery tickets and Nevada to tide me over until the next weekend's charity casino in Orillia. But what was I going to do about the missing $6,000 from the deposit?

Maybe I've already won the lottery, I told myself, bolstering my courage for the long, concrete-pillared drive home to Orillia.

Mr. Casino has its offices in an industrial park in the north end of Orillia. Darren, Mike, and I are sitting around an outdoor patio set on a balcony off the second story of their offices. I called ahead and said I needed to talk to them about the money that the Leacock Heritage Festival owed them. I am sure they are hoping I've brought a cheque for $10,532, the amount I owe them for the event in September. They won't be expecting the payment from last week's event, because I haven't even got an invoice yet. As I sit in front of them, I wonder — are they expecting this?

"I wanted to meet with you for two reasons," I start, looking at them eye to eye, back and forth. Like a stool-pigeon spilling his guts, I have their rapt attention. "I am addicted to gambling and

I am in a lot of trouble because I haven't been able to quit. Casino Rama has killed me, to be sure, but it's been going on before that, and I've got to quit."

"That place can eat up a lot of money very quickly," Darren offers. "I'm sure you aren't the only one."

"Well, that certainly is part of it. But I was losing even before it opened and I have to quit going to the charity casinos too. I need you to cut me off from playing at Mr. Casino events too."

"Hell, the reports we always got were that you were murdering us," Mike says; "you must have been losing it somewhere else. We'll respect your wishes, but we'll miss your business."

"This is very serious," I continue. "I am in a deep hole. There is some hope that I can get out of it, but I need to quit gambling, to be straight with you and to ask for your patience." I go on to tell them that the money I owe them is gone. The cheque that I told them I was waiting for from Casino Rama's sponsorship of the Festival has already come and has been eaten up by the overdraft at the Royal Bank. Leacock is overdrawn by $30,000 — due to my gambling — and the bank has cut us off. The last payment I made to Mr. Casino, in August, was part of that overdraft.

"I owe you the $10,532 from September," I say, looking straight at Mike, because I suspect he will be the harder to read. Now that I have started along this precarious course I know I need to be able to read reactions — it's like a poker game — in order to determine what I need to do or say next. "That money was never deposited but ended up in Casino Rama as I was trying to win back all the other money I owe, like the $30,000 to the bank." I see Mike look over to Darren.

"The proceeds from last week," I pause, gripped by emotion, "they're gone too. I spent the weekend at Rama. I went right from the Highwayman Inn on Saturday morning. I was there for 28 hours chasing the Caribbean Stud jackpot — it was $116,000. I went back Sunday night, then again last night. I left broke."

The egregious impact of what I am saying, and to whom, starts to hit home, stripping away my armour of denial, leaving me vulnerable. My words are starting to swell in my throat and, choking, I stop for a moment to get my breath. Darren and Mike aren't saying anything. They may have eyed each other, as I gagged, but if they did, I missed it.

"So I owe you guys $20,000, and," I quickly add, "I want to talk to you about paying it back." I tell them about my meeting with Ed Leichner, his agreement to set up a meeting with Rama president Bobby Yee, and Ed's confidence that Bobby will help me out.

"Bobby's away but I'm supposed to meet with him when he gets back," I say. "So I need some more time from you guys to work this out."

Surprisingly, they are sympathetic, perhaps because they too are gamblers, and maybe because they also believe the Casino will bail me out. We agree that I will get back to them after my meeting with Bobby Yee to tell them the results.

As I arrive back at the Downtown office, still somewhat ambivalent about this new, all-or-nothing strategy, I see the representative from Angel Gaming Agency leaving through the downstairs door. My heart leaps. Reinforcements. *Money!*

Life at St. Mary's College, as in most seminaries, was cloistered. We seldom went to town. In Grade 10 two of my classmates escaped from a hospital visit in Brockville and went downtown.

They got caught shoplifting and by the time we were told about it, at an extended general assembly in the Chapel by a very severe Father Callaghan, they were on the train home. I'm not sure what was unforgivable, the shoplifting or the stupidity.

Father Callaghan used the occasion, however, to warn us of the seriousness, and severe consequences, of getting caught at one of our favourite St. Mary's traditions: "Raiding the kitchen." Serious, yes: you had to be quiet going down, and you did have to wait until the middle of the night. No more than four people, either. We tried it once with seven guys — way too much talking and not a chance of control. The consequences if you were caught (no one had ever been sent home for raiding the kitchen) probably meant cleaning urinals for a month. Washing a bathroom floor with a toothbrush was another possibility, or perhaps kitchen duty — the dishes — for a month. Or even the ultimate punishment (shy of the train ride home): no desserts.

But who was going to get caught? Raiding the kitchen was a master craft, like plumbing. You had to know what you were doing; you had to serve your apprenticeship. The apprenticeship was Grade Nine. For that entire year, you were forced to listen to the war stories of the older students, the Grade Tens and Elevens, on how they did it and what they got. Peanut butter — the big prize — as well as bread, butter, fruit, and left-over desserts like pie and squares. The rice pudding never got raided. One of the keys, you learned, was going when you knew there would be great leftover desserts.

I had the privilege of being part of one of the most celebrated kitchen raids ever perpetrated at St. Mary's. It was executed with military precision, which was a minor miracle in itself, considering my accomplices: Scott Follis, tall and lanky, definitely awkward at fifteen; Stephen Young, not as tall but so thin you had to be careful not to sneeze in his direction; and my bosom buddy, Einstein with straight hair, Paul Kennedy. However, what made the raid so famous was not that we did it or how, but what we found in the foray.

In this celebrated culinary incursion, the spoils went beyond the normal sandwich sustenance and fruit fare: they were a veritable jackpot. Creams — chocolate creams. We'd found the motherlode. Buried deep in the back of the walk-in refrigerator there was a stack of boxes of McCormick's Chocolate Creams. They were treats for High Feast Days, like All Saints Day, the Feast of the Blessed Virgin, or the consummate High Feast Day, Easter. For Grades Nine and Ten we had to stay at the college for Easter, but in Grade Eleven, the rule was relaxed and we were allowed out for a week. I say "out" rather than home because although some guys could go home — Gordie Peters would have only five miles to go — New Brunswick was too far for a week so I went to stay with my two beautiful cousins in Trenton. Naturually, I fell in love with them and with their girlfriend, too. Eventually, more nails in my cross.

Their splendour notwithstanding, it wasn't the chocolate creams themselves that made our tale into a classic. Nor was it what we did with the creams — of course we ate them by the handful — that cemented our fame. It was what we found among the creams that turned us into legends — at least to the Grade Niners. I know it wasn't Paul or I who found it, so it was either Scott or Stephen, I can't remember which.

"Ow," one of them said as he chomped down on one of the chocolate drops. "What the hell . . ." (We were allowed to say that. Not "Christ," but we could say "hell." Not supposed to go there, but we could talk about it. Hey, this was the middle of Vatican II:

things were changing quickly. Maybe in Grade 12 we could have said "Christ." I never found out.)

"What the hell" was a large bronze packing staple, the kind used to fasten cardboard boxes together in shipping. Somehow, this staple went astray, passed through the box, and ended up embedded in one of the strawberry chocolate creams. Gold fever overwhelmed our quick-witted quartet. With visions of much more than sugar plums dancing in our heads we sat down to compose a letter to Mr. McCormick.

Dear Sir:

While sitting around one evening enjoying the wonderful cream drops from one of your twenty-pound boxes of chocolates, we had a near tragic experience. As we shared these delightful candies we were alarmed, no shocked, to find the enclosed packing staple embedded in a strawberry filling just when one of us began to chew down on the tender morsel. Can you imagine the catastrophe if the rest of us hadn't seen the bronze coloured metal twinkling in the beam of our flashlights and yelled, "Don't swallow" in the nick of time.

In the interest of public safety we are bringing this to your attention. You will note the strawberry filling, still affixed to the staple in its original condition, will verify our story. You may also rest assured that the four of us, who are studying to be Catholic priests, would not lie or make up such an incredible tale.

Please, by return mail, inform us as to what your company is going to do to right this wrong and what actions you are going to use in the future about your staples so we will feel

safe in getting more twenty-pound boxes of McCormick's
chocolate creams.

We will anxiously await your reply.

Sincerely,

Douglas I. Little
Paul D. Kennedy
Scott E. Follis
Stephen F. Young
Students,
St. Mary's College
Brockville, Ontario, Canada.
p.s. Please mark your response "confidential."

Given the self-incriminating nature of the letter (it was well known that the priests read our mail), the next time one of us went to the hospital in town, he mailed it to the McCormick company. For the next several weeks we debated among ourselves the wisdom of adding the "confidential" or indeed the wisdom of using the college as the return address at all.

Every morning, after our silent breakfast, mail call was announced on the second floor, just outside the office of the Subsocius, Father Scanlan. If you received a letter, your name was called out by either Father Scanlan, the Capo, or by the Sub Capo. (The Capos were First Arts students who were placed in these positions of authority to police and discipline the rest of us: "Little, two nights of kitchen duty for talking at breakfast." That kind of thing. Serious stuff — shoplifting — went to the Socius and, I suppose, the Rector.)

After a month of hanging around mail call every day, we started asking Father Scanlan if any letters or packages had arrived for us that he may be forgetting. We wondered, surveying his girth, if Father had decided to keep the package for himself once he discovered its contents during the execution of the open-the-mail policy. Finally, one morning at the end of mail call, Father Scanlan announced that Follis, Kennedy, Little, and Young should meet him in his office immediately. We ran around and gathered everyone together, and headed to the far end of the second floor where the Subsocius' office was located.

"It's here," I predicted excitedly. "Yeah, but how come it wasn't just called out at mail call?" Scott questioned. "Maybe they didn't put "confidential" on the package," Stephen added. "We're dead," was Paul's prognostication. When we arrived at Father Scanlan's office, our four faces peering in the sides of the door like puppet heads, we were greeted with his standard line of affection and we knew we were going to be all right: "Kids, I hate kids."

"Get in here, you guys. This parcel has come for you, packed full of cookies, chocolate, and candies, all from McCormick. There is a letter, laughingly marked 'Confidential,' but it just says thanks for your letter, and that they are pleased to send you these samples for you and your family to enjoy."

"Great," I said. "We just sent them a letter about a quality control problem and I guess they appreciated the concern. Nice of them to send us the samples, though." As I spoke, grinning from ear to ear, all the guys were bobbing their heads in agreement, complete with their own silly grins.

"I imagine if I were to put you guys on your honour now, I might hear a story that I may not want to hear outside the confessional, so take this parcel away, and make sure you do what the letter says." We all looked at him, puzzled, as we grabbed for the box.

"Share it with your family!"

As we scrambled out the door and ran down the hall, heading for the stairs to the dorm, we heard behind us an earthy growl and "Kids, I hate kids."

Angel Gaming Agency services the Leacock Heritage Festival's Nevada pull-tab ticket outlet, at Neighbours convenience store and gas bar in the West Street Plaza. It is a good location compared to the one we had last year inside a downtown restaurant that also contained the only off-track betting screens in Orillia. I'd been gung-ho to get the Nevadas inside the off-track betting parlour, figuring those gamblers crowded around the TV screens didn't have any other gambling to do in between races so the Nevada tickets would do well. Was I ever wrong. At the new Neighbours location we go through a couple of Nevada boxes in a week. In the old off-track betting location we were lucky to go through a box in a month. The racetrack gamblers didn't have any interest at all in the pull-tab tickets, concerned instead with analyzing their programs and handicapping the horses to determine their choice for the winner in each race. I was one of the more frequent Nevada players at the restaurant as I dropped in on Sunday afternoons, threw $10 on some long shot in an upcoming race and another $10 into the Super Nevada box. I must admit that I certainly won more in the Nevada box than I won betting on the horses. My system for the latter, like throwing money against the wall to see if it would stick, didn't return a red cent over my dozen or so attempts. In Nevada, at least, I won the bars once.

I am an impulse gambler, looking for action that will get my juices flowing and an uncertain outcome that will keep my heart pumping. I crave the kind of excitement that will make my hands shake and captivate my mind. (That's why today's roller coaster events are so much like gambling to me. They've got me buzzed.) The racetrack guys and the poker players seem a different breed of gambler, relying more on handicap calculation, guile and their "system" rather than on impulse. They'd think I was nuts, running from game to game and from machine to machine trying to keep the adrenaline or endorphin or whatever chemical it is flowing. Still, I will get to know many compulsive gamblers whose main poison was the ponies and in the end, they too couldn't win because they couldn't quit.

The Angel Gaming representative brings us the proceeds of four Nevada boxes, about $2,000. Enough to pay *F*, who should be back soon, the $600 for Johnny; enough to replenish the $800 bingo float for this week; and enough, perhaps, to either give Bob another $500, or make a bingo deposit and report to the City.

Will I use it to go back gambling? Today? Tomorrow? Frankly, I haven't made up my mind. As much as I want this exhausting chase to be over, to pay back all the money I owe and to "straighten up and fly right" (as Doug Little Sr. would say), I also still want to gamble. I want to gamble at a level so deep in my subconscious that my bones ache just thinking about not being able to do it again, as if just thinking about quitting sets off another chemical reaction that makes me crave it even more. If talking about my problems seems like a soothing balm, then worrying about them is like writhing under an itch I just have to scratch. If someone — the

Casino — gives me all the money I owe to pay everything off, I am sure I will change my gambling, gamble less, gamble what I can afford. After all, when I quit bingo, I quit bingo. Yes, I went on to other, possibly more destructive forms of gambling, but I can quit them, too. Maybe I can just play roulette, once or twice a year, or a month, with a set amount of money — a couple of hundred dollars — after which, win or lose, I will leave. Surely there isn't any harm in that? Isn't it just when I lose money I can't afford to lose that I start chasing? And stealing?

My mind is smoking from this debate when Jennifer's voice comes across the intercom telling me someone from the O.P.P., a Pat Lennon, called a few minutes earlier. Who is she, I wonder, as Jen tells me she said she would call back later. Okay, I shrug. A call for me from the Ontario Provincial Police is not unusual, although I don't recognize the name. Almost all of last year I served as the City of Orillia's representative on a committee planning the opening ceremonies for the new hundred-million-dollar Provincial Police Headquarters Building located in Orillia. As one of the few civilians on the committee, it fell to me to raise the money from sponsorships to fund the committee's opening ceremony celebrations. The O.P.P. supplied me with a contact list of their contractors and suppliers and I called each of them to solicit donations. Fortunately all the donations were paid by cheque, and were deposited in a special account, administered by the City of Orillia treasurer. None of that money got caught up in my "gambling cycle."

Just last week I was honoured at a luncheon at the Headquarters by the Commissioner of the O.P.P., Thomas O'Grady, who presented me with a plaque for my work on the committee. Still, I don't remember any Pat Lennon.

In 1995, *Montreal Gazette* humorist Josh Freed won the Leacock Medal for Humour for his book "Fear of Frying." In the rest of Canada he's not as well known but his most famous quotation is readily recognizable — the "neverendum referendum." A very funny commentator on political and social conditions, Josh came to Orillia to receive his Leacock Medal and cheque in June of 1995. I hosted him for his two-day visit, shuttling him to and from the airport, and from reception to reception. Like many of the Medal winners, Freed pumped me for information about Orillia as background for his acceptance speech, and used me, as he put it, as his ". . . funny speech-line tester." One of his best was about Orillia getting the Ontario Provincial Police Headquarters in town but, not having enough crime, they decided they'd better get a casino, too.

My office at the Downtown Management Board is really in the Leacock Heritage Festival's part of the building. We punched a hole through the two closets to join the two offices up, with my office acting, like me, as the lynchpin. You can come directly through the more open Leacock side to get to my office, which is what my friends and associates do, avoiding the secretarial buffer zone. This is what *F.* does when he returns and startles me out of my O.P.P. musings.

"I've got Johnny's six hundred dollars," I say, shooting up from my seat. "It's here in the drawer." I'd counted out thirty twenties from the Nevada proceeds, and placed it in the top drawer of my desk, away from the remainder of the money and all the unfiled reports which were stored in the bottom drawer. I always tell myself all the records are there, that everything I owe can be accounted for, and repaid. "Loans." All the bingo float cheques; the missing bingo deposits; the Nevada deposits; the charity casino deposits; all the expense advances, all the petty cash funds. All can be totalled and repaid. All it will take is money.

"Good," *F.* said. "How is everything else going?" I'm not sure if he's asking how I am making out solving the rest of my money problems or whether I've been back to the casino this afternoon. As I give him the money, I tell him about what has been happening.

"I've had a lot of meetings — I've opened up to a lot of people about my problem with gambling — the vice president of the casino, the guys who own the charity casino company, and a friend of mine, Ken, who was the Leacock Festival treasurer. It has been amazingly positive. Everybody is sympathetic — actually pleased I'm admitting to my problem — and I think I may be able to borrow the rest of the money to get everything paid off, as long as we can keep Johnny hap . . ."

"Don't worry about Johnny anymore. After this, I'm paying him off," *F.* said.

"I'll repay you, I promise, as soon as I get on my feet," I say to *F.*, knowing how ridiculous it would sound if I said "You don't have to do that."

"Never mind, what you have to do now is get all the cancelled cheques from the last few months you used to pay Johnny. He wants them all."

"I have them at home, with my bank statements. I can get them out tonight for you."

"Good," *F.* says. "If you want to really repay me, quit gambling. That will be payment enough for me."

"I will *F.*, I have."

After he leaves, it's almost five o'clock, and I am alone in the office. How I love five o'clock when the rest of the world stops working, the phones stop ringing, and the banks stop counting what you owe them, at least until the next day. In this peace I review the day that has now ended on such a hopeful, upbeat note. All in all, I say to myself, a positive day of problem solving. *Maybe I can make this happen yet.*

I call Roberta to tell her everything with Johnny is looked after. "It was just a misunderstanding and he's got his money now." I tell her I will be home around six, having decided I would take another $500 from the Nevada funds down to Bob, to try to make sure he felt better.

As I am talking to Roberta on the office line, my direct line begins flashing. I have a call. Perhaps it is the DMB chairman, Mike Knight, who always uses that line. I tell Roberta I have to go to answer the other line. As I hang up the phone to put my line on the speaker phone, my mind questions, "Ralph?"

I hit the line button and respond, "Doug Little here."

"Mr. Little, my name is Pat Lennon. I am a constable with the Ontario Provincial Police, seconded to the Ontario Gaming Commission. I am in Orillia doing some routine audits and I would like to review the Leacock Heritage Festival charity casino accounts at a time that is convenient to you."

If my heart were still in my body instead of on the floor, it might explode. My life, as I know it, is over.

CHAPTER ELEVEN

"What did you say you did with the gaming commission?" I ask as

October 22, 1996 — 5 p.m.

I pick up the telephone receiver. It is the only question I can come up with in my petrified panic, knowing I need to fill the dead air between us, need to prevent an inevitably fatal, pregnant pause. I've seen enough politicians slain on the campaign trail by a couple of seconds of hesitation at just the wrong moment. And I know that on the other end of the line, pen and paper at the ready, Constable Lennon is tuned with the fine ear of a seasoned police investigator.

"I am an O.P.P. officer but I am on loan — seconded — to the Ontario Gaming Commission, which oversees all of the lottery and gaming licences in Ontario," she answers. Her manner is open, measured, like someone who is trained to take a question as a question, not a personal attack, and to respond straightforwardly.

"What is it you would like to see, Officer Lennon?" I say.

"I just need to go over the records of the Leacock Heritage Festival Monte Carlo licenses, for which, I understand, you are the contact?"

"I am," I say, taking a minimalist tack on the principle of the less said, the less incriminating.

"You understand under the terms of the licences and the law, you must make the records available upon the request of an official of the gaming commission?"

"Of course. When do you want to see them . . . tonight?" I bluff, strangely, considering I am holding absolutely no cards.

"No, no. Tomorrow will be fine, Mr. Little," the policewoman says directly, knowing she controls the deck. There is no hurry, short of a fire.

"Is tomorrow afternoon at 1 p.m. okay with you? That way I will be able to get all the papers together in the morning," I lie. Of course, everything she needs to see is already in my bottom desk drawer, arranged neatly and chronologically for this eventuality, or for the chance I manage to win enough money to make all the deposits. Yet even though I've long taken all the reports, bank records, and deposit slips from Doug Bell to make sure neither he, nor anyone else, gets caught up in my whirlwind, Constable Lennon's single call makes me realize how naïve I have been. Everyone is about to get sucked into my vortex.

"Thirteen hundred hours is fine. Is the address still 25 Mississaga Street East?"

"Yes, it's on the main street, upstairs over Radio Shack. You can park in the front or the back."

"Thanks. I am in civilian clothes with a civilian car, so it will be very discreet and routine."

"I'll see you tomorrow, then, Officer."

"Thank you, Mr. Little. Goodnight."

"Goodnight." The line goes dead in my hand. My body is paralyzed, unmoving; for not only have all the balls fallen, but all my illusions, like balloons, are bursting. I once managed the Canadian Hot Air Balloon Championships in Barrie. Balloonists are great souvenir-pin collectors, each pilot with his own colour-enamelled replica of his airship for trading or promotion. One pin I have shows a balloon flying upside down, with an attached bubble containing the words of the unfortunate pilot: "Oh shit!"

If I could move at all I might just jump from my chair and directly out the twelve-foot window beside my desk, rolling out on my shoulder and back — like in the movies — so as not to cut myself on the glass. Several years ago in Timmins I walked through a ten-foot double plate glass sliding window in the 101 mall where I was putting up a Christmas display. I was using an empty store as my base of operations, running back and forth for things I needed. In my rush I forgot I had closed the sliding window behind me. Distracted and needing some part or other back in the store I spun around and, with my head down and in full stride, I walked straight into the glass, shattering it with the left corner of my forehead. I knew instinctively there was no going back, that my momentum was too strong. Trying to reverse would have resulted in stopping, right under the lethal shards of glass above my head. Impulsively, I dove, bringing my hands up to protect my head and face as I passed through the second plate. I ended up splattered on the store floor, a sliver of glass sticking out of the back of my right hand and a few slight cuts on my knees. Witnesses said a three-foot section of the first plate glass fell like a guillotine behind me.

I have the same impulse now: jump, and save my neck from the blade that's about to come down on it. Except this is only the second story and I somehow don't relish serving my jail sentence in a wheelchair. I recognize that this is a pretty squirrelly way of thinking but often when I am feeling suicidal, the fear of ending up *crippled* (like my sister didn't with polio) or as a vegetable in a coma helps dismiss the delusion that death is the best way out.

"Everyone will be better off if I'm dead," I tell myself, thinking of the pain and shame I am about to bring on my family, Roberta, Melanie — brilliant budding author Melanie Little whose father was a gambler and a criminal — my mother and sisters, my friends. What about the people who believed in me, who defended me, fought for me, for my unorthodox way of getting things done? Certainly Roberta will be better off with me dead. She'll get the insurance money and will be able to disappear, change her name and rebuild a better life. The devastation this is going to have on my wife's life brings me to tears, clogging my sinuses, forcing me to hang up the phone and reach for my handkerchief to blow my nose.

My mother — the shame and disgrace of having a criminal for a son. For all the dysfunction, addiction, and craziness that exist among my brothers and sisters, no one has ever gone to jail. How ironic that, for years, I rationalized my isolation from my family by saying I didn't want to be a burden to my mother. Still, I know her religious beliefs couldn't allow her to accept suicide as a solution and maybe mine couldn't either. (As far as religion is concerned, my nightly prayers are testament to my willingness to hedge my bets.) My panic makes it difficult to accept the thought of my mother's understanding and forgiveness, but still it comes involuntarily to mind.

Just the vision of my sister Veronica gives me hope. "We'll fight this, we'll get through it, together," I can hear her saying, dismissing out of hand any thought of suicide, or even that life is over.

Melanie. Night after night the fear of destroying Melanie's incredible future — one that I battled so hard to give her — has saved me from all the concrete pillars and watery graves from Windsor to Orillia. Plainly, she would be devastated by my self-destruction, and I wouldn't be here to help her get over it. Sure, she'd get money too, but — I can't help but smile through my tears — that wouldn't even pay off her student loans. Hey, maybe I'll give her something to write about though I'm sure my haywire behaviour over the years already has.

There will come a day when I will believe I suffer from an emotional illness of which my gambling, my drinking, my escape into work and my need to soothe myself with food are but symptoms. The proof that this is an illness, beyond all doubt, beyond any evidence to the contrary for me, is my contemplation of suicide. So much do I love life, being there, creating, contributing, making things happen, and so much do I enjoy watching Melanie's life unfold, that the mere thought that I seriously considered suicide is astonishing. Only a disease of monumental proportion could have brought me to this place. I will learn I am not alone.

The first time I saw my newborn daughter her head was squished sideways, angled like a parallelogram. To me she looked like a rain-soaked softball, pushed out of shape by some awful accident. Fortunately doctors and nurses have seen that horror-struck look on fathers' faces before and ours were quick to assure me she would be okay. "It's natural; the head is soft on newborns and it will take its normal shape in fifteen or twenty minutes."

"Your child is a healthy baby girl, Mr. Little, and Mrs. Little is fine although exhausted, as you can imagine," the nurse said to me. They had called me, without explanation, out of the waiting room about twenty minutes after I had left Roberta on her way into the delivery room, and I worried that something was wrong.

As I put on a green hospital gown the nurse assured me everything was fine.

"You can go in to see your wife in a few minutes. We'll bring in your baby after we clean her up and weigh her. She's beautiful."

"Did you see her?" Robbie asked, as soon as I came through the door of the recovery room. "Is she okay? I didn't see her very much and I couldn't tell. They said she was perfect but is she? Is she okay?"

"She's wonderful, perfect, a beautiful little girl. She looks just like you," I said, leaving out the twisted head, trusting it would be gone the next time we saw "Melanie."

"Melanie Jessica," Roberta pronounced amidst both our tears as we hugged, and the salt from our eyes mixed with the salt of Robbie's perspiration as we buried our faces together. I held her like a doll, afraid to break her now that the birthing was over. Quite a contrast to the tug and pull battle we waged together in the labour room a half hour earlier. She was no fragile china doll then, but a strong and magnificent woman.

The nurse said they would bring Melanie to us for a few minutes but then Roberta needed to rest before they moved her to her own room. Then her mother could visit her. As soon as I knew both baby and mother were okay I ran back to tell Roberteen, "She's a girl!" and that Roberta was fine.

The doctors were right: Melanie was perfect when they brought her back to us, her head now a wonderful oval shape surrounding the tiniest nose (her mother's), lips like little paint brushes, and coal-coloured eyes, which they said would lighten in the days and weeks to come. She had a little hair and minuscule eyebrows that forecast her dark brown hair. She did look just like Roberta. I was so proud.

If someone had walked in that day with a contract that said Here are the conditions upon which you are given this child: no drinking; no smoking; no drugs; no gambling; no fighting; no working too long; no running away; no whatever. . . . I would have signed. I was in love, with two girls. Two babies.

In the real world, baby Robbie was afraid of baby Melanie, frightened of hurting her when feeding, bathing, and even holding the little seven-pound, thirteen-and-a-half-ounce bundle. "She's so tiny, and I'm so scared I'm going to do something wrong."

One night, I arrived at the hospital — probably direct from the celebrations at the pub after work — and found Roberta lying in bed with Melanie in her arms but tears streaming down her face.

"What?," I said, "I'm okay, I only had one or two and I hurried right here. I have to work."

"It's not that," Roberta said looking up at me with her tear-filled eyes, eyes that matched the moist dark pupils of our little angel lying with her on the bed.

"I want to go home . . . home to Timmins."

So once again, not dying means living, and, it seems, facing the consequences of what I have done. The fear of having go home and face Roberta, of having to tell her, not just that I fucked up again but that I have destroyed our lives, brings the tremors in my stomach up into my throat in a sour acidic bile. I am frozen in the solitude of my office, sitting in my desk chair and staring at the wall. I might wish to stay here forever but I know this office won't be a pleasant place to be tomorrow afternoon. Retribution in the form of an O.P.P. officer seconded to the Gaming Commission arrives at the next thirteen hundred hours, and I'd better be ready for it. What did Ken McMullen say? "You need to start thinking about how you are going to deal with this, Doug."

I pull myself up in my seat, open the bottom left-hand drawer of my desk and look down at the cash, the fourteen hundred dollars left from the Nevada deposit. Behind it are all the unfiled or doctored bingo, Nevada or charity casino reports — Officer Lennon's unholy grail — and the Royal Bank deposit books for the Leacock accounts. I take the files out of the drawer and place them by category around the desktop, like I would a project, the research for a story, and the plan for a campaign or the marketing of a special event. First, a situation analysis: What do we have here? In any of those other scenarios, my first step would be to review everything, so I do.

The bingo reports make three piles. The first: no deposit, no money — these are the latest forms, not filed with the City of Orillia. The second: deposit faked, no money, filed with the City of Orillia. The last pile: reports completed, deposit slips faked but eventually made, money in the bank and filed with the City of Orillia. This is the "oops, sloppy paperwork" pile that I hoped would pass any cursory examination when all the money was paid back. "We had to use the money for other expenses before we deposited it: sorry, we won't do it again." It was the pile I wished the other two piles to become, once I won my big jackpot.

The Nevada reports consisted of the same three piles, although somewhat smaller. Today's two-thousand-dollar reports aren't even completed yet. I make a mental note to move the money from the desk drawer.

The charity casino reports, the Monte Carlo events that Officer Lennon will want to see tomorrow, are, if that's possible, even more problematic. There are only three reports. One is from May, a two-day event where the proceeds were $6,500 dollars. The deposit slip was faked and the fudged report filed with the Ontario Gaming Commission. The deposit was never made, although the slips are prepared, ready for the big win. The operator, Mr. Casino, was paid its $6,000 in August, just after the Leacock Heritage Festival, putting the Royal Bank charity casino account into a $6,000 overdraft, before any money ever went into the account. The report from the second event, which took place at the beginning of September, was similarly gerrymandered: deposit not made; slip rigged; a fraudulent report filed with the O.G.C. but no payment made to Mr. Casino. The "win" — as they call it in the big casinos — from that event was just over $10,000 and it was *lost* at Casino Rama, by me, in less time than it took all of us to win it from a hundred other people at the charity event.

The third event was just last weekend so the report hasn't been completed. What Officer Lennon will be looking for in this case will be a copy of the Pit Boss' report and the deposit slips verifying the money was actually deposited, which to my increasing regret, it wasn't.

Now if I am really going to do a number on this "project," I have to quit the bullshit and look at the "good, the bad and the ugly." The good: umm . . . The bad: forgery — doctored documents and reports. The ugly: the Royal Bank statements for the last ten months (still hiding, cowering in the back of the drawer) showing that the alleged deposits have not been made.

Even a perfunctory routine audit — an oxymoron if I've ever

heard one — couldn't help but discover some forty to fifty thousand dollars in missing funds. Any conscientious independent analyst, at this point, even so early in the game, would be recommending *folding, flight or fire.*

Folding — Ken's option. *Flight* — has possibilities but it will mean leaving everyone else holding the bag. Roberta: alone, broke, and disgraced. Suicide would be kinder. Doug Bell: maybe he'd even get blamed as an accomplice instead of being recognized as the victim he really is in all of this. Melanie, Ken, *F.*, Bob, the list goes on. Add to it the charge of Grand Theft Auto, for my flight would have to be via the company van.

Fire. Arson. A criminal crime. Far from "borrowing" from the petty cash or bingo float, and awfully difficult to rationalize. Besides, it would be all for nothing anyway: bank records are also kept at banks and phoney reports with photocopies of phoney deposit slips are at the gaming commission in Toronto, if not in a neat file folder, then under the arm of one Constable Pat Lennon.

No flight, no fire. Which leaves only the recommended folding. Perhaps, I think, my rational hat on, but quickly the gambler recalls I never was much for folding. Maybe I should see if there any more cards to be played before, as Leonard Cohen put it, "giving up the holy game of poker."

I pile the reports back into the drawer, where they will await their doom. Not wanting to face my own, I start to wonder about how the police and the Ontario Gaming Commission found out. Maybe it is just a routine audit, I think, but can't give much credence to the thought. Occasionally, even when I was gambling, a moment of clarity would make me question how I would cover up a routine audit. Even more disturbing was the thought that no matter how big a win I had, I could not quietly pay back the money without arousing suspicion. The casino makes as much fuss as it can about its winners, so if I had a big jackpot win — like I needed — it would be all over the newspaper, all over town. Suddenly all the Leacock and Winter Carnival accounts are no longer overdrawn and bills are getting paid. "Just what did you do with that $80,000 jackpot you won, Doug?" I can hear my friends and enemies asking, not to mention Roberta.

Roberta. *How can I tell Roberta?* The very thought of her knocks me back into that despondent state where even movement hurts.

Ralph?

Cipolla's name is the only spectre I can summon who is powerful enough to push away the image of my devastated wife and get my blood flowing again. Ralph! Ralph! Ralph! Maybe Ralph? Possibly Ralph? *Dirty old Ralph, you bastard.* Maybe Jennifer, more of a spy than I or she realized, or than I am willing to accept, told Ralph about other money being used for my gambling from the Leacock accounts. It is possible. So is the fact Ralph himself could have drawn the same conclusions from his own desire for vengeance and had his suspicions confirmed when he heard about the Downtown Management Board money going to my gambling. "Douglas, Ralph is after your nuts," Dave Shaw had said.

"He may well have them," I confess to my unhearing confidant, who may join in the gelding once he knows how extensive our "family problem" is about to become.

Still, I wonder, how would Ralph get to the Ontario Gaming Commission, or even know to go there? He may have just gone to the police and then they called in the O.G.C.; obviously they are pretty closely linked. Casino Rama has an attachment of O.P.P. officers, not just patrolling around the casino, but actually inside, purportedly looking for cheaters and any infiltration by organized crime. Peering through those 530 video cameras, the "eyes in the skies," it wouldn't be too hard to observe, night after night, the frantic, whacked-out downtown manager from across the lake running desperately around the casino from machine to machine, game to game, and wonder, "Where the hell is he getting his money?" Even those four-in-the-morning stints when I felt practically alone, shuttered up, in my dream world — the cameras caught it all. Not that anybody will ever admit it. The last thing Ontario's casinos and their government masters want their customers, tourists and locals, to worry about is whether their play is being monitored by the province's law enforcement agency.

The best odds, however, are on the player who is involved directly in this ménage à trois — Mr. Casino. It is licensed by the Ontario Gaming Commission, the same way that charities like the Leacock Heritage Festival are. Darren and Mike would know who to call, and, God knows, they had reasons enough, everything from protecting their own licence after I admitted what I was doing to them to looking for their missing twenty-thousand dollars. This scenario doesn't leave Ralph out of the loop either. Given the small town that Orillia is, it is not inconceivable that Darren Burns called Ralph about our little meeting. If they weren't friends, they were, like all of us, certainly associates.[6]

How about the Casino? Maybe Ed called Casino President Bobby Yee about our meeting and he felt he had to call in the Gaming Commission. I don't believe Ed would do it, given the tone of our meeting and our relationship, but I don't know about

Bobby Yee. Of course this is all speculation because I don't know — and never will — know who called the cops. As for who told on me, I have absolutely no doubt: I told on myself.

I was always a good confessor. Oh yeah, at first I'd try to lie or weasel my way out, but once the chips were down, I'd spill my guts. Especially, I recall, if someone innocent was going to be blamed. A favourite threat of my father's was that others would share in the punishment, which usually involved the leather strap. As my sisters — older and younger — were usually my sinless co-accused, I was usually singing my guilt before the belt was out of the loops. The only time I recall having murder in my heart as a child was when my father was strapping my sisters. One night when we lived upstairs over the restaurant, Veronica and I were doing the dishes. Our kitchen was connected to the living room on two sides, one way through the dining room, and the other through a hallway beside the stairs, which led to the street and the restaurant below. I was 10 years old and Veronica was 12. She was washing; I was drying. As I dried a dish, I wandered over to the dining room corner to look into the living room and watch "Car 54" on television. You know: "Car 54, Where Are You?" It was a slow process but eventually the dishes got done. Veronica, unfortunately, also got caught up in the show at the opposite side of the living room, from the hallway corner. I couldn't see her and she couldn't see me. We both thought the water was running down the drain of the rinse sink. I didn't worry because I knew "Wonkie was there washing."

"I thought Dougie was there drying," Veronica pleaded. "I'm sorrieeee," she screamed as my father's lash struck her in my parent's bedroom. Back in the kitchen, my seething rage burned hotter than anything he had done to my ass. The tears and dance I did under his whipping arm were nothing compared to this stifling, wet-faced anger I bounced around with as he hit her over and over. "You fucker," I screamed, running down the hall to the bedroom door, "you fucker — leave her alone or I'll kill you." Stunned, my father stopped. I turned, ran back down the hall, around the painted banister, flew down the stairs three at a time and out into the night. Fortunately, the girls were seldom strapped.

For me, on the other hand, beatings were a way of life. Maybe I deserved them. Considering what I have done, I can hear some people saying, "Maybe he should have been whipped more often." But frankly, for a few years there, I don't think "more often" would have been possible.

I have no memory of lying and stealing, or being beaten by my father's strap before I was eight years old. Nothing terrible happened while we were living in Rockwood Court.

Stealing started in Milford, as did my running to escape. I would get up early in the morning, before everyone in the whole house, leave for the day and come back late at night to an inevitable and terrifying beating. The money I stole — quarters or dollars — was used to soothe my hunger and fears during those long, fugitive days. Not that I didn't have fun running and playing with kids in the woods — but the fun was always tinged with the guilt that I shouldn't be there and the fear of the punishment that faced me when I got home that night.

Father Callaghan at Saint Mary's used to tell us that anticipation was the greater part of joy. When you come from a big family, holidays like Christmas and Easter are celebrations eagerly anticipated and long remembered. The Milford Easter, when I was nine years old, lives on today at the edge of my consciousness like an echoing nightmare. It's not a beating I remember — although I imagine there was one — it was being kept in my room all that day, while my six brothers and sisters found and ate Easter chocolate, and enjoyed the holiday feast. *I no longer belonged.*

When we moved from Milford to East Saint John later that year, my behaviour hardly improved, although I did have a new childhood misconception about our life. I thought, because my parents owned a restaurant, that we were rich. How come I wondered, if we were rich, I didn't have toys like Alec? Alec Taylor was the kid from across the street, one holy terror, whose parents, who seemed a million years old, owned Kane's Corner Grocery. Alec was adopted by Mr. and Mrs. Taylor — "Now Alec Dear, don't yell at me please and tell your little friend to go home now, please Alec" — who were well into their fifties, and clearly needed to fill some lonely hole in their lives. They got more than they bargained for with Alec, who, while bribed with every toy and doohickey on the market in the nineteen-fifties, still terrorized and bullied his cowering parents every moment of every day I knew him. He was not a nice kid, but he had great toys.

I can still hear Veronica, my rescuer and counsel for the defense even then, pleading my case: "He takes it (a dollar, change off my father's dresser) because Alec Taylor always has money and he can't understand why we have nothing." Thanks for trying, Veronica, but it never saved me from my destiny under the belt. Around that time my father tried another tack that also haunts my waking and sleeping dreams.

For one of my lying and stealing crimes I was sentenced to

223

my room — after the beating — and told to take all my clothes out of my dresser drawers, as I didn't deserve to live with my family any longer. With my clothes piled on my brother's lower bunk, I sat for what seemed like hours waiting for my father to come with a bag or a box to cart me off to some God-knows-where home. Eventually my father opened my bedroom door and said, "Come on, fella, get yourself out here, we're going for a drive."

"What about my clothes," I cried, slinking back into my room, afraid of the swing of his hand on the back of my head if I passed by him while he was standing in the doorway.

"Never mind your clothes, we'll send them after you or just give them to poor. Where you're going you won't need these clothes," my father said angrily. "Get moving, mister."

"I'm sorry Daddy, don't take me away. I'll be good," I said. Tears streamed down my face as I passed out of room looking around the house for my mother and sisters to rescue me from this bewildering punishment that felt more like damnation than correction. But I was alone. This object lesson was for my benefit only. I scrambled my way down the stairs keeping a couple of feet ahead of my father's menacing hands.

"Get in the car, and not another word out of you or I'll give you something to cry about right here in the parking lot."

"Please, Daddy, I'll be good! I promise."

"It's too late for that, mister, we've had it with you. Now you're going somewhere where they know how to deal with little thieves like you."

As my father backed out of the parking lot, and turned, not towards town, but in the opposite direction, towards Loch Lomond, I knew where we were — where I — was going. The

Boys' Industrial Home. If you lived and went to school in East Saint John, the Boys' Industrial Home was a dark and arcane reformatory whispered about at the end of the schoolyard or behind the bleachers in the park.

"They have a machine that whips your bare arse until it's raw every week, just for being there," one kid said, who knew somebody's brother who was once on the inside. There were rumours of worse things they did to the kids, but to my ten-year-old mind it was all part of a harrowing netherworld little boys scared each other with far from the ears of their parents.

To have it brought into my real world, to believe I was being taken to this wicked institution that housed all kinds of evil, deranged bullies and sadistic, hooligan guards, frightened me to my core. How I kept from peeing my pants as my father pulled into the Industrial Home parking lot is a wonder.

"You stay in the car, you little bugger, while I go up and talk to them about taking you off my hands, and you make sure you stay there, too." He may have added the last threat fearing I would run, though he knew I was normally an early-morning runaway. There was nothing normal about this ordeal.

My father left me in the car and walked up the front door of this juvenile jail, and he knocked. In a moment a man, dressed in white, answered the door. The man stood listening to my father, who talked, looking and pointing back at me, making his case, I was sure, for my admission to hell. All I could see the other man do was nod his head as my father talked. Finally my father and the man finished talking, and he said something with the wave of his hand as my father turned to look and start walking back towards me. Was it *bring him to me?* Or *goodbye?* I couldn't tell, but then the man went inside and closed the door. As my father walked closer I saw him suppress a mocking smirk and I started to cry out loud and scream "No, no, no" because I knew it was all fooling. *All a sick-fuck of a game of fooling.*

At least now, if I go to jail, at 48 years old, I won't have to worry about some perverted guard or sex-starved inmate trying to fuck with anything beside my mind.

The light is flashing on my private line. I look at my watch — almost six o'clock. It's Roberta. How am I going to be able to face her? "Don't worry about it" sure as hell isn't going to wash.

Roberta told me: "I hated you in Sault Ste. Marie." We went there in June to attend an economic development conference as part of my investigation of other communities that had casinos nearby in anticipation of the opening of Casino Rama in Orillia at the end of July. Part of the conference included sessions on the economic impact of casinos and gambling, plus a visit across the border for a tour of Vegas Kewadin in Sault, Michigan, the casino owned by the Chippewa Tribe of Sault Ste. Marie, tribal relatives of the Chippewas of Rama. I had been at the casino over a year ago, four nights in a row, until I was broke every night and had to borrow to get myself back home.

I took my wife with me to the Sault this time because she had applied for a job at Casino Rama and she had little concept as to what the operation of a casino entailed. I knew she would put a crimp in my gambling style — perhaps I even wanted that — but even I didn't realize how little influence she would have on me. We arrived in Sault Ste. Marie in the middle of the night, having driven from Orillia with two other economic development officials. It was midnight when I left Roberta in the hotel and went across the bridge at the border to the casino. The last time I was here I didn't get past the slot machines and now I was determined I was going to play roulette, my favourite game, and blackjack, which I had since mastered in the charity casinos in Orillia and Barrie.

I had a terrible night at blackjack and I couldn't get near the one operational roulette table because of the crowd. By 3:00 a.m. I had lost all the money I brought across the border with me, around five or six hundred dollars. From experience I had left enough cash in the van for the toll fees to get back across the border. Roberta woke up as I came into the hotel room to get the rest of my money. I just told her to go back to sleep; I was down and I had to go back to win back what I had lost. "I can't afford to lose," I said, using true words to tell my lie at 3:30 in the morning. I went back to more bad luck at the casino and arrived back at the hotel at nine o'clock, sleepless and broke. No money for food, hotel bills, or even gas to get home. I showered quickly, ignoring Roberta's reproaches as I concentrated on the immediate crisis of getting money, not only to cover the cost of the trip, but also to get back to gambling. Poor Roberta. She had seen me out of control so often in the past eighteen months, not even the lunacy of my staying up all night surprised her. Of course she didn't know I was broke or that I had just lost $1,200 of somebody else's money.

I went down to the conference and borrowed a hundred dollars from City of Orillia development officer Joan Wilkinson until, I told her, I could get to a bank machine: "It was a tough night at the Casino." Of course there was nothing in the bank account, which was overdrawn by several hundred dollars from previous gambling. I had come to Sault Ste. Marie to win, to dig myself out of the hole. I couldn't afford to lose and I couldn't afford to quit. I had to get back in the game.

From a pay phone in the hotel lobby, I called my assistant at the downtown office and told her I was broke — no explanation needed. "Jennifer, go to the City" (the City of Orillia managed the payroll for my employers, the Downtown Orillia Management Board), "and get an advance on my next pay and wire it to me in Sault Ste. Marie."

A day of pins and needles, frenzied phone calls, and messages back and forth to Orillia was spent procuring the money. "It's a personal emergency," I argued with the treasury officials who were reluctant to issue the cheque, "Just forward Friday's pay, that's hardly an advance." I told Jen to just leave messages for me at the hotel front desk and I would call her back; I didn't want Roberta to know I was broke. It took all day to arrange. Then, due to forgetfulness, carelessness, or perhaps the fact that she did care, Jennifer's phone call went to my wife in our hotel room, saying the money had been wired to the Royal Bank in Sault Ste. Marie. *Shit!*

Fortunately no amount was mentioned and I was able to convince — or at least tell — my wife that I had only $300 wired up so that we wouldn't be short because I got carried away, had a rough night and lost a couple of hundred dollars. Obviously my lying was pathological. At this point I would say anything and do anything to stay in action. The lies were part of what made it so difficult for everyone else to see how severe I was hooked, to see that I had gone beyond the joking observation, "Doug is just being compulsive again."

228

Alcoholics. Everyone sees them falling-down drunk, and it's pointed out with varying degrees of insistence by wives, families, friends, and employers, "You better get help." My gambling was a secretive addiction, not readily apparent in its severity even to Roberta until I had progressed to the brink of disaster and beyond.

Roberta was exasperated, enraged, and afflicted, but resigned. Before we returned to the casino that night as part of a reception, I gave her $250 so we'd have the money, regardless of what I did, to pay the hotel and get home. I proceeded to gamble lightly, at least in my mind. To her I still looked like someone possessed, running from slot machine to slot machine and game to game. I took her back to the hotel at 10 p.m. and returned to the casino alone where I gambled until 4 a.m. and lost another $800.

In the morning I gave her the two hundred dollars I had left and fabricated: "See, I won last night and got half of what I lost back. In gambling that's the way it goes, up and down, and if you know what you're doing, up again." She took the money, but by this time it was all appearances. She didn't believe a word I said.

"Are you coming home for supper?" she asks when I finally screw up my courage to answer the phone.

"I have a couple of calls still to make," I say. "I don't feel much like eating, but I am coming home soon. We need to talk."

"I would say it's beyond talk," she return-volleys as she hangs up the phone.

"Little do you know, Rob . . ." I whisper, the words dying in my throat.

CHAPTER TWELVE

My impulse is to not tell Roberta, at least not until the absolute last **October 22, 1996 — 6 p.m.** minute, just on the chance — the slightest chance — that I can worm my way out of this catastrophe. I am loath to deal with any emotional confrontation, but especially when I know how badly it is going to end. She is already angry, exasperated, embittered, and depressed. Me, I am frightened, anxious, bewildered, and desperate. This volatile, visceral cocktail would be frightening under the best of circumstances, but these are the worst. Murder is possible. I could count on bloodshed if this were twenty years ago and I came in to the house with the news that I had just flushed our lives down a Casino Rama toilet bowl. Roberta was always cross and I had to be well fortified before I faced her wrath.

We went back to Timmins in August of 1969. Three children. The one in diapers, Melanie Jessica the newborn, was both adored and feared. Roberta, the very young mother, had awakened, only to find that her dream man was worse than penniless, and a duplicitous drunk. With him she had just parented an angel who scared the wits out of her. By far the youngest was the boy: immature, self-centred, and addicted to, among other things, alcohol. I thought my job was to get up each day, go, work hard — make whatever money was possible — just have a drink or three when I felt like it, come home to play with my beautiful daughter, whom I loved like air — *I was a great father* — when I had time, and make love to my beautiful but somewhat difficult wife when I wanted to, and oh, yeah, get high. That's who I was. That's what I asked from life. I did want to be a writer — a real writer — but since it didn't come instantly out of a bottle, a magic mushroom, or some other self-indulgence, I lacked the courage to pay the price. I could only continue to fake it.

The three kids moved in with mom and dad. Roy, that poor fellow who had answered the door to the long-haired hippie looking to find his misplaced girlfriend in the middle of the night, now had to call me "son." To his credit he buried his disappointment and went through all the motions of having a son-in-law in his life. I was welcome as long as I didn't talk during his hockey broadcasts or muck with his food: "These mashed potatoes are like soup — soup," he huffed after I pulverized the lumps and chunks before dinner one night. As the years passed most of the sins of the father — me — would be forgiven in the name of the daughter, for Grandpa loved the new cherub in his life, Melanie.

I went back to the newspaper in Timmins when I returned but I also had to work in a bar at nights to make ends meet. While that job interfered with the newspaper job, being a waiter paid more. I ended up kissing off the paper completely, slinging beer at night and working for Roberta's dad in his welding shop by day. I worked at an automatic welder that rebuilt mining car wheels and then I'd go to the bar half-blinded by something called "flashes" which felt like someone was sandpapering my eyeballs. Looking directly at the welding flashes, which were impossible to avoid on the automatic welder, caused this occasional condition. Tea bags on the eyes were the prescribed antidote, and were fortunately a staple in the Major household. But, tea bags were impossible to navigate with at Leone's Restaurant and Strip Bar, particularly while trying to count change out of one clouded eye and catch the Dance of the Seven Veils with the other.

I jumped from the Major Welding and Machine Shop into the bowels of the Pamour Porcupine Gold Mine and took my family out of the Major house into a small half-lot war zone on Wende Avenue, a block away. In the gold mine — the lowest-grade mine in all of Canada — I dreamed of high-grading riches and became obsessed with a mineshaft tragedy that happened 25 years earlier. As a Maritimer, I grew up with the haunting images of the Springhill Mine disasters of the 1950s. I remembered families waiting futilely outside the coalmine head frames: it was my first realization that not everything on television had a happy ending. Perhaps this explains my obsession with mining tragedy and the constant fore-boding I felt descending 2000 feet underground in the mineshaft cage. Since I still considered myself a writer, "researching for a novel" became my story as to what I was doing working in the gold mine. Even today I have a considerable folder of research including the blueprints of the "dog-legs" of the cage and several premature beginnings of a play called, what else, "The Gold Miner."

There are times when your palms sweat and your stomach churns in the underground shaft of a gold mine . . .

I became bedevilled by the Paymaster Mine Disaster and the happenstance that saved one miner from his certain demise. On February 2, 1945 sixteen men plunged 2500 feet down the Timmins Paymaster mineshaft, falling to their deaths inside the metal elevator cage. The hoisting cable broke and the emergency doglegs on the sides of the cage failed to bite into the timber guides to prevent its freefall. Thirty-nine-year-old miner Don Trench, for the only time in his life, missed his bus that morning, ending up a half-hour late and missing that ill-fated ride down the cage. Rescuers, including the lucky Don Trench, worked all day to retrieve the sixteen bodies from the crushed two-compartment cage. After an hour and a half of cutting through twisted metal with a blowtorch, the rescue team discovered three men still alive and thirteen crushed beyond hope. Sadly, even these three injured, cut, and maimed men would bleed to death while they were being transported in the wire baskets on the long and difficult 2500-foot climb up the laddered manway, their blood drenching the rescue crew pushing the baskets from beneath.

My novel was going to centre on twenty-four hours in the life of a fictionalized character who missed the cage and would bring illicit sex, violence, and high-grading into the story, in all of which, I am sure, Mr. Trench was not involved.

But if he wasn't a high-grader — stealing gold from the mines — I was. Not just as a metaphor for my life, either. Undeterred by my fool's gold escapade on my first day as a miner, I continued to try my luck, albeit at such a petty level — like so many of my crimes — that it was laughable even when the spoils were real. My jobs, as an engineering survey assistant and then as a surveyor, gave me more freedom to come and go underground than the normal miner had; thus, bringing gold ore to the surface and to my street locker was relatively easy. What was difficult in Pamour was finding any gold worth taking. High-grade by other gold mine standards didn't exist at Pamour Porcupine Mines. Of course this is why security was lax, and in my case, non-existent. Pamour officials were more concerned with workers stealing their tools than their gold ore. My welding father-in-law made me a rounded metal crushing pot, as well as a crushing tool, shaped like the mortar and pestle pharmacists used for mixing medicine, so I could separate the gold flakes from the quartz and granite rock. In the two and a half years I worked at Pamour, during two separate periods, I extracted only enough gold to make a single ounce, which I sold to an old Ukrainian man named Pete for twenty-five dollars in 1974. I also made a few souvenir magnified glass paper-weights, one of which sits in my saintly mother's living room. My rationalization then was "oh, everybody high-grades" and, as with gambling, I was sure they were all a lot better at it than I was.

In 1998, I wrote an article for the Northern Ontario newsmagazine *HighGrader* in which I compared our governments' addiction to my own:

> Today I believe that our Provincial Governments in Canada — and some municipal governments — are addicted to gambling. More accurately they are addicted to the money gambling provides. I believe they are exhibiting the same classic addictive characteristics of denial, rationalization, minimization, and delusion that I experienced in my compulsive gambling binge.
>
> I should make it clear that I am not opposed to gambling per se, any more than I am opposed to drinking alcohol. What I am opposed to, however, is the government being in the gambling promotion and

gambling expansion business. As with liquor, drugs, and tobacco, I feel government should be in the gambling control business.

Gambling like other potentially addictive and abusive pastimes has inherent problems. These need to be met with caution, awareness, and education. Not denial, rationalization, minimization, and delusion. Not confusion, double-speak, secret deals, and collusion.

The first step, as it is for all addicts, is to break through the veil of denial and get governments to admit there is a problem. John Ralston Saul[7], Canadian philosopher, and Governor General's Award winner, points out that in Canada "the governments of the citizen are now devoting themselves to the corruption of the citizen."

You may have noticed I never say "gaming industry." Well keep your eyes peeled because the government and the gambling industry never say gambling — the sanitized name is "gaming" — part of the newspeak.

Gambling is not a very nice business but it has been sanitized and sanctified by the gambling industry and our governments.[8]

My drinking became the cause of a constant battle between Roberta and me in the early 1970s. My side of the story was that everything would have been fine if she would just let me have one or two beers after work without making a fuss — then I'd happily come home to my waiting family. As it was, since I knew I was in for hell anyway, once I started, I always drank until I got drunk and could drink no more, ran out of money or friends, or more likely, the bars closed. Like little Dougie playing at end of Milford Road, I knew I was in for it when I got home, so I always stayed away as long as I could. Now I drank as much as I could before heading home with a confusing and intoxicating jumble of emotions: guilt, remorse, anger, and resentment. Like my father before her, Roberta was always waiting for me, and our verbal and physical interaction often became violent, usually with her hitting me. But, I confess there were times in my alcoholic fog that I slapped her and hurt her by pushing and grabbing. Did I abuse her physically? I didn't think so — but I recognize that my memory of the reality of those days is not a verifiable source. Of my later verbal and emotional abuse, I am certain.

Following these battles we would always make up on my promise that I would not do it again, that I would only drink at home, and even then have just a couple a week. How often I fell off this wagon is difficult to recall: suffice to say it was frequent, and usually around payday. Gambling was also part of these bi-weekly or monthly binges. It was normally bullshit poker in the bar or a shuffleboard game for money, but occasionally I'd end up in a poker game or at a "Millionaire's Night" stag, with its all-included booze, food and all-night card games.

"Where's your paycheque, Doug?" Roberta asked, accosting me at the door as I sheepishly dragged myself home after one of these crapulous losing nights, and I would spend the next several weeks struggling financially, begging forgiveness and promising never to do anything so stupid again. Until the next time.

Impulsively, and to Roberta's chagrin, I quit the mine in 1971 to work full-time as an organizer for the New Democratic Party, campaigning for MPP Bill Ferrier in the Ontario election against former Cochrane South Cabinet Minister, Wilf Spooner. Ferrier had first defeated Spooner in the previous election, with the help of a newspaper picture of Wilf sleeping in the Ontario Legislature. Working as a bar waiter at night, I would spend my days in the campaign headquarters and knocking on doors canvassing. A bonus, Roberta had to admit, was that being so busy, I didn't drink, and what money I did make was therefore safe from my inebriated betting. We won the election and I stayed sober through the victory party only to explode the next day, not prepared for or understanding the post-event letdown.

I went from working the election to helping organize the Timmins Winter Carnival, which at the time was little more than a booze fest during which we shocked ourselves sober with daily saunas and polar-bear dipping in the frigid Mattagami River. I went on to co-ordinate the Town of Timmins Diamond Jubilee celebrations throughout 1972, including the World Wrist-Wrestling Championships, the Ontario Amateur Boxing Championships, a Korean War Veterans Reunion, Timmins Homecoming Week and a Miner's Festival. One of the ways the committee financed its events was through a $10,000 Lottery, with the early-bird and the final draws live on the Timmins-based CFCL Television Station. The grand prize was $5,000, with a second winner for $3,000 and a third prize of a grand: considerable prizes for the pre-government lottery days of 1972. We also had an early-bird draw for a thousand dollars to encourage everyone to get their tickets before the summer events. The early-bird draw was held in May; but when we went to make the final draws in August, we discovered the television station had destroyed all the tickets, thinking the draw was over. We had to postpone the draw date and go out publicly offering everyone who bought a ticket, or said they did, the opportunity to fill in a new free ballot. When we finally made the draw at City Hall in October, one of the members of the committee, City Alderman Mike Doody, was asked to draw the ticket for the third prize of $1,000. "God," he said, when he saw the ballot, "What else can go wrong!" He had drawn his own wife's name. We'd had enough grief with our initiation into the lottery business: Mike quickly drew another name and Charlene Doody was out a thousand dollars.

I wondered what I would have done had it been Roberta's name pulled out of the drum because by the time the draw was made, the year and my drinking had taken their toll and we were separated. In my ongoing debate as to whether my drinking was the problem or Roberta was the problem, blaming my wife won. One night I stopped going home, taking a room upstairs over one of my watering holes until the 1972 federal election campaign found me living with the former New Democrat MP, and now once again candidate, Murdo Martin. This was the same man whose political demise newspaper editor John Wilson was celebrating when I first came to town in 1968.

The United Steelworkers of America hired me on contract, first to help with the NDP election campaign and then to carry out a survey of the work force of Texasgulf — they wanted me to see if there was any chance in hell they would sign up to join the miners' union. While in the end most of my surveying was done in the various Timmins bars, the conclusion was the same as it would have been if I had used conventional techniques. *No* chance in hell. Texasgulf was a massive copper and zinc mine built on a deposit discovered north of Timmins in 1964 — just in the nick of time for the town, as the major gold reserves of the Hollinger and MacIntyre Mines were quickly being depleted. The anti-union base metal producer kept its workforce happy by staying a considerable distance ahead of the gold mines in both wages and benefits.

If I thought Roberta was difficult to live with, she proved intolerable to be separated from. From my perspective at the time, she made my life miserable over support, over access to Melanie and of course, over my continued and accelerating drinking. Roberta's point of view would certainly be that I didn't give her enough money to live on or to provide for my daughter; and that I was always drinking, so she worried about putting Melanie in my care. After six months of separation, my work with the union complete, I left Timmins for New Brunswick, basically abandoning her and the little girl I loved more than air, but, apparently, less than alcohol.

My memories of New Brunswick are a haze of Happy Hours at the Cosmo Club and of solitary walks smoking marijuana. My older brother David blamed me, years later, for his marriage troubles, saying I introduced him to grass during an extended visit at his home in Moncton, just before I returned to Timmins. He might be right: it's a visit of which I remember very little other than having a torrid affair with his maid after he introduced both of us to porno films.

That summer I also had an affair with a wonderfully exciting woman named Judy, who was the wife of my oldest brother's partner in a travelling magic show. Judy assured me — correctly it seems — that she and her magician husband had an open relationship that allowed for such extramarital holidays. Perhaps it was my time with Judy, flogging magic show tickets in the Town of Stellarton, another Nova Scotia coal mining town just down the road from Springhill, that gave me the sexual awakening that Roberta could never understand or accept.

In Fredericton I shared a house with a couple of law students (I couldn't believe how hard they studied) and took an extension course in Canadian Literature. I wrote and sold one newspaper article to the *Fredericton Gleaner*, an exposé about another nocturnal wanderer I encountered on the streets more often than I could believe. It was called "Everything you wanted to know about Skunks."

In my fantasy world, this was the year I took off work to try to make it as a writer. The skunk story was, appropriately, the only thing I had published.

Near the end of 1973, my life completely in chaos due to my never-ending one-two regimen of booze and weed, I called home and escaped back to Timmins and my family.

For the next year I returned to underground surveying at the Pamour Mine and tried once again to take the pledge to stop drinking, only to fail with monthly regularity — and to fail to deal with all the feelings of regret, remorse and guilt just made me want to drink some more. Roberta, jealous over the year we spent apart, was unable to control her anger and resentment, making our lives and Melanie's life completely miserable. At least that was the excuse I used to justify not coming home for a year one night at the beginning of 1975. The fact that I was being considered for the job as a shift-boss and that mining was beginning to become my career path by default added fuel to my flight.

I ran away to London, Ontario, where my sister Veronica was now living with her own alcoholic husband. Shortly after I arrived, whether through inspiration or synchronicity, Veronica decided she'd had enough of her abusive relationship and I helped spirit her and her two young children away in the night and into their own apartment. I got a job as an instrument operator for a land survey office in London and got involved in an amateur theatre group with a neurotic director named Peter North. I did a little script re-writing, and a lot of drugs.

At a pool party one night with Peter and the cast, bombed out of our minds, I broke my big toe on the concrete side of the pool while chasing a water polo ball across the grass. Unable to work in the fields and construction sites, I lost my surveying job just in time to take on the position, as "a seasoned election organizer from Northern Ontario," of Campaign Manager for the NDP in London North. My candidate, David Warren, was an acknowledged homosexual before it was acceptable to admit such things in politics, and I found myself immersed in the gay community of London. For me, only two things of significance happened during this campaign and both happened not in London, but in Toronto. At a pre-campaign meeting of all Ontario NDP candidates and campaign managers, party leader Stephen Lewis was the keynote speaker. Before his speech, I was out in the hallway using a telephone and watching him prepare to make his entrance into the room. I soon realized he was trying to psych himself up for his speech, and there, before my eyes (though he didn't know that), Stephen Lewis made himself cry. They were tears that I saw several times during that "Tomorrow starts today" campaign on television and back in London as Lewis trotted out the victims of all manner of social problems and demonstrated his sensibilities. It was a scene that helped assuage my conscience two years later when I jumped the political fence in Timmins to work on the campaign team of a young lawyer friend running for the Conservatives against my old NDP comrades.

My other significant happening also involved a relationship with the NDP leadership, in this case my older-woman affair with the ex-wife of an NDP federal leadership candidate, who she described as "a real bastard." She was about forty-five and I was twenty-seven, but she was incredible in bed, ranking up there with Judy in helping to develop my sexuality.

The rest of the year I had one of the greatest writing jobs of my life as the senior staff writer for an urban affairs newsmagazine in London called *The Satellite*. The pièce de résistance of this job was that the magazine was a monthly. Trained as a daily news reporter with deadlines every morning I found the monthly deadline a luxury, leaving me a great deal of time for my other pastimes. I smoked at least a ton of grass that year and even tried a few hits of LSD, something I hadn't done since 1968. I found it more than a little intense and frightening.

In the spring of 1976, during one of my phone calls to Melanie, Roberta told me she wanted to come to London to visit me, which she did, and I had an affair with my wife — drugs and sex — just like we had in 1968. It was great. In July my daughter told me she wanted me to come visit her as her birthday present. I hitch-hiked to Timmins for the party — she was seven — and we made the decision that I was coming home for good. I thumbed back to London, packed up my life and hitched a ride back to Timmins — all within twenty-four hours. I am not sure if my speed was a symptom of my desire to get back home or my need to vacate the screwed-up life I had in London.

In an effort to make a fresh start I declared personal bank-ruptcy to stop the tax department garnishees that had been a plague on my income over the last few years once the tax depart-ment caught up with me.

I went back to the *Timmins Daily Press* as the City Hall Reporter and stayed there for the next few months until I was approached to become the editor of the weekly *Timmins-Porcupine News* where I began to make a name for myself as a lethal columnist: "Doug Little's poison pen," union leader Peter Malenchuk called it.

My drinking was not as bad as it had been in London, but soon it picked up again as an irritant in my relationship with Roberta, and then a new element entered into the equation. The weekly newspaper editor's job came with a company car. At 28 years old, I got my father-in-law to teach me how to drive. On the third try, I finally was able to stop at the stop sign at the corner of Third Avenue and Spruce Street in front of the Timmins train station, and I got my driver's licence.

I only drove drunk once. The City of Timmins' outside workers were on strike in a particularly bitter winter labour dispute. Essential snow plowing on the main roads was still being done but the city was almost paralyzed by the snow that was piling up everywhere. In a normal winter Timmins had six-foot snow banks — with the strike it was a city of tunnels. The council appealed to local contractors to come forward to help clean up the mess. A home-made bomb had already exploded under a front-end loader as part the dialogue, so everyone expected trouble. City Hall became the command post for the clean-up operation. It was to be an all-night campaign and there was a party atmosphere to it. Contractors, councillors, and department heads came and went throughout the bitterly cold night. The alcohol flowed freely and free alcohol was an old friend of mine. As a reporter, at receptions and conferences and after council meetings, I seldom paid for drinks. There was always a politician willing to buy the next round. I started out with vodka and orange juice: Roberta would never know I had just one, or two. After three, I got angry that she *would* know: *I might as well get smashed.*

As I drove around checking on the snow removal, the press car was surreally floating forward through the snow-covered streets, drifting through a smoky haze that was a combination of the frost on the windshield, the whiffs of frozen condensation from any heat source in the forty-below weather and the murkiness in my brain. Fortunately I didn't harm anyone and I wasn't caught. It was the last time alcohol was ever allowed in Timmins City Hall.

In the spring of 1977, I left my editor's job to work on the Ontario election campaign full-time for the Conservatives. I was doing — to borrow a term from my daughter's figure skating — my own double jump. I was jumping out of the newspaper before I was pushed out due to my drinking and I was hopping the political fence, a move correctly characterized by my new political enemies on the left as opportunist rather than philosophical. As Bob Dylan said in his 1976 hit song about boxer Rubin "Hurricane" Carter: "It's my work, I say; And, I do it for pay."

About the same time, I made my first feeble attempt to get help with my drinking addiction by attending a couple of Alcoholics Anonymous meetings. I went to placate Roberta in one of my guilt-ridden, morning-after, falling-off-the-wagon despondencies. But, between how busy I was with the election campaign and how much Roberta hated me being out of the house anyway, it was easy to say "I'm okay, I don't need to go to those meetings anymore." As I did in 1971, I stayed sober through the election-victory party, but the next day I exploded and ended up in a bar.

After the election I spent a couple of weeks helping the newly-elected Member of Provincial Parliament, Alan Pope, set up his constituency offices and then ended up going back to my fallback career, surveying on a construction site for a company called Praise Building Corporation. It was a subdivision being developed as "God's work" by a couple of evangelical fanatics. Their morning on-site business meetings began on their knees, which is exactly where the project took them within a year. As in so many other places in this hard-rock mining region, "God" had put bedrock where Praise Building's plans called for roads and foundations. The cost of drilling and blasting for the streets drove the company and its faithful backers into bankruptcy, but not before their high-paying construction wages fuelled the expansion of Melanie's figure skating lessons as well as my final few flings with alcohol.

Construction workers were not the ideal peer group with which to attempt abstinence from alcohol, but then again, for me, neither were editors and reporters, or lawyers and politicians. Over the approximately ten months that Praise Building Corporation existed I drank less than once a month, invariably on payday. I drank two days before Christmas, but not wanting to ruin the holiday — which would have been unforgivable — I didn't stay at the bar all night. I went home, half in the bag, and faced a milder version of the wrath of Roberta as well as the absolute torture of having to push a shopping cart around the mall semi-sloshed.

In AA, they say, "If you can't remember your last drunk, you haven't had it." I remember February 3rd, 1978, in minute detail. It was unusual in that it was the second time I went drinking within a week — by then, there was usually a month or two between my benders — and I ended up drinking when I had sworn, not only to Roberta, but to myself, that I wouldn't. As I had no car I pooled with one of the other construction workers who wanted to stop and have a couple of beers, and cash his cheque at the South Porcupine tavern on our way home. "No," I argued, "I have to get right home after work, I promised my old lady. She'll kill me if I stop and have a drink. I'm still in the doghouse for the last time."

"Don't drink, then," the burly heavy equipment operator said. "You don't even have to come in if you don't want to; I won't be that long."

I'd just drink pop, I told myself. Besides, it would give me a chance to cash my cheque so Roberta wouldn't know exactly how much I made and I could salt some away. I sat down with the other "boys" and being who I was and where I was, I ordered a vodka and orange. *I'll just have one.* Of course that led to two and three, and soon I was being reluctantly dragged out of the bar by my driver who wanted to go home to Timmins. For me it was too late to go home: my inebriation impossible to mask, I had to keep drinking. I transferred bars along with some of the other guys and proceeded to pontificate on politics, religion, and marriage throughout the night, moving from table to table and bar to bar, to wherever there was a familiar face in this town where I'd lived and drank, off and on, for nearly ten years.

The next day I remembered that I almost got in a fight in one of the bars and recalled walking smashed along the streets looking for some poor — and obviously weak — soul upon whom I could take out my anger. Fortunately I didn't find anybody. When I got home, Roberta, doing what I always told her she should do, ignored me and made like she was sleeping. Of course I knew what she was thinking and woke her so I could argue in my defence, precipitating the kind of verbal brawl I remembered from my Russell Street home twenty years earlier. Now Melanie was eight years old — almost the same age as I was when a punch in the stomach told me I no longer belonged and that I should run like hell — and she no longer slept through the wars. I knew, in more ways than one, I was about to lose her for good.

The next day I felt so bad, so despairing, I just had to do something to alleviate the pain and give myself, and my family, some hope. I picked up the phone and called Pete H., who I'd met a year earlier during my first visit to AA. Ironically, he was the father of a kid I almost got busted with ten years earlier for marijuana possession when the R.C.M.P. (the narcs as we called them) had a snitch among the kids on the street. Roberta and I had been sitting in the Paradise Restaurant, me with a small chunk of hashish in my breast pocket, when, by chance, I turned sideways in my seat and saw the narcs coming through the restaurant door in time to first fumble and finally swallow the hash before they grabbed me. Joel was not so fortunate. The police found a dime — ten dollars worth — of hash under his table and said they saw him throw it there. The police let Roberta go after searching her purse but took me back to their detachment office, a house-like building in the city's north-end, along with Joel. I can still hear Joel's father yelling at him through the walls, as I am sure my father would have yelled had he been there, and had I not had the luck to see the narcs coming. In what was an insanely ignorant and punitive period of judicial folly Joel received a one-year jail term for a first offense of simple possession of a ten-dollar chunk of hashish. The few times, years later, that I saw him after that night, I thought it had destroyed his life.

Pete picked me up and took me back to an AA meeting, and

though I still believed I had more of a wife problem than a drinking problem, I came to accept, as well as admit, that I was an alcoholic. February 3, 1978, was the last day I ever drank or did drugs. I was twenty-nine years old.

Now, almost nineteen years later, I remember believing then — quite fallaciously — that I was what we called a "high-bottom drunk" because I quit before ending up in the hospital, jail, or on skid row. Ha! In 1967 I ended up living in a room on John Street in west downtown Toronto, which may be a stylish area today, but back then was as close to skid row as I ever want to get. The apartment where I lived in downtown London seven years later was just a step up; the low-life I hung around with, a step down. I avoided jail by fluke, and the ulcer that grew out of my drinking was the precursor of the heart attack I would have at forty-three, five years younger than my alcoholic father was when he had his. Now as I sit here in my office, the absurdity of my current predicament hits me like a slap: "I'm riding the garbage truck the rest of the way to the dump."

In the Catholic church one of the Stations of the Cross — that penitent journey of my childhood contrition — depicted the women of Jerusalem weeping and wiping the blood and sweat from the face of Jesus Christ as he suffered on the road to his Calvary. One of those saintly women, the one with the cloth, was named Veronica. Hey, not that I mean to compare myself, or my misadventures, to Christ or crucifixion (I am quick to acknowledge I am no innocent martyr), but I need to hear my Veronica's soothing voice.

"Hi, Veronica, it's your little brother, Dougie," I say into the phone trying to summon her familial instincts for the calamitous news I am about to tell her.

"Hi, Doug," she answers with her characteristic exuberance. "Our sister Mary is here and we're having a bit of supper, just the two of us. Bobby is out on a call."

"Veronica, I am in major trouble. I am going to go to jail. My gambling . . ."

"Oh, no Dougie, what have you done?" Veronica asks in alarm, the joy in her voice dropping like a curtain.

"The police just called. They want to do an audit of my Leacock Heritage Festival books . . . tomorrow," I tell her, measuring my words so they will fit in between the gaps of emotion breaking up my voice. "They're going to find I owe — I took to gamble — probably about seventy to eighty thousand dollars. Most of it is from Leacock, but there is also some from the Winter Carnival and from the Downtown. The Downtown Board knows about the gambling and they say they want to help me."

"Does Roberta know yet?"

"No, I'm still at the office," I answer. "I have to go home soon but I don't know how I can tell her. It will kill her, if she doesn't kill me first."

"Is there any way of getting the money and putting it back before they do the audit?" Veronica asks again, utilizing the parenting techniques she learned so well raising her and her second husband Bob's five children. She has also carried on with her childhood role as the surrogate mother for most of our brothers and sisters; our own mother has her hands full, as she always did, with our father, except now instead of his addictions and idiosyncrasies being out of control, it's his mind with his Alzheimer's disease.

"No . . . I don't know," I answer, as I automatically look towards the incriminating desk drawer, wishing it would just disappear and me with it. "I have been looking for months, that's why the amount is so high now, I've been betting more and more trying to win back what I already lost, so I could put it back." Veronica is well aware of my frantic search for money since more than once I have called her looking for a bail-out, but as with everyone else, I never fully levelled with her about how much I owed or how bad my gambling was getting.

"You're not going to win your way out of this, Doug," she says sadly, knowing she is pulling away my shroud of self-denial and striking at my already damaged heart.

"No, I know," I answer. "Now I'm trying to talk my way out of it and force myself to stay away from the casino, because right now I'd rather hide there for the rest of my life than face Roberta with this."

"It's an expensive place to hide," Veronica says. After forty-eight years, give or take a couple of decades when I hid even from her, Veronica knows me better than I know myself.

"Yeah, I know; and I haven't got the money to prove it."

"Doug, are you okay?" Veronica asks, perhaps worrying now more about my head than my heart. I am sure that on this day everybody — Officer Lennon and Ralph Cipolla excepted — was worrying about my heart seizing and me literally dying in front of their eyes.

"I'm okay," I say. "I'll be okay."

"Doug, Mary and I are going to drive up. Maybe we can help with Roberta."

"Okay," I answer resignedly, realizing this means I have to tell Roberta tonight, rather than at the last minute in the morning when I'd tell her to pack her bags and run, or maybe not tell her and let her read about it in the newspaper — "Downtown Manager Arrested — Stole $80,000 to Gamble." Or on the radio: "This is Janice Lee with a CFOR up-to-the-minute news bulletin: Doug Little, Downtown Orillia's flamboyant manager and festival organizer — Mr. Downtown — was arrested today on charges of embezzlement. Police say they have proof Little gambled away $80,000 in stolen funds — *not to mention his life, the turkey.*"

How different these imaginings are from the "It's A Wonderful Life" fantasies I once entertained. I imagined how I would explain I was addicted to gambling, live at a news conference, and there would be a spontaneous outpouring of sympathy and community campaigns to help raise the money to repay what I took. Not that there isn't some sympathy; Ken's reaction and that of the DMB are evidence that people will be sympathetic — some of them, anyway — but nobody is going to say, "The poor schlep, let's kick in to bail him out." Mostly, there will be disbelief.

When I left Soldiers' Memorial Hospital after my heart attack in 1991, I had to go from room to room on the Harvey One wing to give away all the flowers and plants that had been sent to me. Get Well flowers and gifts from city council, the chamber of commerce, Orillia Convention & Visitors Association, my downtown board, the *Packet & Times* newspaper, *Orillia Today* newspaper, CFOR Radio, the Orillia Opera House, and Ontario Downtowns, as well as flowers and books from businesses and friends in Orillia. Stored away in a Downtown Orillia plastic shopping bag,

I have fourteen gift cards as well as 42 Get Well cards, several signed by groups of colleagues, volunteers, and friends. There are cards from across Ontario, from other downtown managers, festival organizers, and entertainers. Bill Powell, from Hamilton's Festival of Friends (who helped start Festivals Ontario in 1986), wrote me a note:

> *What the hell are you doing to yourself? A heart attack — I thought a tough old nut like you didn't have a heart. Stress will do it good buddy.*
>
> *I think the job description for a festival co-ordinator should include the phrase "hide like rhino" or "Valium tolerant." Anyway let's run a stress workshop at the next Festival's Ontario meeting.*
>
> *I hope you take care of yourself and not drop out altogether. You are too valuable a man to lose.*

Among the cards I found one that said: "Our lives have just begun. You will feel well and strong soon, and we will do all the things we love to do." It was signed: "Love, always & forever. Robbie."

I first got my appetite for alcohol, women and writing while I was studying to be a priest. At Saint Mary's College there was a student newspaper, *Scholacta*, which came fully to my attention and that of my classmates with the publication of an article by a First Arts student, John Doyle, a brain from Newfoundland. "No Niners," the headline asserted, the article arguing that thirteen-

and fourteen-year-old boys were not mature enough to make an unencumbered decision to become a priest. As we likely hadn't even reached puberty, the elder Doyle argued, how could we make the commitment to celibacy that the priesthood required? Although we only vaguely understood the concepts of puberty and celibacy, we "Niners" were damn well outraged that this upstart Newfie dare judge us as unworthy to be priests. Of course he hadn't, but since the headline attacked our very presence at Saint Mary's, we responded with indignation, anger, and rhetoric. However inadequate our response was, the process fascinated me. I was captivated by the idea of being able to say what I thought, whether right or wrong, and to have it printed in a newspaper or magazine which somehow transformed my words, giving them a force I didn't even recognize when I wrote them. It is an impression that has stayed with me my whole life. During that grade-nine year and in the next two I spent at St. Mary's, the monthly newspaper was one of the projects I worked on, even if it was just collating and stapling the issues together. When I finally made up my mind that the priesthood was not for me, I felt no hesitation: I told everyone I was going to be a writer.

I may have had my first drink, like normal people, in the confines of my parents' home. If I did, I don't remember it. My memories of alcohol at home are memories of crisis and violence. My mother hated my father's drinking so he did it away from home. I didn't know he was an alcoholic. I just thought he was a bully. He was someone I had to stay away from as much as I could. Running from this pain worked. Maybe if I had understood that alcoholism was the cause of his nastiness I would have been reluctant to try drinking myself. However, I have heard many alcoholics say they *never* wanted to be like an alcoholic parent and then wind up exactly that way in spite of their best intentions.

The purveyor of my first remembered drink was "Uncle Paul," a happy drunk and the bachelor uncle of my college friend Paul Kennedy. It was during my sixteenth summer, between grades ten and eleven, on one of the many nights Paul and I stayed at his uncle's place in Saint John. We both worked in the maintenance department of St. Joseph's Hospital, jobs with the Sisters of Charity that we had as fringe benefits of our being minor seminarians. We got drunk that night, and sick. The next thing I remember about drinking and intoxication was the two of us sneaking the wine in the cell-like rooms we called the "crypts" that were used each morning to say Mass by the priest-teachers at St. Mary's College. Then there was sniffing carbon tetrachloride in the college darkroom. But that night at Uncle Paul's was another watershed, for after that good-time drunk my interest in St. Mary's College and the priesthood started to wane. I had learned of another escape, or two.

In the middle of grade eleven, at Christmas time, I was seduced by Nancy Landry, a girl I had met at a Catholic high school dance. Nancy introduced me to the intoxication of infatuation and sexual fantasy. All I did was touch her bare breasts. But, for the Catholic boy who, in grade four, threw rocks at the guy next door when he told me my parents fucked, it was incredibly exciting. Not unlike my other compulsions. For the next three months, our two imaginations combined to create a feverish letter-writing romance that had even the mailman blushing as he delivered her perfume-soaked letters to the holy school along the Saint Lawrence River. The priests, still opening and reading our mail, were beside themselves — at first, I am sure, with amusement. They soon grew impatient and exasperated, though, as Nancy's verbal titillations and my excited responses continued week after week, even after I was admonished to end the escapade or to at least feign discretion. Instead, I mounted a human rights campaign against the opening of our mail and slept every night with Nancy's perfumed envelopes beneath my pillow in the all-boys' dormitory.

The priests got to say "We told you so" when my "true love" Nancy nonchalantly wrote me to tell me she was getting married and for me to have a good life as a priest. A "Dear John" letter — perfumed!

At the end of Grade Eleven, the priests and I decided I needed to take a year off — to see if I really wanted to become a priest. Of course, I told my mother it was my decision, setting myself up for her wrath because she wanted me to go back. By the end of the summer, my reintroduction into the increasing chaos of my family's home, combined with my own drinking, had me begging to go back. I was greeted with a firm "No — take the year to decide." I had lost that home, family, community, and school, leaving only my confused reputation behind.

Veronica's promise that she and Mary will come up tonight to help deal with Roberta means that I have to go home and tell Roberta the whole truth before they arrive. As nervous as I am of her reaction, I cannot abide the thought of anyone else hearing directly from my mouth the tale of lies, deception, stealing, and cover-up that I am going to have to spread at

Roberta's feet. As much as I dread her subsequent hatred and possible violence, I also fear the revulsion of anyone else who hears the whole truth.

As I pack my bag to head home from the office, perhaps for the final time, I look around to see what I should take with me.

I settle on the fourteen hundred dollars from the desk drawer.

CHAPTER THIRTEEN

I give my neigh-
bour the banker
the finger as I
walk from the van

October 22, 1996 — 7 p.m.

into the house, mouthing to myself: "Thanks for the phone call
heads-up, George." His bouncing my overdraft — the meteor that
started this star-crossed day — seems like a lifetime ago. I know it
is my own fault, but it feels good to give someone else shit for a
moment. Besides, I am about to hit the motherlode of shit. Tuffy
comes padding across the floor to greet me. If he could talk I
know he'd warn, "The woman is in one mean mood." I could
sense it on the phone. Now, she is sitting in the kitchen at the
small two-seat breakfast table where we have all our meals except
for the once or twice a year when we use the oak dining-room set
we bought after we moved into this house. Interestingly, that
move came right on the heels of my heart attack. Moving was
another one of those things that Roberta just did, figuring I wasn't
interested and thus not telling me until it was *fait accompli.*

One day in a session, psychiatrist Mark Filipczuk will explain to
me that a woman has an instinctual need to feel secure, and she
has difficulty expressing affection or sexual responsiveness if she
does not have this basic need looked after. Men, on the other

259

hand, and some men in particular, have no need for security and enjoy an element of risk in life. They do, however, have a deep need to feel wanted and loved. When that love is not forthcoming, these men tend to isolate, fearing rejection, and look for other avenues of self-expression and pleasure, often in risk-taking.

"Your dinner is in the oven. What took you so long to get home?" Roberta asks as I climb the stairs and head down the hall to my room. I hate things in my pockets once I am home — keys, change, casino chips, whatever, everything goes on the dresser except my handkerchief and my Otrivin. Have I mentioned my screwed-up sinuses and my 25-year addiction to Otrivin and Dristan nasal sprays? It drives my heart doctors crazy. But they don't have to sleep with a facial mask over their nose to breathe, which is difficult when your nose is always plugged.

"I had to make some calls and go over a few things for tomorrow," I answer from my bedroom. She says I mumble anyway so it probably doesn't matter if she can hear me. Roberta and I have lived separate lives for many years — I cannot remember how many years it has been since we made love. Since my heart attack in 1991, I could count the times on one hand, and on a couple of hands for years before that. Our drift apart was pretty well determined almost as soon as we got back together in the seventies when we declared a truce on passion and love in order to raise Melanie and provide for her.

"What's this Johnny guy calling here about, Doug? And don't give me that bullshit about meeting him at a charity casino," she says, looking at me with sunken and tired-looking eyes, her lids lined in red like so many times before. "This guy is scaring me."

"You don't have to worry about him any more, he's all paid off. That's the truth," I add, an attempt to separate this statement from the other things I have said to her that were lies, lies about Johnny and so many other things. Gambling and lying seem to be two sides of the same coin. Heads you gamble, tails you lie. You lie about how much you gamble, how often you gamble, how long you were at the casino, how much you lost, how much you won, how much you took with you, where you got the money, and what you did to get there.

"What do you mean he's all paid off? Paid off for what? Who is he?"

"He's a loan shark. *F.* introduced him to me a couple of months ago when I needed money real bad to pay back some more money at work, you know, money I took for gambling." I think this may be as good a place as any to start; at least it begins on a positive note. "Anyway, *F.* paid him off, so we don't have to worry about him anymore."

"How could you do that?" Roberta starts to yell, surprising me with her intensity. She's hardly heard anything yet. "He has our telephone number. Does he know where we live? How could you put your family in this kind of danger?"

I never thought I was putting anyone in danger when I borrowed the money earlier this year. That's it — I never thought — I just wanted the money. The quick fix. Christ, I even tried to leverage old Johnny in June when I called him to tell him I was in trouble and needed to borrow another $20,000, quick, and this time I'd be willing to pay loan shark, err . . . — I didn't use those exact terms — high interest rates. Johnny's answer made me think I was dealing with Canada Trust.

"No, I never lend money to anyone until the first loan is paid off," he said, and hung up the phone.

"There was no danger," I lie again. "He was a friend of *F.*'s who loaned me some money at a time when *F.*'s cash flow was too low for him to lend it to me. I was only paying three-percent interest, for Christ sakes, that's lower than the bank. Anyway, Johnny is the least of my problems tonight." I look around the kitchen, trying to find a place from which I am going to tell her, a place where I won't feel like a caged lion or a trapped rat. The entrances to the kitchen are on either end of the table Roberta is sitting at. Her back is to the outside patio door, and the other side empties into the hall. The rest of the kitchen is like a box, affording no escape unless I plan to do my dive through the window trick. I opt for the seat opposite her at the table and sit down to deliver the news to my wife of twenty-seven years (give or take a few) — the news that our life in Orillia, and maybe anywhere, is over.

"You're in trouble again, aren't you? Just like I said. Your gambling is . . ."

"Roberta, wait. Let me tell you before I lose the nerve to tell you. You need to hear this and decide what you are going to do. My advice is for you to pack up your clothes, hop in your car tomorrow morning, and drive back to Timmins. Get out of here."

"Get out of here?" She yells, her eyes welling up with tears. I hate it when she cries. "Why would I get out of here, this is my home, this is Melanie's home. Timmins is not my home."

"The police called me this afternoon," I say calmly, a contrast to her hysterics but then I've already had a couple of hours for my emotional bingeing. "They are coming to do an audit of the

Leacock Festival books. They are going to find out about the money I took. I'll probably be arrested. It is going to be splashed all over the media. You don't want to be here for that."

"The money you took? What money? Is that what you've been using to gamble? Night after night when you tell me you've been winning?" Roberta's first reaction to most things has always been anger but it's an attestation to her mellowing that I haven't yet had my face slapped or hair pulled sitting this close to her delivering such devastating news.

"I owe a lot of money around the office. Money to Leacock from the bingo funds . . ."

"Bingo? You told me you quit bingo last year after we borrowed the money from our insurance and my father. " She is now crying as she speaks, the tears are running down her face, a little remnant of her eye mascara creating a black shadow under her eyes.

"I'm not playing bingo, for God's sake. I'm at the Casino, I'm at the Casino almost every night. Who the hell needs bingo when we have a mega-casino just ten minutes across the lake!"

"Where did you get this money? How are the police going to know?" Roberta asks through her veil of tears. I'm looking at the clock and thinking we sure could use St. Veronica and her sacred soothing cloth right about now.

"The money is from, mostly from, the Leacock Festival accounts. It's money from their bingo account, the bingo float and deposits that I gambled trying to win back other money that I owed. I have always owed money. Even after your father's loan I wasn't able to pay everything off and so I started gambling again to win back what I still owed." This is a bit of gaslighting, to be sure, I think as I say it. *If only we had borrowed enough money,* is the bullshit message. I am good at confession but I'm not above manipulating the story to suit my purpose. Still, I'm ashamed I said it as soon as it comes out of my mouth.

(In the next couple of months I'll meet a man named Tibor Barsony, the Executive Director of the Canadian Foundation for Compulsive Gamblers, who will suggest that I never paid off all my debts after each bailout or win so I would have an excuse to go back gambling.)

"I owe money to the Leacock charity casino deposits — that's one of the biggest things. Rather than depositing the money from the last couple of events, I've gambled it . . ."

"On the weekend. I knew you were in trouble," Roberta says.

On Sunday night I had gone back to Casino Rama after Roberta went to bed. After my two days without sleep, I didn't get up until 8:00 p.m. and, her bath over, Roberta was already settled in her room, her television on. She was in her own dream world and like all of us ostriches, she didn't want anyone pulling her head out of the sand, at least not that night. I knew as soon as it was ten o'clock I could head out the door for another late-night rendezvous with Lady Luck. Now rested, and still with a substantial stake, I was sure I could mount a comeback and maybe even win that Caribbean Stud jackpot and my way out of gambling purgatory.

If this was to be my Odyssey, the Cyclops had already arrived by the time I came onto the gaming floor, furtively, from the side door. The $116,432 Caribbean Stud jackpot had been won that afternoon. Oh no, I thought, *while I was sleeping.* A setback to be sure, but with $3800 in my pocket, 149 table games and over three-thousand slot machines just waiting to be plucked: *I'll get over it.*

As usual, I went straight to roulette. Late Sunday nights aren't as busy in Casino Rama as the Torontonians head back to the big city for their Monday morning jobs — and to refuel for next weekend's journey into cottage country. Certainly hunting and camping trips up North will never be the same now that there is the Casino Rama pit stop along the way. I can't count how many well-intentioned hunters and fishermen I've met in that place who stopped in "for an hour or so" on Friday afternoon on the way to the camp and hadn't left by Sunday. Obviously, they were younger than me: two days was my record.

There was plenty of room at the tables, so I moved from wheel to wheel, playing nickels — five-dollar chips — on my main numbers. Seven, seventeen, six-nine on the line, nineteen, and twenty-seven. I also threw a five on the zero, double-zero line and on the number that last won.

I put three coins on seventeen and two on seven, and started praying: "Seven-seventeen, come on seven-seventeen," as I moved to the next table to place my bets there while the wheel spun at the first table. I knew I'd only get away with this until the pit boss noticed or got a call from the eye in the sky. "That crazy asshole Little is at it again; tell him he can only play one table at a time."

"Mr. Little, please, you must just play one roulette wheel at a time," the pit boss said, offering me my choice of seats.

"Okay, Okay, right after these spins, okay?" I said, thinking: What the hell's the difference to them? But I know that every square inch of this place is planned, the layout, the colours, where this table and that machine goes and what bells and whistles go off and when, all designed to maximize the number of bets we will make on a given day. Everything they do here has one reason — money. That must be why I'm not allowed to run from table to table.

Roulette was not happening. They jinxed it. I picked up the balance of my two hundred dollars in nickels and headed for the other jackpot poker game — "Let It Ride." It was a game I liked better than Caribbean Stud anyway; however, Let It Ride's biggest jackpot was only $50,000 and up until today I'd been chasing the bigger prize.

"Mr. Little, you're back," the pit boss said like I was his long-lost brother. "Here is your chair, Sir. I heard it was one of the guys that was sitting at your table that won the Caribbean Stud jackpot. I hope some of his luck rubs off on you."

"Thanks," I said, but I didn't believe his bullshit. I know that Mary-Anne, Bob's wife, teaches these guys to say crap like that in her job as Manager of VIP Services. Not that I'm a VIP. Losing fifty or sixty thousand dollars in two and a half months around here doesn't make you a high roller. You're a good customer, you're treated like a muckety-muck, complimentary food, free valet parking, a room in a hotel occasionally if you want it, but no limo, no suite, no hand-holding from the VIP hosts.

"Make sure you let me know, Mr. Little, if you need dinner or valet parking; I'll be pleased to look after you," the pit boss adds. Some day, one of the statistical comparisons that will jump out at me is that, while the government of Ontario spent less than a million dollars on treatment for compulsive gambling in 1996, their three casinos spent over $25 million on "comps" to encourage chumps like me to gamble more. That's not even counting the millions spent on advertising and promotion.

But this night I didn't care about that. All I cared about was winning. The play in Let It Ride starts with making three bets of equal size, the minimum, which now was $25, or higher, in each of the three circles in front of where one sat. The dealer then gives each player three cards and places two "community cards" face down. After seeing my three cards, I had the choice to take back one of my bets or to "let it ride." The strategy was supposed to be that I only let it ride if I had a winning hand or was working on Three of a Kind, or had three cards in a Straight or Flush possibility. When all the players have made their decisions to pull back or stay in, the dealer turns over one of the common cards. Now I had the option, again, to pull back another bet or to "let it ride." Again I was only supposed to stay in if I had a Pair of Tens or better or if I just needed one card to complete a high Straight or any Flush. This included the jackpot Straight and Royal Flushes which paid 200-to-one and 1,000-to-one respectively. At Casino Rama, there was a limit of $50,000 that could be paid out on any one round of Let It Ride. This was the big one I was chasing.

I placed $500 in fifties on the table, Queen's face down, fanspread in groups of five, just like we regulars were trained to do for the cameras up above. The dealer called out "five hundred in" and the pit boss turned and glanced at my money then nodded to the dealer, who took my money.

"Quarters," I said, and the dealer placed two piles of ten $25 chips and called out "twenty quarters out." After the nod from the pit boss he pushed the two piles in my direction. I was sitting in my lucky seat on what is called "first base" at a gambling table, the far right-hand side where you get the first cards in the deal. I wasn't completely hung up on this — there were too many nights when the seat was taken and I wouldn't let a silly superstition interfere with my actual ability to gamble — but if it was available I would take it. Often, if things were not going well in a game, I would change seats in an attempt to change my luck. If it continued going badly I'd change my game, hit the slots, or even try a little blackjack on the run. If it was going *real* badly, as I guess it must have fairly often for me to be down seventy thousand dollars, I would even change casinos if I had that option, spending a few hours back in a charity casino trying to build a stake playing VIP blackjack. I would do this especially if I was broke or near-broke because I could cash a cheque at Mr. Casino and play with the house's money, leaving when I had enough money to retrieve the cheque and had enough cash left to return to the big times. Included in the $5,000 my bank kicked back was a $1,000 cheque to Mr. Casino for a recent night when things didn't go "according to Hoyle."

The Let It Ride dealer had an automatic shuffler with three different decks, each used separately (unlike blackjack where six decks are used together to discourage card counting by the professionals) which cut down on delays between hands. About every eight hours the Casino goes through an elaborate procedure to change the three decks, bagging and tagging the old ones like they're gathering evidence at a murder scene, and then breaking open and spreading out each of the new decks to verify that every card is there and unmarked. These rituals and precautions, aimed at preventing cheating and basically securing the money they are without question going to win each and every day anyway, pervade every corner of the Casino. I have eventually come to realize that a casino is really a bank. All they have to do is secure the assets. The games themselves, in essence as rigged, fixed, or set with a pre-determined house advantage as they were when the mob ran them (or worse, because the mob gave better odds than the government), guarantee the money will keep rolling from the pockets of the suckers sitting around the tables and cranking on the machines. All the Casino has to do is guard against cheating and theft, and count the money. When Casino Rama came to town, the businesses that were impacted most by employees jumping ship were the banks. Former policemen probably made up the next closest career group.

Knowing all of this — and believing it — didn't save me from myself. For me it had to be different. I just had to win because I just had to play and winning was the only way I could stay in the game. Surely at least one of my Gods — the God of my youth or my luck deity — understood that; surely I only needed to keep in the game and my lucky break, my manna, my godsend, would fall from the sky. *God,* I prayed, *make it soon.*

Three cards were dealt to each player and the dealer put the two community cards face down in the little boxes marked on the table in front of her. "You may look at your hands, ladies and gentlemen." I didn't have the recommended minimum requirement hand but I "let it ride" anyway, gambling — it was gambling, after all — on the two cards the dealer had hidden in front of her. After the dealer had checked with each person as to what they were going to do she flipped one of the hidden cards over: Seven of spades. I now had two Sevens, not enough to win.

As John Wayne's Davy Crockett said in The Alamo, one of my all-time favourite films, "discretion seems like a better part of valour," and I withdrew my second bet. Still I had a hundred dollars on the table when the last card was flipped over and showed a Four of hearts. I lost, as did everyone else at the table.

Crossing Colonel Trask's line in the sand, I decided to make this table, this "Let It Ride" — a poker game of all things — my last stand, my Alamo, against the beautiful and colourful marching multitudes of Casino Rama — "the prettiest army I ever did see." I upped my bet to a hundred dollars a spot, three hundred dollars a hand. "Remember the Alamo!" I said aloud, passing my fingers across the back of my neck, across my cheek and ear, and fanning them across my face to my other cheek and chin. Nobody looked at me as if I'd said anything out of the ordinary, figuring, I suppose, I was performing some kind of fortuity ritual. The guy across from me just said: "Yeah, Geronimo!"

After another few hands of chasing Flushes, Straights and low Pairs I was down seven hundred dollars and thinking about moving to another game when I ended up with a Pair of pocket Jacks, and an Eight of diamonds. "Alright, let it ride!" I shouted as soon as I saw my cards. The first card the dealer turned over was another Jack. Three of a Kind! It paid three to one, nine hundred dollars. I was better than even — for the night. *Now I'm playing with their money* was the next thought in my head.

"Hey, buddy, what've you got? Four of a Kind?" The Geronimo guy's question brought the potential I had in front of me to my attention. "Not yet," I answered, but as I looked at the payout schedule stencilled on the felt tablecloth I could hardly contain myself. "Four of a Kind — 50 to one!" On three hundred dollars, that would be $15,000, not fifty thousand but not bad. At least I'd be able to make the charity casino deposit and still have a good-size stake to keep winning back the rest of the money I owed. I couldn't sit still while the dealer went around the table to ask if the other players were playing their option or letting it ride. I stood up pushing my chair away behind me. *It all comes down to a turn of a card.*

"Jack. Jack. Jack. Jack," I chanted, zeroing all my concentration on it, trying to will the face of the card I couldn't see to be what I wanted. "Come on, be there, be there, Jack!"

"Come on, Jack," Geronimo whooped in.

Flip. Eight. "Shit! — sorry, but it was supposed to be a Jack,"

I said as I turned my cards over, slapping them on the table, showing the Pair of Jacks.

"Full House," the dealer and Geronimo said at the same time, and I realized I had another Eight, making the complete hand three Jacks and a Pair of Eights — a Full House. "Pays eleven to one," the dealer announced. "Thirty-three hundred dollars."

"All right, buddy!" Geronimo congratulated me along with the rest of the table, but they were more excited than I was.

It might have been one-twentieth of what I needed, and I thought I may have, as they say in the vernacular, just "shot my wad" in the luck department. In my insane karmic rulebook, having thought it, I made it happen. I lost seven hands in a row, fortunately not all at the full three-hundred-dollar "Let It Ride" three-spot ante. By the time I dragged myself away from the table during one of those three-deck replacement ceremonials, I had lost more than half of what I had won and I was now back to where I was when I came in, give or take a hundred dollars, and it was getting late, or early, very early, in the morning. I stopped off at an empty seat in the Caribbean Stud corral, and threw three hundred dollars after a Pair of Twos, only to have the dealer qualify with a Pair of Aces. "Poker, broker," I sang to myself, the same little ditty I'd used in the charity casinos to keep my grandiose ego from dragging me to the sacrifice at the poker pits.

Back to blackjack was my next move, playing two spots at fifty dollars each, but I started to be haunted by Avery Cardoza's "scared money" warning and I couldn't concentrate on the cards. Reality was sneaking in at two a.m. and with only twenty-five hundred dollars left of the ten grand I'd started the weekend with, I was about ready to test that "If I am losing, I can go home and come back another day" theory.

I went to the cashier, avoiding Ralph Cipolla's wife Diane, who was working that night and with whom I had cashed in before. What can I tell you? It's a small town. As I cashed in the 13 one-hundred-dollar black chips and got 13 crisp one-hundred-dollar bills from the cashier, the *clink-clink-clink* and *ring-a-ding-ding-ding* of the high-end slots — the hundreds, the twenties and the fives — near the bathroom called my name on my way to having a pee. *I wish.* It was me calling their names, cherries, bells, bars, Blazing Sevens, and Haywire, hoping one of them would answer back.

My business done, I walked around to the hundred dollar slots — there were only four of them — just to have a look-see. An older, well-dressed woman who I recognized as a regular was playing one. The hundred-dollar slots were right next to the Let It Ride tables. I looked towards the two machines that were sitting unused around the corner away from the small crowd that was watching her bet three hundred dollars a spin — the maximum bet and amounting to, the way these machines zip along, about three grand a minute. "Ohhh . . ." they groaned when she got two triple bars and the third one appeared just above the line barely missing a thirty-thousand-dollar payout. "Yaaaay" when she got three bars in a row, another ten thousand dollars in credits she'd spend in less than five minutes. As for me, I snuck a hundred-dollar bill into a machine that looked like it wanted to give me ten G's and as I pushed the one-coin button, in the back of my mind I heard that little old lady in Sault Ste. Marie, a lifetime ago, saying "always play maximum." Shit, lady, I thought, it's a hundred bucks! When the reels stopped spinning I might as well have flushed the hundred dollars down the toilet along with the rest of my crap.

Next I fed two one-hundred dollar bills into the twenty-dollar slots, giving me ten credits, with which I played maximum, winning and losing for about ten minutes until the house's edge chipped away at my money, grinding it into nothing.

Here's where the mob definitely gives better odds than the government. While Vegas slots are reportedly set at ninety-two to ninety-six percent payback, Ontario's are more likely in the eighty-three or eighty-four percent range. After all, they have no competition. Regardless, an eighty to ninety percent payback sounds good, doesn't it? *Sounds* good, for sure. What's really going on with my two hundred dollars (well, it's not really mine is it?) is that with every spin I am betting sixty dollars, and the house, the government's casino, is taking an eight-dollar rake. After the first spin I have $192 left. The next spin I'm down to $184. Next $176. Then $168. And $160. So it goes on at the rate of twenty spins a minute until after about two minutes my two hundred bucks is gone. And this is regardless of winning or losing on any particular spin over the long run. While winning may be random on these "one-armed bandits," losing is completely programmed.

I look at Roberta, trying to somehow figure out how to ease her into the reality of the madness I have been living, but in the end I can only say it as a matter of fact: "I lost $10,000 between Saturday morning and last night."

"Ten thousand dollars! Are you crazy?" she screams. *Yes,* I'm thinking with an equal certainty. She continues her emotional venting — it's okay, I tell myself; it's just words, at least so far. "That's the down payment on this house, or a year in university for Melanie. How could you gamble away $10,000 in two days? You told me you were winning."

"It was three days. Rob, forget anything I ever told you, it was all bullshit. I'm addicted to gambling. I can't stop, and I'll do anything, say anything, and take anything to keep gambling. You need to just get the hell away from me and out of here before the shit hits the fan tomorrow."

"What? This is my home! Where am I going to go? Why tomorrow?"

"I've spent all day trying to fix things, to buy some time until I could get all the money back," I say, seeing the panic in her eyes, "and I hoped everything might be okay, but then, just before five o'clock, I got a call from an O.P.P. officer. She said she was working for the Ontario Gaming Commission and she wanted to do a routine audit of the Leacock Charity Casino books."

"Routine." Roberta grabbed on to the word like it was a safety net. "If it's just routine can't you get things fixed?"

"First, I don't think it's routine. I met with Mr. Casino an hour earlier to tell them the money Leacock owed them was gone, that I had gambled it away. I also met with Ed Leichner from the Casino this afternoon to see if I could borrow all the money from them so I could put it all back before I got caught. Somebody must have talked."

"Will they lend it to you?" Roberta asked, still hoping against hope for a rescue.

"He was optimistic and understanding. I think this kind of thing happens often in his business. I have to meet with Bobby Yee, you know, the Casino president, to find out. Ed was supposed to set the meeting up, but now it's probably too late."

"Why is it too late? If you put all the money back . . ."

"Maybe it will help but it's not going to save me. All the records are there in my office and at the bank. It's going to be clear to the police that I have taken the money, whether it's paid back now or not. It's too late — maybe it always was," I add, trying to bring her slowly, but bring her nonetheless, to a clear realization of what I am telling her.

"How much do you owe?" Roberta asks in a half-talking, half-crying voice that reflects her own growing anguish.

"Maybe $80,000 dollars," I answer with new resignation. It's a figure I have become familiar with. "I don't know exactly. It's been growing ever since Casino Rama opened."

"How could you do this to us?" Roberta screams, banging her hand on the table, making her cigarettes and lighter jump. She knows I wouldn't dare stop her so she reaches for them as she continues to yell. "We don't even own a house. We'll never be able to pay $80,000 back no matter who lends it to you."

"I didn't do it to us. I just gambled to relax. I had to keep borrowing money to win back what I lost, but I kept losing. It was a never-ending cycle like a balloon that kept getting bigger and bigger, and now it's exploded."

Lighting her cigarette inside the house for the first time in five years — since I had my heart attack — she looks at me through the smoke and tears. "I have nothing, no money, no job, nowhere to go. How could you do this to me? What about Melanie? This is going to destroy her."

"How?" I snap back, surprising myself with my vehemence. "Melanie is in Vancouver for Christ's sake. Sure, she's going to be upset, but it's not going to harm her life." Knowing the life-and-death decisions I have made over the past few days based on what

275

I thought would destroy Melanie's life, it is taking all my will-power, boosted by the knowledge that my big sister is on her way here, for me not to run out the door and go you-know-where.

That one time I won big — or relatively big — at Casino Rama and got out with the money in my pocket was on a Thursday night, a week after it opened, when I knew I had to go to Montreal the next day to pick up Melanie. Before she went to B.C., she was coming home for a few weeks and before that, she and I were going to take a vacation alone together for the first time in our lives. We were going to travel to the Maritimes to visit my parents and search for warm beaches. I also had, as we have seen, the ulterior motive of going to ask my oldest brother, Jimmy, to loan me twenty-five thou-sand dollars, which was what I owed at the beginning of August.

In alcohol recovery programs there is a tenet that alcohol is "cunning and baffling." When you least expect it, no matter how many times you've sworn you aren't going to drink, you find somebody who shows up with a bottle or puts a drink in your hand. On the night before this excursion to New Brunswick, a trip on which I was ready to bear my soul, to admit my problem with gambling and to desperately beg the only member of my family who I thought had the money to bail me out — I experienced gambling's serendipitous respite.

At the Casino it was one of those nights that gamblers eulo-gize, the one you always remember more than the hundred losing nights combined. Roulette was hot, so hot it reminded me of my last night in Puerto Plata at the Paradise Resort, except now I *was* playing for dollars. My "Lucky Seventeen" hit three or four times when I had a twenty-five-dollar bet straight up. I could do no wrong.

"Five thousand dollars," I yelled in the van heading back to town, hardly able to contain my excitement. Now I had money to put in the bank to cover my overdraft (somewhat lower then), some to give Doug Bell to make a deposit or two, and three thousand dollars extra to take on vacation with my daughter to see her grandparents and look for New Brunswick's "warmest beaches north of Virginia." All thought of approaching my brother Jimmy for the loan was banished. *If I can win $5,000 in one night starting with a couple of hundred, shit, I can win the $25,000 easily when I get back.*

"Hi Doll, it's your Dad," I start the conversation the way I always do, although I am not sure what I am going to say next or how I am going to say it. I just know that I have to tell her this before her mother does and before she reads about it in the newspapers. Somehow I want to make her understand that I never meant for it to happen and, for sure, I don't want it to change her life.

"Hi Daddy, how come you're calling on a week night?"

"I've got a problem and I need to talk to you about it," I say, opting for the direct delivery as the quickest and hopefully least painful method of telling her. I have to admit, as much as I love Melanie, it's me I am worried about here. How she reacts to what I have done, her acceptance or rejection of me, may just be one of the pivotal moments in my life. I'll soon know whether life is worth living. "Mel, my gambling has got me in a lot of trouble, and it's trouble that is going to affect you and your mother."

"Oh, Daddy," Melanie says, "I've been so worried about you. Ever since the summer, I knew you were out of control."

"Yeah, I know. The gambling trip from hell."

"No, we had a good time and it wasn't just all gambling, but it was obvious you were obsessed every time we went near one of those places and now, oh, great, you've got one in Orillia."

"Yeah, 'oh, great,' at least that's what I thought at the beginning — I'd be able to control it better because it was close to home. I didn't need to go nuts just because I couldn't go back the next day. It didn't matter and maybe it's worse, because now some days, I go back two and three times, after I've found more money."

"Is it the money?" she asks. Melanie is well aware of our lifelong struggle with money, and she knows I don't have the kind of money that I have been gambling.

"Yeah, it's the money. I owe a lot of money at work, mainly to the Leacock Festival accounts, ironically to the gambling accounts — bingo, Nevada, and the charity casinos we've been running." I tell her about my "borrowing" and my gambling cycle that has taken me to this point where I owe $80,000, to accounts in my trust that I shouldn't have touched. The police . . .

"What is happening, Dad?" Melanie asks at the mention of police.

"The police called me this afternoon to say they want to do an audit of the books tomorrow," I tell her. "I've kept all the records there so I could pay it back, eventually. They're going to find everything."

"Oh, Dad."

"I'm probably going to end up arrested tomorrow, maybe thrown in jail. I am trying to get your mother to go to Timmins so she won't have to deal with the publicity . . . the shame."

"Don't push her, Dad," Melanie advised. "You just look after you. You are the one who's going to have to deal with this; there's not much she can do. Do you have a lawyer?"

"No, there's a lawyer in Timmins I can call, someone I knew when I was a reporter. I'm going to call him next."

"Good, do what he tells you to do. Dad, don't try to do this on your own."

"I won't. I'll be okay. I just don't want this to interfere with you, your school and your writing." My voice is starting to quiver, tears are in my eyes and emotion is stabbing at my heart. "You know, Melanie, that I love you and I didn't mean to do anything that would hurt you or your mother. I just couldn't stop or stay away."

"Dad, I know you love me, your life has been for me. Now you need to concentrate on you, on getting over this gambling, on getting help and through this. I love you and I'm going to be there for you just like you've always been there for me. Call me tomorrow and let me know what is happening. If you need money — you know — for bail or anything, call me and maybe I can find it."

Bail. I haven't thought of bail, but I suppose Veronica and her husband Bob will figure out something if it comes to that. Usually I'd just think of Bob Willsey, but after what I've done I'm not sure the "Bank of Bob" will ever re-open again, even under these circumstances.

"Don't worry about that," I say, "I don't think it will come to that but I'm sure I can get money from Veronica if it does. She's on her way here tonight to try to help us get through this."

"Let me talk to Mom, and Dad, take it easy. I love you and you're still the greatest dad in the world."

"Okay Doll," I say, fighting back the tears. I yell at Roberta, who is upstairs, to take the phone.

CHAPTER FOURTEEN

I always joked that, if I ever killed anyone, I would call Lorenzo Girones.

October 22, 1996 — 7:30 p.m.

I met Lorenzo as a young reporter in Timmins and through the years I observed him as a talented, tenacious and aggressive lawyer, more than capable of handling those expert advocates who, by the Northern Ontario definition of my old "deep throat" Timmins Alderman Dan Kelly, "got off the plane with a briefcase." He represented a variety of clients in a mixed bag of cases, both criminal and civil, whose common denominator seemed to be controversy. He was the lawyer for the union during the snow strike in early 1977, the one in which a person or persons unknown dynamited a contractor's front-end loader. A few years later there was a feud on city council between Albert Ristimaki and Hank Beilik, which spilled into the slander and libel courts, with Lorenzo defending Ristimaki. There were also criminal cases that I read about, including murder defenses. What I remember was that Lorenzo always seemed to be defending the guilty, the losers or the desperate. Given those qualifications, I am his ideal client.

I find Lorenzo's home telephone number in an old Timmins telephone book I have stashed away in one of my orange storage boxes, a hoard of memorabilia — clippings, campaign publications, and project files — that helped define who I was during those initially liquid and then bumptious early years. A woman, I assume Lorenzo's wife, answers the telephone and I ask for Lorenzo, whom she calls.

He says hello and I am surprised to hear the age in his voice, but his Spanish accent is as distinct as it was twenty-five years ago. I explain who I am, that he might remember me as a reporter with the *Timmins Daily Press* and as a columnist. I can't come out and say "the guy you used to feed information to on the q.t.," and as a result he says: "I'm sorry but I don't remember you — but what can I do to help you?"

"I need a lawyer. When I was in Timmins I always had a great deal of respect for you. Now I am living in Orillia, where I am the manager of the Downtown Business Association. I am very involved in the community and I have had access to a lot of money. We just got a new casino here and now I am addicted to gambling. I have taken money to gamble from various accounts I control — telling myself I was borrowing but always taking from Paul to pay Peter and never getting caught up." I pause to catch my breath but jump back in before he has a chance to comment, wanting to finish first.

"Lately I have started looking for help, and in trying to borrow money to pay back what I owe, I may have told on myself. This afternoon a policewoman, an O.P.P. officer, called and said she wanted to do an audit of one of the accounts tomorrow. All the details of what I owe are there — I kept records so I could pay it back — so she's going to easily find that I took the money. I need to know, how do I deal with this?"

"Mr. Little — Doug — how much money are you talking about?"

"Maybe eighty thousand dollars altogether from eight accounts. Ironically, a lot of it is the proceeds from gambling itself, from our bingo and charity casinos that I ran for my

Festival. The O.P.P. officer said she was doing the audit for Ontario Gaming Commission."

"Doug, you did this, right?" Lorenzo's question is direct, but there is compassion in his tone.

"Yes," I answer, the admission suddenly overwhelming me with guilt.

"And you are going to plead guilty, correct?"

"I am guilty," I choke on the words, and he waits silently until I can go on. "But all the money went to gambling."

"Yes, I know, and that's a mitigating factor that will definitely be considered for sure," he says. "Doug, I cannot come to Orillia to be your lawyer but you don't need me anyway. What you need to do is find a criminal lawyer — preferably someone in Orillia who knows you and who you know, and someone you trust. You need to find a lawyer who is going to explain the law to you and help you through this, not some hot shot looking to make a name. Someone to help you co-operate and to put yourself at the mercy of the court. Unfortunately I do not know any lawyers in Orillia so I can't recommend anyone to you. Do you know anyone like this?"

"I think I may."

"That's good. You need to contact him or her as soon as possible and tell them what you have told me."

"Thank you very much. I am sorry to bother you at home, I just didn't know where to turn."

"That's okay. Hope for the best, Doug."

"Thank you."

Even as Lorenzo talked, the image of Brian Turnbull came into my mind. I had met Brian thirteen years ago when I was just new in Orillia — curiously, through Ralph Cipolla. In order to attract tourists to Orillia, Ralph had become the chairman and driving force behind the Orillia Perch Festival, a fishing derby he had the Chamber of Commerce sponsor. I was the manager of the regional Huronia Tourist Association and to get involved in the individual communities I had volunteered to help with publicity on the Perch Festival. Brian was the other person on the communications committee. He owned a security and alarm business that he ran from his home, and from his wheelchair. One day I showed up at his house and he was bubbling with excitement. He had just been accepted at the University of Windsor law school as a mature student. Forty-five years old at the time, he sold his business and hit the books. I remember marvelling at his tremendous courage. Since that time I watched his law practice from afar, occasionally seeing his name in the papers defending some youth or Rama Reserve native in trouble. I'd see his office sign in a small building next to the movie theatre in Orillia, that Friday night oasis for Bob, Mary-Anne and I.

Brian and I would run into each other occasionally, exchange pleasantries and invariably talk about getting together socially sometime. However, I don't think either of us was very sociable. Certainly part of my community image was that I was outgoing, gregarious, and outspoken — a typical extrovert. Really, I am quite introverted and I am uncomfortable meeting new people, and mixing at public gatherings. Often I would make appearances at receptions just to be seen and escape at the earliest possible moment, often back to work to get the show ready for the next day or week.

Brian's home phone number was in the Orillia telephone book.

"Brian, this is Doug Little, I'm sorry to disturb you at home."

"Hi, Doug, don't worry about that," he replied with genuine warmth. "What can I do for you?"

"I am addicted to gambling and I am in very big trouble. I have taken money to gamble that doesn't belong to me."

"Oh, Doug I'm sorry to hear this. Tell me what is happening."

"I need your help as a lawyer. I am going to be arrested, maybe tomorrow, and I need you to guide me through facing up to what I have done."

"Doug, I want to tell you, I am really touched that you've called me," Brian says. "You have done so much for this community; I would be honoured to help you."

"Maybe you won't be so anxious when I tell you what I've done, Brian, how I've destroyed a lot of that good."

"I'm here to help. Now tell me, what's the problem?" For the next twenty minutes I tell Brian about my gambling binge, my "borrowing" from the eight bank accounts, the juggling, the balls falling, my confessions today and the call from Constable Lennon. When I finish Brian doesn't pull any punches.

"Doug, these are very serious crimes. You are probably facing a number of fraud and breach of trust charges, and you are likely looking at jail time as a result. The fact that this is your first offence, and the gambling, will be circumstances considered at sentencing, but the Supreme Court has ruled on a number of occasions that breach of trust warrants a sentence of incarceration."

"I imagined that," I say but I can't help but marvel at the contrast between the way I felt when I had fantasized about jail as some kind of grim sanctuary on those losing nights, and the stark terror I am feeling at this moment, hearing the reality of his words. To be honest, I usually dismissed the possibility of jail with the delusion that somehow by explaining the pressures of work or my health, by underlining my naiveté about gambling or by pleading temporary insanity, all would be forgiven. My "It's A

Wonderful Life" rationale. Or even if I went to jail, I imagined how I would be able to write, read, and study — kind of an idyllic vacation. Now listening to a lawyer — my lawyer — tell me I am going to go to jail — real jail — seizes my mind and body with anguish. As my mind panics, my heart clenches and my breathing struggles, my being, my right-down-to-the-toes essence, wants to run. I want to run out the door and lose myself forever. No doubt about it, I want to go gambling.

On Sunday night, as my losing continued at Rama, the terrifying truth of my desperation slipped through the chrome veneer of the slot machines. I needed a bigger, faster, more powerful fix. I needed a VLT — video lottery terminal — recently tagged as the "crack-cocaine of gambling."

In 1995, when I quit bingo after being bailed out by Roberta's father and our insurance, I had to deal with horrendous feelings of guilt, anger, resentment and self-pity, all feelings that I preferred to run away from, rather than face. I had Roberta repeatedly reminding me about what I did and how she had to ask her father for money to pay my gambling debts. And me, I was equally infuriated that I had even told her in the first place.

"I wish I had killed myself rather than telling you about the money I took," I yelled back at her as I ran to some secluded part of the house, trying to escape her wrath and my feelings. "I swear I'll never tell you anything again."

My sanctuary within our house was my computer; except now I wasn't using it for work: I was playing video gambling games. No, not Internet gambling, which was still in its infancy in 1995, and would not have been of much use to me anyway due to my lack of credit cards and my inability to get credit. Also, I am more than a little sceptical about the integrity of even the wheels, machines and cards that I can see face to face; I am not about to trust some phantom computer at the other end of the earth to be above-board. No, I was just playing, practising — getting ready for some future return to real gambling when I'd be able to use the skills I was developing to have better results than I'd had during the bingo phase. Later, I practised blackjack on the computer in between charity casino dates, perfecting my skill and knowledge of the intricacies of the game I knew as a child as "Twenty-one." But, initially, I played slots and roulette. I knew from how easily I won that the computer games were programmed that way, since they didn't have to pay out any money. I would constantly look for more and more sophisticated programs that would give that real casino experience, the rush I recalled from my visits to Puerto Plata and The Sault. The games were just temporary substitutes until I served my penance for the trouble caused by my bingo phase. Besides, I was in the busy summer period for both the downtown and the festivals, not to mention the official opening of the O.P.P. Headquarters in September.

I kept hearing about the illegal VLTs that were said to be in the bars and poolrooms but I could never find any during my occasional cruises around the city. That's not to say they weren't there, but their keepers certainly weren't going to point them out to some stranger who just walked in the door. And being who I was in Orillia, I couldn't exactly come out and ask.

That, however, did not stop me from the degrading, hours-on-end visits to the combination dry-cleaner/laundromat where I discovered a "for-fun" video gambling machine. Imagine the picture I presented, the "Czar of Downtown Orillia," as the *Orillia Sun* once called me, skulking in the corner of this dingy domicile of washers and dryers, feeding quarters by the roll into this spinning, whirling, flashing fruit machine for no other reason than being there and beating the machine.

My experience with the real VLTs (apart from those nickel machines at the Cosmo Club, twenty-four years ago) was limited to my holiday with Roberta on the P.E.I. ferry, the corner store in Fredericton which my unretentive father can't find anymore and a couple of bars and corner stores during the Bet & Beach Tour Melanie and I took in August. The main features of the video gambling machines — for me — were how mesmerizing they were and how much I wanted to get back to playing them.[9]

While the Government of Ontario had expanded the access to the more mechanical, slower slot machines throughout the province, and claimed to have banned these electronic VLTs, I still managed to find some in Casino Rama (at least I did in 1996). They were fiddled with to make them "Video Slot Machines" but with the exception of how you got your payout, I saw no difference. For the desired drug-like rush, the action, the excitement, the fix that I needed in those dwindling hours of my two-year orgy of betting, these babies were the real thing — in spades. These weren't the ten-cent a spin types — which of course you could max-out ("always play maximum") thirty-two different ways for $3.20 a spin once you became experienced — but were a dollar a line with a maximum of $8.00 each spin. This bank of twelve or so dollar video slots and their twenty-five cent counterparts on the other side of the aisle have been the third corner in my casino triangle in this last, increasingly desperate, month. The routine has been roulette, poker, video slots, and then if I was lucky, more roulette, poker, and video slots until I either ran out of luck or out of energy, whichever came first.

Although the video slots were late additions to the casino, installed after it had been open several weeks, the quarter machines have proven so popular they are already adding more rows of them. Often on the weekends you have to stand and wait until a free seat comes open, which I would seldom do. One of the advantages of playing clandestinely in the middle of the night is that there are fewer crowds — but even at three o'clock in the morning the video slots are crowded. The one-dollar machines, though, are more accessible — if you have, as gamblers say, "the legs," enough money to play eight dollars a pop.

Early Monday morning at the end of this weekend from hell, almost seventy hours after I entered Casino Rama with my pockets bulging with the illicit $10,000 stake, my "legs" were battered, bruised, and maimed but I still had enough money left to crawl up to the video slot machine and feed a couple of hundred dollars into the bill feeder. Enough money to start banging buttons to make those bells, cherries and prunes spin, the *ding-a-ling-a-ling* music chime, the *ding-ding-ding* of a win ring and the *doo-doo-doo-da-loop* of a loss mewl. There was a $10,000 jackpot, not as big as the five-dollar slots, but considering I was then seventy-five hundred dollars deeper in the hole than I was on Friday, a ten-grand win would have been a miracle from heaven right about then. I lost another thousand dollars before the news that I was falling asleep in front of the screen finally penetrated my stupor and I left for home, eighty-five hundred dollars gone, but taking some comfort in the fifteen-hundred dollars I still had to come back with tomorrow. Appropriately, what came to mind were Scarlett O'Hara's final words in *Gone with the Wind*, "After all, tomorrow is another day!"

Brian says he wants to be with me when I meet with the O.P.P. Officer but he has to be in court on Wednesday. He suggests I try to contact Officer Lennon first thing in the morning and tell her that while I want to cooperate fully, I am not able to make the 1:00 p.m. meeting, and to try to reschedule it for the next day. Meanwhile, Brian tells me to start preparing a statement — a written confession — that I could give to him and to the police when we do finally meet. We talk about getting together at his office the next day, once we know the schedule with the police.

"Doug," he says, concluding the conversation, "I want you to keep your spirits up. We're going to deal with this in a straight-forward manner, but we'll get through this together."

"Okay," I say, fighting back my emotions. "Thanks for tonight, Brian."

Of all the lawyers in Orillia Brian was probably the one most involved in working with the Chippewas of Rama, in defending Natives, and in the exploration of Native-administered justice and healing circles. My involvement with the Chippewas of Rama went back a few years before the casino was even conceived, when I was invited to a meeting between the native community, interested

Orillians, and the Government of Canada. We were to discuss the archeologically significant fishing weirs at the Atherley Narrows, which were interfering with the building of a second bridge to span the narrow channel that joined Lakes Simcoe and Couchiching. As the leader of the downtown merchants, I suppose I was sent to push the cause of progress and the free flow of traffic. Instead I found myself championing dialogue and compromise. This lead to a wonderfully spiritual meeting at the Leacock Home at which Rama Native Mark Douglas told a traditional tale of the Mnjikaning people, who were charged with the care of the ancient "Fish Fence." Mark told us that the Chippewa of Rama's traditional name, Mnjikaning, meant "Fish Fence Minders." He also said the Narrows were a sacred place of peace where Indian peoples from different tribes would come to meet and catch fish, safe from conflict and war. As for the weirs themselves, they were posts or stakes, and while they should be treated with historic and spiritual respect, nothing was stopping their careful removal from under the bridge and preservation in a museum or other appropriate venue. He suggested such an attraction be developed at the Narrows to celebrate its history as a place of peace. On that night we formed the Fish Fence Circle and began work on the promulgation of such a centre. I developed a personal friendship with Mark Douglas, who at the time was the executive director of the Ojibwa Tribal Council but would soon, once the casino was announced, become the Senior Planner for Economic Development for the Chippewas of Mnjikaning. While most times we met at Circle meetings, occasionally we would run into each other at City Tickets and split a couple of handfuls of Nevadas, urging each other on in our mutual obsession, something we both took with a great deal of amusement at the time. Mark told me that he, too, gambled ferociously when he visited other casinos and was starting to be grateful that he would not be able to gamble at Casino Rama because he was an employee of the Rama Band Council. Me, I couldn't wait.

The first time I went to Windsor it was, ostensibly, to get a job. In reality, I was going to gamble. Maybe it was because I couldn't wait for the casino in Orillia to open that I applied for the job as executive director of the downtown Windsor business association. It was the fall of 1995 and after a summer of work and no gambling — I had quit bingo in June — I was ready to escape, big time. A geographic cure had its appeal. I knew I was burned out but what could I do about it? Along with all of the other stuff I did for my eighty-hour-a-week job and the festivals this summer, I also served as the City of Orillia's representative on the Official Opening Ceremonies committee for the new one-hundred-million dollar Ontario Provincial Police Headquarters. I was also on the steering committee of a $150,000 study on tourism in the region, largely overhauling an organization that I once managed. Although there were rumours, it was a little-known secret that I resigned that position due to borrowing from office cash in the mid 1980s. Then I was paying for Melanie's figure skating and chasing another kind of dream world.

In order to maintain my illusion of control, to hide things I was doing now, I couldn't say no when anyone asked me to serve on committees or take on new responsibilities. I couldn't say no, and I couldn't unload any of the things I had going. My job, the

Festival, Winter Carnival, and even Canada Day were all wrapped up together, first in my need to prove myself, and then in my need to hide what I was doing with the money.

A new job and a new town, not to mention a new casino, were attractive. The plan was to kill two birds with one stone. Do the interview and win enough money to get these accounts under control. That was my goal at Casino Windsor: twelve hundred dollars and some hot luck. Then I'd be free to do whatever I wanted, even move to Windsor.

Casino Windsor, the Government of Ontario's first casino, opened in 1994. By all the accounts I'd heard it was a raving success. Downtown Windsor was looking to share in the benefits and wanted a new manager. I was asked to come down to Windsor for an interview. It was a five-hour trip and while I was just driving a van, it seemed like I flew.

One thing that puzzled me on the way was the lack of billboard or road signs announcing Casino Windsor along Highway 401 from Toronto. Even within the city, directional signs were lacking. I guessed I was coming from the wrong direction to catch the casino's target marketing. It must have all been aimed across the river at Detroit, from which, I bet, the directions were exact. Being able to attract American gamblers and U.S. dollars was a key rationale for establishing this first casino in the border city of Windsor. *Money in. Problems out.* Orillia was being sold its casino on a similar basis: Increasing tourism by attracting Toronto and southern Ontario residents who will come to gamble but will also stay and shop. Less than five percent of Casino Rama's *win* would come from the local market. *Money in. Problems out.* I just happened to be part of the small local percentage that couldn't wait.

I tried doubling back from the U.S. border and found my way past the casino's twinkling front lights with ease. While my heart raced at the sight, I was stoic in my patience. I wanted to find the location of the agency where the interview was to take place at two o'clock. I had two hours; this way I would know exactly where I had to go, how long it would take to get there from the casino and exactly how long I had to gamble. Surprisingly I was able to park right next to the casino.

Where were the thousands of cars and jammed parking lots we kept hearing about in Orillia? It reminded me of the other big casino I'd been to in April, in Sault Ste. Marie, Michigan. There, we'd had to take the worst, most convoluted back roads into the middle of nowhere. The Sault casino was made up of a menagerie of buildings, built the same way as a mining town, in both haste and hesitation, not much money spent in case it didn't last. Only the flashy Kewadin Vegas sign had met my expectations of gambling paradise. However, you could park at the door, at least during the weekends in April when I was there every night for four nights during that Festivals Ontario conference. And there were no traffic jams.

Casino Windsor was also stuffed into an unimpressive building, its temporary site in an old art gallery. Its flashy lighted façade and signage, however, were more reminiscent of the Las Vegas movies I had seen and the heat of my excitement was rising as I walked through the doors. Inside it was a palace, three floors of glitter and neon. All the bells and whistles to literally set my heart fluttering. There was even a non-smoking floor. Two hours, I reminded myself as I dashed around the building like the proverbial kid in a candy store with a pocketful of money from his mother's purse.

Even though I'd been learning blackjack on the computer and working on a system for my first love in gambling — roulette, just like my first casino visit at Kewadin, I couldn't get past the slot machines. The *ding-ding-ding* and *clink-clink-clink* of winning coins dropping, the spinning reels, the siren sounds and flashing lights of jackpot winners enthralled me as I wandered up and down the aisles looking for *my machine*. From my April visit in Kewadin I knew my favourites, the ones with a "Haywire" icon and the crazy action where the reels go erratic, spinning out of control and racking up bonus winning credits. I couldn't find any as I sped around the casino looking from side to side, floor to floor. Maybe it was an American thing. I couldn't waste any more precious gambling time.

I settled on the non-smoking floor, a nod to the sensitivity of my nose, and it was among these rows of slots that I passed the next hour and forty-five minutes. Before I even started I was flushed, sweating and hyperactive. I could feel my blood boiling.

I bought five $20-rolls of dollar tokens and five $10 quarter rolls from the coin change cart as soon as I hit the floor. *Clang!* I whacked the roll of tokens against the side of the coin tray at the bottom of the slot machine and flipped the tokens out of the paper wrapper into the coin tray with a crescendo of clinks and clanks as the coins bounced around. In swooped my hand grabbing a handful from the tray and deftly moving up over the coin slot, dropping three coins in rapid succession. *Click! Click! Click!* If they went too fast one coin fell all the way through and I had to swoop down again grab another token and reload. It was a precision I'd learned at Kewadin and now it seemed second nature. The next move was to the maximum button — playing the three-coin maximum — and then I pulled the lever on the right side of the machine to crank it down and start the wheels spinning.

Whirl, whirl, whirl. Ka-chunk. One wheel stopped — bar. *Ka-chunk.* Second wheel — two bars. My heart raced, my mind went tizzy. *Ka-chunk* — three bars. *I won.* I tried to keep myself cool, to keep from dancing in the aisles and making a fool out of myself. *Clink, clink, clink.* The coins dropped into the waiting tray, clinging off my coins that were already there.

I looked quickly to the top of the slot where there was a payout menu. Three single bars — twenty. Three double bars — forty. Three triple bars — sixty. I couldn't figure what I'd won until the clinking stopped and the flashing LED showed twenty.

Swoop. Click. Click. Click. Whack the maximum button and crank the lever. *No, you should have tried the button, just to change things up.* The reels spun. I needed to calm down. *You can't expect to win every pull, relax.* I looked over at the elderly woman, leaning from her stool in front of one machine to slap the buttons on the adjacent machine. *Wow! She's playing two machines at once.* She reminded me of the women at bingo who could play twenty-four cards at once on the regular games and then thirty-six for the jackpot game.

Ka-chunk. Ka-chunk. Ka-chunk. Nothing, except there was a "Wild" symbol almost in the middle window. Breathing in deeply and blowing out like a sigh, I checked out the three Wilds payout — "2400." *Wow!*

Swoop. Click. Click. Click. Whack. Crank. Whirl. Ka-chunk. One double bar. *Ka-chunk.* Two double bars. *Ka-chunk.* Wild. *Clink. Clink. Clink.* The machine started spitting out dollar tokens as I searched the menu for what two double bars and a Wild symbol means. Eighty dollars. *The tray is going to be full.* While the coins were dropping, I gathered up three tokens and leaned over to the next machine. *Clink, clink, clink. Whack* and *whack.* I hit the maximum button and the spin button. Cranking the one arm bandit had lost its novelty. The reels of the second slot spun. It was a "Blazing Sevens," with an icon of three sevens coming out of what looked like the fires of Mel Brooks' *Blazing Saddles* logo. One Seven. Two Blazing Sevens. Two Sevens. Nothing.

Back at "Wild Bars" my winnings are scattered all over the tray, although not nearly filling it as much as I imagined. I remembered a button that I pushed in Sault Ste. Marie that retained your winnings as credits so you didn't have to keep feeding in the coins each play. No *swoop.* No *click, click, click.* I whacked the button and fed a handful of tokens down the coin slot.

"It wants to pay," I said to myself out loud as I whacked the buttons and set the reels to wheeling once again. *Concentrate; keep your eyes on the wheels. Ka-chunk* — Wild. I felt my heat rise. Bar. Double bar on the line. *Ding. Ding. Ding. Ding. Ding. Ding.* The new sound confused me.

"Did I win?" I looked up to the menu as the slot recorded six electronic credits to the four I still had left. There it was. One "Wild" — Six.

Back to the buttons. *Whack. Whack.* The reels were whirling again. Another two wilds and a third one on the line. Oh, so close. Twenty-four hundred dollars. Instead I won twelve bucks.

So the machine teased me, enticed me with the occasional win and lured me to add more coins — I went back to the change cart three times — another three hundred dollars.

The only reality able to penetrate my absorption in these one-armed bandits was the two o'clock appointment, likely because it was connected to the gambling, to my being able to get back here again. I checked my watch hundreds of times while I played hundreds of games, over and over, winning and losing and checking, winning and losing and checking. As much as I wanted to win, I didn't mind losing as long as I could stay there. I hadn't won a big jackpot, the kind where they came and gave you the money in cash and reset your machine. I was up considerably at one point but I continued to gamble until all the credits were gone and then all of the special slot coins were gone.

One forty-five p.m. It was time to go to the interview.

I got in my van and raced along my predetermined beeline to the agency in time for my two o'clock appointment with the job recruiter and her assistant. No Windsor committee. It was a screening interview. My ego was in full bloom, bolstered by two hours of gambling action. I could do this job standing on my head. I was the former president of Ontario Downtowns, four years the president of Festivals Ontario, vice-president of the Canadian Association . . . blah, blah, blah. I didn't care about the job. I just wanted to gamble.

My blood pressure was still through the roof throughout the interview and I fidgeted in my chair like a schoolboy needing to pee, or worse. *Let's get the questions over and get back to the real task at hand — winning back my five hundred dollars along with piles more of Casino Windsor's money.*

Funny, I didn't expect I'd get a call back. Too bad. Poor Windsor. It didn't know what it would be missing. I didn't care. I'd come to gamble.

Another beeline back to the casino. This time it would be different. I could concentrate on the game now that the stupid interview was out of the way. *The nerve of them, dragging me all the way down here and not even a member of the board there.*

♥ ♦ ♣ ♠

Later, in the spring of 1996, with some encouragement from my friend Mark Douglas, and with my mind vacillating about the relative merits of having a casino ten minutes from home (by this time I had lost my shirt in four visits to the major casinos) I applied for a job with the Chippewas of Rama Economic Development Corporation. This was the group that we were working with, along with the casino operators, Carnival Hotel & Casinos, on the Community Casino Task Force, so they knew me and knew my abilities. It was a shot in the dark as they were likely to hire a native. With one of the key promises of the casino being to hire more native workers, it was unlikely a high-profile white guy from across the lake was going to get the tribal plum. Still, it was worth the gamble. By this time, Bob's wife Mary-Anne had rediscovered her native ancestry and claimed her status as a member of the reserve scoring a high-paid, high-placed management position and, as a member of the reserve working on the reserve, her salary was tax-free! Only an idiot wouldn't apply, gambling or no gambling. Of course I didn't get the job; in fact I didn't even get a phone call or an acknowledgement. Oh, well, I thought, I'd probably blow the interview, stopping off at the corner store across from the nearly constructed casino and getting wired and weird on Nevada tickets.

Still I had expected a little gratitude for the role I'd played in supporting the native community in its campaign to be the chosen host for the casino from among all the other Reserves around the Province. My letter on behalf of the Downtown Merchants had been the first to support their bid. Along with being a key player on the Task Force, I was a loud voice criticizing the Ontario Government when it suspended construction in order to blackmail the Chippewas and the Ontario Indian Bands into accepting a twenty percent win tax. The previous NDP Government had promised all the proceeds would go to Native communities but now the new Conservative Government wanted twenty percent off the top to go to the general government coffers. I was among a delegation of area mayors and business leaders who accompanied Chief Lorraine McRae to Queen's Park to confront Premier Mike Harris in the halls of the legislature. Instead we were corralled into a conference room with the Minister of Economic Development.

During the meeting I championed the economic impact that was being delayed by the shutdown and argued that it was going to cause my merchants to miss the ideal opportunity of having the casino launched at the beginning of the tourism season. In the end, everyone took a Valium — there was lots of *win* to go around I guess — construction got underway and Casino Rama, much to my initial delight, and now to my chagrin, opened well into the tourism season, at the end of July. Not that it made any difference to my members from a tourism point of view. For all our efforts — shuttle bus services, boat shuttles, trains, and electronic tourism kiosks, not to mention Players' Club discounts — the gamblers came to gamble and did little else outside the casino save buy the occasional tank of gas and a donut on the trip back home, if, by that time, they could afford it. A few hotels housed the casino's guests but restaurants actually suffered as the casino's three restaurants and snack bar literally gave away food to entice people to gamble more. It's hard to compete with "free." As players we'd call these the "three-thousand-dollar *free* dinners" given as a reward for gambling high enough and long enough to lose that much money.

My eighty thousand dollars in losses bought me all the free meals I could eat. My last free lunch there would be with Casino President Bobby Yee.

The job that I do have, which I am obviously about to blow, is Manager and CEO of an arm's-length board of the City of Orillia, which means that, although I am an employee of the Downtown Orillia Management Board, I am also legally an employee of the City of Orillia and on its payroll. However, this arm's-length position also allows me the opportunity to continue to dabble in political campaigning, and I have been the Mayor of Orillia's campaign manager in the last two elections. Knowing what is about to happen to me, I want him and the city manager to hear it from me first so I call him at home and arrange to have a meeting with them both in his office at 9:30 a.m. the next morning.

Also, I must call my boss, Mike Knight, the chairman of the Downtown Board and tell him that things have deteriorated considerably since we last talked four or five hours ago. Now instead of owing a thousand or so dollars to an account or two around the office, I have discovered I really owe another $79,000 to some seven or eight different bank accounts. Who's counting any more? The forensic auditors will figure it out soon enough. Not only have I uncovered this new information, Mike, but I'll also be sharing it with the police tomorrow, in a neatly typed confession. Then, I expect I will be summarily locked up until my crying-towel-bearing sister Veronica does literally what she has been doing figuratively for the last forty years: bails me out.

"Mike, it's Doug. I am sorry to call you at home." I'm always sorry to call anyone at home because I hate getting called at home. Home is still, despite everything, a sanctuary against the outside world, a place to hide from the trials and tribulations that I have to deal with on a daily and nightly basis downtown.

"Mike, my gambling is a lot worse than the Board thinks, and it has gotten me in a lot more trouble that you or even Ralph could imagine."

"Doug, I don't . . ." I cut him off before he has a chance to tell me we would talk about it later and that I shouldn't worry, that everything will work out. I know better.

"No, Mike, I mean real trouble: police. I have a meeting with a constable from the O.P.P. tomorrow afternoon to go over the Leacock Heritage Festival books and they are going to find money missing — a lot of money. I could be arrested." It would be easier to make him understand if I would just came out and say "I stole eighty-thousand dollars" rather than all this gambling addict talk and skating around the amount. Of course I really don't know how much I owe but also Brian has cautioned me not to discuss the details of my crimes with anyone until we have met with the police and eventually a judge.

Given these omissions, Mike can't help but continue to be optimistic that things will get worked out and "all of this will blow over." It's a denial I recognize, and one that I wish I could embrace. But tonight I am on the wrong side of Lake Couchiching for such a dream world. Tonight my house of cards is crashing down.

CHAPTER FIFTEEN

Writing out my confession for Brian and the police appeals to

October 22, 1996 — 8 p.m.

me. It will allow me to avoid further discussion and confrontation with Roberta — at least until I have some measure of protection when my sisters arrive — and it will allow me to explain things, like how what happened wasn't supposed to happen. Maybe I could even create a little of the sympathy I used to fantasize about in my dream world, where they were holding benefit concerts to help pay back the money I "borrowed."

I don't know enough about gambling addiction, yet, to explain my actions in terms of not being able to stop, in the language of compulsivity and obsession. I can't simply write: "I couldn't stop gambling and because I couldn't stop, I couldn't win; then, when I didn't win, I had to have more and more money to keep playing to win back what I lost because I couldn't stop. Unfortunately, I had access to that money." If I had the language to say this, I'd just have to sign my name.

From where I am tonight, the confession is all about what happened, yes, but also all about my excuses and rationalizations for what happened. I start: "This statement is given on the basis that it will be the sequence of facts as I best can remember them and that my memory may have to be verified by the actual bookkeeping and records on the issues that I will deal with. I suffer from a sleeping disorder, sleep apnea, which does affect my memory." I write this truthfully, not having realized, in the fog of the past two years, that the treatment I have been taking for the sleep apnea, the c-pap breathing machine, actually allows me to sleep better and therefore should have improved my memory and concentration. Why hasn't it? Obviously I've taken the improved sleep that I've been getting — when I've slept — as a licence to sleep less. As a result, as if my body has given me permission, I've gambled more frequently in the middle of the nights often getting by on little or no rest. In addition, the anxiety I have been suffering about the money I stole has completely destroyed my concentration, unless of course I am excitedly focused on a flip of a card or the spin of a wheel. Like the old adage, "there's nothing like a hanging to focus one's attention," if I am facing an imminent critical deadline, like tomorrow's meeting with Constable Lennon, then concentration, like hindsight, is twenty-twenty.

I never gave the treatment for sleep apnea a chance, as my late-night getaways in the bingo halls started almost as soon as I got my breathing machine in December of 1994. During one of those fanciful moments, looking for justification for my actions, I asked my sleeping disorder specialist if there had been any studies done on sleep apnea sufferers and insane behaviour.

Next in my statement I give my reasons for creating the Leacock Heritage Festival, "to produce a celebration in Orillia that would have an economic tourism impact and, as a cultural event, to celebrate the legacy of Mariposa that Stephen Leacock left to Orillia by writing *Sunshine Sketches of a Little Town*." Then my writing is heavy on the "funded by money raised primarily by me" and "with me as its Managing Chairman, without pay." I then explain about running Orillia's Canada Day celebrations and creating the Orillia Winter Carnival, being its volunteer, *unpaid* coordinator and treasurer.

"During the period of 1989 to December of 1994, I probably worked, between my job and my volunteer activities, about 80 to 100 hours a week. To say that there was a grey area between what was work and what was volunteer is an understatement other than as it relates to remuneration, as I was only paid for one forty-hour job." I also relate the story of how I often mixed expense accounts, travel accounts, et cetera, so everyone will understand how my "borrowing" started: "It was also not unusual for me to use expense money for my personal use and reimburse the organization fund the same as it would reimburse me when I used personal money for its business. I utilized this system with varying degrees of accountability for almost six years and explain it here because it contributed to the problems that I have today."

I then write: "I have an addictive personality. The way I work testifies to this. Anybody who knows me knows I jump with both feet into all things and I do nothing in moderation. I am a non-practising alcoholic, having been sober from February 3, 1978 through the help of AA, to now, almost 19 years. I smoked from 1967 to 1983 — almost three packs a day in the end. I quit Weedless Wednesday, January 26, 1983, cold turkey and haven't smoked since. My father was an alcoholic among his other addictions, most of which I have, and addictions are prevalent with my brothers and sisters.

"Since December of 1994, I have been addicted to gambling and have lived in the chaos that this addiction brings. My gambling addiction went from bingo to Nevada tickets, to Lottery Corporation scratch tickets and other lottery games. Then the addiction went to charity casino black jack and to real casino gambling in Sault Ste. Marie and Windsor when we investigated other casino communities as part of my job. My addiction then moved into the big leagues with the opening of Casino Rama where I was an almost daily patron. I quit gambling on October 22. I am seeking treatment. I am still living with the chaos. I hope this is the beginning of the end of that chaos." The chaos stuff is good, and true.

I explain the beginning of my bingo phase which was tied into the Leacock Festival's foray into bingo: "I also remember remarking that bingo wasn't what people imagined it to be, that it was really electronic gambling. Once you got familiar with it you could play 15–18 cards at a time and it provided the rush. In addition the hall also had Nevada tickets that could be played in between, during and after bingo games. It is not difficult to spend, progressively, $60, $80, and $100 a bingo session. Sometimes I went to two sessions a night. Sometimes I won, especially at Nevada but the money really just got poured back into more tickets. I only have a relatively fixed income, so I started paying for bingo and Nevada with Leacock Festival expense advances and Winter Carnival revenues. This began a two-year shell game of taking money from one pot to cover a short-fall in another, all the time hoping to win a jackpot that would be big enough to get me even and repay all the advances."

Then I relate the trips to the major casinos in Sault Ste. Marie and Windsor, how I lost my shirt each time and dug myself deeper into the accounts to which I had access. "My next gambling phase, however, would be blackjack at the charity casinos in Orillia and Barrie. I can't remember when I started gambling heavily at the charity casinos, whether it was September, October or November of 1995. The accounting records may tell us but they may not because

I was pretty lucky and became a good blackjack player, taught by other players, and may have been able to keep the revolving advances under control especially through the Leacock accounts.

"The Orillia Winter Carnival accounts and my own personal overdraft were also likely factors in feeding the blackjack of late 1995 and early '96. I recall writing cheques on the Winter Carnival account for what was supposed to be expense money, bingo float or for cash, and these moneys would be used for blackjack. Again a reconstruction of the books and access to the Winter Carnival bank, the Laurentian, will shed more light.

"The charity casinos were to the first half of 1996 what bingo was to the same period in 1995 except instead of gambling $100 to $200 a night I progressed from a few hundred to $500 to $1,000 and even more. Everybody thought that I always won. In a casino, everybody always thinks that everybody wins. (I certainly didn't tell anyone different.) I used bingo float money, deposit money, and cheques written for expenses to pay for gambling, which I was doing to repay the float money, the deposits and replace the cash. I began to be overdrawn at the Leacock bank — the Royal — and I had to begin my many calls to explain that we were expecting this cheque or that cheque to cover the overdraft.

"The next phase was the desperation phase," I write. "I gambled at the charity casinos heavily trying to get enough money to make the deposits, and file the bingo and Nevada reports. I fell behind in making the reports to the City of Orillia. By that time it was summer and I used the excuse that we were too busy with our summer events to complete the reports and file them. In reality I didn't have the money to make the deposits. We ran another charity casino in June and I think I used the deposits from that one to pay some of the deposits for bingo and Nevada, and file some reports. I recall Mr. Casino, the operator of our charity casino, looking for a cheque in July and I put them off indicating we were overdrawn in our main account and needed to keep the charity casino money in the bank until I received the $10,000 sponsorship cheque from Casino Rama which couldn't be paid until August, after the opening. In the end I arranged an increased overdraft for the Leacock Heritage Festival and that Mr. Casino cheque went through the account in August and the account remains in overdraft today.

"Given my state of mind, my panic at not being able to get even, I think I saw the opening of Casino Rama as my way out. Of course it wasn't. Sitting here writing this, having just related my experiences in Windsor and the Sault — five for five, broke — it's incredulous that I could have thought Casino Rama was going to save me, but I did. I must have, because I gambled everything I could in trying to win a solution at Casino Rama. In the end, what I saw as my mountain of a problem grew to be the whole mountain range."

I confess the obvious: "I didn't win. I won some and often lost it all the same night. More often, I lost — period. I used the same sources of money, except now any money that I did win was used to cover overdrafts at the Royal, or overdrafts at my bank or to replace cheques that bounced because the Royal Bank was fed up with the size of the overdraft. The 1996 Leacock Heritage Festival, held at the end of July and the beginning of August, was not a good festival money-wise, which made things worse because there was little money available for paying down the overdraft.

"I had stopped filing reports because there was no money for the deposits. However, now that the festival and summer were over, I no longer had an excuse and the City of Orillia was putting on pressure for the reports. I would have Doug Bell, the festival manager, complete and sign the report, giving it to me with a prepared deposit which I said I would look after. I filed the reports without making the deposits; instead just photocopying the deposit slips as if I had made the deposits. I had hoped I could get even and make the deposits after the fact."

Over the sound of my typing, even from my room with the door closed, I hear the doorbell. Ah, I think, my sisters. I quickly conclude my train of thought: "I don't know how many (phoney) reports I filed like this but it will be clear to the police upon review. There were also a number of reports and deposit slips prepared which were not filed yet and these will be turned over to the police."

I conclude for now: "The Royal Bank started bouncing cheques, many of them back on my personal account. Cheques that had been written out as cash advances, expenses and floats. This in turn started my bank bouncing cheques that I had cashed around the Downtown so I could gamble. The scramble and chaos that this created seemed to bring me to the reality that I wasn't going to win my way out of the mess."

My sister Veronica worked, to her dismay I am sure, as the school secretary at Simonds Regional High School at the same time I attended Grade 12 after I left the priesthood. Back home, my alcoholism and escapism accelerated into rebellion and pretension. I started living an image of myself, fed by the adolescent fantasies of my latest girlfriend, Donna, who saw us as "Bob Dylan and Joan Baez." I looked to her for validation of who I was. My image was enhanced by the beautiful girl by my side.

At school I played a schizophrenic-like character that swung between being the class clown and the leader of the opposition with the school principal as my adversary and the teachers as my rivals. I even made teachers that I liked cry.

Mrs. Hale's husband Fred owned the corner store on Russell Street near our house. During the short time I had a paper route when I was twelve, it was there that I picked up my papers and also ended my route. *A candy store for heavens sake!* It was only a few months later my mother had to bail me out for "eating the profits" — as we used to say at the restaurant — and I was out of my first newspaper job. Fred and I used to have some great old discussions while I devoured his candy counter and it was here that I first met his wife, who would be my biology teacher some six years later. Biology had always been a breeze to me. Remember the carpenter ants and earthworm Science Fair projects, complete with the experiments in how the worms regenerated if you cut them in half, and how the ants always found their way home, even after you blocked their existing tunnels? Grade 12 in New Brunswick was generally behind the kind of private school education I had received at St. Mary's, and nowhere was this more apparent than in biology, thus providing me with ample opportunity to enhance my comic reputation without destroying my high school diploma. Hell, I even had Perry Nice, my childhood extortionist, laughing. Unfortunately, it was at Mrs. Hale's expense, as she would run crying from the classroom when I'd show the class how to roast frog's legs with a Bunsen burner during the anatomy bisection class. I was legendary among my peers.

The tearful relationship between his wife and I never seemed to interfere with the rapport I had with Fred. It was like the connection you have with your bartender, and Hale's Grocery would become a place I would visit every time I returned to Saint John until the day it closed and Fred retreated into the sanctum of the house he and Rita — Mrs. Hale — shared behind the store. After the store closed I never saw him again, nor have I ever told Rita I was sorry for making her the patsy for my insecurities.

If I were to run into Mr. McDonald, my first History teacher of that year, I wouldn't be so apologetic. He called me "the import from Ontario" in the first class. I swore my vengeance and we made each other's lives miserable until they transferred me to another history teacher's class.

I led a school protest, complete with "unfair" placards and the news media, when my friend Bruce Garnet was first threatened and then suspended for not shaving off a beard he had grown for a school play. "You're next, Little," the principal, Billy Bishop — Veronica's boss — snarled at me across his desk once he kicked the television station cameras off school property.

Drinking became a greater part of my life — sneaking into bars, going to tailgate and bush parties, and drinking at dances. Did that cost me Donna? Who knows? The folkies were into another kind of intoxicant by that time and I wouldn't catch up for a few years. It's not easy living up to an image.

Throughout the year my mother and I remained at logger-heads over me "quitting" St. Mary's. Knowing that I basically got kicked out, I resented her attitude even more. It's not that she expected me to be a priest. It was the missed opportunity to go to university that she regretted. I could always find the moral high ground. "I couldn't pretend to want to be a priest just to get a free education," I told her.

However, I wasn't above pretending I wanted to be a soldier to achieve the same end. At the end of Grade 12, my friend Dave

Landry and I went to Centralia, Ontario, to try out for the Regular Officers Training Program. In ROTP, the armed forces would pay for your university education if you signed up for the military for a few years. To be a pilot in the Navy was my new fantasy, but I also wanted to go to journalism school at Carleton University in Ottawa. The flying reporter?

After 10 days of testing by day, and drinking and chasing girls by night in nearby Stratford and Strathroy, the Navy and I mutually decided that I wasn't suited for the structured life of the armed forces. Everybody seemed to believe me when I said I wasn't the type to take orders. Translation: I didn't get in.

After I flunked out of the military prior to enlisting, I decided to go back to Ontario — Toronto specifically. Another escape? I left family, home, school, community and what reputation I had.

The arrival of my sisters is a welcome respite from both the confession I am writing in my room and the guilt I am feeling in the rest of the house. Without their arrival I may never have come out of my refuge except to make a beeline for the door and back across the lake to finish myself off with one last plunge into the netherworld, one last immersion in the fever of gambling, there to implode, literally, so I would never have to face any of this again. When I quit drinking, everything got better. When I quit smoking I felt better after a few days. Now I have to quit gambling, yet I know things are going to get a lot worse. For the first time in two years I have to face the cold reality of the mess I have created without the hope that I can make it all go away with a big win. Wracked with worry, I find no hope even in the lottery tickets I bought earlier today. Now there is no winning. There is no escape.

Roberta has already let Veronica and Mary in by the time I come out of my bedroom, and they are almost in the kitchen when I meet them in the hall. I put my arms around Veronica and feel myself sob into her shoulder as I look behind her at the tears streaming down Roberta's face, brought on, I am sure, by a similar embrace at the door. I envy Roberta her tears, even her anger. She is so demonstrative of her feelings while mine are — except for the occasional choking snivel — stuffed down to fester and smoulder only to erupt at the most inappropriate time in a white-heat anger that robs me of my reason and my control. I have long mistrusted my emotions and hide them beneath an insulating exterior.

"Have you heard anything more from the police?" Veronica asks as we pull out chairs to sit around the kitchen table. Might as well get right to the point. That was always Veronica's way. Tears are fine but let's get down to business. My younger sister Mary, on the other hand, has always worn her emotions on her sleeve, and she joins Roberta with a box of Kleenex.

"No," I answer, and at the mention of police bounce out of my chair almost as soon as I sit down. "I don't expect anything more until we meet tomorrow or maybe the next day. I talked to a lawyer earlier tonight and he wants me to try to postpone the appointment until Thursday because he's in court tomorrow and he wants to be there." Earlier I tried to call Rod Williams, one of my contacts in the O.P.P., an inspector at Headquarters with whom I had worked closely on the opening ceremonies. I left a message to see if he could contact Officer Lennon and have her call me first thing in the morning.

"So you have contacted a lawyer?" Veronica asks the obvious, but what she really wants to know is whether he is any good.

"He's a guy I used to work with on a committee. He's older; he went back to law school about ten years ago. I trust him which, considering the circumstances, is probably the most important thing." I tell them about my call to Lorenzo and his advice, as well the conversation with Brian. I hang for dear life on his words, "I'd be honoured."

"Well, that's a good step. What do you think is going to happen next?"

"I'm not sure," I answer. "I have to hand everything over to the police either tomorrow or the next day and Brian has me writing out a statement which he wants to see before I give it to the police. That's what I was doing when you arrived." I tell them that the reports and accounts of what I took from the charity casinos — which is what Constable Lennon is looking for — will clearly show what I did. "I was borrowing, or at least that was what I kept telling myself. I always had records of what I owed so I could pay it back." As I say this I can see Roberta's incredulity and anger rising. No doubt she thinks the worst. "Of course, while the money I took from the casinos, bingo and Nevada tickets will be relatively easy to track, it will be a little more difficult to figure out how much I owe to the bank accounts as a result of my writing cheques on one account and cashing them at another. Still, all the records are somewhere and I am going to commit to help the police with the accounting."

Veronica and Mary accept my confession as a first step, and tell me they are going to lend what support they can to both me and Roberta to see us through the next few days.

"What about publicity?" Veronica asks.

"I'm not sure," I reply. "There is nothing yet but I suppose if they arrest me tomorrow then it will be all over the newspapers, radio and television. My position in Orillia is going to make this front-page news here, and my involvement in the Casino and the festival could make it news right across the country." My journalistic instinct tells me the irony of the community casino promoter being arrested for stealing to gamble will be front-page news coast to coast.[10]

"I'm not going to be able to show my face in town," Roberta cries. "How could you do this to us?"

"I didn't do it to you — or at least I didn't mean to — I was trying to win back the money. I couldn't stop. Besides, that's why I want you to go, to just pack your clothes and leave first thing in the morning. Go home to Timmins." I am pacing back and forth in the kitchen like I am already imprisoned, unable to run out because they are barring all the doorways. The Nevada ticket money, hidden in the glove compartment of the van, appears wistfully in my mind.

"I have nowhere to go," Roberta cries. "Timmins is not my home. Everything I have is here except Melanie. This is going to destroy Melanie."

"Doug, Roberta, stop. This isn't helping anybody. Roberta, why don't you go into the living room with Mary so Doug and I can talk about what we are all going to do together."

"Don't you dare run away, you bastard," Roberta snaps at me though her tears. "That would be just like you."

"Maybe I should have run a long time ago," I answer, more to myself than her but then aloud I yell after her, "Melanie is fine. I talked to Melanie. At least she's trying to understand."

Veronica separates the two of us, admonishing me not to respond to Rob's anger, explaining to me that she is entitled to her anger. She didn't gamble away our lives. How I want to deny that I have, but tonight all my delusions have come crashing down.

"Doug," Veronica says softly, once she's calmed me down. "We have to call Mom."

"How can I?"

Annie MacKinnon met Doug Little Sr., in a small rural New Brunswick village of Hampton not far from the hamlet of Apohaqui where he had been raised by his mother, Martha, and his stepfather — a crusty, mean old man I only knew as "Brownie." I learned that Brownie was a son-of-a-bitch when it came to his treatment of my father, employing physical and verbal abuse that eventually drove my father from their home and community when he was fifteen years old. Brownie was also an alcoholic. Dad was fifteen and Mom was thirteen when they first met; he had come to Hampton to live with his cousins, the Giggys. I grew up never quite under-standing how I could have just two cousins named MacKinnon on my mother's side and yet a myriad of relatives named Little, Brown, Baxter, Daigle, and Giggy in my father's family. As I grew older some of the family connections became clearer. Of course I always knew my dad's father, Arthur Little, died of tuberculosis when my father was three. My widowed Grandmother had her hands full with six kids, with the oldest, Aunt Lola, blinded at birth by a nurse pouring the wrong chemical into her eyes. Nanny

Brown, as I knew her, remarried and she and "Brownie" had two other children.

Growing up we saw the Browns and Littles often as we visited Apohaqui to see my Grandmother. Aunt Lola's family, the Baxters, lived in Saint John. There was also our Daigle cousin, Ruthie, who lived with us for a while, related to my father's mother Martha, whose maiden name was Daigle — establishing our French-Canadian Acadian roots. Then, at least once a year, usually around Christmas, this obscure cousin, Bert Giggy would make an appearance at our house.

In his later life, my Uncle Gordon became an amateur genealogist and family historian. He believed the Giggy connection came from a "Little" family scandal involving my father's grandfather, another handsome and enigmatic David Little. Dad's father, Arthur, was born a Giggy but was adopted by his neighbour David Little when Mrs. Giggy died at childbirth. What Uncle Gordon concluded was that David Little was "a fence jumper." However, in defence of my great-great grandmother's honour, the fact is Mr. Giggy was blind and unable to care for his children without her, and all the children were adopted by different families. Gordon's "Little" ego may not have allowed him to accept he really was — a Giggy.

If I came from a dysfunctional family and crisis household, and if I "came by my addictions honestly," as my mother would tell me this night, so did my father. Alcoholism is a condition I can confirm in at least one of his brothers, my Uncle Jimmy, who once tried to fondle me in a drunken stupor when I stayed at his home at the age of sixteen. I wasn't close enough to my other uncles to judge their ability to drink but I do know they have suffered heart diseases and cancers that seem to be genetically linked throughout my father's family.

My mother didn't even know my father drank when she married him and would not have married him if she had known. A strict Baptist, she converted to the Roman Catholic Church in order to marry my father in 1940. My oldest brother Jimmy was born in the next year, followed three years later by David in 1944, Veronica in 1946, and me in 1948. My mother told me she was devastated the first time my father came home drunk. Perhaps she would have left him were it not for her fervent faith in the Catholic Church and its no-divorce decree, and the fact she had given birth to a child every second year until 1952. The birth of her last two children, born in 1958 and 1960, almost killed her due to the exhaustion she suffered dealing with my father's drinking, his career crisis, and his under-capitalized entry into the restaurant business. She was taking care of six and seven of her own kids plus caring for, and eventually adopting, the child of her oldest son. In 1959 Jimmy's seventeen-year-old girlfriend Sheila gave birth to my brother Kevin and her mother would not let her keep the baby. My mother took him in, along with Sheila for a time, and it wasn't until he was in his teens that Kevin knew his oldest brother was actually his father. These births coincided with a huge crisis in my father's life, the death of his boss at Green's Restaurant, and the beginning of the monumental task of creating his own restaurant with little or no money. My father's drinking accelerated, as did my mother's vehemence against it, resulting in World War Three every time my father came home drunk. I've learned that my mother's stance with the sideboard from new bunk beds she was building — from my childhood memory — was not just a defensive pose against harm but also her own version of *no means no* to my father's drunken amorous overtures. Like me if I hadn't had

Roberta, I have to wonder: How long would my father have lived if he'd had a submissive woman who just let him drink himself to death?

Veronica is right. As much as I dread telling my mother what I have done and hate the shame I am about to bring upon the family name, I can't let her read about it in the newspaper or hear about it from some catty neighbour in Fredericton. I once did a freelance article for the *Fredericton Gleaner*, and someone might remember me and use the angle of former-local-boy-does-bad to splash my story all over the front page. While my first instincts were not to tell anyone tonight, I am grateful I have taken this path because I'm not sure that in my self-centred survival mode I would have remembered or had the courage to call my mother. I mention only my mother because, even though I will talk to both my mother and father, my father's Alzheimer's has progressed to the point where, while he'll understand what I am telling him at the time, he'll forget that I said it in a minute or two. When I visited Fredericton with Melanie in August, I learned of the death of my father's beloved dog. Thunder was a massive half-Siberian Husky, half-malamute who excavated the back yard of my parents' Sunset Boulevard home for several years once all the kids were finally gone. In a particularly cruel manifestation of his disease, my father's memory loss would cause him to regularly head out to feed Thunder, only to have to be told that Thunder was dead. Each time, he would live through the pain of his loss and mourning all over again.

But tonight, I am not in a very pro-Doug Little mood, whether the Doug in question be Jr. or Sr. I don't suppose I know it yet, but I have come to this place by avoiding both Doug Littles.

Veronica primes them for the bad news, getting my mother and father on the extension phones. She tells them she is at my house and that while I am well health-wise (she doesn't want to scare them into thinking I've had another heart attack, or worse), I am in trouble and need to talk to them.

"Hi Mom, Hi Dad," I start reluctantly. Even as I prepare to confess to my parents the devastation that gambling has brought to me and my family, I want more than anything to be standing in front of a dozen casino roulette wheels yelling for all my life, "Seventeen! Come on seventeen! Lucky seventeen!"

In May of 1978 I was celebrating three months without drinking at an AA meeting while my mother and father were visiting us in Timmins. I invited them to the meeting.

"There's too much cigarette smoke at those meetings, my heart can't take all that smoke," my father said, referring to his series of heart attacks and the addiction he conquered flat on his back in the intensive care ward of St. Joseph's Hospital. "You better quit smoking, Doug, or it'll kill you quicker than alcohol ever will."

Dad had it down to a science. His doctors told him to quit smoking or die, so he did; but they also said a shot of whisky a day was good for his heart, good to relieve the stress and tension that comes with just being a Little male, especially a Doug Little one. So he had to drink for his health, and if occasionally, unintentionally, he drank too much, it was a small price to pay to keep the heart attack stress at bay. *A classic Doug Little rationalization.*

All of a sudden my father had to get back on the road and they weren't able to attend my celebration. Afterwards I gave myself credit for showing my father the way into Alcoholics Anonymous, for he joined less than a year later and the last seventeen years of my parents' fifty-six year marriage have been a relative heaven for my mother in comparison to the previous thirty-nine. A few years ago my parents went on a trailer-home trip through the United States with Veronica and her husband Bob. Somehow my father got his hands on an American beer and drank it amidst protests from my mother and sisters. "That's not real beer," he scoffed, "it's just like soda pop." In the first stages of undiagnosed Alzheimer's, my father forgot he was an alcoholic. Fortunately, because of the disease, he quickly forgot that he had broken his abstinence and went back to sobriety.

Shortly after my parents left Timmins in 1978, I had what I used to call my "spiritual awakening" in AA. One night I was sitting alone in our kitchen, having come home after a meeting to find everyone in bed. Why did I drink? I asked myself. Why did I drink beer, wine, vodka, and rum? Why did I smoke pot, and for the few times I did do it, drop acid?

To get stoned. Buzzed. Drunk. The more I thought about it that was the only reason to drink, or do drugs — to get smashed. I didn't think about why I had to get "smashed": it was revelation enough for me that I knew that I did. So-called "normal drinkers" don't drink just to get drunk.

Why would anybody want to drink for any other reason? What the hell good were one or two beers? All that would have done was make me tired, cranky. I had no desire to be a social drinker; in fact, I abhorred the idea.

It was perhaps the first time I came to the realization that I didn't have a wife problem. I had a drinking problem. That night I accepted that I was an alcoholic and could never drink normally again, not that I ever had. There have been few times in my life when I have been brought to a place where I might just admit that my way is not the best way. In 1978, after years of battling alcoholism, poised to lose my family — and especially my daughter — as well as my home, job, and community, I found myself in such a place within the rooms of Alcoholics Anonymous. I accepted that drugs were the same trip for me as alcohol, and at the very least would lead me back to the booze. I gave them up at the same time. I attended meetings — a couple a week — where we shared our experience, strength, and hope with each other, and it was in these meetings I came to view my sobriety as a gift. I thought quitting for me was relatively easy compared to others I saw in the AA program who were struggling, trying hard to quit and yet slipping and, in at least one case, dying. I believed I was a "high-bottom" drunk because I hadn't hit skid row, hadn't been institutionalized — hospitals or jail — or hadn't been caught driving drunk. Of course these were all rationalizations, but at the time I had no inclination to learn the truth about myself, I was just looking for a way out. Another escape. That I never owned a car, that I only started driving a year or so before I quit, was chalked up to luck. I gave no thought to the possibility that I instinctively avoided driving for years as self-preservation. I had escaped alcoholism just in time to save myself. A survivor, until the next thing. What I did take from this high-bottom myth was a belief that somehow I had been blessed with the ability to quit — a gift — but, should I ever drink (or do drugs) again, I would not be able to quit a second time.

Even during the nightmare of those desperate mornings after gambling and losing I never drank. (Melanie has told me that this was her greatest fear after our emotional phone call.) The image of alcohol that came to reside with me from those AA meetings was of poison, bottles with the skull and crossbones symbol, hidden under the sink. Bottles with corks never to be opened, at least not by me.

While I do not want to make light of my five years in AA, because no doubt about it, it did save my life, acceptance that I was an alcoholic and that alcohol was for me lethal were the only lessons I learned. I saw the "Twelve Steps" to recovery as something nobody really did and believed that as long as I quit drinking I would be okay. I had nothing from which to recover. I just had to stop. If that was my attitude, it was reinforced at home. Roberta grew to dislike me going to meetings almost as much as she hated my drinking, claiming, accurately perhaps, that the meetings were just a way to get out of the house, the same as my drinking.

The other sadness was that drugs and alcohol were always such a large part of our physical sexual relationship, and their lack, especially grass, which we never had again, created another barrier to intimacy. That, combined with Roberta's unwillingness to accept my sexual evolution or in her words "perversion," meant that our sex life became non-existent. In AA there is a joke about sex and recovery: a new member goes to his sponsor, an old-timer wise in the AA way, and says he's heard you are not supposed to have sex for at least a year after joining AA. "That's a gall-darn lie," the old-timer says. "You can have all the sex you want in your first year in AA, and then, in the second year, you can start having it with other people."

Of course I contributed to this in an ongoing manner, just as I likely caused it all with my earlier patterns of coming and going. It was easy to bury myself in work. I had been trained in the newspaper business and our need for money to pay for Melanie's figure skating was growing. When the Praise Building Corporation finally exasperated the patience of its God and went into bankruptcy, I wound up straddling a fence between journalism and marketing. I started a small public relations company called Little Services from which I coordinated marketing for a Timmins mall, worked with a small supermarket chain and ran election campaigns for the Tories and various municipal candidates. The weekly that I had abandoned in 1977 ceased to publish and a new newspaper called *NorthStar*, patterned off the hugely successful *Toronto Sun*, came after me to be its editor and columnist. I was the editor until the next federal election in 1979, when I stepped down to become the Timmins-Chapleau campaign manager for the Conservatives in Joe Clark's modest and short-lived national election victory, which we lost locally. Actually, we weren't supposed to win. In an unwritten, unspoken pact between the Liberals and Conservatives in Timmins, the way we kept the NDP out of office both provincially and federally was for the Tories to run a weak candidate in the federal elections, allowing the Liberals to win, and for the Liberals to run a weak candidate in the provincial election, thus not splitting the anti-socialist — as we used to call it — vote and electing the Conservative. While I gave up my editorship — which I didn't like anyway — I kept writing my two columns: "My Little Opinion" and "Little's Street Talk." The opinion column was where I could engage in investigative reporting, exposés and general muckraking. Street Talk was a great *little* page — patterned, I suppose, after Gary Dunford's highly successful Page Six in the *Toronto Sun* — of irreverent rumours, anecdotes, gossip, and news scoops. My threat was, "If you don't read it this week, you'll be in it next."

The young Little Family circa 1951. From the left in the back: Veronica, Doug Jr. sitting on Doug Sr., Baby Mary with Mom Anne, and David. Sitting up in the front: Jimmy.

Christmas 1953 — Dougie and sister Veronica.

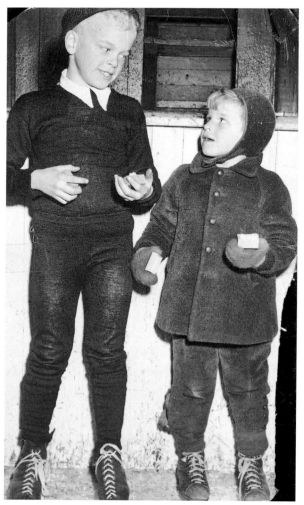

Medal winners — 1954
Dave and Doug Little at
the Maritime Speed
Skating Championships.

May 1954 — A day out
from under Sister
Noberta's desk.

Circa 1964 — Fellow seminarians Paul Kennedy and Doug
take a summer break at the beach.

Circa 1974 — Roberta and Melanie at the rink.

1979 — Smokin' PC Campaign Manager in Timmins.

1989 — Roberta and Doug at the inaugural
Mariposa Ball celebrating the premiere
Leacock Heritage Festival.

1990 — Unveiling the award-winning poster for the Second Annual Leacock Heritage Festival.

1991 — Presentation of the limited edition print to Prime Minister Brian Mulroney.

1992 — When gambling was still just for fun.

February 25, 1997 Published in Orillia since 1870 75¢ GST incl.

Court appearance

Little: 'I'll take responsibility'

By Colin McKim
The Packet & Times

Downtown manager Doug Little admitted yesterday he is receiving treatment for a gambling addiction, and says he will face the consequences of his actions head on.

"I've got to take responsibility for what I did and I'm going to," Little said, following a brief appearance in Orillia court yesterday morning.

The 48-year-old manager of Orillia's downtown management board was charged with criminal breach of trust and theft in late January, following the disappearance $80,000 in funds from bingos and charitable casinos.

Little has cooperated with police since the Orillia OPP began looking into the possible misappropriation of funds from the Leacock Heritage Festival, which Little chairs.

A few days after the investigation became public, Little took a sick leave to receive treatment for compulsive gambling.

Coming to grips with the consequences of his addiction has been difficult, Little told The Packet & Times yesterday.

"It's something that's very regrettable. I'm still bewildered by myself. But we'll deal with it."

Little said he is staying with relatives in Toronto and is enrolled in a problem-gambling program at the Donwood Institute.

"I'm also getting psychiatric help," he said.

Whatever the outcome of the court case, Little says it's unlikely he will move back to Orillia.

"It would be pretty difficult to return to Orillia. I have to turn pages in my life."

Little sat by himself in the Orillia courthouse.

After leaving the courtroom Little stopped to talk to reporters and pose for a photograph with his lawyer Brian Turnbull.

Little is charged with six counts of criminal breach of trust; five counts of theft over $5,000; one count of theft under $5,000; and three counts of breach of terms under which a lottery licence is issued.

"Breach of trust is a serious offence," said Brian Turnbull, Little's lawyer.

Anyone convicted could be sentenced to several years in jail, said Turnbull.

Turnbull intends to tell the court about Little's gambling addiction and call expert witnesses to shed light on the problem.

But gambling addiction itself is not a defence, said Turnbull.

"A judge would probably consider that (gambling addiction) on sentencing."

Little's case has been remanded until March 24.

At that point he can ask for a preliminary hearing or to have the case transferred to a higher court, said Turnbull.

Anyone with a gambling problem should seek immediate help, said Little, pulling out business cards for the Donwood Institute and the Canadian Foundation of Compulsive Gambling from his wallet.

"If anybody has a problem, they should seek treatment," he said.

When the court case concludes, Little promises to tell all.

"When it's over I will talk."

P&T

Court date

Doug Little and his lawyer Brian Turnbull pos... Orillia courthouse Monday morning for photogra... with breach of trust and theft of charitable funds, L... in court March 24.

Little supported by friends, family

By Joanna Frape
The Packet & Times

Many Orillians still support former downtown manager Doug Little despite his admitted guilt to defrauding three local organizations of almost $70,000, a provincial court heard yesterday.

Defence lawyer Brian Turnbull presented 33 character letters, mostly from prominent Orillia citizens including Mayor Clayt French, former MP Doug Lewis and Stephen Leacock Board Member Doug Bell, to the court before Little's sentencing.

"All of the letters have the same theme, an exceptional worker, tireless efforts to the community" said Turnbull.

"People thought enough about his work to write these letters."

Turnbull also swept his arms around the courtroom filled with Orillia supporters, including French and Alderman Ron McLean, as proof of the community's continued support to the man who "created Mariposa."

Little pleaded guilty May 23 to three counts of fraud and one count of breaking the terms of a lottery licence.

Mariposa Market owner Robert Willsey took the stand to testify to the long hours Little dedicated to Orillia and the lead-ing role h...

Tulip Festival in Ottawa who testified Little was a leader in setting up Festivals Ontario. Gauthier also told the court he still respects Little and has offered him a job.

"Doug has always been generous and has been there for everyone. He is always committed," said Gauthier. "If he wants it, Doug has a job."

The defence painted a picture of a man struggling with a gambling addiction so out of control it ended with him hitting rock bottom and wanting to kill himself. Turnbull told the court Little didn't run away from his problems but decided to take responsibility for his actions and get help with his addiction.

"His cooperation was exceptional," said Turnbull.

A psychiatrist and a therapist at Donwood Institute in Toronto where Little went to get treatment both testified Little is a pathological gambler who has done everything he can to get help. Little is also a recovered alcoholic.

Michael O'Brien a member of Gamblers Anonymous testified Little regularly attends meetings.

"He has become a role model for other clients because of his commitment and his desire," said O'Brien.

Turnbull ... ets his ... the ... to ... d ... is

Receiving therapy

Little a 'gambling addict'

By Colin McKim
The Packet & Times

Downtown manager Doug Little, charged in the disappearance of more than $80,000, has "a serious gambling addiction."

"He's receiving therapy in Toronto for a serious gambling addiction that he's developed," his lawyer Brian Turnbull confirmed yesterday.

"I suspect he's had the problem for a couple of years and it's been getting worse," said Turnbull, an Orillia law...

fy at Little's trial, which begins Feb. 24 in Orillia provincial court.

"I'll be bringing expert evidence to shed light on some of the aspects of his illness."

Turnbull said the trial will offer startling insight into the pathological side of gambling.

"It will all come out."

Little has apparently moved out of the city and could not be reached for comment.

Little asked for a medical leave from his job as downtown manager ... ched ... cock ... ated

Exclusive

The investigation grew to include money missing from the Downtown Management Board (DMB) and the winter carnival. Little is the treasurer of the carnival.

The OPP and Ontario Gaming Control Commission laid 15 charges against Little last week, including criminal breach of trust and theft.

Mayor Clayt French said he has been aware for some time that Little has been getting help for a compulsive gambling problem.

When police began investigating the misappropriation of funds from the Leacock Heritage Festival, Little informed the mayor and city manager Ian Brown that he had a gambling addiction, said French.

"Doug made a point of telling me. My understanding is it's a medical illness."

Mike Knight, chairman of the downtown management board, refused to disclose the nature of Little's illness.

But members of the board knew the problem was related to gambling, said one board member.

"It was pretty well understood," said the board member, who asked not to be identified.

Little was known to gamble at Casino Rama, local charity casinos and bingo halls, and with lottery tickets.

The final sum of money missing has yet to be determined, said OPP spokesman Gail Webster.

Little has been assisting the police in their investigation, said Webster.

"He's being very helpful."

Mayor French said he was shocked at the sum of money that has gone missing.

"I had no idea it was that high."

Beating bushes

Festival landlord seeks rent

By Colin McKim
The Packet & Times

Call it a case of mistaken indemnity.

The landlord of the offices for the Leacock Heritage Festival has tried to collect six months of overdue rent from several groups and individuals unconnected with the festival.

And that has at least one group worried about negative publicity.

The chairman of the Stephen Leacock Associates was shocked to receive a letter from a landlord, saying the Leacock Heritage Festival was $3,400 behind in its rent.

"I don't know why this happened," said Judith Rapson. "They somehow thought I might have been a director of the festival."

The Stephen Leacock Museum has also been pursued by the same festival creditors, said curator Daphne Mainprize.

"I called my lawyer to find out my liability," said Mainprize.

She was relieved to discover the festival is incorporated.

"Nobody is liable because it's a numbered company."

But Mainprize still wonders how her name came to be on a list of festival directors.

It's been more that two years since she attended a festival board meeting and then only as a liaison between the museum and the festival.

"I didn't know my name existed as an officer of that company."

Rapson said her involvement with the festival was also strictly as a liaison.

She was just as surprised as Mainprize to find the landlord considered her a director.

The Leacock Associates and the Leacock Heritage Festival are completely different organizations, Rapson stressed.

"We are not associated with the festival. When someone else uses the Leacock name people get confused."

The summer festival is under investigation for the possible misappropriation of charitable funds. Festival chairman Doug Little is on a sick leave connected with the investigation.

"We don't want our association smeared in any kind of way," Rapson said.

A number of other people loosely connected with the festival also received copies of the letter from Consortium Capital Projects.

Sheldon Godfrey, a principal in the Toronto company, said the letter was sent to try and flush out someone to take responsibility for the rent owed by the festival.

"We don't know who to speak to," said Godfrey.

...nday ...rch 17, 1997 CityLife News Editor Randy Richmond 325-1357 Page 3 Orillia Packet & Times

...ittle's fall from grace

...wntown boss details ...scent into nightmare

...dy Richmond
...ET AND TIMES

...Little did nothing by ...ncluding destroying his

...he type of person who ...o everything with two ...e says, speaking from his ...ome near Toronto. ...beginning of the inter... nervous, tentative, his ...y, but by the end he is ...te, outspoken and gre... ...tle that ran the city's

..., has been charged in ...80,000 from the ...itage Festival, the ...ival and the Downtown ... Board. He was chair... ...stival, treasurer of the ... manager of the ... board.

... admitted his gambling ...he Packet & Times, ...nt indepth interview, ...scent.

... work here in 1988 as ...f the downtown, ...te the city's core

...inence grew each ...d the Leacock ...l, a highly success... ...nt in the summer,

...ark mutton chops ...ume, Little looked, ..., like a riverboat

...re was a down... ...ity festival, Little ... Farmers' ...ay celebrations, ...ask force - Little worked for or helped manage them all.

... recalls feeling.

"I created my own mini-casinos I had bingo cards in the middle, a pile of Nevada tickets at my left hand and scratch tickets at my right. I was pretty ferocious with my Nevada tickets. I could open them with one hand while I played bingo with the other."

He went through $300 to $400 a night, first at the bingo halls from 10 p.m. until closing at 1 a.m., then with the scratch tickets for an hour at home.

He began borrowing money from the accounts he oversaw, says Little.

"I had access to all these accounts and started juggling them."

And he began visiting charity casinos in Orillia and Barrie.

The first few times he played blackjack he lost, so he began teaching himself the game on computer.

"I was looking for the big jackpot to get me out from problems," he says.

In the spring of 1995 he visited a casino in Sault, Mich. while on a conference for Festivals Ontario, a ...

... wired up.

He went back the next day and blew that too.

In less than 24 hours, he had lost about $3,000.

"I jumped from the frying pan into the raging fire"

...ing, Casino Rama was the perfect solution.

"I saw it as my salvation."

He could leave when he was losing and come back later to win.

"This is going to be perfect," he remembers thinking. "In reality, I never left."

He gambled "eight days a week. If I wasn't there every day, I was there often enough, two or three times a day, to make up for it. I would gamble after my wife went to sleep, until four in the morning, then get three hours sleep and go to work. I did three months in Casino Rama, day in and day out. By the end I was in there in the day time. I'd go to work with no sleep. I went to casino task force meetings after gambling all night."

Just before the crash, a person he knows who works for the casino asked him if he was in trouble.

"I said I was fine. I believed it even when I was going crazy."

He had to play three slot machines at once, or all the spots at ...

...lem. Others heard about the investigation and soon the news was public.

His wife has since moved to be with her family in Timmins, while Little lives with his near Toronto to get treatment. His daughter is attending university in British Columbia.

His case is still before a judge, but Little has no problem admitting guilt.

"It was a crime. It's that stark."

He wishes there was a way to get help before he fell so deeply into gambling.

Casino Rama has recently begun a self-help program for people worried about gambling. A local Gamblers' Anonymous has sprung up and Georgian College will offer programs this fall on dealing with gambling addiction.

Little applauds all these moves.

"There really wasn't anywhere I could reach out and turn to," he says.

Still, he doesn't know if he would have reached out for help even it was available.

"It's tough to penetrate the denial and the rationalization. I blame myself."

"A few times since I've quit, I've been in danger of going back. In times of distress I think, 'What the hell, I might as well go and end it all.'"

Naturally, the thought of jail frightens him. In one respect, it reminds him of the nightmare of gambling.

"For people like me, the loss of control is frightening. I have absolutely no control over what is going to happen."

Equally troublesome, he is still figuring out who Doug Little is.

June 28, 1997   Published in Orillia since 1870   75¢ GST incl.

Doug Little pleads guilty

By Sarah Papple
The Packet & Times

Doug Little, the former manager of the Downtown Management Board, pleaded guilty to four of 15 charges Friday morning in Barrie. The other 11 charges were dropped.

Little, 49, pleaded guilty to criminal breach of trust with intent to defraud the Orillia winter carnival, criminal breach of trust with intent to defraud the Downtown Management Board, breach of terms and conditions, and theft of more than $5,000.

Little will be sentenced June 27.

Brian Turnbull, Little's lawyer, said he was pleased 11 other charges were dropped.

"The Crown Attorney and I have been negotiating since day one," said Turnbull.

"The Crown was satisfied that ...

Community service
...ittle spared jail term

By ... Frape
... Times

... Little, an admitted gam-... walked out of Barrie ... man yesterday after a ... judge decided the former ... manager would not go to jail for defrauding three Orillia organizations of almost $70,000.

Little, who pleaded guilty on May 23 to three counts of fraud and one count of breaching the terms of a lottery licence, was sentenced to 12 months yesterday to be served in the community instead of prison.

He was also ordered to pay $200 a month to the court in restitution and to eventually pay back the $69,852.07 he owes the downtown management board, the Orillia Winter Carnival and the Leacock Heritage Festival.

"The charges to which Mr.

Little pleaded guilty are extremely serious not only in the amount of money but because by breaching this trust he has betrayed every citizen of Orillia," said Judge Paul Hermiston during sentencing.

Looking at a courtroom packed with Orillia supporters for Little, including Mayor Clayt French and Alderman Ron McLean, Hermiston said, "It is evident to me this community supports Little even today and I'm satisfied his compulsion to gamble and his predisposition to addiction caused his present difficulties."

Defence lawyer Brian Turnbull asked the court for the conditional sentence and had to prove Little was not a threat to the community and the circumstances of the crimes were exceptional.

"His past and present addiction is an illness that creates exceptional circumstances," said Hermiston.

The judge allowed Little's guilty plea showed remorse and his significant contributions to Orillia should not be forgotten. Hermiston also took into consideration that Little is currently receiving treatment for his pathological gambling.

"It's not in the public's interest to unduly interrupt this process by

He plans to increase awareness of compulsive gambling and assist other gambling addicts to find help.

Little, 49, who now lives in Mississauga, is sorry for the harm he has caused Orillians.

His family is glad to have the shameful affair behind, he said.

"It was like a roller coaster ride when the judge was talking. I was uncertain and nervous," said Little. "It was a tough day and I never want to go through a day like this again ever in my life."

Mayor Clayt French assured Orillians justice was done yesterday.

"When you consider the hard work Doug has done for the main street of Orillia, the sentence is adequate," said French, who pointed out Little has a recognized illness that contributed to his crimes.

Crown attorney John Alexander who asked the judge to give Little 18 months in jail, said fraud cases involving trust are too serious to receive conditional sentences and there needs to be a stronger deterrent for others who might consider committing the same crime.

"The provision is new and is generally confined to theft and fraud cases that do not involve the nature of breech of trust we have here," said Alexander.

Alexander hinted there could be an appeal.

Little must meet as part of his sentence a curfew from 10 p.m. to 6

P&T photo/Rod Frketich

Festival investigation expands
Winter carnival probed

By Colin McKim
The Packet & Times

The Orillia Winter Carnival has been drawn into a police investigation of the Leacock Heritage Festival.

Late last month The Packet & Times learned the OPP and the province's Gaming Control Commission were investigating the Leacock Heritage Festival for possible misappropriation of charitable funds.

The two-week festival was run by Doug Little, manager of the city's Downtown Management Board (DMB).

Two days after news of the

investigation broke, Little notified the Downtown Management Board (DMB) he was taking a sick leave because of an unspecified illness.

At the time Little acknowledged the sick leave was connected to ... investigation.

Yesterday Little, who was ... treasurer of the Winter Carni... confirmed the Winter Carni... financial records have been t... over to investigators.

"The books are in the ha ... the police," he said.

The Winter Carnival ... about $4,500 to the Orillia ... District Construction Asso... for blocks of ice purchased ... last year's ice castle.

Carnival chairman Ron McLean told The Packet he originally thought the bill had been paid.

McLean said he wondered what ... when he learned the ...

"It will all come out in time," he said.

Numerous local businesses claim they are owed money by the Leacock Heritage Festival.

One of the largest claims, from Mr. Casino, is for close to $20,000.

... he hoped the ...

said McLean.

The Packet & Times

November 27, 1996   Published in Orillia since 1870   75¢ GST incl.

Misappropriation of funds?
Leacock Festival probed

By Colin McKim
... Times

Leacock Heritage Festival ... investigated for possible ... opriation of funds. The ... community services officer at the ... Times has learned.

... Ontario Gaming Control ... ion is investigating the ... the Leacock Heritage ... old Ali-Campion, director ... lations for the Ministry ... er and Commercial

The OPP Central Region Crime Unit is also involved in the investigation, said Sgt. Gail Webster, a community services officer at the general headquarters in Orillia.

The investigation involves possible misappropriation of funds, said Webster.

"My understanding is police have an investigation going on and ... he's co-operating," said Doug Little, chairman of the Leacock

Heritage Festival board. Little is also manager of the downtown management board.

Little would not comment any further on the investigation.

The Heritage Festival runs for two weeks in the summer in Orillia, and includes a downtown sidewalk sale, entertainment and other events celebrating Stephen Leacock, the world famous author who summered in Orillia.

The Leacock Heritage Festival

derives much of its revenue from bingo, charity casinos and the sale of Nevada tickets.

A Monte Carlo Night for the festival, scheduled to run three days this week, was suspended as a result of the investigation, said Campion.

The festival has an annual budget of $90,000 to $100,000, said former board member Ken McMullen.

McMullen keeps the books for the festival from its inception in

1989 until he resigned in March of this year.

"I got complete records. Everything balanced when I did the books."

The board has not been active recently and McMullen could not think of anyone other than Little who is still a member.

"Doug was the driving force always has been the driving force."

DMB manager
Sick leave tied to OPP probe

By Colin McKim
The Packet & Times

Orillia's downtown manager Doug Little said today his sick leave is connected to a police investigation into the Leacock Heritage Festival.

"There's no use in denying that," Little told The Packet & Times this morning.

However Little would not specify the illness.

"An illness is a private thing."

The Downtown Management Board (DMB) announced this morning that Little is taking sick leave for an undisclosed illness.

"Doug Little will be unavailable for work for an indefinite period of time due to illness," said a one-paragraph release from the board.

DMB chairman Mike Knight said he didn't know the nature of Little's illness.

"I have no idea. I'm not a physician."

Little is the DMB manager. He is also chairman of the Leacock Heritage Festival, which runs for two wee... brates ... The ... is bein... and th... Commi... proprie...

Li... ating ... to com... Lit... and N... Leaco... police...

The festival's licensing privileges for a charity casinos have also been suspended by the Ontario Gaming Control Commission.

Little has been manager of the DMB since the late 1980s, promoting the downtown and becoming a driving force behind a number of ... festivals including the

---

March 1, 1997   Published in Orillia since 1870   75¢ GST incl.

No replacement
Downtown to fire Little

By Colin McKim
The Packet & Times

Orillia's Downtown Management Board (DMB) has taken legal steps to fire its manager Doug Little, The Packet & Times has learned.

And they may eliminate the position of manager altogether.

"There are no plans in place to replace Doug," said board chairman Mike Knight.

"The Downtown Management Board is functioning very well right now."

A self-confessed gambling addict, Little

faces 15 charges of breach of trust and theft in connection with the disappearance of more than $60,000 in charitable funds.

Little requested a sick leave in late November, shortly after the police investigation into the Leacock Heritage Festival, which he chairs, became public.

The sick leave expires March 24, the same day Little will make his second appearance in Orillia court.

At a recent meeting the board passed a motion directing their solicitor to notify Little in writing that he is dismissed, said two board members who asked to

remain anonymous.

Knight would not comment on the firing, but outlined plans for the future of the DMB.

The board of directors will take a more active role in the running of the DMB office, said Knight.

"It's time to make some changes. We need to re-evaluate the direction the board has been going for the last few years."

In the fall the board will decide whether to eliminate the position of manager completely.

"We don't need a manager," said DMB board member Bruce Jones.

"All the directors have picked up the slack. Now the board can be the architect of its own success."

There was concern among board members that Little, who has run his own marketing company and was involved in a number of community festivals and projects, should have confined his activities solely to the downtown.

"We want the board to be more downtown-oriented and get back to basics," said Jones. Sometimes Little supported positions, such as Sunday shopping, that contradicted the majority of downtown merchants.

1993 — Receiving the
Canada 125 Medal from
Minister of Transport
Doug Lewis.

1994 — Sharing four Festivals of Ontario
marketing awards with the Leacock
Heritage Festival creative team.

October 1996 —
Receiving an award
from Ontario
Provincial Police
Commissioner
Thomas O'Grady
a week before my
house of cards came
tumbling down.

Eventually, *NorthStar* went the way of most of the independent weeklies that tried to compete with Thompson Newspapers: it folded as the *Timmins Daily Press* undercut advertising rates to bring about its demise. It was to be my last major journalistic foray as the financial rewards of marketing, managing and campaigning overtook my writing career.

"Hi, Doug," my mother says, followed by my father's echoing, "Hi, Doug."

"I want you to hear this from me, but I don't want you to worry. I will deal with it *straightforwardly*," I say, using Brian's word, "and I will come out the other end — perhaps better."

"What's going on, Doug?" my father asks. I realize I can't speak in riddles anymore if he is going to comprehend what I am saying, and if I am going to have the opportunity to say it without his interrupting questions. The pathological liar, the incessant twister, face to face with an imperative to tell the truth, to be straightforward.

"I am addicted to gambling and it's got me in a lot of trouble. I have been taking money from work and the festivals I run here in Orillia, to gamble, chasing what I had already lost, and now there is going to be a police investigation."

"Oh, Dougie," my mother whispers and my father asks, "What happened?"

"I have been gambling for about two years — out of control — starting with bingo of all things, but progressing right up to the big casino that opened here in July. I have been gambling there almost every night for the past three months, except for the two weeks Melanie and I came down to visit you. But even then I found every gambling nook and cranny I could during the trip."

"How much?" my mother asks. I curse myself for not getting that out in the beginning, sensing in my mother's voice some hint of hopefulness. They had bailed me out once before, ten years ago, when I was over my head owing money to the tourist association due to figure skating bills. Then also, Veronica had been my intercessor, helping me borrow a thousand dollars from my father, about half of which I probably still haven't paid back.

"A lot. I'm not really sure, but it may be as high as eighty thousand dollars. There is no chance of paying it back and regardless, the police have already called and want to see the books tomorrow. I probably told on myself as I've been trying to borrow and buy some time to get things worked out. Now I am going to have to face the consequences."

"Have you stopped gambling?" my mother asks but before I can reassure her, in the background I hear sobs, sobs from the extension line. *That bastard is crying.* I am raging inside. *He's ashamed and he's crying that one of his children is going to go to jail.*

Fuck you, Doug Little! The doors of the East Saint John Industrial Home flash through my mind. I cover the mouthpiece on the phone to tell Veronica: "He's crying, that bastard is crying."

"Let it go, Doug, he won't even remember the conversation five minutes from now. It's Mom we're calling."

"Mom," I say, choking back my own emotions. "Yes I've quit. I had quit even before the police called but I was still trying to borrow money to pay back what I took. I kept telling myself that I was just borrowing the money and I was going to pay it back as soon as I had a big win, but I never won."

"Doug, your father and I are going to pray for you, that you will have the courage and strength to face this. How is Roberta? And Melanie?"

"Melanie's in Vancouver doing another degree at UBC. I talked to her earlier tonight and told her. She's all right, I think. She was very supportive."

"Roberta?"

"Roberta's here, downstairs with Mary. She's pretty upset. Devastated. Angry. She'd probably kill me if she had her way and I guess I'd probably deserve it although, you know, I never did any of this on purpose. I never meant to hurt her or you guys."

"I know," my mother says. "You come by your addictions honestly."

CHAPTER SIXTEEN

When I get off the phone with my parents, I have to get some air.

October 22, 1996 — 9 p.m.

Roberta's cigarette smoke is now being augmented by Mary's sympathetic fumes wafting up from the basement and I am beginning to whine to myself about how I will never be able to sleep with the house full of the smell of tobacco. Not that I ever let the reek of cigarettes stop me from gambling, but to give the devil its due, the Casino's state-of-the-art ventilation system did a pretty good job of lifting the smoke straight off the end of the cigarette and up. This made avoiding the unavoidable chain-smoking gamblers less necessary than it ever was in the charity casinos or in the bingo halls. It's a good thing, too, because the oxygen they pumped in to keep all of us nighthawks awake at four o'clock in the morning also caused the cigarettes to burn like torches. At bingo, although there was a non-smoking room, I still had to pass through the smoking areas to go to the bathroom, purchase my bingo cards and Nevada tickets, or visit the snack bar. Just that was enough to make me want to fumigate myself before I went home, but not enough to keep me away.

I quit smoking when I was almost thirty-five years old, as I said in my confession, on Weedless Wednesday, January 23, 1983, eleven days shy of my fifth anniversary of not drinking. I had been an insatiable smoker, having progressed to between sixty and seventy-five non-filter Export cigarettes a day by the time I quit. People who knew me in Timmins could barely recognize me without a cigarette in my hand and a cloud of smoke about my head. What motivated me to quit? I was persuaded — as most of us are when we give up our addictions — by fear and self-preservation. I was almost thirty-five-years old. My father had been having heart attacks for the past fifteen years and, believing I had all his genes, I hoped quitting early would help me avoid his fate. (Of course, despite quitting, I had my heart attack at forty-three years of age, five years younger than his first.) The other motivating factor was that I needed to do something positive in a particularly difficult time. In early 1983, I found myself in Orillia with little work and even less money. The sense of accomplishment, as well as the money saved by quitting, helped me weather this dismal period.

The way I quit was similar, yet different, to how I quit my other addictions. I piggy-backed on the Weedless campaign and I talked a lot about it, telling everyone I was quitting or that I had quit, thus closing the door to my impulsive return to smoking. The biggest differences, however, were how I defied tobacco and how I built my abstinence upon never wanting to have to feel the pain of withdrawal again. Reasoning that I always wanted to smoke more when I was out of cigarettes or matches (over the previous fifteen years I had plenty of memories of frantically searching the house for butts, lighters, or coins to buy cigarettes), I quit with a full package of cigarettes in my breast pocket at all times. In those first few hours and days, I often took both the package and individual smokes out, held them in front of me and defied them. As I achieved one hour, one day, one week, and so on, for the first few months, I slammed the door on ever returning by vowing I would never feel so crappy again. The pain of withdrawal from cigarettes was much greater for me than any agony that came from quitting alcohol. With alcohol, all the pain came before I quit. When it was tobacco's turn, it was all about quitting, with the cravings and physical need to smoke manifesting themselves so fiercely that I was sure it was just like getting off heroin or other so-called hard drugs. I'd always — and it seems a bitter irony to me now — avoided heroin, speed, and in the main, cocaine, owing to my fear of becoming addicted.

The urges and pain of withdrawal I am feeling tonight about quitting gambling are reminiscent of my quitting smoking, and I am sure are equal to the misery of getting off hard drugs. Tonight, facing jail, the destruction of my Festival, and the loss of my job, family, and community — losing Mariposa — I feel as wretched as I have ever felt in my life. As terrible as "Ring the bell Daddy, ring the bell"; as alone as spending Easter in my room; as terrified as shaking outside the East Saint John Industrial Home; and as frightened as scrambling down my father's back as I ran out the door. I feel as alienated as I was when I was Perry Nice's chump; as guilty as I did about sexual urges at puberty in the seminary; as rejected as when I left St. Mary's; as confused as in Grade 12; and as crushed as I was when I lost my first loves. Here is shame greater than being caught in my lies at University; fear as palpable as what I experienced in Roberta's labour room; desperation as acute as that which I faced finding myself once again drunk and devastated by the prospect of losing my daughter. The loneliness of my heart attack; the isolation of an empty bed; the dissatisfaction of work that is never quite enough; and the despair of the ride back over the sacred Atherley Narrows Bridge. I am as despicable as an inveterate gambler. Feelings. Very bad feelings. *I don't do feelings!*

Have evasion, delusion, and escape abandoned me? I ask myself as I look out past our backyard and across the frigid waters of Lake Simcoe imagining the Atherley Narrows and Lake Couchiching's Rama Reserve shoreline.

God, how I want to gamble!

On my second visit to Casino Windsor — actually to its riverboat Northern Belle Casino overflow location — I finally got to a roulette wheel. We came as a business delegation from Orillia in January of 1996, me as the Downtown manager, my best friend's wife, Mary-Anne Willsey, as my boss and chairman, and Rita Dennis, as the president of the Chamber of Commerce. We were the guests of the Downtown Windsor Business Improvement Area (I got to meet the board this trip) and its chairman, Paul Twig. While I had not met Paul on my previous excursion to Windsor under the pretext of a job interview, shortly thereafter I did talk to him and invite him to be the guest speaker at the Downtown Orillia BIA annual meeting. Our visit to Windsor was a reciprocal hosting and the continuation of our agreement to share information and ideas as Ontario's two "casino communities."

Our whirlwind overnight trip (were they ever anything else?) included a tour of the Downtown (still a lot of empty stores and a lack of revitalization), a tour of the casinos, and dinner with the Downtown Board. You can imagine my restlessness as we quietly toured the casinos, supposedly for the first time. I had to restrain myself from running madly from machine to machine as I had on my prior covert journey. At least during the tour I was able to identify the locations of the roulette wheels for later consumption. When we finally finished the blah, blah, blah of Downtown

Windsor's dubious efforts to benefit from the casinos (as would be the case in Orillia, the large payroll and the shopping, eating, and drinking of the casino's employees seemed to be the substantive benefits — everything else was speculative) we broke before dinner for a little R&R, which for me meant Roulette and Roulette.

True to gambling's inexplicable essence, my re-introduction to roulette (this was the first time I had actually played since Puerto Plata) was an intoxicating and, appropriate to its Riverboat surroundings, swashbuckling affair where I won eleven hundred dollars in the hour or so we had between the tour and dinner with the Downtown Board. I had picked up where I had left off that last night in the Dominican Republic, parlaying my wager of fifty dollars into this incredible windfall. *Roulette was my game.*

Dinner-time beckoning, I had to quit while I was ahead, but in the process made what I believed to be an unlucky, as well as stupid decision. I left the roulette table with eleven one hundred dollar chips and headed for the cashier's wicket. Once there I excitedly plopped my black stack on the counter and watched the casino teller ritualistically replace them in two piles of five chips each, with the single hundred along side.

"One, two, three, four, five," she counted. "Five hundred, five hundred and one hundred. Eleven hundred dollars?" she smiled looking for my agreement, which I, spellbound, readily gave. "Great," I said.

"Would you like a one-thousand dollar bill?" she asked, taking me by surprise, waving the pink one thousand denomination in front of my eyes.

"Umm . . . Nnn . . . no," I stammered impulsively, not expecting the question and being totally unprepared as to what I would do with such a large bill.

"Hundreds, then?" she asked, to which I grunted my agreement, still distracted by the image of the thousand-dollar bill, and debating whether I should have taken it and salted it away in some prudent place.

Throughout dinner I was haunted by misgivings as to what I should have done. The significance of my decision took on some foreboding metaphysical meaning. Like an unshakeable negative affirmation, I knew I was going to lose. True to form, however — knowing never saved me — after dinner, when our socializing turned back to gambling, I lost myself and my eleven one-hundred-dollar bills back at the various Northern Belle Casino roulette tables along with a couple of hundred other dollars I brought with me to Windsor. At about midnight I walked Mary-Anne back to the hotel under the pretence that I, too, was going to bed, and then I snuck back to the Riverboat, playing slot machines and blackjack until four in the morning when I quit because I was broke.

Addiction treatment is next on my sister's checklist for redemption. With a lawyer contacted, my employer called, and my family burdened, the only positive thing left to do is seek treatment for my gambling addiction. The first step, we agree, is to get into Dr. Strickland's office tomorrow and get referred to the psychologist Ken McMullen had suggested. Veronica has a psychiatrist in Toronto who she has seen to work through some of her childhood "issues." We agree to get Dr. Strickland to refer me to this Dr. Daniel Kappon — Veronica would put in a call to his office to see if I could jump the queue. Also, my sister Mary has been a volunteer at a residential treatment centre in Guelph, Homewood, where her husband was treated for alcoholism. She says that while they may not have a specific treatment program for gambling yet, they treat all kinds of addictions and she's sure I can get in, if there is space. If I have an EAP at work — Employee Assistance Program — that will cover the costs, and I can get in immediately. Otherwise, for government-financed care, there usually is a long waiting list. I will ask about any City of Orillia EAP programs during the meeting I have arranged with the City Manager and the Mayor in the morning.

I had AA friends in Timmins who went away to treatment programs twenty years ago but it was something my "high-bottom drunk" belief made unnecessary for me. What's that expression? "If your foresight was as good as your hindsight, you'd be too smart by a damn sight." Maybe if I had gone into treatment I would have dealt with all of my addictions or whatever was underneath that keeps festering and raising its ugly head again and again in this self-destructive behaviour. Maybe I wouldn't have just jumped out of the drug and alcohol frying pan into the workahol fire, reinforcing my image as the *great* Doug Little by wearing my quitting as a badge of honour and using it like a weapon, especially against Roberta. "I quit drinking for you," was used to justify much of my selfishness and in the end, my descent into the abyss of gambling.

Workahol: I see now I did more harm to other people, Roberta and Melanie excepted, with my addiction to power and control, than I ever did with alcoholism or gambling. I was getting things done and God help anybody that got in the way. Not that I was intentionally cruel. I just didn't take the time to think about it, or to worry about it. I could be a million miles away right in front of people. Volunteers, board members, or friends could be standing in my face talking to me. I would smile, nod my head, and respond with my studied "ah huh," not hearing a word they said. My mind and attention were somewhere else more important. The end justified the means because I defined myself by the end result. *I got things done.*

The Internet came into my life in 1996. I'd heard there were gambling sites on the web, but I couldn't imagine ever trusting some computer in Antigua or Australia not to rig the games. Besides, they required a credit card, and all of ours were in Roberta's name. It wasn't possible to spend the bingo float on the World Wide Web.

What I did find in the Fall of 1996, however, was the Twenty Questions of Gamblers Anonymous, ironically on the web site of the New Brunswick Coin Operated Machines Association who were in partnership with the New Brunswick Provincial Government in operating VLTs in every corner store, restaurant and bar in my home province. The NBCOMA was looking to retain their lucrative share of the gambling market by feigning concern for problem gamblers. It's a charade that goes on across North America, often with the gambling industry's massive financial resources co-opting researchers, universities, consultants, and even organizations like the Canadian Foundation for Compulsive Gambling.

My first review of Gamblers Anonymous' Twenty Questions was typical of the addict's rationalization and minimization. I remember thinking, any gambler's gonna answer yes to these questions. Gamblers Anonymous says, "Most compulsive gamblers will answer yes to at least seven of these questions." When I drank in the taverns and beverage rooms of Timmins, I used to think everyone drank like I did and therefore there was nothing wrong with my drinking. I was conveniently unaware that I was surrounding myself with people who drank like I did, consciously or unconsciously excluding normal or social drinkers.

During the six months I spent in the bingo hall, I saw the same faces night after night. Playing Nevada tickets from store to store in Orillia was like being on a circuit, seeing the same players, day after day. In the charity casinos, we were like a club, the same hundred people from Orillia and Barrie that you saw at every event. When I graduated to the big leagues and my 78 days at Casino Rama, I saw the same faces every night, the same core group of gamblers. Of course we'd all answer yes to at least seven of these questions — and some of us would answer yes to all twenty by the time we were done.

1. Did you ever lose time from work due to gambling?

For the first twenty-one months of my gambling I would have said no to this question. The fact that I was going to work on two or three hours sleep some days wouldn't have counted, nor would the fact that much of my daily focus would have been on getting money to gamble or getting money to replace money I "borrowed" to gamble. By the time I crashed, there was no doubt I missed meetings, came to work late and left early. When I was there, I spent my time putting out fires. It was crisis management. By this time, gambling was my job.

2. Has gambling ever made your home life unhappy?

For a long time I believed I was gambling because my home life was already unhappy. It was my escape, now replacing work as my drug of choice. Unfortunately, while I was escaping all these negative feelings, all I was doing was making everything worse.

However, I could rationalize that all gamblers would answer yes to this question and fear of unhappiness at home was why gamblers went to such lengths of lying, sneaking around and hiding their gambling activities from their families.

3. Did gambling affect your reputation?

It would be hard to argue otherwise, even back at the beginning, when I sat around the bingo hall night after night, Mr. Downtown Orillia and all, the mayor's campaign manager to boot. I played two sessions of bingo a night and visited corner stores to play Nevada tickets throughout the day. What about standing in that laundromat watching those fruit reels spin around for hours? It was easy to minimize the impact on my reputation or to dismiss my detractors as not understanding my need to relax. To tell myself I didn't care what they thought. In the end, the devastation I brought on my life and on the lives of my family and friends, people I cared about even in the depths of my addiction, brought me great shame and destroyed my reputation.

4. Have you ever felt remorse after gambling?

A thousand times yes, even right from the beginning. Losing money you can't afford to lose, not to mention money that doesn't belong to you brings remorse, regret, and panic. Early in my gambling, however, I just believed everyone felt this way, and that the solution was to get more money and win back what I lost. At the end, I had to admit that the nightly contemplation of self-destruction crossing the Atherley Narrows was a little bit more than a passing regret.

5. Did you ever gamble to get money with which to pay debts or otherwise solve financial difficulties?

In my gambling binge I was always chasing my losses, trying to win back money that I borrowed from petty cash, my expense accounts, the bingo floats, the unmade deposits, the kited cheques, or from my loan shark. I was always trying to get out from under. Undeniably yes, but then again I thought all serious gamblers were the same way although they may not have had my specific sources of revolving credit.

6. Did gambling cause a decrease in your ambition or your efficiency?

Yes, but I had no idea to how great a degree. One of the apparent side effects of marijuana use, at least for me twenty to thirty years ago, was a loss of ambition. The three laziest, least accomplished years of my life were the ones when I was using grass heavily, starting with my one year in university. Gambling, however, didn't make me lazy. On the contrary, I worked very hard at it — either wagering or running around getting money to bet — night and day. It took over my mind and my life. When I wasn't gambling, I was thinking about gambling. When I was doing something else it became a task I had to do in order to get gambling. I ate, drank, and slept gambling. The rest of my life didn't get any airtime.

7. After losing did you feel you must return as soon as possible and win back your losses?

Amen. Every time. Often two or three times a day.

8. After a win did you have a strong urge to return and win more?

Winning was worse than losing. My self-delusion had me dwelling on the wins and dismissing the losses. I told everyone I won, reinforcing the lies I was telling myself. For many of my colleagues and even gambling buddies, the first admission that I ever lost was in the headlines of the newspaper. The truth is I didn't win because I didn't quit, and even when I did win, it was like I was just holding the money temporarily — a loan — until I gave it all back the next time. This was the crux of my compulsive gambling, but it was an essence I would deny until the end, until I had no more money, and no more sources of money, with which to stay in my denial.

9. Did you often gamble until your last dollar was gone?

Every time. The only times I ever got out of a gambling session with money in my pocket was when the event was over, the casino closed, and I was too exhausted to keep gambling or had something I absolutely had to do. When I hit the twenty-four-hour-a-day Casino Rama, the only times I left with money were the ones when I was falling asleep at the tables.

10. Did you ever borrow to finance your gambling?

Even the legitimate borrowing I did, from friends, family, and other gamblers, had that desperate, frantic aspect about it. *How about Johnny?*

11. Have you ever sold anything to finance gambling?

Other than my soul, I thought, this one was definitely a no, until I remembered my old car that I sold for six hundred dollars, money that was supposed to go to pay down the bank loan on the other car, which didn't happen for several weeks because I gambled the money away.

12. Were you reluctant to use "gambling money" for normal expenditures?

In order to maintain my façade, my normal money went to keep up our day-to-day expenses, and sometimes to cover my stealing, but certainly every spare cent I had went to gambling, covering up gambling, buying forgiveness or assuaging guilt caused by gambling. Shortly before the end, I gave Roberta money from my "winnings" to buy new living room coffee and end tables. Soon we'd return them.

13. Did gambling make you careless of the welfare of yourself or your family?

When I was gambling I could refute I was being uncaring as if it were an accusation — and did. Once I faced what I had done, I took out the "or" and replaced it with an "and."

14. Did you ever gamble longer than you had planned?

Every time. In AA there are also twenty questions, but I've often heard they could be boiled down to two questions — "Have you ever drank when you didn't want to?" and "Once you started drinking, could you stop?" My answers to these questions convinced me I was an alcoholic. With GA's questions, I believe if anyone could honestly — and I do mean honestly, remembering what a pathological liar I had become when I was in gambling's thrall — answer no to this question or to question nine, about gambling until your last dollar was gone, then I don't think they could be a compulsive gambler.

15. Have you ever gambled to escape worry or trouble?

When I first started I said gambling was about relaxation — an escape from my workaholic life and troubles at home. It grew to become an even more critical refuge as my troubles grew increasingly more desperate because of my gambling and the money I was losing. This was the recurring chaos, my gambling cycle, my hell on earth. I gambled to escape my troubles but the more I gambled, the more troubles I had and the more I needed to gamble. A vicious circle, spiralling out of control.

16. Have you ever committed, or considered committing, an illegal act to finance gambling?

When I first read this question, although I already owed about fifty thousand dollars and knew what I was doing was illegal, I was amazed. I thought what I was doing to get money to gamble was unique. The existence of such a question brought home to me just how sick I was. Of course I didn't want to be sick. No one wants to have an "illness" and I continued for a few more weeks to hold onto that desperate dream that I would win my way out of trouble and out of what clearly was my addiction.

17. Did gambling cause you to have difficulty in sleeping?

I knew every night the only way I could even possibly get to sleep was to first be exhausted. "Fall-down tired" I used to call it. In addition, I needed to cry out for the intercession of my two gods: the God of my youth, through the recitation of both the Lord's Prayer and the Serenity Prayer, over and over, until I dropped off for a few hours of unconsciousness; and my gambling god, Luck, who I prayed to by making sure I had a pocketful of lottery tickets on that night's draw.

18. Do arguments, disappointments or frustrations create within you an urge to gamble?

Do negative emotions make me want to gamble? Yes, yesterday. Yes, today and yes, tomorrow. Arguments, disappointments and frustrations pretty well sum up what I have been running away from since I was nine years old, and what I still want to run away from tonight.

19. Did you ever have an urge to celebrate any good fortune by a few hours of gambling?

I didn't have a propensity for good fortune by the time I discovered these questions. I was definitely on the downhill slippery slope. Still, if I could beg, borrow or steal money, that was good fortune and I headed right to the casino to celebrate. In my self-denial, I initially dismissed the question with *what good fortune?*

20. Have you ever considered self-destruction as a result of your gambling?

342

Dammit, when I read this question for the first time I resented the hell out of it. It was like an arrow piercing the armour of my delusions. I was suicidal when I was reading the questions, desperately searching for a way out of my dilemma. But there was no solution to my financial problem of where I was going to get $50,000 to return to all the accounts I owed, which was what I thought all my problems were. Now here on the screen was a question that I could not shrug off, that told me clearly that my nightly thoughts about killing myself were a symptom of gambling addiction.

I don't remember whether the New Brunswick VLT pushers had the GA quote about the seven "yes" answers on their web site. I didn't add up my answers at the time anyway. My anxiety about needing to win or borrow my way out of trouble wouldn't have let me accept the truth regardless. The truth, as you plainly see, is that I must answer yes to twenty out of twenty questions. As my friend Bob's wife Mary-Anne would say: "You just have to be perfect."

On Monday, October 21, after losing $8,500 on the weekend, but still having $1500 left to play with, I itched all day to get back to Casino Rama. The remnants of my job and my workaholic ways conspired against me. Unfortunately I had a "Shop Orillia First" meeting — kind of a strategic planning session — that evening. This was an organization of all of the various "centres of shopping" in Orillia that I had founded to combat out-of-town shopping a few years ago. Of late, our relationships had been strained, as the Orillia Square and the Downtown were at odds over a new "Power Centre" that promised to bring big-box shopping, including Wal-Mart and a new Canadian Tire store, to Orillia. The Square and Zellers were opposed to this new competition while the Downtown, seeing the inevitability of new retail, was supporting the proposal. We felt that the larger stores and joint marketing could stop the increasing trend of Orillians, and of those living north of us in Muskoka, who rushed down the highway to Barrie to shop in its mega-malls and big-box centres. That evening's session was supposed to help us reinvigorate the joint efforts we could make in the meantime to reduce this out-of-town shopping trend.

For me, the meeting was just going through the motions. My mind wasn't a million miles away: it was in its usual place, just a few kilometres across the Lake. As it turned out, so was the Downtown's: it was also fighting to make sure there was no shopping on Rama Road to distract the out-of-town gamblers from coming into Orillia for their essential needs. What a joke! Gamblers are pretty much focused on one thing and one thing only when they come to Casino Rama — gambling. That is their one essential need.

The one good thing about the meeting was that it provided me with a convenient and legitimate excuse not to go home until near enough to Roberta's bedtime that it didn't matter, at least to me. I was free to hit the casino as soon as the meeting was over.

All day I had been trying to pump myself up, to banish negativity. I was still spooked by the downturn in my luck at Let It Ride the night before, precipitated solely, it seemed, by my thought about having "shot my wad" of luck with that Full House. This luck deity of mine would have felt right at home among the Greek Gods, high up on Mount Olympus playing with Achilles and the Trojans like Alec Taylor and I would throw around his tin soldiers. "Let's let Little win a few so we can see him whine when he loses.

He's such a great whiner." These kinds of thoughts kept tormenting me all day as I struggled in vain to develop the enthusiastic positive winning attitude I knew I needed to defy the gods.

Still, having $1500 in my pockets going into the Casino was a great motivator.

The first time I visited my psychiatrist Mark Filipczuk at St. Joseph's Hospital Health Centre in Toronto I found myself in an old-fashioned elevator, the kind where you open the door and slide the metal cage aside to enter. I pushed the button for the fourth floor and waited as the cage lurched upward, thinking about the ancient department store elevators in the old MRAS (Manchester, Robertson, and Allison) in Saint John, New Brunswick. A scene from my childhood was replaying itself in my mind: a crime scene. A Jim Bowie (another of The Alamo's heroes) rubber knife I was trying to shoplift fell to the floor from under my jacket right in front of the sales clerk. What can I say? I was an incompetent thief from the beginning. What did I do? I ran, of course.

Mark Filipczuk was one of two Toronto psychiatrists treating compulsive gamblers. The other was Ralph Pohlman, a flamboyant and outspoken physician who I once heard call the government "whores" for their role in promoting gambling. I remember thinking I'd characterize them more as pimps — living off the avails of the prostitution, as well as lining up the Johns with their marketing and promotion. "Here, have some of this. This is good for you," governments seem to be saying with their "Imagine the Freedom" advertising and their determination to place a gambling casino of one ilk or another in every corner of Canada. My answer to ads was a little cartoon I drew depicting me standing behind bars saying, "Imagine the Freedom."

Both Filipczuk and Pohlman were on the Board of Directors of the Canadian Foundation for Compulsive Gambling. Both they and the board had links to Gamblers Anonymous in Toronto. Certainly Filipczuk was a believer in GA, but he was uncomfortable with the current tendency of the CFCG to cozy up to the casino industry for funding and he was thinking about resigning, which he eventually did. My therapist, Roger Horbay, referred me to Dr. Filipczuk and arranged this first appointment. Filipczuk and Horbay would both play an important part in my recovery as well as my legal defence.

As I watched the floors pass in that ancient elevator at St. Joe's, I marvelled at the poetic justice of the elevator plaque, on the left, just above the buttons: "Car 17."

Plato is credited with saying that "The unexamined life is not worth living." For all my forty-eight years I was afraid of what I might find. I hit puberty while I was at St. Mary's College, as my infatuation with Nancy readily attests. I'm not sure just when I discovered masturbation. There was a dirty old man in my life — a pedophile we'd call him today — but I can't pin down his identity or my age. I do remember he lived on a side street off Waterloo Road in Saint John, just above Haymarket Square. I don't recall where or when I met him, just that he lured me to his house where he had pictures of naked women — on the backs of playing cards — and he'd jerk me off when I got hard. He wanted to do other things but I didn't let him. Of course I wasn't going to tell Father Kinsella about him, or what we did.

In Grade 10, in the dormitories at St. Mary's College, one of the older students approached me one day, saying that if I didn't stop "abusing myself," I was going to get kicked out. He said he could help me stop. Of course I denied I was doing anything — how the hell could he know what I was doing under my blankets when he was at the other end of the dormitory? But he spooked me. I went to the Socius, tough-as-nails Father Callaghan, and told him what this guy had said to me and about his unexplained offer to help me stop. To his credit Father Callaghan never even asked if my self-abuse was true — he knew that was between me and the confessional — and he assured me that the student wouldn't bother me again. St. Mary's was my last confession — until now — and leaving there was the beginning of a life lived in a very dangerous, solitary place — my head. What I perceived to be the Roman Catholic Church's antiquated attitudes towards sex, the circumscription of a priest's right to marry, of the use of birth control, of a woman's right to choose to have a child or not, and of dissent within the Church, were among the reasons I initially rejected what I call the "religion of my youth." In Grade 11, two of my favourite priests, Father Gilbert Golden and Father Gregory Sullivan, left the college and, reportedly, the priesthood. They were young reformers who had given up.

In March of 1998, my daughter Melanie sent me a copy of a story that she'd written that was soon to be published in an anthology of the best up-and-coming writers in North America. Canadian author and Pulitzer Prize winner Carol Shields had chosen her story to be included in *Scribner's Best of the Fiction Workshops 1998* published by Simon and Schuster, New York. Editor Shields and reviewers hailed these 22 writers as the fresh new voices of North American fiction.

Melanie's story was called "Apnea." It was loosely based upon some of my idiosyncrasies and on some of my ailments, recent and otherwise, including my gambling. When she sent me the copy of the story, she attached this note:

> *Well, I'm finally getting around to this. When you read it you'll understand the delay, but I want you to see it this way first. I really, really, really hope this doesn't hurt you too much, but I know that a lot of it will make you uncomfortable. This is FIC-TION but as you'll see, I borrowed liberally (and not always delicately) from life. I was unable to think about anything else but what you (and we) were going through ALL LAST YEAR and I wasn't able to write anything that wasn't terribly personal, and I only wrote this because I had to write SOMETHING.*
>
> *As I say, it's fiction, and I hope you won't be hurt by anything in it. You know how much I love and esteem you, and I'm sorry if you've been such a big part of my consciousness that I can't keep you out of the writing!*
>
> *That being said, the story is really about the narrator, and it in no way succeeds or even attempts to capture you — the "dad" is a construct, of course. One of these days I'll write something that does you guys justice — but it won't be fiction!*

The story didn't hurt me or make me feel uncomfortable. It was incredibly well written. I thought it captured the gambling addict quite well, and I at least, knew the fiction from the reality.

In Melanie's "Apnea" story she has the daughter secretly follow the father to a Quebec bar where she witnesses his playing VLTs. I'm sure she didn't tag along during my real life sneaking around, but her images of the bar, and of me, are dead on.

I picked Melanie up in Montreal the day after my big $5,000 win at Casino Rama, and, of course, I wanted to visit the Montreal Casino before we headed for New Brunswick the next day. As Melanie had yet to witness the feverish spectacle of my gambling, she had no qualms about going for a visit and having dinner there. The Montreal Casino, at least on the outside, was the most ornate casino I had ever seen. Built in the former "Pavilion de la France" from Expo 67 on the island site of Man and His World, its isolated location was meant to control crime, robberies and the like, which struck me as odd. Too bad, as the Government surely knows but won't admit, that most of the crime is committed by people getting money from other places to take to the island casino. The cost of this crime in terms of both money and human misery was not something that was included in the economic impact studies that, when I was fighting to bring Casino Rama to Orillia, I bought into hook, line, and sinker.

When Casino Rama was under construction, it was touted as "Canada's largest casino." By the time it opened on July 29, 1996, it had already been relegated to "Canada's most unique." Casino Montreal, bowing to the demands of long line-ups, had expanded. Well, there were no lineups on the summer Friday night when Melanie and I visited. The casino was crowded, though, and

349

inside, its hodge-podge construction made it difficult to navigate. We found several roulette wheels in one area of the casino but the crowds were too thick to get a seat to play. Standing on the outside row of players I was able to bet colour — using actual casino chips rather than roulette chips — as long as I bet green, $25 a spot. By startling coincidence — an instance of gambling's "cunning and baffling" that will never cease to amaze me — precisely as in my first bet in Casino Rama, on Number 17, I won with a $25 bet — thirty-five to one — $925.

"Wow!" I said to Melanie as I gave her $50 to go play the slots. "My luck continues."

I am not sure which of my deities gets incensed by this bragging, cocky attitude, but the words were no sooner out of my mouth than I began losing. I threw a couple more green "quarters" at the cluster of roulette wheels and lost. Not being able to get a seat at the roulette wheel in order to play dollars or fives, I wandered off to the blackjack tables where I came up against Quebec's unique rules. Since it was Friday night and packed, the table minimum was $50 a bet for your first square and five times that amount, $250 a bet, for a second square. *So much for the social night out for entertainment, eh?* This being August 8, even Casino Rama had only been open for a week or so, meaning my system of blackjack — from the charity casinos — was to still play as many spots as possible and try to get control of the table. That's what had worked in Rama with Arnold the night before. For gamblers, systems that gave us an edge were our acts of faith. But I knew $250 for a second spot, and $500 in the VIP area into which I had foolishly wandered, would spell a short vacation. Playing one spot without luck had me meandering from table to table searching for another elusive windfall or just a break in what seemed to be the beginning of a losing streak. After I had given back the entire $925 plus a few hundred of my own, I went looking for Melanie among the slot machines and announced it was time to eat.

While my sisters and I are talking about options for treatment my lawyer, Brian Turnbull, calls back.

"Doug, I got the name of a treatment program in Toronto for gambling addiction from Byron Stiles of the Chippewas of Rama." Stiles is involved in the Chippewas' social services programs and was setting something up to deal with gambling problems among the Native community. Brian often worked with his department in dealing with Native clients.

"Did you tell him . . ." I start to ask, but Brian cuts me off with a little impatience.

"Of course not. Doug, what you say to me is confidential, privileged. I am allowed to tell someone else only what we agree upon. That statement for the police, have you started it?"

"Yes, I'm about halfway through but my two sisters from Toronto have arrived and we're also trying to find some kind of treatment program. Listen Brian, I didn't mean to . . ."

"Forget it. I just want you to understand the rules. I am on your side," he says. "On the top of each page of the statement, I want you to write, 'For My Solicitor's Eyes Only.' This makes the statement privileged, too, until we have a chance to go over it and hand it over to the police. In fact, put that at the top of the page on everything you write."

"Okay, I'm doing it on the computer and I can just add it as a header on each page."

"Good," Brian says. "The treatment program is the Donwood Problem Gambling Program and the Director's name is Jim Milligen. I suggest you try calling them tonight, even if you just leave a message. It will be good if we have initiated treatment before meeting with the police."

I take the telephone number and tell him I am going to see my family doctor tomorrow to get referred to psychologist Alan MacLeod. He says that's good but to make the call to the problem gambling program tonight. We agree to talk again in the morning and say good-bye.

By October 22, Casino Rama had been open almost three months, yet there hadn't even been a whisper about problem gambling, let alone steps taken to institute a program of gambling addiction awareness. While my delusions and desperation were so great that such a program would probably not have stopped me, I have often wondered what would have happened if I could have reached out for help. What if I had made a call after one of those despairing nights of leaving the Casino broke once again, making that precarious trip across the Atherley Narrows contemplating suicide?

Very soon after my meeting with Casino Rama's Ed Leichner, the marketing vice-president, and before news of my addiction and crime hit the news, the Casino announced it was partnering with the Canadian Foundation for Compulsive Gambling (CFCG) to promote awareness of the dangers of problem gambling in Orillia and at the Casino. "Bet with your Head, Not over it!" was the slogan in newspaper ads announcing the initiative in Orillia. My Donwood therapist and I thought it was an odd slogan to aim at problem and compulsive gamblers, who have a difficult if not impossible time controlling their gambling by using their heads. At least, however, the posters had a telephone number to call for help.

There was a time when I thought about suing Casino Rama and the Ontario Casino Corporation for not having put such an awareness program in place when it first opened. At that time the CFCG was already working with Casino Windsor and the Ontario Casino Corporation at that location. It remains inexplicable to me why Casino Rama would not have had such a program right from the get-go. In the end, I didn't think I was an ideal plaintiff, given that I already was addicted to gambling when the casino opened, and in fact was already into my "borrowing" crime. I never believed Casino Rama caused my addiction or my legal problems, but it certainly made them worse. Someday, someone will come along and successfully sue the casinos, opening the floodgates. They will be like so many I have seen — some widow with three kids who had never gambled in her life, someone who went to one of the casinos for a "night of entertainment," got addicted and woke up two years later having gambled away her husband's insurance and children's inheritance.

Twenty years down the road there will be lawsuits and revelations about the gambling industry and the involvement of Canadian governments that will rival today's headlines about the tobacco industry. The cigarette marketers also said at one time, "Try this, it's good for you." Isn't this what our governments are saying, to the tune of $43 million a year," promoting one form or another of the "Imagine the Freedom" dream world?

Melanie and I had our meal at Casino Montreal. I had seafood pasta but wasn't impressed, especially considering the price tag. I was used to getting my meals free in a casino — this one, by my count, had already cost me over a thousand dollars. Accounting for me, as you may have noticed, was a matter of some flexibility. One day I would have felt like a winner because I still had a couple of thousand dollars left after a few hours in a casino. Another day I would have bragged about winning $925 on the first spin of the night and conveniently forgotten about giving it all back, plus another couple of hundred. On other days, I would forget that the money I just lost was money I had just won. What was that joke? "It wasn't a win, it was a loan."

We played the slot machines — Melanie with quarters and me with dollars — for another hour and decided we had had enough of Casino Montreal. The fact that Melanie was with me certainly was a governor on my activities — more than Roberta was in Sault Ste. Marie — but so was the fact that I had one of these back home, ten minutes from my house, and I didn't have to blow my brains out gambling here because I couldn't come back. Also the prospect of Video Lottery Terminals in the United States and in New Brunswick provided me with plenty of antic-ipatory excitement. Often, the action of getting ready to gamble

— getting the money, the travelling, and the dream world of all the money I was going to win — was almost as good as gambling itself. Especially on this trip because, with the $5,000 win behind me, my optimism was bubbling. I could still make this happen.

CHAPTER SEVENTEEN

I put in a call to the Donwood Problem Gambling Program while my

October 22, 1996 — 10 p.m.

sisters are still at the house. A woman answers and I ask for Jim Milligen. I am asked to hold on. While I am waiting my sister Veronica offers to allow me to stay at her house if I need to travel to Toronto for treatment or for therapy sessions.

The Donwood woman comes back on the line: "I'm sorry but I have to go, I have a crisis call on the other line. Could you please call back tomorrow?" Before I can respond to defend my own crisis status, she is gone.

"She hung up on me," I say in disbelief. "She said she had a crisis call and could I please call back tomorrow and she hung up. Aren't I a crisis?"

According to its literature the "Donwood Institute is a publicly-supported centre of excellence committed to preventing and reducing the harm to individuals, families, and communities associated with addictive disorders." Eighteen years ago, a friend of mine went there for treatment of his alcohol addiction. It didn't take me long to learn that Donwood's current "harm reduction" approach was controversial with both Alcoholics Anonymous for alcoholic treatment, and Gamblers Anonymous for gambling treatment. Although I was curious about the conflict and the politics of addiction treatment, I rightfully concluded that my own recovery was my priority and that I would take what would benefit me from all of the programs. I needed all the help I could get and would seek help wherever it was available. Up to this point I had only heard of Gamblers Anonymous in passing, as a joke among gamblers — "You need to go to Gamblers Anonymous" — or through the twenty questions I'd found on the New Brunswick Coin Machine Operators web site. When I was running the bingo at the Magic Dabber Bingo Hall, early in 1995, one of the regular customers complained that her husband had made her go to Gamblers Anonymous, but she decided it was easier to quit the husband than to quit gambling. Certainly there was no "GA" in Orillia.

I later e-mailed Jim Milligen, not wanting to risk a repeat call with an inadequately demonstrative display of the hysterics necessary to convince the woman on the phone that I too, was in crisis. In my note, I said, "I guess because I asked for you by name she assumed I was not a crisis.

"Certainly I am a crisis as you will learn and perhaps your operators should be forewarned not to make such assumptions. Very soon my addiction to gambling and the financial and legal chaos that the last two years have created will be public. I am now under police investigation and will cooperate fully with the police. I have been looking for help locally for some time.

"I am a non-practicing alcoholic having been sober for 19 years. I need urgent help. I quit gambling and while I may be safe from returning at the current time, the chaos, the consequences, and the despair that my two-year gambling binge have created for me and my wife are monumental. Could you please contact me as soon as possible so we can discuss what steps I need to take to get treatment for me and my wife?"

I included my work and home telephone numbers and I must have impressed him with my urgency and "crisis" status because I received his call the next morning and the first thing he asked me was, "Are you suicidal?"

Satisfied I wasn't going to drive the van over the Atherley Bridge or into a concrete highway pillar, Jim Milligen made an appointment for Roberta and I for 9:30 a.m. the next day in Toronto. I was to see Certified Gambling Counsellor Roger Horbay and Roberta would meet with another therapist, Nina Littman-Sharpe.

At the beginning of treatment, Donwood administered another series of diagnostic questions called the South Oaks Gambling Screen after the American treatment centre where it was developed. The questions were similar to the GA 20 Questions except they asked about the type of gambling I did (everything but sports betting), how often I gambled at each (once a week or more often), and the most I spent in a day ($1,000 to $10,000). Within my twelve-step recovery program, the amount wagered was said to be unimportant — "you'll gamble whatever amount you have access to" — and only relevant to what people can afford. I met people who had lost thousands, even millions. One man who hasn't gambled in over ten years, the former president of a pharmaceutical company, went through three million dollars but when he was in treatment at the pioneering John Hopkins Treatment Centre he met a man who had lost $43 million. It all depends on how much you have or, as in my case, how much you have access to.

Question Three asked, "Which of the following people in your life have (or had) a gambling problem?" I check-marked next to "father." While the rest of the questions were like the GA questions

I'd answered, Question Sixteen had several parts related to the sources of money borrowed to gamble and among others — like loan shark — I answered yes to this euphemistic question, which with my talent for minimization I could have written: "(h) Have you borrowed on your checking account (passed bad cheques)?"

I answered no to (e) from credit cards, (g) you cashed in stocks, bonds or other securities, (i) you sold personal or family property, because I didn't have any of these things. I also answered no to (j) you have (had) a credit line with a bookie, and (k) you have (had) a credit line with the casino, because I couldn't get one. Of course I could have answered yes to a few of my own unique sources of "borrowing" such as cash deposits, petty cash, travel expenses, and cash floats that would have more than offset my "no's" to give me that all important perfect, high-achiever score.

I would learn that the Donwood Problem Gambling program began in 1995 as a pilot project in cooperation with the Ministry of Health. Around the same time, Homewood, in Guelph, and Bellwood, in Toronto, began residential programs where gamblers were mixed with patients with other addictions. Within a few years there would be forty-four agencies operating similar problem-gambling programs across Ontario as well as other addictions facilities offering treatment for compulsive and problem gambling. It was to become one of the growth industries of the 90s.

Last night, after the "Shop Orillia First" meeting, by the time I hit the casino, my delusional armour was shining like the glittering cuirass the god Hephaestus made for Achilles for use on the battle-fields of Troy. The fifteen hundred dollars from the weekend's

$10,000 "loan" was still large enough of an ante to get me into the battle, provided all my gods were with me. I could win back the eight grand that I'd lost if I could just get ahead of the game, win a little and gamble with "the casino's money." I made token testimony to my faith in this theory by leaving a thousand dollars hidden in the glove compartment of the van, swearing I wouldn't have to go out and get it. I resolved that, by the end of the night, I would add several thousand dollars to it, just like I did in August with just $250 to start. No negative thinking, I admonished myself.

What do you think? After 77 days and the equivalent in thousands of dollars lost, isn't it time for a change? How about reversing the order, play blackjack first and roulette last? No! No! That's just the kind of doubting head-game that screws up luck. How do I know tonight's not the night for roulette — a night like I had at Paradise Resort except with stacks of chips worth five dollars each instead of a peso? Or a night of blackjack like I used to have in the charity casinos, when we broke the table at five and ten dollars a spot? Except tonight it'll be $50 a bet.

I remembered Steve and his wife Chris, the couple who taught me to play blackjack, telling me that night if I'd been in Vegas playing for "real money" I would have won fifteen to twenty thousand dollars. *Well, why not here, in Casino Rama? — Las Vegas come to Mariposa — why not now? Surely I am due!*

Thus began what was to be my final frenzied quest for elusive luck in Casino Rama. It began again, with me running fruitlessly from roulette wheel to roulette wheel, losing and winning, losing and winning in a futile game of ping-pong that I had neither the time nor the money to play. I needed a big win. I scrambled from roulette table to the five-dollar slots where I threw a hundred dollars at the $50,000 jackpot.

Zip! — the bill slot took the hundred, giving me twenty credits. *Whap!* Maximum. *Whap!* Spin. *Whirl. Whirl. Whirl. Ka-chunk!* One bar. *Whirl. Ka-chunk!* Two bars. Alright! *Whirl. Ka-chunk!* On the line. *Shit. Whap!* The previous night's dismal slot performance began to haunt me along with empty bank deposit bags. *Whirl.* I had to fight the temptation to slip another hundred in the machine next door, a trick that might — for a few moments — have blocked out the negativity that was seeping, uninvited, into my consciousness. That was the problem, thought — consciousness. I pissed away the rest of the hundred bucks in a matter of minutes, hardly noticing what was happening on the machine. I certainly wasn't focused on *making it happen* with my positive thinking and concentration.

Since it was Monday night there were plenty of chairs open at the poker games. The Caribbean Stud game wasn't worth playing, however, with the $116,000 jackpot having been won while I was sleeping on Sunday. Still, I couldn't resist taking a chance — after all, even $21,000 would help; at least it would replace the ten thousand I "borrowed" on the weekend and give me another stake and some breathing room on everything else I owed. But I'd no sooner sat down than the futility of such a win struck me. Everyone would know I'd won a jackpot. "What did you do with the money, Doug?" More reality. I put a hundred dollars in the ante circle and told myself to focus on the task at hand and to cross the bridge of what to do about winning when I came to it. I couldn't help but smirk at myself. *I've lost eighty thousand dollars in the last three months and now I'm worrying about winning.*

Throwing a hundred-dollar chip into the ante circle meant I'd be putting all of the money I had left in my pocket (not counting the stash in the van) on the table if I got a half-decent hand and had to make the additional bet of $200. I got a Pair of Threes and a King in my five-card hand. The dealer turned over an Eight, which I saw as neutral. Since a Pair was a winning hand — provided the dealer didn't have a better combination — I bet. Two other players folded and two also bet, although they were at fifteen and twenty-five dollar ante.

"Good luck, pal," one of the other players said. "I hope you've got a Royal Flush!" I was about to assure him I hadn't any such hand, but remembered such banter was frowned upon in Caribbean Stud and while it likely didn't matter in this hand, it might in the future. How acquiescent! To no avail. The dealer turned over his four other cards and failed to get even a Pair, therefore "Dealer does not qualify" and he only had to pay even money on our ante. I won a hundred bucks on my three hundred dollar bet. That didn't seem to be very good odds even to me who never worried too much about such things, preferring instead to follow my instincts, inclinations, hunches, and of all things, feelings. "I feel this machine is going to pay a big jackpot," I'd often told myself, feeding endless dollar tokens into its mouth before I'd concede that, just maybe, it had all been my imagination.

Well, I didn't feel anything about Caribbean Stud, so I took my $100 winnings and moved to the blackjack tables where I was long overdue. I hadn't had a good night of blackjack since I won that night before I picked up Melanie in Montreal. Since there were lots of open seats, I started playing at one table, one spot at $25; and I'd go to two spots if I won and move tables if I lost. Cherry picking. I hated when other players did it, coming into a table, upsetting the rhythm, ruining the shoe, and then moving on. Tonight I didn't care about anyone else. I was beyond gambling etiquette. It was every loser for himself. Amidst the blackjack tables there were a number of faces I recognized, other members of the club, but I avoided everyone. I worried my desperation was written all over my face and the last thing I wanted was someone to tell me so.

After being up and down on single hands at a number of tables, I settled at one table where there was only the dealer and I. Having won the first hand at $25, I placed my two green chips in the circles at the anchor and second-last positions. That way, if some other interloper came along, at least I'd control the third-base position. Not that it mattered in Casino Rama, because the dealer already had his two cards, but the familiar illusion felt comforting. The dealer dealt me a card up on each spot. A Ten and a Three. He then dealt his card down. My second card on the first spot was a King — twenty. I'd stay. The next card was a Seven for a total of ten. The dealer then dealt his second card up. It was an Ace. *Shit.*

"Insurance?" he asked. When the dealer has an Ace showing, players can bet half their wager (against themselves) that he has a Ten in the hole and therefore a winning blackjack. "Sucker's bet," I said to myself as I placed my $25 on the insurance line, covering both my bets. The dealer then peeked at his down card using the small-mirrored square beside his cards. "Dealer has no Blackjack," he announced as he scooped up my *chickenshit* bet.

I waved him off my twenty as I stayed on the first hand. I scratched the table behind the second set of cards, telling him I wanted another card on my total of ten. In my mind, I traced the cards again: Ten, Three, dealer (*if it follows pattern it should be a small card*), King, Seven, and Ace. Following Sherrie Darling's

364

theory, "They always seem to be together," this next one should have been a Ten giving me two pat hands against what should have been a poor hand for the dealer.

"Four, fourteen" the dealer said as he plopped the terrible card in front of my second square. I was already looking for a new table as I scratched the felt knowing that now it had to be a Ten. "Tens are due," I moaned, against all restraint.

"Twenty-four, bust" the dealer called politely as he picked up my losing cards and slid the green quarter chip into his tray. "Sorry."

"Me, too," I murmured as I remembered what it was that I no longer liked about blackjack: *thinking*.

"Dealer has Ace — Four, five or fifteen." As he said it, I visualized his number Six card and no sooner had the thought hit my consciousness than the card hit the table. Before he had a chance to mouth the words I was on my feet in disgust, and I heard behind me: "Dealer has twenty-one."

There was a time when I revelled in predicting the fall of the cards — that bystanders' cheer "You're on fire, Buddy!" echoing in my head — but now the significance of losing, the apprehension and anxiety, had taken the joy out of any conscious thought. I needed to win, yes, but failing that, I needed to be numb.

I decided it was time to head out to the van for a refill. I hated it when I walked past the security guard at the side door of the Casino and he said goodnight because I knew I'd be walking back past him again in a few minutes. I really hated it the second time. I wondered if he knew who I was. The Chief of Security at the Casino was Gord Pye, the former city police sergeant who had called me, what seems like a lifetime ago, about the Leacock Festival sponsoring a bingo at the new Bingo Hall, thus opening my Pandora's Box. *Where is my escape now?* And while I wondered about the security guards, the dealers, and other Casino workers who saw me night after night, what about the 530 "eyes in the sky" which had seen and recorded everything I did for the past three months? They saw me three, and sometimes four times a day. They saw me leave broke and return an hour later with a bundle of 50 five-dollar bills, feeding them frantically into three slot machines at a time. How many videotapes recorded my repetitive visits to the change counters where I unburdened my pockets of rolled loonies, toonies, quarters, dimes, and even nickels as I pitifully came to the end of the bingo float on so many nights? How many slot machine jackpots have they recorded me giving back, almost as soon as I won them? How many expressions of despair have they captured? What are the odds I've grimaced into all 530 cameras? *How about putting those faces in the television ads?*

I am not sure at which point I gave up on any hope of winning and decided what I needed more was unending stupefaction, but that was what I craved as I stumbled around the Casino floor in the middle of that last night. I knew luck had deserted me: all I wanted was to drown myself, not in the spiked Atherley Narrows, but in a sea of spellbinding whirling reels, dinging bells, and spinning wheels. Here, if they let me, I would stay forever.

I never got to Las Vegas. Not the old Las Vegas or the new Las Vegas, the Disney-fied Las Vegas. I was finished before I got there. During treatment I would meet a man who, while he hadn't been there for over twenty-five years, still vividly recalled his last ignominious visit. Harvey S. is the veritable backbone of recovery from gambling in Toronto and tells of being a high roller in Vegas, fêted on each trip with airfare, hotel rooms, and limousines. At the end of his gambling, broke — busted completely — he asked the casino operators for a last ride back to the airport. Reluctantly, they finally supplied him with his final chauffeured exit: "They had a maintenance worker drive me to the airport in a beat-up pickup truck. I was out of money and they were through with me."

My sisters Veronica and Mary leave shortly after 10 p.m. They've accomplished all they can and they're fairly certain Roberta won't murder me in the night. Of course I'm being facetious; however, literature I will one day find on the Donwood bulletin board points out that "the family members of pathological gamblers commonly experience anger or rage when the depths of their financial losses due to gambling are disclosed during treatment.

"They exhibit tremendous hostility, almost a vengeful indignation. 'What do you mean you didn't pay the income taxes in April?' a man bellowed at his wife. 'How could you do this to me?' 'Don't tell me about any disease!' thundered one wife of a pathological gambler. 'That's just an excuse!'"[12]

The flyer quotes Steve Dentinger of Gamblers Intervention Services as saying: "Inherent in pathological gambling is dishonesty, manipulation, and isolation from loved ones. Family members are left confused and angry.

"A study of violence in families where pathological gambling is a factor found explosive anger that is engendered in the family members of pathological gamblers (The National Council on

Problem Gambling). The family members of alcoholics may have reason to fear violence from their alcoholic, but the family members of a pathological gambler seem to be more likely to perpetrate the violent acts."

Roberta seeks the seclusion of her bathroom after they leave and I head back to my room and my confession for the police. "When I quit drinking," I write in my statement, "everything got better. When I quit smoking, I felt better after a few days. When I quit gambling, things just got worse. For the first time in two years I had to face the cold reality of the mess I had created without the hope that I could make it all go away with the spin of a wheel, or the flip of a card, or the purchase of a lottery ticket. Now that hope was gone.

"I have tried to borrow money to repay what I took from almost everyone I could talk to. No one knows all of the details, but I indicated that I was addicted to gambling, my life was in financial chaos and I was going to have legal problems if I didn't get money fast. Hardly a risk-free application for a loan. The results were predictable. I found a lot of sympathy and understanding but no financial solution."

I confess to buying time by talking to the banks while I tried to find money. "I met with the Royal Bank, provided them with a list of expected revenues that we could use to get the Leacock Heritage Festival out of overdraft. We agreed that we would communicate weekly and that they would process further cheques provided adequate deposits were made to cover those cheques, thus not increasing the overdraft.

"I have also looked for help with my gambling addiction. I raised the issue with my family doctor as far back as a year ago, although it was pretty shrouded in the problems my wife and I were having in the aftermath of having to borrow money in July of 1995 to repay some of what I owed."

I continue with the statement: "I went back seeking advice on where I could get help in the summer of 1996 and we found that the Orillia and Simcoe County agencies and therapists were just getting into gambling addictions and there was no local resource. I obtained some sleeping pills to help me sleep nights so that I could think clearer in dealing with both the gambling problem and the financial mess." The first time I took a sleeping pill in the middle of the night, it whacked me out completely for seven or eight hours, plus had me groggy for the rest of the next day. Afterwards, I would usually take only half or quarter of a pill, enough to augment my lottery tickets and prayers in fighting off my anxiety so I could get to sleep. I was also afraid of getting hooked on the medication, a legitimate fear I suppose. Did I have enough pills to commit suicide? I doubt it, as the prescription was only for a couple of week's supply, which I stretched to a couple of months by only taking them as a last resort and in smaller doses. Frankly, I never contemplated taking pills to kill myself. I've always been afraid I'd change my mind as I waited for the pills to work. Besides, the pills weren't in the van during those lonely rides home at 4:00 a.m. when I'd just lost another pile of money that didn't belong to me.

"I certainly wasn't committed to seeking treatment for the gambling as I still felt I needed to solve the financial problems or else they would turn into legal problems."

My confession then goes on to detail my meetings with

Darren Burns and Mike Timpano of Mr. Casino, and Ed Leichner of Casino Rama. I also tell them of the Downtown Management Board's awareness of my gambling problem and its commitment as my employer to help me with treatment and with my financial difficulties. "Of course we did not get into the details or the size of the financial mess or any discussions of the legal issues."

I say that as late as today, "I was still hopeful a combination of family and friends' personal loans, a business loan to myself, and help from the DOMB combined with the advance of Casino Rama's 1997 sponsorship would get me even enough to survive and eventually repay all the debt. I was probably fooling myself.

"I received the call from Const. Pat Lennon about the audit of the charity casino accounts and I knew there would be no financial solution. I resolved to cooperate fully with the police. I know the records will clearly indicate what happened because records were kept so that I could repay the monies.

"These are the facts as best I can recall and relate them," I write, summing up. "I am responsible for these acts. No one else either participated or benefited from these acts. Volunteer committee members on both the Leacock Heritage Festival and Orillia Winter Carnival had no knowledge that I was using the funds to gamble although some may have suspected something was wrong and distanced themselves from my actions. I kept control.

"The same holds true for my employee, Festival Manager Doug Bell. He was always acting under my instructions and I kept him in the dark as to the full implications of my actions. He was concerned about the financial affairs of the Leacock Heritage Festival and about me but I assured him constantly that the solution was just around the corner.

"I dealt with the banks, I falsified the deposit slips and filed the reports. He merely carried out my instructions, as my employee, in preparing reports and forms. Where there were two signatures needed on Leacock Heritage Festival cheques or Orillia Winter Carnival cheques, the second signature was signed on blank cheques and only I knew to whom and for what the cheque was written."

The only time Doug Bell had seen me gamble, other than playing Nevadas at the bingo hall, was on my final visit to Casino Windsor in April of 1996. We'd been attending a Festivals Ontario Conference in London, two hours to the east. After we made the five-hour trip from Orillia to London the night before the conference opened, I convinced him we needed to take the opportunity to visit Casino Windsor to "check it out." He had all the expense money we'd need for the conference, and I had a cache of gambling money when we hit the casino at about 11:00 p.m. What he witnessed must have frightened the hell out of him. As usual, when I was betting in these places away from home, I was insatiable. I ran from floor to floor (and casino to casino, alternating between the Riverboat and the art-gallery locations), roulette wheel to roulette wheel and slot machine to slot machine. I went through the several hundred dollars that I had brought with me, and started borrowing from the expense money he had, disregarding how reluctant he was to give it to me. By the end of the night, or early morning, I had gone through it all, plus the daily limit on my bank card. We had to use a Festival cheque to pay for our hotel rooms, plus cash another one for expenses with the conference organizers. I also arranged to borrow another $500 from the conference funds to return to Windsor the next night but I couldn't find anyone to go with me. I knew $500 wouldn't begin to be enough if I went alone.

My confession ends with a statement of remorse: "I deeply regret my actions of the past two years. I regret the pain and suffering that I have brought upon my wife and family. I regret the pain and anxiety I have brought onto my colleagues, both my staff and volunteers. I am sorry for the pain and trouble I have caused and will cause for other people at the banks and the businesses that will be affected by what has happened.

"I am sorry for the problems this will create for my employers and the members of the Downtown Orillia Management Board. I am sorry that I have probably destroyed two of the most important things that I helped to create with hundreds of community volunteers — the Leacock Heritage Festival and the Orillia Winter Carnival. I apologize and I will try to make whatever amends that I can."

In the months that followed all of this, I had a tremendous amount of support in dealing with my addictions. Therapists, psychiatrists, psychologists, other compulsive gamblers, my lawyer, my daughter and my family. One of the most difficult and most dangerous aspects to cope with was the tremendous sense of guilt I felt about what I did and the destruction I caused, not only in my own life, but also in Roberta's life. One night I was feeling particularly down while I was taking the 90-minute bus and subway ride to a Wednesday recovery meeting in Woodbine — the community, not the racetrack. I was psychiatrically diagnosed at the time as suffering, along with pathological gambling, from depression, swinging from anxiety to despondency, fearing the consequence of jail and despairing of what I had done with my life. I had gone to enough meetings and therapy sessions to know I was dangerously close to a so-called mental blank spot where I could just say "fuck it" and return to my great escape of gambling and "screw the consequences."

Suddenly, I realized I was wallowing in a deluge of self-pity, feeling sorry for myself and drowning myself in it. In my pocket I had a letter from my wonderful, supportive mother, which I had salted away because I knew it would cheer me up. It was then I realized that my sea of guilt was so close to self-pity that I could not afford to indulge it any longer and turned instead to the task of making something good come out of what I did — first by staying abstinent from gambling myself and then in helping others like me through the self-help programs. I resolved, as opportunity arose, to speak out to create awareness about compulsive gambling as the devastating disease it is. It was that night, on the Toronto Bloor-Danforth Subway line, that my recovery really took hold.

My mother's letter was inspirational. She wrote:

> *I wish you could have been spared this ordeal, but I am proud of the way you are facing up to what you have done and what you must now do, and have already begun the*

journey to sanity. Life is a series of journeys with many twists and turns but it's not hopeless, as long as we are alive, there is recovery.

I don't know how the seeds of addiction are planted but I know we all have our share, some like bad weeds in a neglected garden run wild and some are more deadly than others, but the plants must be dug up and destroyed or they will spring up from the roots again. That's where your program comes in. The knowledge, sharing, and pointing to our Higher Power. Sometimes, most times if we want to grow spiritually, the God we knew in our childhood is not the God of an adult, much the same as the alphabet is not the skill of a mature reader. We must put it into practice and develop it.

Somewhere you seem to have gotten off track and I am praying for the experience for you to find your way again. God never leaves us, all he asks is for us to admit that ours is not the right way, and to pick ourselves up and try again.

We must not wallow in self-pity which I thank God you are not doing.

I try to live one day at a time and not project. I ask God to help me handle what comes along and he has not failed yet, even when my pleas are urgent and no more than "God help me with this man I love, at this moment my thoughts are not loving just pure frustration, and I am overwhelmed just now with worry." He truly takes my hand.

I realize family relationships are hurting and I ask your forgiveness for my shortcomings in that department, they were committed by frustration and lack of understanding, certainly not lack of love. I love you all equally, all ten of you and I don't expect perfection.

You must remember you grew up in a home with the shadow of alcoholism, gambling and more commitment to work than family, but that too was not lack of love just being mixed up and not knowing how to show love.

Remember the letter your dad wrote to you in the early eighties. I don't know what he said, but you told me you were happy when you read it. I know, or I feel, he lacks sensitivity and perception sometimes, other times he surprised me.

When you called he felt very bad for you but there was no condemnation, only sorrow. Shortly after it was all forgotten, only a vague feeling that something is wrong with Dougie. He grills me and I tell him Roberta has left and you are going through a tough time.

If I were to keep him informed, the initial reaction would be repeated each time. He cannot retain memory of new experiences or happenings — before two or three years ago, no problem. He does not watch games because he cannot retain the scores and that was an important part of his viewing; the same with drama. He can do puzzles because that calls for past learning not current remembering.

I hope you get to the bottom of your problem with your search. I hope you discover that while you were part of a large family, you were valued and loved as if you were the only one, although we may have failed to impart that to you.

You have just been to a written spiritual meeting with your mom. Please try to understand my love and concern for you.

Many years ago at a family reunion for my parents' fortieth wedding anniversary (the first time in our lives that all ten of us siblings were together in one place), I obtained a copy of a manuscript of a memoir my mother was starting to write about the family. In it she wrote, "Doug, the child in the middle, was a good student, but sort of got lost in the shuffle." Later my mother told me she stopped writing the family autobiography because she didn't want to hurt people by writing the truth.

All my life, while I may have been, as Melanie called me in "Apnea," the "god of doorways," I have also been somewhat of a pack-rat in my comings and goings, lugging six orange plastic packing crates that contain the story of my life. Newspaper clippings, columns, children's book drawings, samples of my marketing and communications publications and awards over the years, souvenirs of the festivals and events I've organized, and cards and letters I've received. The only period I have little to show for is my early creative writing from the late sixties and early seventies, much of which I destroyed in fits of anger and self-destruction as I battled with Roberta and my alcoholism.

My mother's letter sent me on a search through the stacked cartons until I found the letter my father wrote to me on March 25, 1984, just prior to my thirty-sixth birthday and his quadruple bypass heart surgery at the age of sixty-four. He would have been very nearly five years sober at the time. I thought, and perhaps my mother did too, that this was his effort at making amends. In fact, it was the first and only letter I ever received from my father, not counting a note I got when I was at St. Mary's College along with a baggage-claim ticket for my trunk, which he shipped by passenger train because he knew someone in the railway office. The note had simply said, "It's cheaper this way" and was signed "D.A. Little."

His 1984 letter started:

Mum thought it would be nice if I sat down and wrote to you as your birthday is near and I agreed to make an effort. We both love you and hope your birthday will be a happy 36.

He went on to describe the new small one-bedroom house he and Mom had recently bought, having sold the large home they had in Fredericton which had had a penchant for attracting one or another, or two, of us wayward children back home from our fractured marriages. I know I gravitated there in 1972 when Roberta and I separated for the first time and found it so chaotic that I didn't even consider it an option during our second split in 1975. He also took great pride in telling me about his pet who lived in their backyard.

Thunder my big sled dog lives out there. I have a big dog-house for him but he likes to come into the house when it rains. He is half Malamute and half Siberian Husky, he weighs about ninety pounds. He's friendly, loves kids — only rough and loves to wrestle. He, for some reason, hates the mailman.

We keep him chained, but I had a forty-foot cable tied to two trees with a pulley to his chain so he does get to be able to run. His coat is starting to shed so it keeps me busy grooming him. I guess I am giving you the idea I like him.

He said he was going to enclose a picture but he forgot. Today a painting of Thunder, whose death he lived over and over again, hangs on the wall of his room in the locked-care Alzheimer's ward of the Loch Lomond Villa, along with a picture of his family taken at the subsequent fiftieth wedding anniversary, when we all came together once again.

> *I suppose you have heard, I have to have heart surgery, a triple bypass of three coronary arteries that feed the tissue of the heart muscle. I am waiting word from the Victoria General Hospital in Halifax when to go. Their cardiac team there is recognized as good as anywhere. So I hope and pray I will be okay. And I know if it's God's will I will be better.*
>
> *It was getting so that I was having more and more pain so the doctors here sent me to Halifax on March 6 and they did a catheterization and angiogram and it showed one artery completely blocked and two about eighty percent blocked. Also I have the main arteries to my legs blocked in the groin area. This means another separate operation sometime later after the heart operation.*

I was always amazed at my father's ability to describe in detail the diagnosis of his heart disease and all of the medications he was taking. Me, all I knew was I had a heart attack (myocardial infraction) took a beta-blocker and a coated aspirin. Today they tell me I have both hardening of the arteries (arteriosclerosis, if I have a dictionary handy) and a deteriorating heart valve due to a defective heart at birth (congenital heart disease). While he could always rhyme off the specific names of his medications I only knew I was progressively treated with the beta-blocker, a calcium blocker, and now an ace inhibitor as I progressed through various cardiologists. At one time I also took a pill for blood pressure but now I take something called Lipitor that inhibits the production of cholesterol in the liver, thus, hopefully, reducing the deposits in my arteries. Odd: as I get older, my need for information seems to get more exacting.

> *So you see your old father is getting old and a little bit worn.*
> *But, thank God I am as well as I am. I still have all my facul-*
> *ties and I'm sober.*

The rest of the letter talks about his AA group in Fredericton and asks about Melanie and Roberta. He concludes with:

> *Doug, I want you to know I love you, and hope and pray you*
> *are getting along good. Don't forget the strength of your Higher*
> *Power and seek his direction.*
> *I'm praying for you every day and I will offer up the pain*
> *and suffering that I have to go through in the next while for*
> *all our children and grandchildren that their lives may all be*
> *happy and Godlike as well as prosperous.*

He signed it your loving Dad, with four Xs and four Os.

When I read my mother's letter — and her reference to Dad's letter — I was sure I didn't remember any apology or confession that I thought she implied. Certainly my initial re-reading of the letter didn't reveal any overt admissions or contrition. That wasn't Staff Sergeant Douglas A. Little's forte. My cardiologist, however, recently told me that in five to eight years I would have to have open-heart surgery to replace the deteriorating heart valve caused by my congenital heart defect. The image of my own pried-open chest and the resultant cross-like scar somehow gives me a deeper appreciation of what my father was trying to say in his letter.

Roberta is downstairs watching television when I finish my confession. She has lit a fire in the family-room woodstove, taking the chilling edge off the October night. I join her without saying a word, sitting in the chair closest to the picture window that looks out onto our back yard, the small park and Lake Simcoe beyond. It always exasperates me that Roberta has put curtain flanges on this window — they hang exactly at eye level and block the incredible view. Her chair is several feet to my left and several feet back from the crackling wood stove. The television is in the remaining corner of the room. It becomes readily apparent the show is good American fare; I am able to pick up the plot in about thirty seconds and realize quickly it is a movie about child abuse.

Roberta is already well sedated, first by her bath, and now television. I am still a little wired from the confession — even it seemed a bit like action, a gamble. It doesn't take me long to get sucked into the television program — if it weren't for my absolute distaste for commercials I wouldn't come up for air while watching TV. With commercial television, the only way I can tolerate it is with some other distraction, some sort of mechanical work. I've gone through computer desktop publishing, logic puzzles, jigsaw puzzles (in a particularly obsessive period after my heart attack), and, of course, computer gambling games. Other coping mechanisms involve channel surfing which Roberta, and every other woman in the world, it seems, hates, and watching only the last ten minutes of a show — which is what I am doing tonight.

I didn't catch the name of it but it is clearly a movie about the sexual abuse of children, mesmerizing as most topical made-for-television American movies are. Canadian movies are different in that to follow them you have to concentrate and watch at least most of the movie. (It's a pet theory of mine that our Catholic guilt and Protestant work ethic prevent us Canadians from creating "entertainment.") Not that this is entertainment. It's too disturbing. Child abuse of any kind, physical or sexual, bothers me a great deal. Perhaps it's my own experience of childhood beatings, or the fuzzy memories of fondling priests and cackling perverts. I only slapped my daughter once in my life, on the back of the hand one night when she was two and wouldn't calm down and go to sleep. It so shocked her that it devastated me and I never did it again.

"How could anyone do that?" I say to Roberta as the movie draws to a close, the perpetrators dealt with, and the victims portrayed as moving on with their lives. It is a just a comment. I don't expect a response — certainly not the one I get.

During my therapy sessions at the weekly group I attended at Donwood, the group leader, Nina Littman-Sharpe, provided us with an illustration about relapse — going back to gambling. She drew a picture of a hill and likened our journey in recovery to a walk in the woods. The hill represented triggers and our urge to gamble; the bottom of the hill, actual gambling. We begin our trip down the hill when we entertain thoughts about gambling. Near the top of the hill we can choose to get off and continue our walk.

If we keep going down the hill, there is a point at which we choose to go gambling: for the rest of the slide down the hill we are merely getting ready. We've already decided.

Question 18 in the Gamblers Anonymous handbook is the only one of the Twenty Questions in the present tense. "Do arguments, disappointments, or frustrations create within you an urge to gamble?"

For all my good intentions — as Father Callaghan would say, "The road to Hell is paved with good intentions" — I made my decision to go down the hill when I put that $1400 in Nevada ticket proceeds in the van. What Roberta says next merely provides my excuse.

Turning from the television show, tears of anger and hurt welling in her eyes, she says: "Why do you think what you did to us is any different?"

CHAPTER EIGHTEEN

"Fuck you!" I holler, my body trembling as I bounce from my

October 22, 1996 — 11 p.m.

chair and bound up the split-level stairs towards my room. "And fuck me too," I'm mumbling as I grab my change, the few dollars I have on my dresser and the van keys. Roberta is still down in the basement as I make my way back down the hallway, towards the front door.

"Where are you going?" she yells through her tears, too exhausted and despairing to do anything else. Maybe she wants me to kill myself, I think unfairly; certainly she'd be better off.

"Out." I yell back as I — the god of doorways — reach the door, open it, pass through and slam it behind me. I jump into the van and open the glove compartment to check to see that the money is still there — it seems a lifetime ago that I put it there — and start the engine with a loud and excessive roar of the engine, again raising my finger in salute at my banker neighbour, yelling "and fuck you, George" as I turn the headlight brights on and put the van in reverse, squealing the tires first as I back out of the driveway onto the cul-de-sac, and then roaring down Maple Leaf Avenue to Highway 12, to the Atherley Narrows Bridge and Rama Road.

I met Bobby Yee for lunch, at his suggestion, at Traditions Restaurant inside the Casino. It was the only time I had ever eaten there without gambling. It was my norm to have a middle-of-the-night breakfast, a steak and eggs entrée that was the most expensive item on the overnight menu: my 'comp' coupon was usually $30 or more — you didn't get change — and this used most of it. Casino Rama had two other restaurants, one a buffet and the other a high-end Chinese dining room. I seldom ate at the Chinese restaurant — too slow — and the buffet was rarely open when I was there, catering as it did to mealtimes and seniors' groups. Occasionally, after an all-night session, I would have a falling-asleep breakfast at the buffet before slinking home to bed. Towards the end of my gambling, I seldom ate at the restaurant for I had come to blame it when my luck turned bad after stopping to eat.

I wondered what, if anything, Ed Leichner had told Bobby about my problems; I quickly learned that all he knew was that I wanted to have a meeting with him and that Ed had arranged it. Given my position as the manager of the Downtown, I am sure Bobby didn't perceive it as an extraordinary request.

Once we had ordered — I had steak and eggs for old time's sake — and exchanged pleasantries — the casino attendance was already exceeding all projections — I began to tell him my troubles. I kept my voice down, because we were surrounded by other clientele as well as the constant comings and goings of waiters out to impress the boss.

I told him about getting ready for Casino Rama by gambling at charity casinos, and by the visits to Sault Ste. Marie and Windsor.

I skipped the bingo and pull-ticket phases, too ashamed to admit to this "lowbrow" insanity.

"I didn't realize I had a problem when I lost every time I went to one of those other casinos," I said, "I just thought it was because I was away that I went overboard." As I spoke I could see that while he was attentive, he was uncomfortable, shifting in his seat, looking around to make sure others were not overhearing my confession.

"I didn't know," was his first response.

"By the time Casino Rama opened I was already over my head, maybe $20,000. I was about to arrange a loan with my brother shortly after the opening, when I won — $5,000 in one night." I went on to tell him about figuring if I could win $5,000 in one night then I could win back the twenty I owed and that I kept gambling "almost every night, sometimes two or three times a night as I gambled mostly late at night."

"That is why I didn't see you very often," he said. "I'm here mostly in the day."

"Yeah, I know," I responded. "The few times I saw Ed or any of his staff I was embarrassed, but it didn't seem to stop me." Looking warily around for any prying ears I leaned forward, signalling Bobby to lean forward as well.

"I am in big trouble, Bobby, and I need your help. After seventy-eight days in here I owe $80,000 that doesn't belong to me and if I don't pay it back I could go to ja . . ." Before I could finish the word Bobby cryptically waved his hand, like a blackjack player waving off a card, and silently flicked his index finger upward, warning me of the overhead camera, and perhaps, a microphone.

"I can't know this, Doug," he said quietly. "I am sorry you are in trouble but be careful what you say. If I could talk to someone for you or if there is anything I could do to help, I would do it."

With that my dream world spouted out my mouth. "Lend me the money I owe. I could pay you back in marketing services. Ed thinks there are things that I could do for the marketing department in the region that would be worthwhile."

"If this were Nevada I would do it in a minute," he said, "but here all the money goes to the government first, and it is tightly controlled. The only thing we could do is process a credit application and from what you tell me you'd never qualify for the credit."

My last balloon had burst. The rest of the meal went quickly, both of us extremely uncomfortable. He told me I should call 1-800-Gambler, and maybe they could suggest some financial counselling or something. I apologized for burdening him with this and told him I still hoped to work things out, but I had quit gambling so he wouldn't see me back at Casino Rama. I tried the 1-800 number, but it didn't work from Canada. Later I learned it was the New Jersey compulsive gambling help line.

The last time I talked to Ed he told me Bobby walked into his office after the lunch while Ed was on the phone and just sat in a chair. A few minutes went by and Bobby got up and left the office without saying anything. Ed said he never mentioned it thereafter.

Now that I have finished the theatrics of leaving the house and squealing the tires, this has become a tortured, and I know, dangerous ride. There is no excitement, no heart-pumping adrenaline, no giddy anticipation. No hope. The fourteen hundred dollars in the glove compartment no longer offers anything approaching optimism. The apprehension is harrowing. It's another crime, maybe another charge. Winning is no longer winning: at best it would be a mitigating factor, helping to pay down what I owe. Even then it would be a two-sided coin: "Yes, you paid some of it back, but the only reason you did was because you had a lucky night at the casino — restitution but hardly evidence of any repentance."

As I pass the Atherley Narrows I recall the image of the Chippewa of Rama Elders carrying the ancient fishing weir stakes in their arms, cradling them like babies, handing them over to the Parks Canada conservationists to be catalogued and stored in a vault in Ottawa. "They'll be preserved there, and they can be brought back whenever a suitable facility is constructed here to display them," the Parks Canada official had announced. Mark's words from that first Fish Weir Circle gathering at the Leacock home so long ago echo in my head: "They're just stakes."

Stakes.

Ron Barbaro, the new President of the Ontario Casino Corporation was quoted in the *Globe and Mail* on the occasion of the opening of Casino Windsor's new $505 million permanent casino as being so "churned up with excitement and the possibilities of future growth for this development, I'm not even sleeping nights." He reminded me of me.

> Casinos are "what the public wants," insisted Mr. Barbaro, a non-gambler. "When 77 per cent of the people of Windsor vote in favour of a second casino, it tells you that a shift has taken place on a broad base. If this is what the people want to do, if this is their form of entertainment, you can't suppress that.

"Every industry has its wake," Mr. Barbaro said. "Drinking has its wake, but we don't close all the liquor stores. It's how you deal with it."[13]

So, we're just a wake.
Stakes and wake.

What was maybe the toughest letter of my life came to me indirectly, through my psychiatrist Mark Filipczuk. During my treatment in May 1997, he sent me to a psychologist to have a psychological test called a MMPI-2 (Minnesota Multiphasic Personality Inventory-Revised). The letter was a report on that test in which, the psychologist, a Dr. Poon, states I took "two hours to complete the 567 test-items (average time is about 1½ hours)."

"This is a valid profile," he wrote. "This individual appears to have responded frankly to items dealing with common human frailties. This indicates a willingness to admit minor faults and shortcomings. It may indicate self-confidence. Similar patients have a balanced self-appraisal which includes appropriate self-disclosure and self-protection. The presence of coping resources and typical level of effectiveness in every day functioning is suggested." I interpret this as saying I was honest on the test, which I certainly was because, as the fact I have the letter attests, it was an appraisal done for me so I could better understand myself. Dr. Filipczuk warned me the test results were just a guideline, not a diagnosis and should be analyzed in relation to other information and facts, things neither the test nor the psychologist know about.

The next section was entitled "Affect." I wasn't sure of the word's meaning so I looked it up in the dictionary and found a definition specific to psychology: "an emotion or mood associated with certain ideas." The reported continued: "People with this profile are typically seen as depressed, agitated, frustrated, restless, and hostile. Their depression is often a reaction to constraints in their life, such as incarceration. Expect a low frustration tolerance and intense dissatisfaction with present life." Considering I was facing jail at the time, I'd say this was accurate.

"Resentment is often conspicuous, especially when demands are made by others. Prominent feelings probably include hostility and resentment. Family members are likely to be the focus of at least a part of these feelings.

"Periodic anxiety attacks are possible. In general, emotions are probably over-controlled. The thought of expressing negative emotions, such as anger, probably produces considerable discomfort."

When I decided I wanted to get serious about telling my story in a way that people would be interested in reading, rather than in the straight journalistic form in which I was trained, I turned to the Toronto Humber School for Writers' mentoring program. The school, which was heralded by the *Globe and Mail* as one of the best such programs in North America, is run by Joe Kertes, whom I knew because I hosted him in Orillia when he won the 1989 Leacock Medal of Humour for his first novel, *Winter Tulips*. Joe and his family also joined us in Orillia for the first Leacock Heritage Festival, when he was Honorary Chairman, and he returned regularly throughout the Festival's next eight years as an author participating in the Leacock Medal of Humour Readings. Paul Quarrington, who would become my mentor in the Humber program, was also a regular participant in the Festival, having won the Leacock Medal in 1988 for *King Leary* and having served as Honorary Chairman in 1990, the year he won the Governor General's Award for Fiction for his novel *Whale Music*. Paul had also lived in Orillia for a year, serving as writer-in-residence at the Public Library and making a substantial contribution to the Festival over the years as a participating author, as well as an entertainer. Paul's brother Tony Quarrington became my artistic director for a wonderfully successful event we called the "Leacock Evening of Humorous Song," an eclectic outdoor stage show of Canadian humorous singer-songwriters including, over the years, Nancy White, Moxy Früvous, The Arrogant Worms, and Corky and the Juice Pigs, as well as ex-band member Paul Quarrington, both as a solo act and in a reunion of his previous band, Joe Hall and the Continental Drift.

At first I was reluctant to have Paul as my mentor in the writing of this book because he was, as I saw it, a part of the story. My destruction of the Leacock Heritage Festival was one of the sad consequences of my two-year gambling binge, a fact I lamented to him at a meeting we had in Toronto shortly after my court case.

"One of my great regrets," I said, "was the destruction of the Festival, something which I created and worked hard for over eight years to sustain." Paul's answer, epitomizing, I am sure, the feelings of dozens, if not hundreds of other Orillian volunteers, has always made me realize how self-centred I still was.

"You know, Doug, you weren't the only one that put a lot of effort into making the Leacock Heritage Festival a success, and for the rest of us who didn't have anything to do with its destruction, it is just as gone." The meeting was the last time we talked for several years until I called him to ask if he would be willing to mentor me in writing this book through the Humber program. While I was reluctant at first to ask him, Melanie encouraged me to choose him because she felt he would be straightforward with me, and he has been.

After reading my initial outline and first few chapters of this project, one of which was published in *Reader's Digest* under the title "I was Addicted to Gambling . . .What's the Government's Excuse?" Paul wrote to me:

> *Your training as a journalist is evident. I'm not convinced that is a good thing. I think what I must try to do is dampen and subdue some of that journalistic training. The secret to this creative non-fiction is employing the tricks of the novelist. What I lack, reading these pages, is* subjectivity. *That's what I want.*
>
> *I want to know what you felt while all this was going on. So what I think you should do is, if you will, put all thoughts of books and publication out of your mind for a little while. (I'm talking about an hour here, don't get panicky.) I want you to write something that only I will read. I want you to remember one occasion when you were gambling, one particular instant in time, and write about that with as much subjective detail as you can muster.*
>
> *There are a few internal doors we must bust down, so I'm going to start hammering right away.*

Knowing me well, he concluded the letter with the challenging, "Are you up for it?"

What I *felt*. Certainly, by the time Paul wrote me this letter, I had come to terms with the fact that feelings were what I had been running away from all these years. Dr. Poon's talk of negative emotions still made me uncomfortable. I have heard other compulsive gamblers describe it as being "uncomfortable in your own skin." I wondered if Paul understood what a tall order he was asking of me, just how big a challenge he had issued when he asked me to write about how I felt.

Under the "Personality/Behavior" title Dr. Poon's report stated: "Most of these people are immature, egocentric, and have difficulty delaying gratification. Impulse control problems are prominent. Recurrence of acting out is followed by remorse and guilt. They are unlikely to follow through with their convincing resolutions to change behavioral patterns." I also read this as a challenge, of course, but when I recalled my years of struggle trying to quit drinking it rang true. As far as gambling was concerned, I knew I couldn't quit alone, that I needed all the help I could get, including that of this annoying psychologist.

"A strong tendency to addiction is frequently accompanied by excessive use of alcohol. Stress tends to result in drug abuse. A few of these individuals attempt suicide in order to make others feel guilty." While I never attempted suicide, I certainly thought about it often during my gambling and after, as I dealt with the consequences. My motivation, I believe, was hopelessness after losing and, after I quit gambling, despair of ever being able to have meaning in my life again. If I ever wanted to commit suicide to blame anyone, it would only have been to blame the casino industry and the government, which to me would have been clearly ineffective.

The report continued: "Paranoid traits may include oversensitivity and rigidity. Hysteroid [Merriam-Webster defines this as "resembling or tending towards hysteria"] traits are probable including egocentricity, immaturity, optimism, suggestibility, and naiveté." I was not sure what they had to do with hysteria — "an emotional state caused by grief or fear" — but I sure recognized the traits.

"Passivity or refined characteristics are suggested. Men with a college education often score within this range. Exhibitionism and self-indulgence can be present." My friend Mary-Anne used to tease that if I had a TV show it would be called "Enough About You," and I have to wonder: are self-indulgence and exhibitionism what I am engaging in by telling my story?

The next section on "Interpersonal" was tough to take, which, with me, usually means that it's hitting true.

"Their personality promotes marital and family turmoil. They tend to overreact to social stimuli and be argumentative. Strong demands may be made on others for affection or attention. Manipulative means may be used to meet these needs. Such individuals can overemphasize getting along with others and being socially involved. Relationships can be immature and superficial.

"These are typically gregarious, outgoing, sociable individuals who have good social techniques. Although they may need to be with other people relationships are apt to be superficial and insincere. They may provoke resentment and hostility in others." Certainly my workaholic ways in the community were characterized by these traits, leaving me with more enemies than I would care to count, some of whom took great glee in my downfall.

In the "Cognitive" category Dr. Poon wrote: "These individuals often see themselves as trapped. They may vacillate between self-pity and blaming others. Underneath they often have unmet dependence needs.

"Projection is probable. A thought disorder and paranoid features are possibilities. Feelings of being mistreated and suspicious may be apparent. Excessive use of repression and denial can create a lack of insight and a resistance to insight.

"Aesthetic and artistic interests, such as art, music, and literature, are probable.

"SOMATIC: Physical problems tend to develop after periods of stress. Conversion symptoms are a possibility. Physical symptoms may be unconsciously used for secondary gain, such as avoidance of responsibility. Common complaints include headaches [*none*] chest pains [*none*] tachycardia [*rapid heartbeat — no*], and weakness." I have no doubt my experiences have created stress that has resulted in real physical consequences; however, my multiplicity of ailments seems to be backed up by real evidence — electrocardiograms, echo-cardiograms, nuclear scans, blood tests, and sleep labs.

Dr. Poon completed his report with his "Diagnostic Considerations": "These individuals are very often given a diagnosis which addresses their alcohol abuse or substance abuse. Another frequent diagnosis is adjustment reaction with depression." In fact, Dr. Filipczuk had already diagnosed me as suffering primarily from pathological gambling and secondarily, as having "adjustment disorder with depression.

"A prepsychotic state is also cited in connection with this profile type. The diagnosis of a personality trait disturbance or personality disorder such as passive-dependent or psychopathic, may be appropriate."

To certify I was a diagnosed compulsive — or, in medical terms, pathological — gambler, Dr. Filipczuk had to determine whether I met the criteria of the American Psychiatric Association DSM-IV (Diagnostic and Statistical Manual of Mental Disorders, 4th Edition). The DSM-IV classifies the disease as an "Impulse Control Disorder," and says the "essential feature of Pathological Gambling is persistent and recurrent maladaptive gambling behaviour that disrupts personal, family, or vocational pursuits." I garnered another perfect score on its criteria.

Dr. Poon pointed out some additional sections of the manual to be checked out: "Related DSM-IV Categories: Alcohol Abuse/ Dependence 305.0/303.9; Psychoactive Substance Abuse/Dependence 305/304; Adjustment Disorder with Depressed Mood 309.0; Schizotypal Traits/Personality 301.22, Dependent Traits/Personality 301.60; Antisocial Traits/Personality 301.70, Narcissistic Traits/ Personality, 301.81."

This end of the report disturbed me, of course, even with Dr. Filipczuk's admonition to just look it as a guide, not a fact. Words like *prepsychotic, personality disorder, psychopathic, schizotypal, anti-social,* and *narcissistic* were almost impossible to swallow, as was much of his report in May of 1997, when I was just six months away from gambling. They are still difficult today. As I write this, I recognize much of the report itself, as a guide, strikes a chord. I can even find some truth in the words that are hard to accept. I recognize some prepsychosis in my delusions and a loss of external reality regarding my gambling and my stealing. Also, I certainly had a passive-dependent personality disorder regarding my escapes and my failed marriage, doing anything to avoid dealing with the very real problems.

But psychopathic? Certainly I was "mentally or emotionally

unstable," one of the *Oxford Canadian Dictionary* definitions, but was I "suffering from chronic mental disorder especially with abnormal or violent social behaviour?" If I buy my own PR — certainly used in our case before the courts — I suffer from a mental illness called 'pathological gambling' and I did display abnormal social behaviour — stealing $80,000 — as a result. Outside of the gambling there is even something to be said about a lifetime of escape in and out of a variety of addictions that bring with them the "abnormal social behaviour" of lying, cheating, and stealing.

Schizotypal? The definition of schizophrenia is frighteningly close to the reality of compulsive gambling: "a mental disease marked by a breakdown in the relation between thoughts, feelings, and actions, frequently accompanied by delusions and retreat from social life."

Antisocial — you can't get much more antisocial than stealing $80,000 from a bunch of community non-profit groups and friends.

Narcissism — "an excessive or erotic interest in oneself." Narcissus, of course, was a handsome youth who rejected the nymph Echo and fell in love with his own reflection in a pool of water, eventually changing into the flower that bears his name. "Narcissistic" is a word I have heard often to describe addicts in general and compulsive gamblers in particular. This is from the Gamblers Anonymous "Combo" book: "Also, a compulsive gambler seems to have a strong inner urge to be a 'big shot' and needs to have a feeling of being all-powerful. The compulsive gambler is willing to do anything (often of an anti-social nature) to maintain the image he or she wants others to see."

Dr. Poon's letter concludes with a brief statement about *Treatment Considerations*: "Assess suicidal ideation."

♥ ♦ ♣ ♠

When I first moved to Orillia in 1983, I didn't have a job and was scratching out subsistence with temporary contracts, hocking Roberta's wedding diamond (which she had made into a necklace during our 1975 separation) and my 35-mm camera. Although we were still paying hundreds of dollars a month on skating, for food we were desperate. When I lived in Timmins, I helped elect Alan Pope, a Conservative member of the legislature who was then the Minister of Natural Resources. I visited him in his offices and had lunch with him to talk about a government job in Toronto, either among his staff or in the ministry's communications branch. The prospect of commuting from Orillia to Queen's Park seemed ludicrous to me but others, I learned, were doing it and I didn't seem to have a lot of choice.

I had never commuted to Toronto before, but I was told to park my car at the Wilson subway station in the north end and take the subway south to Queen's Park. Alan and I had lunch at Winston's, a posh downtown restaurant where Toronto's politicos dine. We fought over the chocolate-covered strawberries and left the job issue unsettled.

When we were finished at about 2:30 p.m., I had plenty of time to take the subway back to the Wilson station, get to my car, and be at another appointment at the Orillia Square Mall in Orillia at 5:00 p.m. Saying goodbye to Alan, I went to the Queen's Park subway station to catch the train.

I was standing on the subway platform thinking about my meeting — pretty superficial, I'd tell Roberta later. The train came speeding into the station, preceded by a stale wind and a squealing of steel wheels. About ten feet to my right, a woman in a knee-length grey overcoat was standing alone, unexceptionally. Suddenly, in my peripheral vision, I saw a grey shadow move quickly towards the oncoming speeding train. *What the* . . . I thought and then I realized, shouting, "She jumped!" The screeching of the subway train wheels drowned out all other screams.

The next day I scoured the Toronto papers, listened to Toronto radio and watched Toronto television. There was nothing. I learned later that "jumpers" died in the subway system about once a week but they were seldom reported in the media because it encouraged other jumpers.

We were delayed for about an hour in the subway station while ambulance, police, and subway workers "cleaned up." I missed my appointment later that day and took it as a sign I wasn't supposed to commute to Toronto.

"What am I doing here?" I ask myself as I drive by the parking security guard at the entrance to the Casino lot. He's a new addition to the "gaming entertainment experience," put in place to check cars entering the parking lots for children after Casino Rama received national notoriety when some of its patrons left their children playing in the parking lot for hours while they gambled inside. He recognizes my van and waves me on without even a glance inside.

Tonight I don't even care to play games with myself, so I reach in the glove compartment and stuff the entire $1400 into my pockets. I have no illusions about winning, maybe not even any desire. "I'm on the run," I finally answer myself as I cross the parking lot. "Maybe I'll just keep going."

As soon as I enter from the side door, it hits me. The drone of the casino, the clamour of wheels, reels and bells, the trumped-up sound of winners, the din of thousands of voices shouting and moaning. It's not unlike like the hum of my apnea C-PAP machine. I need the casino to keep the chemicals pumping through my bloodstream to keep me numb — dead to the world — just like I need the C-PAP machine pumping air through my throat to keep me breathing and alive. I am wired to gambling as much as I am attached to that pump every night, and without it, I am sure I don't want to live.

I built my confidence by doing. Sure, I approached new things nervously, but I also reasoned I had successfully accomplished equally new things in the past and hadn't let fear stop me then. Maybe that too was gambling, but without dwelling on the differences between taking calculated risks in life and gambling with abandon in a casino, I expect there is a little bit of the risk taker, the gambler, in all of us. The first time I spoke to Timmins City Council — after years of being a political reporter and observing all kinds of municipal presentations — my throat was dry, my hands were shaking, and I spoke in a voice I didn't recognize. Now I could do it, as Stephen Leacock said, "at a hundred yards." The only time I have difficulty speaking today is when I don't know what I am talking about or when I know the audience isn't interested in what I have to say. I have put enough people to sleep with after-dinner speeches on tourism, downtown revitalization, festivals and, yes, even casinos, to know when I haven't got someone's attention.

My ability to talk, my courage to speak, my passion to express what I believe, my power to engender enthusiasm and, perhaps to a lesser degree, my competence at communication, have provided me with the successes I have achieved in my life. That gregarious six year old who lived under the teacher's desk because he couldn't stop talking, who said good morning to strangers on the Saint John buses and who rehearsed his requests in the bathroom mirror used these tools for good — and for bad *(bullshit baffles brains)* — throughout his life. I talked my way into Saint Mary's College where they taught me elocution so I could talk even more. I talked myself in — and out — of the military in a week. I talked myself into my first newspaper job a month and a thousand miles before I even got to Timmins. Love, marriage, jobs, campaigns, organizations, and festivals — talking was what I did best. Oddly, there was little talk in gambling, or even alcoholism or being a workaholic. Sure, I talked when I drank, but it was empty, meaningless talk and it always ended in solitude. I certainly talked my way into a lot of work, but in the depths of that addiction, words were weapons that hurt people, and the work was isolating. I preferred to work alone or to just have people do what I told them. Gambling was certainly isolating. I didn't care if I ever talked to another human being again, although I was happy to talk to machines, cards, and little white balls spinning around on the roulette wheel.

In New England with Melanie I had to satisfy myself with lobster, clams and scratch tickets. New Hampshire — the "Live Free or Die" State — was the first American jurisdiction to introduce the lottery and it was working hard to stay on the leading edge with instant lottery tickets. Once we hit New Brunswick, I was able to slip off to the corner store near where my parents lived and play the VLTs. I reflected, as I stood in front of the machine slipping in a fifty dollar bill, that my father probably played this very machine before his Alzheimer's got so bad he couldn't find his way to the store.

Deceptively, the VLT was only ten cents a play. But to play all thirty-two options — to play maximum — it was $3.20 a spin, or thirty-two credits, instantly deducted from the 500 credits bought with my fifty as soon as I hit the maximum button en route to the spin pad.

Click. Click. Whirrl. Whirrl. Whirrl. Whirrl. I was instantly transferred to that longed-for-world of "All Fruit" which I had prepared for on so many days in the laundromat in Orillia. God, I thought, there's so much to watch. I could feel myself being pulled into the video screen as I watched the spinning symbols, entranced by the possibilities and hypnotized by the action. I could feel my blood pressure rising, the blood in my veins percolating, my heartbeat racing so fast I gave myself a scare. "Slow down," I mumbled, "you'll give yourself a heart attack." The wheels stopped spinning and the video graphics flashed that I had won a diagonal line, worth — I tried to look quickly at the guide above the video screen — twenty credits, the video counter recorded faster than I could read. Great, I thought, forgetting momentarily that it had cost me 32 credits for the spin. Still, I hadn't lost it all. *Click. Click. Whirrl. Whirrl. Whirrl. Whirrl.* The colours, the graphics, the flashing lights kept me riveted to the screen. It reminded me of drugs like LSD, and I wondered if this was what that fearful "speed" felt like. *Clink. Clink. Clink. Clink.* Four Credits. One "Fruit Basket" flashing in the centre of the screen. I looked quickly at the payout menu as I pushed the buttons for the next spin. Sixteen Fruit Baskets: 2000 credits — two hundred dollars. Sixteen Horns of Plenty: 3000 credits. Sixteen Fruit Markets: 4000 credits, or $400 — the "Holy Grail" on this machine. A three-dollar-and-twenty-cent bet for a four-hundred-dollar return? This was like the hundred-dollar bars I used to chase on pull-tab tickets. A comparable bet on a casino slot machine would hold out the promise of at least a thirty to forty grand jackpot. These machines, and their low payouts are resounding proof that, for people like me, it's not about money. Of course I'd already proved that when I poured hundreds of dollars in quarters into the pretend VLT in the Orillia laundromat. For me it was about being there.

Other compulsive gamblers, notably from Quebec where VLTs are in all the bars in monumental numbers, have since told me the maximum bet there is usually $2.50 and the maximum payout $500. Again, for them, it isn't about money. One fellow I know walked a mile to play a five-cent machine with just a loonie in his pocket. Getting twenty shots at the Keno, he just had to win. "With VLTs, you were always so close to winning," he said. Again this reminds me of the "paper slot-machine" Nevada tickets, which invariably created that false hope, that "near-win," on every card, enticing you to go on. I had more experience with slot machines but it was similar. I have read enough and learned enough about slot machines to now believe that winning was random, not dependent upon how much money was fed into it, or when it last paid out, as I and so many other delusional gamblers had believed. I am not, however, so sure about the near-win. Like VLTs, and the break-open tickets, the near-win on the slot machines seems to be programmed and programmed for one reason only, to entice gamblers to play more and more. Manipulation brought to you in Canada by your friendly neighbourhood government. Given the confusing roles of governments in regulating gambling on the one hand, and promoting and encouraging gambling on the other (not to mention providing crime enforcement and problem gambling treatment and research along the way) it is impossible for me to believe with any confidence that such manipulation is not going on. In my experience, the near-win is real.

I played VLTs throughout the New Brunswick leg of our trip, sneaking off whenever I could — day and night — when I didn't think it was too obvious or that I was away too long. Because, being on the Community Casino Task Force, I needed to investigate other casinos and their communities — I figured I had a good excuse to visit all the gambling establishments along our route. However, even I realized that extending that rationalization to every grocery store, restaurant and bar in New Brunswick was going to be seen as obsessive. In Quebec, as Melanie points out in her "Apnea" story, I tended to go for inexplicable rides at night and woke up to find myself screwed by a machine, two and three hundred dollars poorer with all the guilt one feels after a one-night stand. Halfway through Quebec I admitted what little muggers these machines were and swore off them forever; just in time, however, to visit the Charlevoix Casino, deep in the country north of Quebec City.

Of all the casinos I could visit Charlevoix was the easiest to justify. Its location far away from an urban setting was similar to Rama and there would be valuable comparatives to analyze. What I learned was that the casino was a great deal smaller than Rama, maybe about a tenth of the size, and that, getting near the end of my financial resources, my needing it to be generous didn't count for squat. I lost $350 of my last $500 playing blackjack and roulette and I was getting worried about having enough gas to get back to Orillia. A planned side trip to see the Casino de Hull, near Ottawa, on the way home was scrapped. "Not enough time," I told Melanie, not wanting her to think there was anything wrong. I knew all I had to do was get back home to Casino Rama and win back what I had lost. I would later learn this was to be called my desperation stage.

When I was the editor of the *Timmins-Porcupine News* in 1977, I wrote a column entitled "The lottery mentality, perhaps we all lose." It had been just a few years since the introduction of lotteries in Canada and at the time there existed just two games in Ontario — a televised Wintario every two weeks and a monthly Provincial draw. Many years and many more lotteries later, I met with a group of community and religious leaders banding together under the acronym OCAGE — Ontario Coalition Against Gambling Expansion. At that meeting, a former Ontario Government cabinet minister from the 1975 Davis Government, Jack McNie, told his new anti-gambling colleagues that around the cabinet table, when lotteries to raise money for arts and recreation were being debated, some members had expressed concern that "it would be the thin edge of the wedge to allow further legalized gambling." In hindsight, the thicker edge of that wedge has proven astronomical. The irony of my column seems just as stupendous.

The Lottery Mentality, Perhaps We All Lose

by Doug Little

Ever the dreamer, I recall many times thinking that someday I'd write a book, sell it and all my financial problems would be over. I'd even tried it a couple of times, starting one literary attempt after another, only to place them away in a cardboard filing cabinet in my home study, perhaps for a later time when more maturity and more time allowed me to complete the efforts. Two years of intense work on illustrating children's books pretty well went the same route, placed aside while I went about the day-to-day task of earning my daily bread. Still the dream was there, and every time we were short of money it would resurface in my consciousness as the solution to all our problems.

I think a great deal of us in one way or another had similar dreams. There was always something that we dreamed of doing that would solve all our financial problems, some initiative we could take ourselves that held at least the hope of returning fortune in varying degrees. Some people would dream of building their own home, and save a considerable amount of money by avoiding the high construction costs and interest payments. Some even dreamed so often they formulated plans, and one day took the daring step and created a dream come true. Some writers have even written the book I often dreamed about, and while, if they were Canadian penmen, it did not solve all their financial problems, it did give them a great deal of satisfaction and some financial reward.

Other people dreamed of starting their own business, to get on that gravy train. Some carried these dreams to reality and now dream of being bricklayers, or plumbers, where they could make twice as much money, with half the headaches.

The point is everyone had a dream that they could conjure up when the going got rough, do a little work upon, a little planning and sometimes, take a little action. It was great therapy and in some cases it was the driving force behind new enterprise and incentive that made the economy work. I talk in the past tense because I am afraid the vast majority of the people now work day to day, slugging it out and spend their dreaming hours, not pondering some elusive goal but working out how they will spend the next $1 million lottery prize.

The odds of winning in the average Wintario are one in 200, and the Provincial odds are one in one-hundred, but these are the chances of winning any prize, most of which are the $25 or other small prizes. In Wintario, for example, for the March 31 (1977) draw when 72 series of 90,000 tickets (6,480,000) were sold, the chances of winning one of the five grand prizes of $100,000 were one chance in about 1.3 million. Similarly in the Provincial, chances of winning one of the five $1 million prizes was one chance in 900,000.

Millions of dreams up in smoke before the television set is even blacked out, and not a chance that they could lead the dreamer into some new enterprise that would benefit himself, his family or his community. All he can do is buy another ticket and begin dreaming of winning again.[14]

I am in no mood to gamble and I know it. The image of me yelling, "Seventeen, come on Seventeen," running from roulette table to roulette table literally throwing money at my so-called lucky numbers brings bile to my throat. I recall the desperation of the weekend's last stand "Alamo" that ended up with me losing another $10,000 and with it, any hope of winning my way out of my troubles. The rest of today rushes into my consciousness and my mind begs for relief.

In 1974 I worked as a full-time election organizer for the NDP, paid by the United Steelworkers of America in Timmins. The campaign manager was another headstrong egotist with his own political ambitions and, of course, we clashed terribly. One evening after a particularly stressful day — I was also warring at home with Roberta — I was in the campaign headquarters and felt like I was at the end of my rope. Then a physical sensation started in my head — a twirling, a spinning. It felt as if my head was lifting off my body, being rapidly unscrewed. Right then, I believe I made one of the best choices of my life. Instinctively, I rushed out of the headquarters and walked. I just walked for about an hour and then went home. I always believed I was on the verge, on the precipice, one step away from a nervous breakdown that night and only saved myself from crossing over that line by going for that walk.

Now, as I stumble around the surreal casino, fending off the images of the day — the bounced cheques, the banks, Bob's anger, secret board meetings, Ralph's glee, the scramble for money, *F.* and Johnny's calls, Roberta's suspicions and tears, my meetings with Ed, Ken and Mr. Casino, my hopes, only to be crushed by Constable Pat Lennon, Ontario Provincial Police Officer, seconded to the Ontario Gaming Commission . . . I feel my head start to twirl, to lift, to unscrew. "I have to get out," I say to myself, audibly but amidst the din of whining machines, snapping cards, reeling wheels and caterwauls. No one is listening. If the "eyes in the sky" are watching, they'll chalk me up as just another loser talking to himself.

"Getting out" on October 22, 1996, meant, not walking, but running — virtual running — in the fastest game I know: Casino Rama's video slot machines. I had ended the previous night by pouring my final few hundred dollars into these video slot machines after a disastrous night of roulette, blackjack, and poker had cleaned out the last whack of the ten grand I stole on the weekend. My last big crime — before tonight, that is. Tonight, as last night, by the time I get to the video slots I am out of hope. I am there to obliterate myself.

I stuff the twenties into the bill feeder until I figure it is satisfied. I am in a daze but not even the hypnotic whirling of the video screen can smother the profound sense of doom I am feeling. *Gambling is failing me.* I slam the maximum button as fast as the reels stop, hardly watching to see if I have won anything. The machine racks up the wins and deducts the losses and the game proceeds to its inevitable end. Angry at the slowness with which the counter is adding a couple of hundred-dollar wins, I lean over and slip another twenty-dollar bill into the video slot next door. Two hits. Maybe that will smack me out.

"Click. Click. Whirl, Whirl, Whirl, Whirl. Click. Click. Whirl, Whirl, Whirl, Whirl. Shiiilp, Shiiilp, Shiiilp, Shiiilp. Doodoodooloop. Shiiilp, Shiiilp, Shiiilp, Shiiilp. Doodoodooloop." Fuck!

"Click. Click. Whirl, Whirl, Whirl, Whirl. Click. Click. Whirl, Whirl, Whirl, Whirl. Shiiilp, Shiiilp, Shiiilp, Shiiilp. Doodoodooloop. Shiiilp, Shiiilp, Shiiilp, Shiiilp. Doodoodooloop." Shit!

So I go on whapping the two machines until I indeed obliterate, not my mind, but a couple of hundred dollars. I am still here. While I finish off the credits I have left in the video slots, I look around for my next poison.

"Remember that we deal with alcohol — cunning, baffling, powerful!"[15]

While I am sitting on the stool, in front of the video slot machines, looking, I am sure, as dejected as any skid row rummy, one of the casino waitresses passes by and asks: "Can I get you a drink?"

CHAPTER NINETEEN

If I was ever ser-
ious about killing
myself, all I had
to do was pick up

**October 22, 1996 —
12 Midnight**

the first drink. My belief about my addiction to alcohol was that
it was a progressive disease, continuing to grow and get worse
inside of me even when I wasn't drinking. Dr. Filipczuk applied
the same progressiveness to my gambling addiction: "While you
are in the meetings," he said, "your addiction is like a tiger outside
the door, doing push ups." On October 22, 1996, my alcoholism
— that mythical high-bottom 1978 recovery notwithstanding —
is eighteen years and nine months worse and, in my heart of
hearts, I believe one drink would unlock the very gates of hell itself
and unleash the behemoth to drag me inside. More than death,
one drink would retroactively destroy all the good — even if it's
hard to fathom tonight — that I have done over the past two
decades. "No hope" would become a reality rather than a feeling.
Despair, a place as opposed to a thought. The ideation of suicide
turned into the consummation of self-murder.

"No, I don't drink," I answer automatically, dismissing the
innocent waitress with an unfair contempt, more angry at myself
than her, or even this place.

How come I didn't know, smart guy that I am, that sitting
down in that bingo hall two years ago was like picking up a drink,
only sixteen years worse? Why didn't I recognize my work as an

addiction? What about the awards, the medals, the accolades? I knew my gambling was out of control — why didn't I care?

That's enough for me. If I'm going to wallow in self-pity and hindsight, I'll do it in some other deity's temple. I came to gamble and dammit, gamble I will.

It was the Depression. I was fifteen, and was working at a part-time job after school. Times were very difficult and I was lucky to have any kind of job. My older brothers were scattered all over the country looking for work, so I was left at home with the younger kids, Mother, and him. I came home one night after work to find him drunk and, from the sound of things, in a particularly mean mood. He was always a tough guy, but when he drank he thought he could lick the world. I had learned to ignore him and stay out of his way during those times.

"I'm sick and tired of your whining about my drinking and accusing me of taking your money," I could hear him yell at Mother in the kitchen as soon as I entered the back porch.

"We can hardly put food on the table, for God's sake, and you're drinking whisky like there is no tomorrow," I heard Mother scream back, obviously at the end of her patience. "If you can't stay sober, then get out of my house," she yelled. Good for her, I thought, I'll help the old bastard pack. After years of living with his abuse and drinking, maybe Mum was ready to deal with him.

I heard a crash, the sound of wood snapping and glass shattering and yelling: "Don't you dare . . ."

"I'll show you whose house . . ."

I barged through the porch door, my anger over years of abuse boiling and my courage fortified by a few quick ones of my own after work. I rushed across the room between him and Mother and I smashed him in the face with my fist. He fell like a sack of potatoes to the kitchen floor.

After he knocked out his stepfather that day, Dad went to live with his Aunt Pearl Giggy, who was also my mother's cousin. Mom was only thirteen and there was nothing romantic about their friendship at the time. After a year or so my father went to New York to work in a restaurant. In 1939, when war broke out, he returned to Saint John to join the army and on a visit back to Hampton he saw 17-year-old Annie once more. They were married in April of 1940.

I go from the video slot machines to the poker tables, playing Caribbean Stud and Let It Ride by jumping from table to table as I would run from blackjack table to blackjack table looking for luck. Tonight I am looking for something even more elusive — oblivion. People that know me, the dealers, the pit bosses, some of the other players, know something is wrong. You can't be a regular for 78 days without somebody noticing, even in a casino. As if I have a smell of defeat about me, no one talks to me. Unlike the other gamblers, I have come to do something other than play. There are no offers of valet service, no "Can I get you anything, Mr. Little?" or "Would you like me to find a chair for you at first base, Mr. Little?" I'm starting to wonder if Ed put out the word that I'm not supposed to be gambling anymore. *God, maybe it's all over the casino, maybe I'm being watched now by the O.P.P., videotaped by the eye in the sky for some future courtroom screening.* Each of Ontario's casinos has a detachment of the O.P.P. inside, supposedly there to prevent the infiltration of organized crime, to catch cheaters, and protect the casino's, and therefore the government's money — there are millions of dollars here at any given time — from robbery. Funny, eh? The police protecting the one-armed bandits.

"Seconded," I say out loud, looking up at the black-mirrored bubble I think must contain one of the 530 video cameras. "O.P.P. Constable Pat Lennon, seconded to the Ontario Gaming Commission." I can't stop myself from giving her a little wave and a sardonic grin. That grin, it's always getting me in trouble. When I was a columnist in Timmins I was attacked at a city council meeting for snooping around city hall trying to find out what the council was doing behind closed doors. Sitting at the media table, my ears burning at hearing my name bandied around by one of the alderman, I was then chastised for having "a silly grin on my face" while he was talking.

My mother told me she didn't think much of the picture on the cover of *Saturday Night* magazine. Maybe it was the "silly grin" or the golf-ball-like lump in the side of my face.

During the photo shoot, as I was being tied down with the red nylon cord to the roulette wheel table, I was imagining the bizarre bondage picture that would be the result. The tune running through my head was *"Get your picture on the cover of —* no, not *Rolling Stone*, but *— Saturday Night!"* Here was another irony. *Under another circumstance, this could have been my sexual fantasy.*

Even in this circumstance, I was strangely submissive. The photographer, the art director, the designer, the stylist, and the make-up artist all marvelled at how patient and co-operative I was as we pre-pared the final scene in what had been a seven-hour photo session. It was resignation, perhaps serenity. I had already fully exposed myself in the article that Paul Palango had written. Now it was going to be the cover story in Canada's premier newsmagazine.

The fact that it was going to be a strange cover for the maga-zine — perhaps ridiculous — was, like the gambling addiction that spawned it, beyond my control. I had decided to try to make some good come from what had happened: to create awareness about the addiction of compulsive gambling. In order to do it, paradoxically, I had to take risks.

It was a story that I had started: first, of course, by my insane gambling and because of who I was in the Orillia community — "Mr. Downtown Orillia." But also, I had pitched *Saturday Night* magazine almost a year before when I sent the magazine an out-line of my story with all its ironies. The one I stressed, and the one that attracted front-page news from coast to coast in Canada, was that as a community-business leader in Orillia and one of the new Casino's biggest boosters, I ended up addicted and stealing $80,000 to gamble.

My friend Tom J., another recovering compulsive gambler, called me to tell me he had read the article in *Saturday Night*, but he didn't think much of the cover picture. "What do you mean?" I asked. "Well, it makes it look like you are enjoying gambling, all dressed up in a tuxedo with the roulette wheel and that silly grin on your face."

"Yes but, did you look inside?" I asked. "Oh yeah," he said, "the pictures in there are better, especially the one where you're scowling at the Casino Rama sign, but the cover makes it look like you are promoting gambling."

"No, Tom," I said. "Inside the cover — it's a fold-down cover — the bottom part shows me barefoot in old jeans, with my pockets turned inside out, broke. It was a before-and-after picture, you know, winning and losing."

There was a pause on the other end of the telephone line. "Oh, I never saw any fold-down cover," he said. It was the first time it occurred to me. Maybe nobody did.

The idea of the "vertical fold-out" cover came from Microsoft marketing. Microsoft had decided to launch Windows 98 in Canada with a multi-million dollar campaign and a series of quirky magazine ads. It bought page three and the inside cover with a drop-down page, instead of the usual foldout page. The ad was booked in a number of Canadian magazines, among them *Toronto Life*, *Harrowsmith*, *Equinox* and *Saturday Night*. It provided the magazine art directors with the unique and interesting challenge of having a two-part, fold-down cover to their magazines. *Saturday Night's* Barbara Solowan had the idea of a before-and-after shot. That's about all I knew when I agreed to be flown from Ottawa to Toronto for a two-day photo shoot that would include going back to Orillia.

One restriction was that I was not allowed inside Casino Rama — or in any other place of gambling — as a condition of my court sentence. At my sentencing hearing, the judge originally said I was not to go in any place where there was gambling. From the prisoners' dock I had to speak up.

"That means every corner store and subway station in Toronto," I said.

"Okay," he said, with more than a little exasperation, "Any place where the main business is gambling." That probably still included a lot of corner stores but the alternative of jail time was still a fresh option in his mind so I bit my lip. Afterwards, away from the courthouse, my friend Bob said: "Leave it to Doug to start arguing with the judge."

If I couldn't go to the casino, then the casino — or at least the roulette wheel table — would come to me. The scene was set up in the photographer's studio. All of the scenes we shot were of me lying on the table, my head resting on the roulette wheel — my "Wheel of Misfortune" as Paul Palango's story would be aptly named. It reminded me of a coffin. I was grateful it wasn't.

In some pictures they had me lie face down on the roulette wheel, still dressed in the antique tuxedo. The facedown, back-of-the-head scene — dead — would have been the fold-down flap, as opposed to the face up, grinning gambler cover. The idea of the bondage scene was me having a good time gambling on the top, and all tied up in my addiction on the bottom.

I first saw the final cover picture chosen via the Internet, on the *Saturday Night* magazine web site. "What did they do to my face?" was my first reaction. It looked like I had a jawbreaker sticking out of the side of my cheek. I hoped it was just a distortion of the computer. *Saturday Night* couriered me a few copies the next day and I saw the defect wasn't totally the fault of the computer. Most people said it didn't look like me. The cause of my puffed out cheek was that I was lying flat on my back for the pictures and gravity gave me a middle-age spread — of the head.

Although I didn't see the article ahead of time, with the meticulous fact-checking done by *Saturday Night* researchers, I had a pretty good idea of the final story line. When it was published, the one surprise in the article for me was the use of the quotations from Stephen Leacock's *Sunshine Sketches of a Little Town* throughout the story.

Even though I had created a festival around Mariposa, it was a testament to the delusion and denial of compulsive gambling that I never saw myself turning into a Leacockian character.

The pictures used inside the magazine had been taken in Orillia outside Casino Rama the day following the "bondage shoot." We did the pictures in front of the Rama sign from the front yard of a disgruntled neighbour of the casino. Knowing the politics of the area, I walked up to the house and asked if they'd mind if we used their property to take the pictures. Whether they knew who I was or not, I don't know, but they said okay. Their house was positioned in the line of the glare of Casino Rama's humongous, twenty-four-hour, Las Vegas-wannabe-flashing sign. Not exactly complementary to this once-rural Native community.

Photographer Rino Noto and designer Scott Gibbs spent the afternoon dodging rain showers and the casino security, shuffling me in and out of the van when the coast, and the skies, were clear. After an hour or so, satisfied they had the right picture of me sneering at the sign, they began to pack up when Rino reached into the back of the van and pulled out a green roulette table cloth — a cape — and a miniature golden roulette wheel — a crown.

"Why don't we just try these? Just to see," he said, trying to fake spontaneity.

I thought: *Captain Casino! King Roulette! Foolette! A Clown!* Then I thought of the bondage photos the day before. My two-year gambling binge. The insanity of my gambling. "Why not," I said.

I head to the regular slot machines, again, seeking oblivion or at least sedation. *What an upside-down world I've created!* I now need to deaden my mind with the very excitement I used to think was the panacea for being alive. Yet, tonight there seems to be no action fast enough, no spinning wild enough and no chance great enough to extinguish the anxiety I feel about the consequences I now have to face. I immediately slide two twenty-dollar bills into two slot machines, and hitting the maximum button on each I reach over to a third machine and feed it another twenty. "Maybe I'll play a whole damn row," I say, looking up at the glass bubbles in the sky. "Or the whole goddamned, bloody lot of them." I push the cash-out button on all three of the machines, not caring whether I won or lost on my initial spins. I want coins. Scooping the dollar tokens from coin trays at the bottom of each slot I grab a plastic pail from the side of a machine and dump the tokens into it. As I move to the next machine and pour three of the coins into the slot's slot and whap the maximum button I'm sure I hear a mournful wail in behind the incessant ringing-dinging-whirling-twirling of this place. Gone is the sound of impending winners that seemed to be piped in under pressure through a tube next to the oxygen line.

Three coins. *"Click, Click, Click. Whap!"* As I move on to the next machine I hear: *"Whirl, Whirl, Whirl."* Again *"Click, Click, Click. Whap!"* on the next machine. *"Whirl, Whirl, Whirl."* Next: *"Click, Click, Click. Whap!"* I hear *"Clink, Clink, Clink, Clink"* somewhere behind me. More bullets. I reach back and scoop the 20 or 30 new coins into the pail, and then resume my ruinous run up and down the banks of slot machines. "Only 2,170 bandits to go!"

During the summer when I was in between Grades 10 and 11 at Saint Mary's College, I worked as a maintenance cleaner at Saint Joseph's Hospital, run by the Sisters of Charity and, incidentally, the birthplace of me and my brothers and sisters. As I was studying to be a priest, the job was one of the perks shared among the Roman Catholic family. I had also worked there the summer before as a laundry worker. Cleaning floors and walls was a considerable step up from sorting operating room and maternity ward laundry in the days before disposable diapers. My college friend Paul worked with me on the maintenance crew and we had a great time engaging in sponge fights while cleaning rooms from the ceiling down after patients had died in them.

I also spent time at our new parish church, St. Anne's, with Father O'Leary, a huge rotund man with both a sharp tongue and a sharp wit, able to dole out equal measures of sarcasm and humour. My parents had changed parishes after the mortgage incident with Father Kinsella at Stella Maris. I was grateful because, for all his quickness of mind and sharpness of tongue, Father O'Leary never questioned my sincerity. On weekends I served his mass as an altar boy on Saturday and usually had breakfast with him at his rectory home. I'm not sure what he thought of me, but I liked him.

During that summer there was a noviciate priest assisting Father O'Leary and one weekend he invited me to a summer home he had access to on the Kingston Peninsula. I suppose today we'd call it a cottage although it wasn't. It likely was an abandoned country house, left by some rural family who had given up commuting and catching ferries and had moved into Saint John. My parents rented a similar house a few years later where Mom took the kids when my father was recovering from his first heart attack.

There was a small beach on the Kennebecasis River not far from the house that made it attractive to me, so we piled into the parish van after mass and breakfast on Saturday. "Don't drown," Father O'Leary ordered as he sent us on our way.

I confess my memory of what happened at that Peninsula house is foggy, and what I do remember may even be a mirage. The whole incident has always seemed like an echo to me rather than a reality. A recent visit to Saint John and St. Anne's helped me reconstruct as much as I've already told. My memory tells me of being asleep. It was a big house, so we had our own rooms. I was awakened by something — or someone — touching me. What I said, or how I stopped him, I don't remember. I never told anyone, dismissing it as something that I didn't want to think about, much less talk about. Like the kissing priest, like "Ring the bell, Daddy, ring the bell," like dancing to my father's leather strap and the dirty old pervert just above Haymarket Square.

The fact that today, some forty years later, I can still feel and taste that Redemptorist Father's tongue pushing into my nine-year-old mouth, and his hands squeezing and caressing my little boy's bum, makes me wonder, between then and now, what I *have* been thinking about all these years.

Escape. Fear. Mistrust. Who could I tell? Deception. Pretension. Unholiness. How could I tell? Alcohol. Fantasy. Duplicity. Why would I tell? Work. Image. Control. How do I dare tell? Gambling. Liar, cheat, and thief. I don't want to tell!

I give up the slot-out at the casino-corral when I'm finally out of dollar coins. There are still a couple of thousand machines to plug but I'm not going to blow any more money on this madness. Instead I head down to the VIP area and the baccarat pit. Baccarat is a simple game of fifty-fifty, like cutting cards or flipping a coin, but with a complicated counting system built around a total of nine as a winning hand. You can bet the player or the bank just like heads or tails, and there is even a tie bet, a long shot like betting that the coin will land on its side. A winning tie bet pays nine to one, and as the dealers will always tell you, "Ties often repeat." I first watched this game in the Rama VIP area in the first month the casino opened, wanting to learn any game that would give me an edge. I quickly learned that, in the VIP area anyway, it is a game for very high rollers, and not one where you would feel comfortable unless you were ready to wager thousands, if not tens of thousands on a single hand. Its clientele are primarily Asian, whom I am told provide forty percent of Casino Rama's win. Tonight I don't care about comfort and I don't care if I blow the rest of the Nevada money. I look into the VIP area and change my mind. Somehow I know I can't pull off pretending I belong in there tonight.

Still, halfway across the room, there's a Mini-Baccarat table, which is essentially the same game with less ritual and theatre than there is in the Baccarat Pit. The table is crowded, with seven or eight Chinese players layered several deep, and a couple of Toronto Italians. I edge my way in at one of the corners and place four fifty-dollar bills on the table. "Two hundred in," the dealer shouts and I ask for quarters. When I get my chips I place four on the Tie line, to which the dealer also shouts "Player on Tie — one hundred," causing the pit boss to eye both me and the bet. Shit, I think, I can feel the camera sniffing around like a drug-smelling canine. I'm also, obviously, the object of jeers and sneers among the Chinese, and although I have no idea what they are saying, the sound of contempt is universal.

Ties don't come, nor do they repeat when, in pride or stupidity, I place another four greens on the tie line. After the second loss, I walk away from the table thinking that at least it was a mental break. The Chinese cheer my departure. Maybe it was a Confucian thing — "Dead man, bad luck."

The first time I identified myself as a compulsive gambler in an AA meeting a woman named Lorraine laughed out loud. As part of my recovery I had started going to AA again, trying to develop a deeper understanding of the 12 steps and spirituality. At the meeting a number of members had introduced themselves as addicts and alcoholics, or alcoholics and drug addicts.

"Hello everyone, my Name is Doug and I am an alcoholic and a compulsive gambler."

Why that triggered a loud guffaw from Lorraine I was never sure; even after I got to know her, I never asked. Oddly, over the next year and a half that I attended AA again I was never comfortable talking about my addiction to gambling, even though it related — in my mind anyway — so closely to my AA experience the first time and my failure to work the steps and deal with the underlying causes of my addictions. In addition, I believe that addiction is a progressive disease that I was 17 years further into when I sat down in that bingo hall in December of 1994, which likely precipitated my rapid slide in to hell.

Perhaps AA's reluctance to talk about other addictions shouldn't have surprised me. In Timmins 19 years ago our AA meetings were held at a hall we called "The Club." It was a place that some AA members had pooled their resources to rent as a clubhouse, and then in turn re-rented to the different AA groups. After the meetings, on many nights, members of the club stayed behind and played cards all night long.

With a proliferation of 12-step programs — Narcotics Anonymous, Overeaters Anonymous, Gamblers Anonymous, Sex Anonymous and on — many AA members and groups have evoked the "primary purpose" clause of AA's Fifth Tradition: "Each group has but one primary purpose — to carry its message to the alcoholic who still suffers." Talk of other addictions is either tacitly or vocally opposed. This is unfortunate, because I, for one, was an alcoholic who was still suffering due to my addictions to other things besides booze. Over the years I have met many other so-called "addictive personalities" who had a history of trading one addiction for another.

Lorraine and I became friends within AA. We talked after the meetings and once I spoke at a meeting she organized in a downtown Toronto homeless centre. One day she told me about a book I should read, *Coyote Blue* by Christopher Moore. After I read it I understood a little more why she laughed aloud.

The Coyote in the book was a Navaho myth come alive, a trickster with a penchant for gambling. Once he took the narrator's credit cards and fed them to a bank machine in Las Vegas, dancing with glee on *winning* several hundred dollars. It's a feeling I've heard shared by many compulsive gamblers.

The book relates a native legend (traditional or fiction, which I am not sure) where Coyote and Beaver bet a night with their wives on a wager about who was the best hunter. Of course Beaver won. Then Coyote proceeded to gamble away everything he owned, his horses, his lodge, his wife and his clothes.

"I'll bet you my ass against everything else," which Coyote proceeded to lose.

When Coyote got home his wife was waiting. "Beaver took the lodge," she said.

"Yep," Coyote said.

"Where's your ass?" she asked.

"Beaver got that too."

"You know," she said, "there's a twelve-step program for gambling. You should look into it."

"Twelve steps." Coyote laughed. "I'll bet I can do it in six."

Back to blackjack. I'm going from table to table where there are two open spots and betting a quarter on each, winning some and losing some, but the flood of emotions I am trying to dam keeps on flowing as my concentration on the game is shot. I try upping the ante to $50 a spot but it has little effect. My mind still isn't in the game. Winning is hollow, as if we are betting play money or matchsticks. No longer can I hope I am going to win my way out of trouble. Losing is terrifying, as it is a harbinger that sooner or later I will be through the rest of the fourteen hundred dollars and have to leave, having gambled away all my resources — all the money I could beg, borrow, or steal — as well my family, home, job, blah, blah, blah. I know it's forever, and that thought terrifies me to nausea. *No escape.*

My secular faith is destroyed. As I now drag myself from table to table, I am no longer looking for luck, but fearing fate, and that feels a whole lot different. Like a bar after everyone else has had a few too many, the casino, now devoid of hope, looks like the inferno of my youthful faith — weeping and gnashing of teeth — and I'm wondering just what the hell I'm doing here.

♥ ♦ ♣ ♠

I was Addicted to Gambling . . .
By Doug Little

The only economic impact studies that have been done of gambling expansion in Canada have been by consultants for the gambling industry (and their government partners) on the impact on communities that host casinos like Orillia, Windsor, and Niagara. These studies are the cheerleader type, assessing the win, the jobs and the spin-off of construction, and they contain nothing about the harmful economic impacts of what gamblers lose. It's a one-sided ledger. It's a lie as an economic impact study. I bought into such a lie for the City of Orillia, believing the casino was going to be an "economic engine" that pulled along the rest of our local economy. On my last visit to Orillia, almost two years after Casino Rama was opened, I counted one new motel, a gas station, and two donut shops. My main street in Downtown Orillia was, if anything, worse off, with more stores closed than ever before. Instead of being an economic engine, the casino has been sucking all the disposable income that used to be spent in the local economy.

Oh yes, there are the tourist dollars (although the American tourist dollars are much more in evidence in Windsor and Niagara than Orillia). However, those tourist dollars are spent mostly in all-inclusive casinos rather than in the broader community once the casinos reach their full potential with hotel rooms, restaurants and entertainment centres.

When Senator Paul Simon of the United States appeared before Congress in 1992 he made a forceful argument. "Gambling is not the only kind of business that can remove dollars from a local economy, but very few remove proportionately as much money for so marginal an increase in public revenue. Given the widespread evidence that gambling hurts a community, what rationale is there for government to act as a conduit for the profits of private promoters? The answer is none. But naive public officials remained convinced that someday they'll hit the jackpot. It's a delusion as old as gambling itself."

By far the biggest selling job in Canada has come from the promise of jobs and one certainly can't deny the casino jobs that are in Orillia, Windsor, and Niagara. However, as Dr. Earl L. Grinols of the Department of Economics of the University of Illinois points out in the Illinois Business Review: "Taking all areas into account, gambling does not create jobs. Rather, it shifts them from one location to another and converts some jobs that would have been devoted to other things into gambling jobs."

These jobs are created at the expense of other businesses. The so-called "entertainment" dollars that are spent on gambling are, in fact, dollars that otherwise would have gone into numerous businesses.

Dr. John Warren Kindt, of the University of Illinois, in "The Economic Impacts of Legalized Gambling

Activities" states: "Gambling interests are competing not just for the consumer's 'entertainment dollar' as they claim, but for all consumer dollars, including the savings dollars. Once discretionary dollars are exhausted, 10% of the public [the problem economic gamblers — PEGS] will draw on their savings accounts."

Dr. Kindt continues: "Subsumed in this 10% are the 1.5% to 5% of the public who are compulsive gamblers and will exhaust an average of $15,000 per year over a maximum 15-year period before 'bottoming out.' In addition compulsive gamblers also go into debt an average of $80,000 to finance their compulsive gambling."

Dr. Grinols, in a paper "Development of Dream Field Delusions: Effects of Casino Gambling" says: "As best as I can determine, problem and pathological gamblers provide just slightly more than half of the revenues of casinos. What makes this a blockbuster in my opinion is the fact that the casino industry is therefore heavily dependent on the revenues of psychologically sick people. They have to know this. They have to be aware of this fact."

In my three-month gambling binge inside Casino Rama I saw the same faces night after night leading me to believe that problem and compulsive gamblers make up a very much larger percentage of casino revenue.

Industry and government seem to have found a way to rationalize the existence of problem and pathological gamblers by setting casinos up along borders and in regions that can draw on outside populations.

In addiction recovery there are no international, provincial, or municipal borders: thus we see the harm done by Casino Niagara and Windsor to our American neighbours, and in Ottawa by the Quebec Hull Casino and in Toronto by the Orillia Casino.

It is the basest rationalization for government to discount the harm it is causing simply because it affects people mainly from another jurisdiction. And yet the prospect of feeding off the neighbours is one of the most effective arguments used by governments and the gambling industry to promote expansion.[16]

Blackjack is just not doing it for me tonight. I pick up my remaining quarter and nickel chips and head to the washroom. There are already rumours that one of the Chinese gamblers has blown his brains out in this washroom, just like there have been stories of loan sharks standing behind the losers at the tables offering them money. It's obvious that no one has ever offered me money, because there's no doubt that if they had, I would have taken it.

As for the suicide story I'm not so sure. Casino officials call these rumours "urban legends" — a term, interestingly enough, you'll also hear them use in Las Vegas, Missouri, Quebec and just about everywhere a casino exists — but my instincts as a reporter tell me "where there's smoke, there's fire."

Looking in that bathroom mirror, I say, "It certainly would make a statement." The memories of my conversations with Melanie and my mother come quickly to my rescue and I mumble in reply: "Don't worry, I'm not going to kill myself."

So as usual, if I am not going to die I am going to have to live and living means something different than what I am doing now. Something other than gambling. People say they love to gamble because the excitement makes them feel so alive — on the edge. Tonight I realize: not me. Gambling has made me dead, dead to life on life's terms. Running. Escaping. Pretending. Intoxicated. High. A big shot. Lying. Cheating. And stealing. Just going through the motions of being alive. A caricature of myself — no, two caricatures — one, the small-town big shot, "Mr. Downtown Orillia," and the other, the gambler, feverishly risking it all to win. I started gambling to escape, to relax from the pressures of my unhappy workaholic life. Little did I know the troubles it would lead me to would multiply my need for elusion tenfold, bringing me to my knees, defeated, and to the very threshold of prison, insanity and death.

I am now faced with only two alternatives: Gamble, continue running off the cliff, surely into prison, continued insanity, and ultimately, death. Or, stop gambling, face the consequences, and try to make some good come out of all of this.

I turn and leave the washroom, passing the ringing and dinging of the five-, twenty- and hundred-dollar slots, around the poker pit with its flashing neon Caribbean Stud jackpot sign — I don't want to know the prize — down a row of blackjack tables, where all those excited happy social gamblers in the ads are supposed to be but aren't, to the first spinning, flashing, shining roulette table I see.

"Playing colour," I shout to the croupier standing behind the table. He is just about to spin the roulette wheel. I reach between the players, across the table and place my last green chip — $25 — on, what else, my lucky 17. Stepping back as the croupier starts the white ball twirling, I turn and walk towards the door. Raising my head and my eyes to the eyes in sky, I say out loud: "I won't be back."

On January 31, 1997, three months after I quit gambling, I travelled back to Orillia for the most ignominious event of my life. After three months of assisting the Ontario Provincial Police and the Ontario Gaming Commission in conducting a forensic audit of the Leacock Heritage Festival books and piecing together the Orillia Winter Carnival accounts, the police were ready to lay charges. Once again my rights were read to me — off a little card in case you are interested and would rather not learn first-hand — and I was arrested on fifteen charges. Six charges were of criminal breach of trust (fraud), one for each the Leacock Festival's bank, bingo, Nevada and charity casino accounts, the winter carnival account and for Downtown Orillia. Five charges were for theft over $5,000 and one charge was for theft under $5,000 (the Downtown) and three charges were for breach of the terms and conditions of lottery licence, one each for bingo, Nevada and the charity casinos.

I was photographed twice, once for my O.P.P. record and once for the RCMP, and I was similarly fingerprinted. While Officer Pat Lennon had attended the several meetings I had over the previous months with her and Constable Dan Anthony, only Constable Anthony officiated at my arrest and carried out the printing and mug shots. Both Officers Anthony and Lennon always treated me with respect and professionalism. On our initial meeting at my office, when I first handed over the charity casino, bingo, and Nevada records to Constable Lennon and told her I would cooperate fully with the investigation, she said she would "try to carry out the investigation with as much compassion as possible," which she did. As we were completing the fingerprinting I was visibly shaken by the experience and Const. Anthony said, "Doug, just remember, this too will pass."

I knew I was not going to be held in custody, as we had already discussed this when the police called me to come to Orillia for the formal arrest and I was released on a promise to appear. I took the bus back to Toronto that afternoon, and then the subway and bus to Mississauga where I was living with my sister. Rather than take the final bus I decided to walk, needing more time to wrestle with my feelings of anxiety and despair following my arrest and the anticipated new volley of publicity before going home.

I know that compulsive gambling is indeed an illness — and that I suffer from it — because of the prevalence of suicidal thoughts in my life over those two years. Prior to that, I could never have imagined myself contemplating self-destruction — I *engaged* in it, certainly in my other addictions, but I never *thought* about it or realized that was what I was doing. I may have been destroying myself by my actions, but I never really acted, or considered acting, to kill myself.

That night, once again, full of guilt, regret and shame on the lonely walk through the streets of Mississauga, which I am sure are the loneliest streets in Canada, I thought of suicide. But quickly, on the tail of this despair, came the thought: "Fuck it, I might as well gamble." It was a godsend.

From that night on, in my soul, gambling has been inextricably linked to suicide, just as alcohol was linked to poison nineteen years earlier. As I had already made up my mind I did not want to die, first for Melanie's sake, but subsequently for me and for the human being I really am, I have not gambled again.

I have been given many gifts since I walked out of Casino Rama on October 22, 1996 — my journey in recovery could fill another book — but one of the most precious has been reading a book by a Viennese psychiatrist, Viktor E. Frankl, entitled *Man's Search for Meaning*. Dr. Frankl was a Jewish prisoner in the Nazi concentration camps, where he gained his essential understanding of life stripped to its core. Having lost his wife, father, mother, and brother to the camps and the infamous gas chambers, having lost every possession, suffering inhumanely from hunger, cold and brutality, and expecting death at any moment, how did he live? How did anyone live under such circumstances and how did so many die so peacefully, as he relates that they did? It was in *Man's Search for Meaning* that I first read the quote from Gothlieb Lessing, an eighteenth-century German playwright, which so aptly described my workaholic life: "There are things which must cause you to lose your reason, or you have none to lose."

Interestingly, Frankl also quoted gambling addict Fyodor Dostoevsky, who once said: "There is only one thing that I dread: not to be worthy of my sufferings."

Frankl wrote: "We who lived in the concentration camps can remember the men who walked through the huts comforting others, giving away their last piece of bread. They may have been few in number, but they offer sufficient proof that everything can be taken from a man but one thing: the last of the human freedoms

433

— to choose one's attitude in any given set of circumstances, to choose one's own way.

"Fundamentally, therefore, any man can, even under such circumstances, decide what shall become of him — mentally and spiritually. He may retain his human dignity even in a concentration camp. It can be said that they were worthy of their sufferings; the way they bore their suffering was a genuine inner achievement. It is this spiritual freedom — which cannot be taken away — that makes life meaningful and purposeful."

This book and the philosophy it espoused were with me in court and helped prepare me for jail.

In May of 1997, Toronto Intergroup published a newsletter for the members of its seventeen area gambling recovery groups. In the same month I pled guilty to three charges of Breach of Trust and one of Breach of Lottery Conditions and I wrote an article for that newsletter. I outlined what happened to me in my gambling binge and what I had learned about myself, as this book has done in detail. This is how I concluded:

> Today my life is still chaotic and certainly much of it is out of my control. For an old control freak, at first, this was among the hardest things to deal with. However, participating in recovery and with the help of my sponsor and my many friends in the program, I have been able to accept this and other realities that I can not change. Guilt and remorse, especially over what has happened to my poor wife, has been a struggle;

however, the realization of how close these feelings are to self-pity has prevented me from wallowing in them.

Now that I am out of action, abstinent from gambling, sober and cognizant of my tendency to go overboard in many areas including work, I have choice. I have what the noted Austrian psychiatrist Viktor Frankl calls the "ultimate freedom — the ability to choose one's attitude in a given set of circumstances."

I choose hope.

I choose to have "the courage to change the things I can" — me.

I choose the 12 Steps — all of them — and I am working on a Fourth Step; seeing, for the first time in my life, what has made me who I am.

I choose recovery.

I choose meaning in the rest of my life.

I choose God, of my understanding.

I choose helping others.

I choose freedom from the bondage of "self-will run riot."[17]

AFTERWORD

I walked out of Casino Rama in the middle of the night on October 22, 1996, to face the consequences of my two-year gambling binge. I met with Constable Pat Lennon and turned over the records of the Leacock Heritage Festival gambling fundraising accounts and offered to cooperate fully with the police investigation. Two days later, my lawyer Brian Turnbull and I attended the Orillia Police Station and I read my ten-page confession into a video camera and answered questions from Const. Lennon and Const. Dan Anthony, the Orillia officer assigned to my case. Throughout the next three months I cooperated with the police in a "straightforward manner" in their investigation of my wrongdoing, a fact that they testified to at my sentencing hearing. The only contentious issue between us came when I was asked about a copy they had from my bank of a bounced $500 cheque to a numbered account in Toronto. I said it was for payment of money I owed, an answer that failed to satisfy their suspicions. As we were taping the session I asked the tape recorder be turned off so I could explain it, "off the record."

"That cheque was to be a partial repayment of a loan I got from a guy in Toronto, who, I suppose, you would call a loan shark. I only knew him as 'Johnny' and I gave him blank post-dated cheques. When my bank manger kicked back my overdraft in October, that cheque bounced."

"Do you still owe him money?" Constable Anthony asked. "Are you in any danger?"

"No, I am not in any danger. The loan has been paid off."

"How did you meet this 'Johnny'?" he asked.

"That's why I don't want to talk about this," I said. "When I was gambling, I was bailed out of trouble on two occasions by a friend here in Orillia. The last time, in April, he gave me $2,000. That was all he could afford but he arranged for me to borrow another $8,000 from this 'Johnny,' but not at loan-shark rates; at only three percent. In the end, when all of my troubles became public, my friend paid 'Johnny' the balance of what I owed him, likely $6,000.

"He didn't do anything wrong but was simply trying to help me out of my troubles as a friend. Since the interest rate was only three percent, it wasn't loan sharking so therefore not a crime."

"How did your friend know 'Johnny?'" Constable Anthony asked.

"I don't know," I answered. Getting flustered, I told the police I would cooperate fully with them on the details of my crimes but insisted: "I will not say anything or cooperate in anyway to get my friend in trouble as he was only trying to help me out as a friend. I am responsible for what I did."

They accepted what I had to say and it was the last I heard of the cheque and 'Johnny.' I still owe my friend the six thousand dollars, and although he insists I don't, someday I plan to repay him.

I started attending the Donwood Problem Gambling Program immediately and became their most frequent visitor as I chose to build an outpatient plan of recovery in Toronto rather than attend a treatment centre I could not afford. In a year I attended 44 one-on-one sessions with my therapist Roger Horbay, as well as four telephone sessions from Orillia. I attended an additional 21 group sessions and workshops at Donwood and had 27 sessions with psychiatrist Mark Filipczuk. In that same year I attended 150 gambling

Twelve Step meetings in the Toronto region, as well as 89 alcoholic Twelve Step meetings. In that first year of recovery, during which time I was on sick leave and disability insurance, I attended 410 treatment sessions, meetings and presentations all told. By the time I stopped keeping a record of my treatment for my probation officer, almost three and a half years after I quit gambling, I had attended 823 sessions of one kind or another that helped me deal with my addictions and with the unravelling of the story of my life. For that first year I was fortunate to have had four months of accumulated sick leave from the Downtown Management Board (which I got to use before they fired me) and after that I was able to qualify for sick benefits from the Unemployment Insurance Fund until I was finally awarded long-term disability payments (and repaid the UI fund) from Mutual Insurance, likely the first time pathological gambling was recognized as the cause of a disability in Canada, combined of course with the depression and anxiety I was feeling over that year. This income allowed me to sustain my family and myself while I attended the intense treatment I needed to deal with my addictions and their consequences. I remain active in recovery programs today.

Shortly after the police investigation began, word leaked to the media and the first of fifteen front-page headlines and countless articles about the investigation, my crime, the gambling addiction, my court cases, and sentence appeared in the *Orillia Packet & Times*. The *Packet* reporters were sympathetic and understanding about the addiction at the beginning but reporter and columnist Randy Richmond told me, "Every time we write something about you, you would not believe the pressure around here." I took this to mean pressure from the Casino but it may have also been a backlash from *Packet* readers. At any rate, the paper, and Randy, turned on me with a vengeance, especially after the sentencing.

When the news came out that one of the key boosters of Casino Rama ended up being a gambling addict charged with stealing $80,000, the irony attracted national attention with the story appearing on the front page of the *Toronto Star* and newspapers across Canada.

From the night I told Roberta, she rarely went out of the house, too ashamed to face our neighbours or other Orillians. We gave notice to the landlord of the house we were renting on Maple Leaf Avenue and on December 31, 1996, I drove Roberta back to Timmins where she still lives, and I went to Toronto to live with my sister Veronica. Melanie continued to attend the University of British Columbia where she obtained her Masters in Creative Writing.

At my first court appearance on February 23, 1997, I was remanded for another month but made a statement to the media at the time that I would take responsibility for my actions and face the consequences head on. At the next appearance we opted to have all the charges heard in Federal Court, which moved the case out of the jurisdiction of the Orillia Provincial Court to Barrie with the next hearing scheduled for May 23, 1997. I was in agreement with my lawyer's advice to move the case to the Barrie Federal Court — it gave us more options and took us away from Orillia and any undue community pressure that might have influenced the court.

On May 23, with sister Veronica in attendance, I pleaded guilty to three counts of breach of trust, one for each organization — the Leacock Heritage Festival, the Orillia Winter Carnival and the Downtown Management Board. I also pled guilty to one count of breaching the terms and conditions of a lottery licence. The other charges were dropped. Judge Paul Hermiston ordered a pre-sentence report and a sentencing hearing was scheduled for June 27 in Barrie. After appearing before Judge Hermiston for my plea, and watching him deal with other cases, I had no problem believing he was stern but Brian also believed he was fair and had an open mind on the gambling addiction, so we would get a fair hearing.

My psychiatrist Mark Filipczuk and Donwood problem gambling therapist Roger Horbay agreed to testify as did a long-term member of my gambling recovery program, Mike O., a man who knew both the disease of compulsive gambling and my efforts at recovery. My friend Bob Willsey from Orillia would also testify as well as Michel Gauthier from Ottawa, my friend and colleague in the festivals and events industry for the previous ten years.

In addition we planned to present the judge with a number of letters from people who would attest to my community involvement and past contributions before the gambling. We also invited people to attend the hearing.

On June 27, Roberta came from Timmins and Melanie from Vancouver to attend the sentencing hearing. Two of my sisters and their husbands also came. My mother, I was sure, was with me in prayer. I never counted the supporters in the room, but between them and the media, the courtroom was crowded. The Mayor of Orillia, my friend Clayt French, attended with his wife Les, as well as Winter Carnival Chairman and City Alderman Ron MacLean. Both were severely criticized in the *Orillia Packet* for this and I was portrayed as having friends in high places that influenced the judge. But, they were there as my friends and people who respected what I had previously contributed regardless of how much they deplored my crimes. Unfortunately, the paper used his support for me to continue a vendetta it was already carrying on against Clayt. While he wasn't running for mayor again anyway, I still felt bad for him; I knew he was being charitable in his support. I also felt bad that Ron lost the next election, partially, I am sure, due to his show of support for me.

Ken McMullen and Doug Bell from the Leacock Heritage Festival attended along with Tim Dixon, the Chairman of Canada Day. Mark Douglas of the Chippewas of Rama attended and wrote a letter to the judge. My previous assistant at the Huronia Tourism Association, now its administrator, Rose Cambourne, attended and wrote a letter.

Along with the member who testified, four other members of the gamblers' twelve-step programs in Toronto travelled to Barrie including my sponsor, Ted, who also wrote a letter.

In all, we had a package of thirty-three letters to present to the judge. References from Orillia, Timmins, the Huronia region, and across the province, written by colleagues from festivals and downtown business organizations. Former MP and cabinet minister Doug Lewis, the man who, four years earlier, presented me with the Canada 125 Medal, wrote a letter of support, as did former Leacock Museum curator and city alderman Jay Cody. The chairman of the Leacock Home Board, Pete McGarvey, and University of Ottawa Dean David Staines, Canada's foremost authority on Leacock, also wrote letters.

My lawyer told the court, "All of the letters have the same theme, an exceptional worker, tireless efforts to the community. People thought enough about his work to write these letters."

One of the letters, written by the former publishers of the *Orillia Sun*, Anderson and Susan Charters — two of the first people I met when I came to Orillia in 1983 — are typical of the content of the letters.

We have known Doug Little since January 1983 when he arrived to live in Orillia. We had just arrived a few months earlier to launch a community newspaper in Orillia.

During the 1980s we were able to follow Doug's active involvement in the community as newspaper publishers. Subsequently we have been able to observe his contributions to the community as residents and as an active family with an interest in our community.

We can attest that through his work and as a volunteer Doug initiated many projects that benefitted our community. He also worked hard to follow through on these projects. Indeed it is hard to think of a major community initiative in Orillia during the last 15 years that he was not involved with.

Although active politically and involved in many political issues, we can never recall Doug Little acting, speaking, or referring to anyone else in a divisive or mean-spirited way. We feel the people of Orillia owe Doug a vote of gratitude and support.

We have been impressed with Doug's willingness to acknowledge his guilt, to co-operate with authorities, to engage in treatment for his gambling addiction, and seek support from friends and colleagues. It is clear that Doug has and will accept responsibility for his wrongdoing. We would also like to make it clear that in many other ways Doug was a model citizen in our community, a fact recognized by the Government of Canada when he was awarded a Canada 125 designation.

We ask The Honourable Court to bear this in consideration when sentencing Doug Little.

To my everlasting shame, Andy Charters, a better man by light years, was one of the Liberal nominees I helped Ralph Cipolla defeat for the Liberal candidacy in 1994. The incongruity of my behaviour compared to my beliefs was typical of my workaholic addiction. Ironically, of course, Andy and Susan's letter, like so many of the others, was praising my workaholic life. The good I did in one addiction saved me from the full consequences of the harm I did in the other.

The sentencing hearing was an emotional day for us all. Roberta was in constant tears, and I choked and wept when I read my statement to the court. Brian Turnbull told me it was the most emotional day he had spent in a court room.

Brian used the witnesses to show the court there was a mental condition called Pathological Gambling, and that I most certainly suffered from it and that it affected my judgement. He also had them testify to my cooperation in treatment. He used Bob and Michel and the letters to show my past "good works," and that the support of my family, friends, colleagues, and community still existed.

In seeking a conditional sentence, allowing me to do my time in the community rather than jail, Brian had to prove that I was not a threat to the community and that the circumstances of my crime were exceptional.

Prosecutor and Crown Attorney John Alexander asked the judge to give me 18 months in jail saying breach of trust is too serious a crime to receive a conditional sentence; there needed, he argued, to be a strong deterrent for others who might consider committing the same crime. Later, Alexander would be quoted in the *Orillia Packet* as saying he didn't think compulsive gambling was a mitigating factor but at the trial he did not argue this, or even cross-examine any of our witnesses. He merely cited case law to argue that a conditional sentence shouldn't apply.

Before the judge retired to make his judgment, I asked to make a statement. This is what I said:

> *I take full responsibility for what I did. I am, I hope, prepared to accept the consequences of my crimes.*
>
> *I am sorry for what I did. Although I deluded myself while gambling that I was just borrowing, I know it was stealing, and wrong. I will do everything in my power never to do anything like this again.*
>
> *I am sorry for the harm I have done, first and foremost, to my wife Roberta, who has innocently had her life destroyed along with mine. She has lost family, home, security, and community, and suffers from the shame and the consequences of my actions.*
>
> *I am sorry for the embarrassment I have caused my daughter and my family. I am sorry I am now a burden to my mother and my sister.*
>
> *I am sorry for the harm and embarrassment I have caused my friends and colleagues. I am sorry for my employer and the hundreds of volunteers who placed their faith in me.*
>
> *I will regret my actions and the harm I have done, forever.*
>
> *I am committed to repaying the money I took and I am willing to take personal responsibility for the debts of the organizations so that creditors have direct recourse to hold me liable.*
>
> *I am committed to making happen whatever good can come from this nightmare by helping other people suffering from the disease of compulsive gambling, and by helping to increase awareness of problem and compulsive gambling and the various treatment programs.*
>
> *I am committed to doing what I can to heal the harm I*

have done with my family and friends. I am grateful for the
support and compassion of my family, friends, and colleagues
that is so evident in the letters and in the court today.

I blame no one for what I have done. I am learning about
myself through the various recovery programs that I am
attending and I will continue my journey for spiritual, mental
and physical recovery. I am grateful to the professionals who
are helping me in treatment and to my lawyer Brian Turnbull
for his wise counsel and hard work.

I am indebted with my life to the other recovering compul-
sive gamblers and alcoholics that are helping me in my
recovery. Without them I am lost.

I have not gambled since October 22, 1996.
I have not drunk since February 3, 1978.

With the help and support of my family, my old friends,
and my new friends in recovery, one day at a time, I will not
need to gamble or drink again, and I will not need to fear
again the wrath and punishment of my country and commu-
nity as I do today.

I had come to the court that day fully prepared to go to jail. I
had brought my c-pap machine with me as well as a letter from
my specialist explaining that I needed it to breathe while I slept. I
had a friend in Barrie, Dave S., from my Balloon Festival days,
who was a member of AA. He had permission to go into the Barrie
Jail and was ready to visit me after I was incarcerated. My sister
and I had already signed affidavits for an appeal that would be
used to have me released on bail, likely after the weekend, as the
twenty-seventh was a Friday. Brian said he would take the appeal
to the Supreme Court if necessary. I had also imprinted Viktor

Frankl's ultimate freedom — "the ability to choose one's attitude in a given set of circumstances" — upon my mind, and thought I was ready, if necessary, to accept jail.

Moments later, standing trembling in the prisoners' dock as Judge Hermiston delivered his stern judgment, I wasn't so sure. As he started, I thought I was going to jail.

"The charges to which Mr. Little pleaded guilty are extremely serious not only in the amount of money but by breaching this trust he has betrayed every citizen of Orillia."

He acknowledged the letters and attendees in the courtroom. "It is evident to me that this community supports Little even today, and I'm satisfied his compulsion to gamble and his predisposition to addiction caused his present difficulties. His past and present addiction is an illness that creates exceptional circumstances."

Even as he said that my cooperation with the police and guilty plea showed remorse, I felt that I was on a roller coaster that could easily have a sharp turn still landing me in jail. He said my significant contributions to Orillia shouldn't be forgotten and that I "still may have much to contribute to society."

When he said he took into consideration that I was receiving treatment for my pathological gambling and that "it's not in the public's interest to interrupt this process by incarcerating him," I knew I wasn't going to jail. There was no treatment in jail.

I was given a twelve-month conditional sentence to be served in the community and two years on probation. Among the conditions during the twelve months, I had a curfew which meant I had to be in my place of residence by 10 o'clock each evening. Throughout the three years I had to abstain from alcohol, to stay out of any premises where the main business was gambling, and report to a probation officer each month. I was also was ordered to make restitution for the $69,852.07 I still owed to the Leacock Heritage Festival and the Orillia Winter Carnival by paying $200 a month for the term of the conditional sentence and probation, after which I would owe the balance to the organizations. I continue to make payments and will for many years.

After the hearing, as I have said, there was an outcry in Orillia about the leniency of my sentence. The *Packet & Times* mounted a campaign to have letters sent to the Crown Attorney urging an appeal. I watched all of this with great anxiety from Mississauga, reading the Orillia newspaper at the library in Toronto and talking regularly to my lawyer. Fortunately, there was no appeal.

I can understand people who think I got off easy, considering that what could have happened — and what I feared would happen — was that I would be sentenced to several years in prison. Recently I read an article in the *Globe and Mail* about the latest spate of executions in Communist China: some 801 executions in the month of April alone. One of them: "Wu Wei, an insurance salesman, was shot by authorities in the city of Kunming for embezzling $70,000 and using it to gamble."[18]

I have been grateful for the outcome of my trial, and this gratitude has been paramount in my new life. As much as I regret the harm my past actions have caused to Roberta and others, I know I cannot live in guilt and remorse for I can twist them to self-pity so quickly. Instead I look to see how my experience can benefit others. I no longer regret being a compulsive gambler nor am I afraid of my past — or of having my life defined as a gambler and a thief. I know who I am today because I know who I want to be in the future.

Judge Hermiston's challenge that I still may have much to offer society has been a principle in my life since that day. I live that principle in three ways. First: by not gambling and continuing in my recovery. Second: by helping other compulsive gamblers in their struggle against this most insidious addiction. Third: by creating awareness about compulsive gambling and speaking out against the mindless expansion of gambling by our governments, more concerned about the promotion of gambling than its control. Like alcohol, drugs, even cigarettes, gambling has inherent problems. Risks. In spite of all the government's talk of "gaming," gambling is not a game. This is how I make amends for the wrong I did Orillians and the harm I did to so many in my life, harm that I can never repay.

My father's Alzheimer's disease has continued to get worse. In early 2000, my brothers and sisters and I helped my mother make the necessary decision to place him in full care in a locked ward. He likes to wander. He still recognizes all of us, but he has no concept of time for our visits, as his short-term memory seems completely gone. It is difficult to fathom what goes on in his mind other than to know it repeats itself over and over, such as his admonition to me that I "better do something about that belly" about every five minutes when I visit him. Fortunately there is an Alzheimer Ward in the seniors' complex where my mother lives in Saint John East and she is able to visit him as often as she desires.

In April of 2000 we celebrated my parents' sixtieth wedding anniversary with a mass at the Cathedral and a family dinner for just them and their children and grandchildren. My sister Veronica and I flew in for the weekend and stayed with Mom. The Sunday morning of the celebration, I was given the task of going down to the ward and getting my father ready for the Mass and festivities. As I helped him shave, comb his hair, put on his socks,

449

pull on his pants, button his shirt, and fix his tie, I realized how symbolic and therapeutic the exercise was: I had no issues with this good man. I loved my father and was grateful for the 21 years of sobriety and love he gave to my mother since he stopped drinking in 1979.

After the sentencing hearing, Roberta returned to Timmins where she continues to live, rebuilding her life. We both shared the joy in June of 2000 of seeing Melanie married to Peter Norman in Vancouver. Melanie met Peter at the University of British Columbia — he's also a writer — and it is apparent they are very much in love. While they continue to struggle financially in launching their careers as Canadian writers, I have great faith in their talents and tenacity.

Later in the summer, when my mother could be convinced my father would not know she was away — or at least would have no recollection of her absence — she came to Ontario to visit my sisters in Toronto and me in Ottawa. She had driven from New Brunswick to Toronto with Veronica and her husband Bob and it was my wonderful task to drive her back home in September through the changing of autumn's leaves. For the first time in my life I had my mother alone for three glorious days.

When I was in Saint John, I visited St. Peter's, the Redemptorist Parish where I launched my first great escape, and the home of my kissing priest. I went to the Rectory looking to confirm the name of the kissing priest, and perhaps to learn if there were other abuses. During my first visit a caretaker told me all the priests were all laying down after the noon meal (I'd forgotten these guys say Mass at six o'clock in the morning). He suggested I come back later and go to the back, through the kitchen, as the receptionist was on holidays.

Father Arthur Connell, the Rector at Saint Mary's College in 1965 with whom I "mutually agreed" I should take my leave, was now living in his retirement in residence at Saint Peter's. When I came back, I found Father Connell in the back yard. We had a pleasant conversation which touched on Saint Mary's, former teachers, and finally, my story. He was friendly, sensitive and genuine, vastly different from the stern, stiff, and unfeeling headmaster I remembered. We talked about my priest, now long dead, not in terms of abuse but as a person who had regarded me as his protégé. But Father Connell wasn't sure who he was and the Parish Rector was not at home. I said I would call back later.

I also met that day with Sergeant Gary Mott, who was in charge of the Family Protection/Youth Unit of the Saint John Police Force. Yes, there had been complaints of child abuse about members of Saint Peter's Redemptorist community, but we couldn't pin down a name. Later in the fall, in Toronto, I went to the Provincial Offices of the Redemptorist Order and found the name of my kissing priest in their archives. By telephone Sergeant Mott confirmed there had been an investigation decades earlier, but what was found didn't warrant charges then.

Also, Sergeant Mott and I discussed my old pervert, but even though I could point out his house, without a name there was no way of obtaining any information.

In recovery I have heard horrific stories of child sexual abuse, physical abuse — guys that actually were inside those sadistic boys' homes — and even childhood rape. Stories that seem much more tragic than mine, which were at the root of other alcoholics and compulsive gamblers beginning to run and escape.

But, to nine-year-old little Dougie Little, as he wandered the Milford Road in fear, mine were just as terrible. For me that's the point. Life on the run began with those childhood perceptions and now has ended with my lifetime of revelations. Now I live today. I live in the now: present to — and knowing what I know, appreciative of — the miracle of life.

My recovery has opened up a new spirituality in my life and a belief in God as my "Higher Power." Defining who that God is has gone as far as knowing *it's not me.* I strive to no longer play God, in my life or anyone else's. I have not returned to the religion of my youth but I could not resist the opportunity to ask Father Connell for his blessing, which he gladly gave. For me it was a reconciliation.

I began writing this story in a variety of forms almost immediately after October 22, 1996, with the preparation of my confession, and through keeping a computer journal and notes on my recovery. It has taken a number of years, however, and a great deal of soul-searching to produce this book. It is vastly different from the book I'd first imagined. Perhaps a future book on my recovery will be equally as unpredictable.

In October of 1997, one year after I quit gambling, I attended a retreat as part of my recovery and was able to complete a Fourth and Fifth Step, major hurdles in my recovery. The Fourth Step — "Made a searching and fearless moral and financial inventory of ourselves" — helped me recognize much of what this book is about. The Fifth Step — "Admitted to ourselves and to another human being the exact nature of out wrongs" — was completed with the help of a very enlightened Roman Catholic priest, Father Vaughan Quinn, who was conducting the non-religious but spiritual retreat.

After telling Father Quinn much of what is in this book I felt a great weight lifted from my mind.

However, having listened to my life, as you have read this story, and recognizing me for the person I am, Father Quinn gave me a warning that I have to keep front and centre, one day at a time, for the rest of my life.

"You have to be careful," he said, "that you don't ever think you won."

NOTES

CHAPTER 1

1. "It's Official Now . . . Small Fry Welcome Spring," *Saint John Evening Times Globe,* 13 (April 14, 1956).

CHAPTER 4

2. Canada's "Neverendum Referendum" on national unity and keeping Quebec in Confederation was soundly defeated across Canada on the basis it gave too much to Quebec and in Quebec on the basis it was not enough. Our "Two Solitudes" continue.

CHAPTER 8

3. "The Man on the Street," *Saint John Evening Times Globe,* 13 (November 9, 1954).

4. *Socius* — Latin for friend.

CHAPTER 9

5. I was pleased to see Orillia, Mariposa and Gordon Lightfoot reconcile their differences and the Festival return to its roots in Orillia in the year 2000 to successfully celebrate its 40th Anniversary, headlined by Gordon Lightfoot. I understand it is staying in Orillia — I hope, forever.

CHAPTER 11

6. The police officer's notes revealed the gaming commission received "an intelligence" that I was gambling with charitable funds. Disclosure provided me with the opportunity to review all the evidence collected by the police including the interviews they conducted with witnesses. Conspicuous was the absence of any evidence from Ralph Cipolla.

CHAPTER 12

7. At the time of my writing, in addition to continuing his private work as essayist and novelist, His Excellency John Ralston Saul participates in many activities with his wife, the Governor General of Canada, Adrienne Clarkson.

8. "I was Addicted to Gambling . . . What's the Government's Excuse?" By Doug Little, *HighGrader* Magazine; November–December; p. 21.

CHAPTER 14

9. VLTs continue to frighten me in my abstinence from gambling. With their captivating speed and hypnotic action I know they still could provide me with the benumbing escape I would need if I re-entered that delusional hell that I am convinced would lead me, the next time, well beyond the gates of prison, insanity and death.

CHAPTER 15

10. When the story did come out it was front page in the *Toronto Star*, and almost every newspaper across Canada. Eventually there was a cover story in *Saturday Night* magazine, in which I collaborated, and I wrote an article in a small Northern Ontario magazine, *HighGrader*, which was reprinted in *Readers' Digest*. In Orillia, I was front page, headline news almost daily for a couple of weeks as the investigation proceeded and then once the charges and my addiction became public, my dual life

was subject to a two-page spread as well as ongoing editorials, columns and letters to the editor.

CHAPTER 16

11. Writing in the *Globe and Mail* on February 21, 1998 ("Long-armed Bandits") Donna Laframboise showed how government advertising has sugar-coated gambling so that what was once considered "a moral and social evil that undermined communities . . . (has become) a socially acceptable pastime. This image makeover is the direct result of what may be the most expensive and most sustained government-funded advertising campaign in Canadian history." Since the early 1970s we have been bombarded with advertising that not only presents gambling in a positive, exciting and fun light, but that has sanctified it as a way of supporting "good causes." The Ontario Lottery Corporation, just one of several government agencies across Canada promoting lotteries, has spent $375 million in advertising over the past 22 years ($17 million a year on average), literally shouting at us to gamble. In 1996 alone, lotteries across Canada spent $43.4-million on advertising compared to a total $42.5 million spent by Provincial and Federal governments urging people to do everything from voting to buying Canada Savings Bonds. "No other single issue has been promoted so relentlessly and so expensively by government," Laframboise stated.

CHAPTER 17

12. From "What Happens to Families . . ." quoting *Pathological Gambling and Chemical Dependency: Similarities and Unique Characteristics* by Sandra Brustuen and Gregory Gabriel.

13. "Gambling Fever Hits Windsor," Column One, *Globe and Mail* (July 27, 1998), Michael Posner.

14. "The lottery mentality, perhaps we all lose," *Timmins Porcupine News*

(May 4, 1977), 5. Doug Little.

15. "How it Works," *Alcoholics Anonymous "Big Book"* (Third Edition, 1976), Alcoholics Anonymous World Services, Inc. New York City, Chapter 5, 59.

CHAPTER 18

16. "I was addicted to gambling . . . ," *HighGrader* Magazine (December 1998), 20–24; abridged and reprinted in *Readers' Digest* (February 2000), 13–18.

17. *"What's New in ____,"* Volume One, Issue 1 (May 1997), Toronto.

AFTERWORD

18. "China's execution factory," *Globe and Mail* (June 14, 2001), Marcus Lee.